ASIA ANNUAL 2010

ASIA ANNUAL 2010

Nationhood and Identity Movements in Asia

Colonial and Post-colonial Times

Edited by
SWARUPA GUPTA

Associate Editors
Rakhee Bhattacharya
Suchandana Chatterjee
Binoda K. Mishra

Maulana Abul Kalam Azad
Institute of Asian Studies
Kolkata

Ministry of Culture
Government of India

MANOHAR
2012

First published 2012

ISBN 978-81-7304-960-6

Published by
Ajay Kumar Jain *for*
Manohar Publishers & Distributors
4753/23 Ansari Road, Daryaganj,
New Delhi 110 002

Printed at
Salasar Imaging Systems
Delhi 110 035

Contents

Contributors

Arpita Basu Roy is Fellow, Maulana Abul Kalam Azad Institute of Asian Studies, Kolkata.

Buddhadev Bhattacharya is former Fellow, Maulana Abul Kalam Azad Institute of Asian Studies, Kolkata.

Rakhee Bhattacharya is Fellow, Maulana Abul Kalam Azad Institute of Asian Studies, Kolkata.

Suchandana Chatterjee is Fellow, Maulana Abul Kalam Azad Institute of Asian Studies, Kolkata.

Ambalika Guha is Fellow, Maulana Abul Kalam Azad Institute of Asian Studies, Kolkata.

Charu Gupta is Associate Professor, Department of History, University of Delhi.

Swarupa Gupta is Fellow, Maulana Abul Kalam Azad Institute of Asian Studies, Kolkata.

Tze-ki Hon is Professor, Department of History, State University of New York at Geneseo, USA.

Monika Mandal is Fellow, Maulana Abul Kalam Azad Institute of Asian Studies, Kolkata.

Binoda K. Mishra is Fellow, Maulana Abul Kalam Azad Institute of Asian Studies, Kolkata.

Sanghamitra Misra is Assistant Professor, Department of History, University of Delhi.

Antara Mitra is Fellow, Maulana Abul Kalam Azad Institute of Asian Studies, Kolkata.

Soumya Kanti Mitra is Fellow, Maulana Abul Kalam Azad Institute of Asian Studies, Kolkata.

Syed Tanveer Nasreen is Reader, Department of History, University of Burdwan, West Bengal, India.

Suvro Parui is Fellow, Maulana Abul Kalam Azad Institute of Asian Studies, Kolkata.

Safoora Razeq is Fellow, Maulana Abul Kalam Azad Institute of Asian Studies, Kolkata.

Peter Robb is Professor, Department of History, School of Oriental and African Studies (SOAS), University of London.

Kaushik Roy is Senior Researcher at the Centre for the Study of Civil War (CSCW) at International Peace Research Institute, Oslo (PRIO), and Reader, Department of History, Jadavpur University, Kolkata.

Daniel J. Rycroft is Lecturer, Department of History, University of East Anglia, United Kingdom; and Founding Editor of the journal, *World Art*.

Abhik Samanta is Fellow, Maulana Abul Kalam Azad Institute of Asian Studies, Kolkata.

Anita Sengupta is Fellow, Maulana Abul Kalam Azad Institute of Asian Studies, Kolkata.

Priya Singh is Fellow, Maulana Abul Kalam Azad Institute of Asian Studies, Kolkata.

Krishnan Srinivasan, former Foreign Secretary, Government of India, is Fellow, Maulana Abul Kalam Azad Institute of Asian Studies, Kolkata.

Acknowledgements

I am grateful to many, more than I am able to acknowledge, for the production of this volume. The writers of the essays and book reviews in this volume (contributors) in India (some of whom are Fellows of the Maulana Abul Kalam Azad Institute of Asian Studies, Calcutta: Ministry of Culture, Government of India) and abroad have made this endeavour an intellectually enriching experience. I am especially grateful to Professor Hari S. Vasudevan (Director of the Maulana Abul Kalam Azad Institute of Asian Studies, Calcutta). His unstinting help, support and kindness, as well as his constructive academic suggestions have sustained, improved and strengthened my efforts. Without his help, the seminar/conference held at the Institute (in October 2010), in which the papers were discussed/presented—would not have been possible. I am also very grateful to Professor Jayanta Kumar Ray for his support and sustenance. The suggestions and comments of Professor Om Prakash Mishra, Professor Purabi Roy, and Professor Kavita Panjabi (who were chairpersons in the conference sessions) were very valuable. I also thank Professor Chittabrata Palit for his help, and for delivering the keynote address of the conference.

Some of the intellectual trajectories explored in this work emanated from my collaboration with Professor Peter van der Veer, Director of the Max Planck Society for the Study of Religious and Ethnic Diversity (Department of Religious Diversity), Gottingen, Germany. I have benefited from his intellectual acumen and expertize, and am grateful to him for inviting me as a Visiting Scientist to the Max Planck Institute in 2009.

I wish to thank the staff of the Library of Maulana Abul Kalam Azad Institute of Asian Studies, and of the National Library, Calcutta for their help in securing primary and secondary sources, which I have used in writing the Introduction to the volume.

I am deeply grateful to my family, especially to my mother, Professor Chhanda Gupta, who has been a source of constant support, guidance and inspiration.

SWARUPA GUPTA

1

Introduction

SWARUPA GUPTA

Asia has long been stereotyped as the exoticized and subjugated 'other' of Orientalism[1] and post-colonial discourses. This volume focuses the spotlight on an awakening Asia emerging through dynamisms/interfaces between two main conceptual sites: (1) nationhood (including the modern nation state, and political and cultural nationalism); and (2) identity movements. How did nations in Asia (from colonial to post-colonial times) fuel and propel identity movements and how did identity movements, in their turn create, recreate and reify nations? This intersection sets Asia in the contested terrain of nationalisms across the world in a specific way. Nationhood in its various incarnations and forms continues to feature centrally in scholarly debate, state policies, international relations, and print literature across the world. In both theory and practice, a continuing influential model is to see colonized worlds as *not* having real nationalisms a la the West,[2] or being the site of 'echoed', 'borrowed',[3] 'modular type' nationalist discourses. On a more nuanced note, the story of nationhood in Asia is one that has a 'different' but 'derived'[4] style. The colonized intelligentsia, imbibing modern post-Enlightenment Western discourses of power, remained, and still remain ensnared in prison houses where nationalism articulated in the 'public' sphere is only a derivation or shadow of Western types. It is only in the so-called 'inner' arena of culture, that nationalism's journey begins, and this nationalism is sharply delinked from public discourses of the outer sphere. What shrouds colonial nationalisms then, is the disillusion of a disjointed discourse (inner /outer),[5] which continues into the post-colonial. What haunts Asia still is the spectre of post-colonial division. What mocks it still is the memory, and belief in the memory of 'cultural mimesis' and

the 'nationalist' mimes of a 'mimic intelligentsia'.[6] Still trapped in Western post-Enlightenment discourses and colonial hegemonic forms of power-knowledge, 'independent' India (using an example) is an 'India against itself'.[7] By extension, countries of Asia—(especially the colonized parts), with their vast, rich cultural heritage, resources, histories, memorializations, and actual people's movements (implied in the point about identity movements, mentioned above)—still remain fragmented, fissured and fissioned. Such division within, and between countries in Asia seems to depict an Asia against itself. Contemporary post-colonial predicaments of fragmentation, separatism, and division are considered as legacies of colonialism. Further, at a time when so-called 'negative' nationalisms (described by Elie Kedourie)[8] characterized by breakaway movements, fundamentalisms, and a divided dystopia still haunt the West, it is time to rethink and qualify the various dimensions of current theories and paradigms of Asian nationalisms.

What do we see when we look deeper with a critical eye? While many still remain under the thrall of theories which see Asian/colonial nationalisms as shadows and derivations of the West, there has been a new, relatively recent trend. Can we really regard the Asian peoples as devoid of subjecthood, and mute and silent actors (or non-actors) in the nationalist stage? Were they only vocal in a derivative sense in the public, political sphere (sequestered from the inner cultural realm)—echoing Western terms and trajectories of nationalism, and remaining prisoners of Western dominant hegemonic discourses? It is more realistic to regard the two spheres/arenas (political and cultural) as connected and hybrid, rather than sharply dichotomous. Instead of regarding nationalism's journey as beginning in a so-called inner cultural sphere, and then moving on to the political arena, the two were interpenetrative, and more or less contemporaneous. The interpenetration of the inner/private and the outer/public has been underscored by C.A. Bayly[9] and Rajat Kanta Ray.[10] Further, the 'outer' arena (civil society) in colonized worlds cannot be regarded as identical to its counterpart in the West.[11] The civil societies of colonized worlds had features, as Sudipta Kaviraj has argued, which could not be fitted into the classic divisive mould of *gemeinschaft* and *gesellschaft*.[12] The story/stories of Asian nationhood must be re-written, going beyond the iconic divide of the 'natural' *gemeinschaft* and the associational, modern, political *gesellschaft*. Cultural and political nationalisms, then, need to be seen as co-eval, sometimes parallel, and sometimes inextricably interlinked.

This aim—to return the Asian peoples their subjecthood, by crafting a methodological mould in which culture and politics intermesh—leads to another vital point. Kedourie's thesis of 'negative nationalisms'[13] resonates to paradigms influenced by Edward Said. These counterpoise community and fragmentation to the modern, political nation-state. Such exultations over fragments splinter communities, regions, and nations in Asia. But was such fragmentation/division, supposedly negating and marginalizing unities, inherent in Asian countries especially in the pre-colonial and colonial periods? Did such intrinsic division form a fertile field for Western, colonial discourses to trap indigenous articulations of identity in prison-houses of Western post-enlightenment discourses, robbing Asian peoples of their subjecthood? Or can we return subjectivity to them by seeing how they adapted, adopted, and also significantly metamorphosed dominant Western discourses? Were there constellations of unity which provide a strong counterpoint, offsetting such division? I have argued elsewhere that there were indigenous terms, institutions and ideas-in-practice, which reflected notions and practices of unity.[14] These unities were reconfigured in the modern period, and they had a modern functionality. Thus identities were not created overnight or *ex nihilo*. To see fragmentation in perspective, rather than over-prioritizing it, is not to succumb to the lure of hegemonic centrality or nationalist meta-narratives sweeping away particularisms. This volume steers a middle course between revelling over fragments and hegemonic centrality. In formulating this methodological orientation, it breaks the age-old stereotyping of Asia as the exoticized, hegemonized and fragmented 'other' of Orientalism and post-colonial discourses. It attempts to reverse the continuing trend of looking toward, and using as reference-points—Western models of nationhood and state building. By delving into the unique experiences of various Asian countries—in colonial and post-colonial times, this volume tries to reverse and return the westward gaze of Asia toward the Asian self. This does not mean that we would then have any single uniform model of Asian nationalism, or even of nationalism *per se*, because nationalism, as a political, cultural, social or economic phenomenon does not have any universalist, single form. What we hope to have are certain different (from European/Western) forms and patterns of nationhood, developing in Asia along specific trajectories. This would help us glimpse and glean new aspects of Asian national identities, their genealogies (often elided in modernist definitions of nationhood), which would help create an

interpretive paradigm for correlation between countries within and beyond Asia.

BEYOND EXISTING MODELS OF ASIAN NATIONALISMS

A recent, if relatively marginal development in the field is the endeavour to discover 'Asian' forms of nationhood, and compare them to European varieties.[15] While trying to break from the thrall of Western political theories seeing Asian nationalisms as shadows and derivations of dominant post-enlightenment discourses, these attempts remain incomplete. Sectional, divided pictures of nationalist experiences in specific Asian countries form the content of volumes dealing with 'Asian Nationalism'. Though it is impossible to describe in nuanced detail, the multifaceted patterns and processes of Asian nationalisms in a single volume, the above-mentioned work leaves the impression of an unfinished story, or a half-drawn picture on an alluring canvas. While sectional and temporally limited essays on nationalisms in China, Japan, Taiwan, Pakistan and Indonesia tell the nationalist tale of what happened in Asia—it seems to be a truncated tale. Essays on nationalisms in Central Asia/Eurasia are conspicuously absent. Though Anthony Smith's influential model of ethno-symbolism is significant, and is successfully deployed to delve the dynamics of Asian nationalism, the polarization of the 'civic' and 'ethnic' types of nationalism seems a trifle artificial. Though Smith admits that civic and ethnic types are not entirely exclusive, but a 'complex continuum', illustrations of this point are lacking in the volume: *Asian Nationalism.* These types (as the present volume would show) often melded at important junctures (seen in the essays on Israel and Chechnya).

Significantly, the European model continues to remain a reference point for discussing Asian nationalism (for instance—in Japan, Russia and other Asian countries).[16] The practice of vernacular mobilization, deployed in the way core *ethnies* move along a political route toward nationhood—absorbing 'peripheral', and 'fringe' areas and groups may work, as Anthony Smith suggests, for eastern Europe, and parts of Asia and Africa. But in South Asia and elsewhere, ethnic nationalism did not always clamour for well-defined, sovereign political nation states. Instead, especially during the mid/late colonial period, cultural nationhood was a more significant trajectory. It entwined with political nationalism at levels, but did not always have an overt (often politicized) territorial teleology.[17] Summing up the Asian experience of nationalism, scholars like James Mayall cannot

get away from the Western, politicized referential index. The main point according to him is: to what extent have Asian nationalisms conformed to the Western norms and practices of international relations, and to what extent have they challenged (if at all) them.[18] In the world stage of international relations, conquered and colonized Asian lands had—according to Mayall—a subordinate role, and articulated identities on Western terms.[19] The result was that even in the afterlife or end of empire, European imprialist' powers continued in the sense that 'they were almost inevitably used as models for nation and state-building'.[20] Asia thus still remains in the penumbra of the West, and is robbed of its possible original and indigenous elements which were intricately interwoven into richly-textured, and internally differentiated discourses on nationhood. Instead of highlighting this, Mayall concludes that 'Asian nationalisms . . . seem to be more similar than dissimilar to those in other parts of the world.' This volume qualifies this contention. It transcends existing paradigms which admit that Asia had/has its own national forms which are not reflections of European or American models, but still think that it is important to believe that 'all Asian nations have been deeply influenced by their relationship to Europe, or rather to 'the "West" as a whole'.[21] While admitting the latter to be true, this volume demurs that Asia's multiple forms of nationhood cannot be neatly fitted into, or put under the three main theoretical rubrics: modernist (Anderson, Kedourie, Hobsbawm and Gellner); post-modernist; and ethno-culturalist (Anthony Smith). Hans Antlov's and Stein Tonnesson's attempts to discover features of 'Asian Forms of the Nation', see Western theory (like *Asian Nationalism* seen above) as a referential point against which non-European nationalisms are to be pitted and with which they are to be compared. But it goes a step further to see whether new theory can come out of Asia. Can we develop new variants of nationalism from Asian experiences and examples, which may then be moulded into paradigms to be followed or used in the rest of the world?[22] This volume tries to build on this in a different way. Without theorizing Asian nationalisms and identity movements, it tries to uncover the dynamics of the politico-cultural mosaic of Asia and (re)discover a new Asia which reconfigures questions in regard to empire, fragmentation, fundamentalisms, state-building, and transnational identities. It seeks to map Asian nationhood over the *longue duree* and meld ideational trajectories (theory) with practice. Existing works on 'Asian Forms of the Nation' or 'Asian Nationalism' do not capture the subtle nuances of how, via continuity through change, Asia has emerged as a key arena in

redefining the connotation and complexion of national movements. This study moves beyond existing models in specific ways: (1) It offers a wider vision of the Asian experience of nationalism, rather than sectional or divided pictures of specific countries trapped in a-historical temporal frames; (2) It does so by situating the different nationalisms in Asia in a comparative grid, to open a heuristic field for seeing how original patterns of nationalism emerge as a contrasting foil to dominant paradigms of the West; (3) It focuses the spotlight on a new Asia emerging through dynamisms/interfaces between two main conceptual sites: (a) nationhood (including the modern nation state, and political and cultural nationalism); and (b) identity movements from the colonial to post-colonial times.

SHIFTS AND NOVELTIES

Wider Visions of the Asian Experience of Nationalism

This volume tries to tell a densely argued, richly-textured story of Asian nationhood, which may then be a foundation for fathoming fascinating, untapped depths of the Asian experience(s) of nationhood. This is of course, not a complete story in the sense that it covers national experiences of all Asian countries, across time and space. What it does—is to focus on particular experiences of countries in West, South, and South-East Asia and knit them into an internally-differentiated ontology of nationhood. By yoking genealogies to modern and post-colonial experiences, it gives a broader and wider basis to the Asian experience of nationalism. Deploying a multidisciplinary methodology, the prisms for studying Asian nationalisms oscillate, and often meld political, social, cultural, economic, and anthropological perspectives. Despite the focus on genealogies, the volume is not entrenched in primordialist, essentialist, and/or perennialist moulds, but melds instrumentalist, political, cultural and sociological parameters of analyses. Thus there is a feeling of evolution—which vividly brings out the experience lying at the heart of nationhood (as compared with political nationalism *per se*)—the ontology of being and becoming a nation. The past, present, and in a sense—possible futures, interlock to give expression to Asian nationhood and identity movements.

This does not imply that Asia is valorized and hagiographed as forming the centre of the world. We are not talking here of an enchanting wonder that was or is—Asia, or of an immemorial Golden Age (as Stewart Gordon puts it): 'when Asia was the

world'.[23] The focus of interest lies in the multiplicity and variations of the nationalisms of this magical mosaic. But despite contestations, differences, and variations—between the interstices of contextual dissonance, there can still be bonds, comparative angles and connectivities. This volume illuminates these connections. Places/sites were connected contextually, as were processes. Such contextual connections may form the foundation for imagining a reincarnated and contextually connected Asian spatiality. This spatiality is/was underpinned by ideology as well as materiality. Thus, though not covering every country of Asia or dealing with numerous identity movements of this vast continent, the volume crafts some thematic sections, to which other (elided) countries, movements, nations—may relate to. This book does not narrate a complete, finished story of Asian nationhood—or a wide-ranging, all-covering experiential, epistemological and ontological spectrum of nationhood. The aim is not to paint a vibgyor, but to trace variations, shades, and blendings in the vibgyor. The intent is to partially weave, as well as disaggregate the multiple strands in Asian nationalisms. Thus, this volume does not offer a symphony of Asian nationalisms, but underscores special notes in the complex polyphony of Asian nationalisms and identity movements. Further, instead of focusing solely on any single master-narrative of nationalism (as done in many existing works) or theorizing about colonial nationalism as a whole, this book illuminates relatively shaded and elided (and, to an extent, seemingly 'marginal') concepts, movements and practices embedded in the multiple experiences of Asian nationhood.

THE INTERFACE BETWEEN NATIONHOOD AND IDENTITY MOVEMENTS

The second point of departure of this volume is to connect nationhood with identity and identity movements in Asia. I use the word 'identity' here in the sense of individual essence and selfhood. It follows that Asia had/has multiple identities which sometimes connect, while at others—deviate from each other. The rationale for linking nationhood with identity lies in the fact that nationhood—or the process of becoming a nation is closely linked with a reinvention of the self/or of a country's identity (in its manifold aspects: social, cultural, economic, religious, political and economic). In Asia, such reinventions took different forms: such as articulations of empowered identities woven around specific indigenous concepts and identity markers, group relations, communities and institutions:

these included *jati* and *samaj*[24] in Bengal, *biradari* in north India, and *qawm*[25] in north-west India and modern Pakistan and Afghanistan. These were reconfigured in 'modern' colonial times, but they had genealogies. They fed into the concept of indigenous identity, which, like nationhood, is protean and multidimensional. It is not frozen, but flexible, having liminal, contextually expanding, inclusive boundaries. It is also in constant flux: and is made and remade due to a variety of contexts and circumstances. What were the levels of interconnection between nationhood and identity in Asian nationalisms? Which identity was prioritized/legitimized over others in claims to nationhood? Which identities were forgotten or submerged? Which identities concatenated? Which identities were rescued from history and reconfigured so that ancient bonds could become modern unities? These are the questions which this volume addresses. Further, this conception of identity, though inevitably rooted in and tied to sets of ideologies, may also break occasionally from their thrall. In this break, real, living experiences begin to emerge and crystallize. The break may also result in a plethora of possibilities with regard to nationhood. Sectional or divided interests may dissolve, façades of fantasy may fade, and social structures may be transformed.[26] This conception of identity is taken a step further. As identities do not operate in a void, this volume traces the trajectories which Asian identities took in the multiple routes to nationhood (the latter implying not just a claim for political, territorially defined, sovereign, limited nations/imagined communities of the Andersonian type, but also nations without political underpinnings, or any fixed governmental structure, and having fluid, Turnerian territorial boundaries or cartographic lines in flux). Talking of identity-trajectories, what become crucial are identity movements with aims. This volume argues that the interface between nationhood and identity movements in various parts of Asia underscores a sense of flow and movement toward specific aims. This implies a discussion of the relationship between centralized, majoritarian identities and so-called fringe-peripheral identities. The volume intends to trace conflicts and comparisons between both centrifugal and centripetal forces. It would steer a middle course between hegemonic centrality, and exultations over 'marginalized', hidden, silent fragments. Exploring the dynamics of 'marginal' as well as 'majoritarian' movements, it would etch three analytic levels: (1) intra or sub-regional (micro studies); (2) inter/trans-regional; and (3) international or transnational. These movements include ethnic, political, religious, linguistic, insurgent, and economic ones. By conjoined focus on these factors, this

discussion would show how the reincarnated Asian spatiality is not merely a utopic vacuum, but strongly underpinned by materialities and infrastructural processes. These analytic trajectories may open a heuristic field of comparison, consonance and dissonance between identity movements in West, Central, South, East, and South-East Asia. In this path of discovery, we may see, feel, and live in a new Asia through a creative reconfiguration of indigenous identities. The paintbrush of time, moving over colonial and post-colonial identity-imaginings, and actualities of movement will draw new ideational and material lineaments. In contradistinction to existing literature in the field, this volume melds and relates nationhood with living, pulsating movements across Asia.

Comparative Grid

The volume seeks to open a field of comparison, consonance and dissonance between nationhood and identity movements in West, Central, South, and South-East Asia. The methodology deployed draws on a new, relatively recent trend of seeing worldwide phenomena through the prism of connected histories. Using a temporal and ideational axis, one may see what happened in different places (within and beyond Asia), in terms of contemporaneity/simultaneity/conceptual connectedness. By formulating this focus, scholars have tried to link roles of ideologues, traveller-actors, politicians and labourers/working classes across the boundaries of the nation state at a given time, to discern patterns of connectedness.[27] Applying this analytic tool, we may draw comparisons between identity movements and nationhood within various parts of South Asia, and beyond. This may help in the envisioning of 'a hundred horizons'[28] and etch trans-regional, national and transnational spaces. Closer home, as an illustration—we may cite the unique spatial, geopolitical and ethno-linguistic location of north-east India and its component regions. Rather than regarding this area as a segregated, paradigmatic site of conflict and separatism, the volume would try to see how specific places in this region formed foci of shared spaces. Extending this model, we can situate India in a comparative grid. This implies the mapping of contrasts, comparisons and connectivity between Indian/South Asian movements, and those in other parts of Asia (this extends the model of 'Origins of Nationality in South Asia' to other parts of Asia beyond India and her neighbours). The volume intends to map shifts/variations between stirrings of identity in India and other parts of Asia to have an internally-differentiated

pattern of Asian identity in temporal spirals of colonial and post-colonial periods. This internal differentiation springs from the unique histories, heritages, governmental systems and ethnic identities of the countries concerned. While, as argued at the beginning, India's national movement cannot be regarded as a 'derivative discourse', but rather as a nuanced story in which politics and culture intersected to produce a complex pattern of reconfiguration of indigenous unities by the intelligentsia, nationalism in Japan followed a different trajectory. Unlike India, Japan was ethnically homogeneous. Nationalist discourses and identity issues in late nineteenth-century Japan followed the European, post-Enlightenment, rationalist, evolutionary and linear path. The idea of *toyoshi* underscoring territorial sovereignty and boundedness, allowed the new nation state to write its history as an enlightened modern nation, and also to valorize a culture rooted in a great Asiatic tradition, that could challenge Western claims of superiority.[29] In a multi-ethnic China, Han Chinese identity was superimposed upon ethnic particularisms. In Vietnam and China, race, ethnic patriotism and territorial sovereignty, were reworked in an anti-alien and political platform. This state of affairs was possible in China because of imperial rule providing a political rubric, and working as a shield against 'barbaric' foreigners. In Vietnam, national memory has increasingly come to be woven around martyrs of the revolutionary war.[30] These examples show that Asian nationalisms were different in many ways, and even within the same country, there could be different types of nationalist and identity movements in different temporal phases. The intention, here is to focus on specific experiences of nationhood and identity movements in Asia, in which commonalities as well as differences may be discerned. Specific threads and trajectories are taken and woven into a richly patterned, textured discourse on nationhood and identity movements, which throws up some interesting differences and originalities, going beyond 'Western' models of nationalism which continue to be planted on Asian soil. It opens a heuristic field for seeing how multiple stories of Asian nationhood had points of consonance as well as dissonance, ideological rendezvous, as well as divergences. There were/are multiple voices and variations. It is not a symphony, but the polyphony of nationhood in Asia that this volume is about.

In this endeavour, 'vanquished' Asia becomes an articulate, role-playing, actor in nationalism's stage. It does not remain in the wings anymore. Nor does it speak in the voice of 'Western' prompters. There is no single voice or type of 'Asian Nationalism'. This volume is about

multiple forms, patterns, ideologies and movements. It does not claim that it gathers all the threads of Asian nationhood's complex idea and practice, and weaves them into a single, integrated, coherent, uncontested or undifferentiated terrain, arraigning it oppositionally against the West. It does not situate Western civic centralized state systems (as in England and France), eroding local particularisms *versus* Asian 'ethnic', particularistic, parochial nationalisms, but positions them *vis-à-vis* each other, and sees how Asia emerges as a key player in the history and contemporaneity of nationalism.

THE COLONIAL AND THE POST-COLONIAL

The story of Asian nationalisms/identity movements as told here, falls into three main categories: (1) those of the colonial period; (2) those which move from the colonial to the post-colonial era; and (3) post-colonial nationalist impulses and identities. A crucial feature which emerges is the contextual melding of the colonial and the post-colonial, rather than a sharp, sudden break. Further, colonial nationalisms also had genealogies in the pre-colonial. Nationalism then, does not always awaken or comes to life through the magic wand of colonial modernity, nor wither away with the end of colonialism, or fade with the end of an empire which was once pushed beyond the limits of the setting sun. This volume deals with transitions, evolutions, reconfigurations and reinventions. It does not compartmentalize the historical discourse of nationalism or split it into a pre-colonial nebulous non-national primordiality, a colonial national modernity[31] and a post-colonial period emerging after the so-called end of empire. This further means that nationalism's story has a history, and that history is not solely political. The historical narrative of the evolution of identities in South Asia and beyond cannot be split up artificially, though links between the modern nation and the historical community from whence it emerged—were neither simple nor continuous. There was no sudden leap from pre-colonial, non-Western, non-scientific historyless-ness and identityless-ness to a modern rationalist project of history-writing geared to writing nationalistic history along Western colonial lines, which dispensed with earlier terms, concepts, traditions and methodologies.[32] Rather than an undeviating linearity, one can talk of temporal spirals of pre-colonial, colonial, and post-colonial. In this frame, while analysing contemporary nationalisms and identities, there need not be convenient post-colonial amnesia—forgetting the fact of empire, anti-colonial struggle, the realities of the colonial past(s), or the

taxonomies and tentacles of imperialism. On the contrary, we can have a richer discourse drawing on charismas of the past.

While milestones and temporal divides are important, one must look beyond them too, and even before them, to have a nuanced, finished story. Post-colonialism—after the demise of the empire, was one such milestone. But as some essays in this volume would show, there were other milestones too: such as the dissolution of the Soviet Union and the creation of new nation states in its wake. As a field of academic enquiry, post-colonialism emerged in a sense, with Said's *Orientalism*, which brought Michel Foucault into the arena of post-colonial studies.[33] Though Said retreated later from the overt Foucauldianism of Orientalism, the otherness of Asia, and the conquest and transformation of that otherness, not just by the force of arms, but through culture, became inbuilt into the new discourses which emerged in *Culture and Imperialism*.[34] Post-modern intellectual discourses proliferated, comprising critical analyses (rather than seeing colonialism as a multifaceted phenomenon, which cannot solely be judged in terms of dominance and hegemony) of the cultural legacy of colonialism. Post-colonialists argued that the intellectual hegemonic power-knowledge of colonialism was/is not something vacuous/airy—but causes, influences and impacts global inequality. Following Said, 'subaltern' historians continued the most scathing tirades, championing post-colonialism under specific banners.[35] The subaltern studies project had an influential following, but one needs to look deeper to understand the dynamics of post-colonialism, especially in the context(s) of nationalism. It is important not to locate the otherness of the other (the colonized) wholly or even solely in the colonial moment, thus eliding pre or non-colonial differences of consequence.[36] Orientalism does not alone wield the wand to animate 'silent shadows' or bestow subjectivity to Asian peoples: rather they create it on their own, through specific reinventions of indigenities and transformations as well as continuations of traditions. They may not speak in the same nationalistic language as in the West, because nationalism, like history, does not have the same meaning in all countries—but they may be actors, or even directors in post-colonial theatres of what Homi K. Bhabha has called 'hybridity'—spaces where 'dominant' and 'marginal' knowledge mix and interact.[37] This volume takes the notion of hybrid spaces a step further by redefining, and contextually obliterating hard divides of the so-called cores and peripheries. Fettered by globalization, these 'peripheries' are 'under siege'. According to Roy Starrs, Asia is especially threatened, and becomes the site of reactionary nationalisms in the post-colonial period, having an economic and political slant. This study is another

addition to the vast array of post-colonial nationalistic studies, viewing Asian nations mainly from political, material and economic angles,[38] rather than weaving the colonial and post-colonial into cultural-political genealogized nationalisms. We need to recognize that post-colonialism is a fluid and plural concept, in which continuation of the colonial is embedded. This continuation does not always have a negative influence, but positive, creative dimensions which shape Asia's today, and to an extent, its tomorrows.

CONCEPTUAL SECTIONS: ESSAYS/CHAPTERS

(I) *Nationhood, Place and History: Specificities, Generalities and Memorializations*

The three essays in this Section explore how place-history, connected and shared spaces, and archetypical sites concatenate to address and resolve the tension between local identities and wider unities: between specific sites and larger interregional spaces; between the sub-regional/regional and the national. While Peter Robb and Sanghamitra Misra set their essays in the colonial temporal frame, Tze-ki Hon outlines a paradigm of re-colonization drawing on nostalgias of the colonial period. His essay thus melds temporally (and, to an extent, ideologically), the colonial and the post-colonial (the point discussed above). Sectioned around the thematic axis mentioned, these three essays spatially extend from north-east India to East Asia (Hong Kong). This shows how we may thematically situate nationhood/national experiences within a grid of connected histories and identities, moving beyond time and space.

Peter Robb in his article 'Place and Difference' contextualizes and explores the dynamics of Indian nationalism with reference to the inevitable conflict between local and generalized identities. At a theoretical level, he problematizes the issue of repression of the one by the other. Deploying a novel methodology, he juxtaposes this issue (with examples), to the related dilemma of dealing with particularisms/minutiae and wider/great processes (master narratives) emanating from multiple changes, including the evolution of nation states. His article ponders over the paradox that both generalities and localism are shaped not only by autochthonous trends but also by external influences. Using the case study of Swedish Baptist missionary activity in twentieth-century north-east India, he suggests that places, people, and societies transform through simultaneous external influences (in this case, the missionaries' roles) as well as by local traditions. Through such explorations, he illuminates the particularities of

distinct and contested groups of Indian citizens, each in their own places, and the importance for them of an experience of difference. Colonialism (in the form of missionary activity), place-making and local indigeneities thus interlock to tell the story of nationhood in a part of South Asia by crafting a model which may well be applied to other national experiences within and beyond South Asia.

Also setting her study in colonial north-east India, Sanghamitra Misra, in 'Practices of Sovereignty, Practices of the Market: Writing Spatial Histories of North-Eastern India', argues that histories of exchange, marketing practices, and trading networks in India's north-eastern borderland region produced shared spaces with liminal boundaries, though the main discourse is focused around Goalpara. The connected places—forming a shared spatiality included the Eastern Duars, Cooch Behar, southern Himalayan foothills of Bhutan, the north-eastern borders of Bengal and the western borders of Assam. This shared borderland was also linked (via frontiers/borders)—with Bhutan, Nepal, Tibet, China and Bangladesh and the rest of India. The central argument is that local/regional histories of exchange and marketing practices relate to wider processes and contexts (that of nationhood). In this tale of connected histories and heritages framing a shared space, Misra argues that markets were important sites. Commercial transactions formed part of a shared social landscape in the region. The article considers how notions of a sacred topography bound the local polities of Tibet, Assam, Bhutan, Bijni and Sidli. Though tracing genealogies of spatial and commercial connections, Misra emphasizes that colonial modernity and its spatial strategies transformed this shared culture of trading. Nebulous and amorphous borders were re-drawn/erased to produce a politically and economically unified territory. But integrations and connections (commercial and cultural), such as local fairs, and traditions of exchange continued despite colonial reifications, and at specific contexts even resisted colonial policies of segregation and rigid demarcations.

In 'Colonial Nostalgia as a Means of Resistance: Historical Discourses in Post-1997 Hong Kong', Tze-ki Hon gives an original dimension to the story of Chinese nationhood. By focusing on how the erstwhile colonized intelligentsia/Western educated professional middle class people of Hong Kong used colonial nostalgia, myths, memories and metaphoricities of colonialism as a strategy of resistance in regard to 're-colonization' by mainland China, Hon highlights a major link in the unfinished discourse on Chinese nationalism. Challenging master-narratives, he shows how a specific

form of place making—applied to Kowloon City and Causeway Bay—articulated a strategy of resistance which fed into the imaging of a 'unique', individualized, cosmopolitan, immigrant identity of Hong Kong. This imaging contrasted sharply with ideas and policy-attitudes of the Beijing government towards Hong Kong. What we have here then, is an identity movement challenging a wider, more general discourse on Chinese nationalism through a unique refraction of the local/particularist/historicist, and the latter's conflict/correlation with more generalized identities.

(II) *Nationalism and State-building*

While the first three essays explore historical settings and reifications of place and space to construct histories of nationalism in the colonial and post-colonial periods, the second section in this volume looks at more concrete, material, infrastructural processes tied to state-building. Formulating a multidisciplinary methodology by grafting sociology and political science, Arpita Basu Roy and Kaushik Roy explore processes of state building and obstacles/challenges to such processes, to see whether and how the idea of nationalism burgeoned and developed in Afghanistan, India and Iraq. As mentioned earlier, this volume explores the interface between nationhood and identity movements. The drive on the part of nations (by this I mean cultural units, which may have some political features and territorial boundaries: they may be nations in the making) to become full-fledged political nation states—is also an identity movement of a specific brand. These roads to becoming a nation state are various. While L. Greenfeld talks about five such roads,[39] the Asian nationalist experiences also had variations, obstacles and challenges in their routes to nation statehood. A nation state may be defined as a state which the great majority of the citizens identify with, seeing it as their own. Nationalism (in the political sense) is the identity movement associated with the formation of such a nation state—an ideological movement for attaining and maintaining a nation state. In Asia, the colonial experience complicated the journey to the nation state as it was fraught with difficulties and strife. In Afghanistan, for instance, it is clear from Basu Roy's article, 'Ethnicity and State-building in Afghanistan', that the national idea remained weak and fragile. Multiple groups in Afghanistan's cultural and social mosaic have resulted in ethnicization of political conflict. The nationalist imaginary, and a clear idea of the nation state and its aspirations found appeal only in a limited group—an educated urban, literate

class. Basu Roy argues that in the contemporary period, the process of nation-building, democratization and institution-building need to be explored and understood through the lens of the societal fissures. Her essay explores the structural constraints and historical heritage inhibiting Afghan nation-building. It also sees whether constitutional provisions guaranteed under the Constitution of Afghanistan in 2004 assume significance, and whether the state is equipped to pursue policies of religious, linguistic and cultural unity. By way of conclusion, the article argues that it would be surprising if a strong state did emerge as the country remains fragmented along ethnic, religious and ideological lines and geographical/topographical lines of segregation.

Kaushik Roy in his essay 'Insurgencies, Counter-Insurgencies and State-building in Asia: A Comparative Analysis' takes Basu Roy's essay further, by situating the issue within a comparative grid comprising Iraq, Afghanistan, Kashmir and Nepal. He explores in detail how in these different countries of Asia, insurgency and its aftermath pose a significant challenge to state-building. From the late twentieth century, Roy argues there has been a proliferation of unconventional war. The latter term refers to intra-state wars. In recent times the term 'insurgency' connotes an organized movement aimed at the overthrow of a constituted government through the use of subversion and armed conflict. Insurgencies include both guerrilla warfare as well as terrorism. His essay examines the rise of insurgencies, responses by the polities (known as counter-insurgency or COIN), and its impact on state building in four regions of Asia (mentioned above). Three of the above-mentioned regions experience 'Islamic' insurgency while the last region has recently undergone a Communist insurgency. The novelty of Roy's essay lies in the comparison and contrast of/between the four cases, and also the attempt to see whether Islamic insurgency differs from Communist insurgency, and further, if all the four insurgencies could be categorized as 'New Wars'. What could be added, however, is (:) what kind of policies the concerned governments may take in the future to assess the individual situations and whether new strategic dimensions of state-building may emerge through comparison of evolving government policies.

(III) *Cultural Nationhood: Ethnicity and Linguistic Identity*

As the experience of nationhood is not merely a linear, political flow towards the formation of nation states, but a complex pheno-

menon in which culture (which sometimes entangles with politics) plays a key role, this section shows how cultural markers such as ethnicity and language played a major part in the evolution of Indian nationalism. More generally, though Walker Connor has argued that nationalism emerged first in the economically advanced 'core' and not in the 'underdeveloped periphery',[40] ethnicity and cultural ties are indispensable in claims to nationhood. The lure of modernist theses (socio-economic developmentalism and the onset of print capitalism)[41] cannot elide the different ways in which Asian nationhood was forged in different countries: these paths often deviated from this so-called beaten track. Ethnicity and culture shaped and directed modernization in many parts of Asia. The two essays in this regard address themes related to cultural nationhood, which are relatively unexplored. Daniel Rycroft, in 'Indian Anthropology and the Construction of "Tribal Ethnicity" before Independence' explores how, in late colonial India, the concept of 'race' was nationalized. Anthropological knowledge and cultural policy were linked domains. Rycroft asks a significant question in this context: how did exponents of Indian anthropology re-formulate 'race' within a nationally-relevant racial studies framework? In an insightful and lucid account, he shows how relational concepts of 'tribe' and ethnic diversity were reconfigured within a new sociological rather than colonialist discourse of race. This set out the terms for a national science. Researchers dispensed with the idea of the 'aboriginal' or the 'indigenous' before 1947: this forms, according to Rycroft, the causal foundation and the counter-ideological background of both Indian anthropology, and the closely related field of Tribal studies. His essay critically focuses on the work of Brajendra Nath Seal, Sarat Chandra Roy and Dhirendra Nath Majumdar who were the main exponents of this emerging discipline.

Rycroft's essay contextualizes ethnicity in regard to so-called 'marginal' or othered ethnic group in the sociological landscape of India—the tribals. While this sheds light on how a new concept of tribal ethnicity was formulated, the second essay in this section deals with a linguistic movement—also of a supposedly marginal and 'excluded' group: the Bhotis. Both the essays bring to the fore the issue of indigeneity, in the sense of having a primordial, pristine dimension to it, un-tarred by the brush of any pseudo-modernity, and not seen only through the prism of colonial scholar-officials and/or a Western-educated professional intelligentsia. The essay entitled: 'Identity Image(s) and Actualities of the Bhoti Language Movement in Post-Colonial India' by Buddhadev Bhattacharya is an insider's (he

was a participant in the movement) view of a 'marginal' linguistic identity-group (the Bhotis). Fleeting references (by British scholar officials such as G.A. Grierson) to the Bhoti language group did nothing, claims Bhattacharya, to crystallize and consolidate them into a significant identity-group. This situation continued in post-colonial times. Clubbing them with the Indian Tibetan speakers could not prevent an explorative odyssey into identity-origins on the part of the Bhotis since the 1960s. Despite inclusion in the Eighth Schedule of the Constitution, the lines of demarcation between this articulate and conscious linguistic group with other related groups have remained hazy. Bhattacharya is indignant that the issue is still unsettled. This cultural nationalist movement based on language as the key identity marker—may be considered as part of a much wider Indian nationalist discourse and practice. It is an illustration of the problems and pitfalls of cultural nationhood in India, and its resolution may have promising consequences—the Bhoti explorative journey may have a microcosmic and symbolic significance for other language-groups in India. It can add new dimensions to the discourse on cultural nationhood and its entanglement with associational politics, which forms the basis of contemporary Indian cultural-cum-political nationhood.

(IV) *Nationalisms in Eurasia*

The story of cultural nationhood (and its entwining with political processes) in South Asia had counterparts in other parts of Asia, albeit with significant differences. This section of three essays set in post-colonial Eurasia explores the complex dynamics of identity formation, nationalism, modernity and challenges to nationhood in Buryatia, Turkey and Chechnya. The leitmotif of contextual connections surfaces in these essays also, linking locales, ideologies and memorializations. What connects these essays despite the difference in their geographical positionings, are their contemporaneity and continuation. Set in the post-colonial, post-Soviet-dissolution stage, the essays explore the problems and possibilities of their national experiences, and contain as a subtext, thoughts, imaginings and realities relating to the future. 'What is', is therefore crucially linked to 'what can be'. Suchandana Chatterjee in 'Shifting Perceptions in Buryat Identity' qualifies the segregation of Buryatia as a 'periphery', and highlights its connections with Buddhist identities, Russia, Mongolia and China. Chatterjee argues that nationhood in Buryatia

is conditioned by local sentiments about collective ethnic memory and East Siberian regionalism on the one hand, and supra-nationalist sentiments like Buddhist spiritualism and pan-Mongolism on the other, qualifying the contention that Buryatia was a segregated Soviet entity. Linking pre- and post-Soviet scenarios, Chatterjee highlights indigenous reactions in regard to ethnicity, ideology, and more generally, culture. She contends that instead of using the Soviet paradigm, we need to deploy a more complex methodology to study the multiple dimensions and facets of Buryat identity. By moving beyond the Soviet model, Chatterjee focuses on certain unique features of the Buryat-Mongol Autonomous Soviet Socialist Republic in 1923, which existed at least theoretically till 1958.

Anita Sengupta in her article, 'Modernity and Denial: The Case of the Kurds in Turkey' concentrates on the pangs of transition, integral in the creation of 'modern' Turkey. What emerges from her study is that hard disjunctions between civic and ethnic nationalisms do not always work; rather, we need to have a more flexible analytic approach, melding civic and ethnic trajectories in the creation and maintenance of nation states. This *modus operandi* is linked to the wider question of (Asian) modernity,[42] and its connection with the creation of nations. The creation of 'modern' Turkey was a contested process in which diversities were erased or submerged. Despite such erasure, heterogeneities remained. This led to an investigation of the 'Kurdish question'. Cultural pluralities of varied groups with their own religious and ethnic identities posed a serious challenge to the modernity-driven discourse and practice of recreating Turkey. The government's 'Islamic' background was an anathema to the ideological stance of the state-building architects: the Kemalists. Assimilative moves could not simplistically transform a majority of Kurds into 'Turks'. Sengupta argues that a neo-Ottoman ethos would be more pluralistic and cosmopolitan. It would be better-equipped to deal with the multiculturalism of Ottoman society. Against this analytic backdrop, Sengupta explores how Turkey was transformed in the years immediately after the establishment of the Republic. Corroborating and illustrating the point about the interpenetration of civic and ethnic nationalisms, Sengupta shows that despite such moves, the Kurds were alienated, thus complicating and occluding integrative ventures.

The third essay in this section also points to the limitations of ethno-nationalism in Eurasia. Antara Mitra in 'One Size Fits (not) All! De-hyphenating Chechen Nationalism from Kremlin's

Rhetoric of "War on Terror"' traces the changing contours of Chechen nationalism, and trends in the traditional discourse and understanding of ethnicity, nationalism and identity-politics. She focuses on Kremlin's rhetoric of 'global jihadist conspiracy' *vis-à-vis* the increasingly militant Chechen ethno-nationalist separatism. Mitra thinks that conceptual distinctions between ethno-nationalism and religious terrorism by thrusting region-specific dynamics of ethno-nationalism unto the Procrustean bed of global jihad, complicates the situation. Significantly, she explores the distinction between Chechen nationhood and *New Chechen Jihad.* Her article traces the historic process of how an originally secular-territorial Chechen ethno-national identity-building movement against Russian colonialism slowed down due to increasing Islamic mobilization. Consequently, Mitra argues, a more distinctively ethno-nationalistic imagined idea of Chechen community has become increasingly subordinated to and absorbed into a meta-identity of global Islamic *ummah*, deviating from its originally nationalistic character.

Mitra's essay offers an insight into how typologies—civic and ethnic nationalism—interpenetrated. Her essay (as well as those of Sengupta and Priya Singh) show how the sinews and strands of such seemingly opposite types of nationhood entangled in the Asian nationalist stage. This volume asks: How were civic/secular nationalisms transformed into ethnic nationalisms with a 'strong religious aura that was more attuned to the needs and outlook of the mobilized people?' Ethnic nationalism could also be transmuted to acquire a civic slant. A key aim of the volume is to trace how vernacular mobilization and ethno-historical appropriation by intellectuals among various Asian populations transformed historical *ethnies* to self-determining political nations. Specifically, how did this occur in West (Priya Singh's essay) and Central Asia (Anita Sengupta's and Antara Mitra's essays)? This would offer insights into the fascinating interface between primordialism and instrumentalism[43] as played out in the Asian theatre. Such interrelations between seemingly opposed methodologies of ethnic identity formation developed in Asia through reinventions of the indigenous.

(V) *Transnational Identities*

The model of comparative grid surfaces strikingly in discussions of historically-mobile peoples (such as the Jews), and the dilemmas, dreams and despairs of Asian diasporas settled in homes away from

home. Here we have actual movement and residence of people and constructions of interconnected social and cultural spatialities, which I feel, is a significant dimension of Asian nationhood. The very experiences of travel to other countries, residence in those places, and interactions with social communities—builds an Asia of connected lands, people and histories. These experiences also reify ideas about the region, locality, province, nation and continental identities, and connect disparate cultures and identities, integral to the modern influential concept of transnationalism. Nostalgias, cultural pulls and impulses from beyond a specific site/country/nation crafted discourses and practices of nationalism from a distance (as seen in the case of Buryatia) or transnationalism in places as diverse as West Asia, South-East Asia and parts of Central Asia. But these transnational identities took different forms.

Priya Singh in 'Comparing Zionism with European Nationalisms' demonstrates that conceptual disjunctions of 'civic' and 'ethnic' nationalisms do not work in specific cases of Asian nationalisms. Though Zionism is regarded as constituting a case of ethno-cultural nationalism, there is no one model of nationalism by which Zionism can be tested. However, in the recent past, studies on Zionism as a nationalist movement from a comparative perspective have started. The essay contends that such comparisons enrich historical research. At the core of the comparison between Zionism and the other (European) national movements lies the deep belief or disbelief in the uniqueness of the Jewish people and the divine purpose for which it exists. Singh concludes that this unique mobile group claims an individual, exclusivist essence for itself, while at the same time—wishes to be like other nations (element of comparison).

At the other end of Asia (South-East), transnationalism had other facets. Binoda K. Mishra's essay 'Shiva's Children in Prophet's Land: The Story of Indians in Malaysia' describes how from the mid-nineteenth century, Indians were taken to Malaysia as indentured labourers by the British East India Company. This exodus to an unknown land and its culture led to fear, apprehension and a sense of isolation and identity-crisis in diasporic minds. Indians protected themselves by a self-imposed Laxman Rekha crossing which meant loss of 'identity'. Though residing in a foreign country—nostalgias, reminiscences and fascinations for their homeland remained the basis of this fragile identity. Mishra describes how the migrant labourers chose to stay back and adopt the new land as their home. This entailed sacrificing their old 'identity' and acquiring a new

'identity' which would facilitate social and cultural inclusion in their adopted home. For the Indians, this was like the dance of Nataraj, symbolizing their death and creation at the same time. Lost in an identity-trance, diasporic Indians became targets of Bumiputras and 'Islamization'. The cosmic dance of Nataraj and the process of death and creation could not be completed, resulting in a state of 'suspended identity' comparable to Trishanku (hanging in mid-air between earth and sky). With this background, this essay tells the story of identity articulations among Indians in Malaysia from mid-nineteenth century till modern times in various phases. By bringing out the differences in the nature of identity in each phase, it challenges the notion that 'identity' is fixed, and argues instead that articulations of identity are dependent and contingent upon a variety of factors, including socio-political stimuli.

(VI) *Gender and Identity Movements*

Nationhood always has its others—sometimes embedded in the nationalist self, sometimes lurking on the margins, waiting to be incorporated,[44] and/or sometimes challenging its master-narrative. Gender forms one such—perhaps imagined or supposed other, which interacted with and impacted nationhood and identity movements in Asia in different ways. This section has three articles which bring out complex and nuanced dimensions of one such so-called 'othered' group: women. Did they, as contended by some scholars, form the site of articulating the 'private', untainted, inner domain in a colonized world where men orchestrated such segregations in a bid to underscoring cultural otherness *vis-à-vis* the colonizer? Were women's voices stilled in nationalist discourses? Were they indeed sequestered in inner domains delinked from the 'outer' political, public arena? How were they iconized (such as the image of Mother India) and representative of nationalist movements? What were their own roles, un-prompted by men, in the colonial stereotyping of India (especially Bengal) as 'feminine' and effete, which was to be conquered, transformed and viewed through the lens of colonial masculinity?[45] And, significantly, did their movements meld with wider identity movements—thus contextually dissolving their supposedly 'marginal' or 'fringe-identity' character? Addressing the debate on whether Asian governments provide constitutional guarantees to protect the rights of minorities, this volume would see how 'marginal' groups such as Muslim women formed the subject of

much wider debates, influenced by Western culture, pan-Islamism and rural-urban relations. It would situate women's movements in north-east India, and the 'othered' within the marginal (iconization of Dalit women) within wider contexts of political unrest, separatisms, and the role of religion to evaluate their mergings with wider nationalist movements and historical processes during colonial and post-colonial phases.

Charu Gupta in her essay 'Gendering Dalit Identities: Retelling "National" Histories of 1857' deals with a double marginality or otherness: (1) Dalits (a marginal group in the Indian social landscape, who had a contested relationship with mainstream Indian nationalist discourse and practice); and (2) Dalit women. The latter form an other within a wider other, and the essay deals with how this double otherness was negotiated in the Revolt of 1857: flashbacks and echoes of which continue to reify Dalit identity even today. The aim of her essay is threefold. The first examines contradictory Dalit voices on 1857, as reflected in contemporary debates, archival records and popular Dalit literature. Second, these voices are specifically related to Dalit identities, particularly to representations of Dalit women. The third aim is to explore possibilities of a radical gendered Dalit politics beyond the rubric of the nation, and one that is not tied just to the tyrannies of 1857. Dalit participation in 1857 has invoked heated debates, where there is condemnation of 1857 on the one hand, and on the other, commemoration of Dalit participation in it. However, both these versions signify the genealogies of ambiguous nationalisms, where the Dalits, from their own standpoint, deal with the selective and restrictive lineages of historical pasts. The essay makes the point that Dalit literature on 1857 was also crucial from a gender perspective. Notwithstanding an attack on feudal patriarchy (recognized as a critical characteristic of 1857), there are also Dalit female heroic icons (*viranganas*) who became the symbols of bravery of particular Dalit castes and ultimately of all Dalits in 1857. Thus the internal other (Dalit women) flows and mingles with the wider otherness (all Dalits). Focusing on the critical relation of this double otherness, the essay is then yoked to the wider questions surrounding Indian history and nationalism. Providing gendered accounts of histories from below, this essay argues that such connections re-present counter-histories of 1857. The 'margins' or others are then positioned in the wider stream of Indian nation and nationalism.

Such gendered identities also drew on, intersected with, and impacted wider identity-struggles and social, cultural, economic

and political issues in north-east India. Rakhee Bhattacharya in 'Identity Consolidation of Meitei Women: Reflections on Women's War' explores how the Meitei women of Manipur resisted external aggressions and exploitations. They asserted their identity through empowered movements and wars for nationhood. The roles of Manipuri women go beyond conventional 'feminine', familial spaces, and move beyond the household level to various socio-economic aspects. Bhattacharya argues that women's market in Manipur has remained one of the largest markets in South Asia from time immemorial. Manipur was the site of a series of women's movements which fought against injustice and oppression. Thus the first *nupi lan* or women's war began in 1904 against colonial rulers. It proved to be a launching pad for Manipuri women, and served as a foundation for the development of their identity formation. This war then never ended. The voices of women were raised again against ruthless economic exploitation of the British rulers and their agents, which culminated in the second *nupi lan* of 1939. This war had a unique dimension, and illustrates the point mentioned above. It moved beyond the issue of women's identity within Manipur; and manifested itself even against the policy decisions of independent India, which according to the people of Manipur, has kept the state perpetually disturbed and destabilized. Bhattacharya analyses and connects women's movements in Manipur to a wider pan-national movement, simultaneously exploring the depths and dimensions of identity formation amongst the Meitei women. The argument of the essay is explicated in three temporal phases, each with its distinct aim: (1) the colonial phase: *nupi lan*, implying women's war against economic exploitation of the colonial rulers; (2) post-colonial period, witnessing the *meira paibee*: a women's war against 'state terrorism' and against Government of India's policy on conflict management; (3) a comparison between women's movements in Manipur with other movements having a wider span and reach.

The third essay in this section is significant because it addresses a double, so-called 'marginal' otherness which is inextricably bound to histories and contemporaneities of India's secular identity, its sociological landscape and interrelation between two conventionally 'opposed' categories: Hinduism and Islam. Tanveer Nasreen in 'Bengali Muslims at Crossroads: Women and Early Encounters with Contemporaneity' rightly remarks that Islam (Hinduism's tyrannized/marginalized or tyrannical other) is not an immutable monolithic system. Muslims of various social strata are conditioned by specific historical contexts, sectarian differences and socio-cultural diversities. In Bengal, Hindu socio-cultural, linguistic identities were

interfused with Muslim religious identities to produce the category of 'Bengali Muslims'. Nasreen contextualizes the evolution of the identity of Muslim middle-class women. Seclusion, or *purdah*, was an integral element in the ideology of *sharafati* upheld before these women. Women were debarred from the right to education, although it contradicted one of the basic theoretical tenets of Islam. The essay argues that education resolved the identity crisis among women to a great extent. The mass of protest literature from women was in Bengali. The essay maps changing social dynamics resulting from education and consequent empowerment of these women. Education among Bengali Muslim women made considerable progress during the first half of the twentieth century and assumed the nature of a movement as many women took up professional employment. At a time when Hindu nationalism iconized nationalism in the form of 'Bharat Mata' (Mother India), Islam deployed a discourse on motherhood as a strategy to legitimize the necessity and scope of women's education. However, the Partition of India caused a major setback to the process. Many Muslim families opted for East Bengal, causing a break in the pattern of development among them. The search for identity among a minority population assumed newer dimensions in the Western part of truncated Bengal after 1947, dispelling many of the possibilities and promises of an Indo-Islamic intellectual/cultural heritage.

CONCLUSION

By studying various forms of Asian nationhood and identity-movements through a multidisciplinary methodology, this volume seeks to re-open and address the debates surrounding the nature of colonial and other nationalisms. Breaking stereotypical binaries of Western and Eastern nationalisms, it will show how reinventions of the indigenous refracted certain key notions that lie at the heart of Western nationalisms. It goes further. Countering the centrality of the West in nationalist discourses, this volume addresses, and also moves beyond the thesis of the West *versus* the rest, which continues to dominate post-colonial studies. It opens a relatively unexplored arena in which intra (within) Asian nationalist voices speak to each other. Asia then becomes a vibrant, internally-differentiated arena where multiple trajectories of nationhood entangle and tell nuanced stories of nationhood. It not only returns subjecthood to the Asian peoples in the making of their own nations, but also opens a field for discovering through insiders' (Asians') eyes, their own experiences and formulations of the national idea. In such experiences, regions and regional sections within and beyond nations—are reified and

contextually connected to form a shared, but particularistic and historicist Asian national and supra-national, reincarnated spatiality. This does not refer to pan-Asianism,[46] or a simplistic and vacuous 'glocal' (global, yoked to the local) Asian utopia. This volume does not project the image of a universalist Asian nationalism, but captures and focuses on hidden and unfinished stories of nationalisms, where multiple trajectories entwine as well as separate. These richly variant strands cannot be woven to formulate any single theory that can explain the enigmas and dynamics of Asian nationalisms. But these strands (as reflected in this volume)—do mark the beginning of a new journey of discovery: at each bend, new insights and patterns of identity may emerge—to inspire and enchant nationalist ideologues, political scientists, sociologists, and anthropologists (as the volume is based on a multidisciplinary methodology). In this path of discovery, new nationalist paradigms may offer interpretive strategies relevant to policy-making, political and cultural cooperation and correlation, economic exchanges and material connections. This may help realize the dream of a possible new Asia.

NOTES

1. Edward Said, *Orientalism*, London: Routledge and Kegan Paul Ltd., 1978.
2. Scholars such as Elie Kedourie contend that nationalism is decidedly a European phenomenon. He dates the beginning of nationalism in Europe to Fichte's addresses to the German nation in 1807.
3. Benedict Anderson contended that nationalism has a modular form and can be transplanted across a wide variety of geographical and cultural terrains. See Anderson, *Imagined Communities: Reflections on the Origin and Nature of Nationalism*, London: Verso, 1983.
4. Partha Chatterjee, *Nationalist Thought and the Colonial World: A Derivative Discourse?*, Delhi: Oxford University Press, 1986.
5. Partha Chatterjee, 'The Nation and its Fragments', in the *Partha Chatterjee Omnibus*, Delhi: Oxford University Press, 1994.
6. Homi Bhabha, *Nation and Narration*, London: Routledge, 1990.
7. The words form the title of Sanjib Baruah's book, *India Against Itself: Assam and the Politics of Nationality*, Delhi: Oxford University Press, 1999.
8. Elie Kedourie (ed.), *Nationalism in Asia and Africa*, London: Weidenfeld and Nicolson, 1970.
9. C.A. Bayly, *Origins of Nationality in South Asia: Patriotism and Ethical Government in the Making of Modern India*, Delhi: Oxford University Press, 1998, 2001.
10. Rajat Kanta Ray, *The Felt Community: Commonalty and Mentality before the Emergence of Indian Nationalism*, Delhi: Oxford University Press, 2003.
11. Jurgen Habermas, *The Structural Transformation of the Public Sphere*, tr. Thomas Burger with the assistance of Frederick Lawrence, Massachusetts: MIT Press, 1989.

12. Sudipta Kaviraj and Sunil Khilnani (eds.), *Civil Society: History and Possibilities*, Delhi: Cambridge University Press, 2001. Also see F. Tonnies, *Gemeinschaft und Gesellschaft*, or *Community and Civil Society*, ed. Jose Harris, and tr. Jose Harris and Margaret Hollis, Cambridge: Cambridge University Press, 2001.
13. See Elie Kedourie, op. cit.
14. Swarupa Gupta, *Notions of Nationhood in Bengal: Perspectives on Samaj, c. 1867-1905*, Leiden, Boston: Brill, 2009.
15. See Michael Leifer (ed.), *Asian Nationalism*, London: Routledge, 2000; and Stein Tonnesson and Hans Antlov (eds.), *Asian Forms of the Nation*, Richmond, Surrey: Curzon, 1998.
16. Anthony Smith, in Leifer (ed.), *Asian Nationalism*, op. cit., p. 15.
17. For details relating to the dynamics of cultural nationhood in Bengal and in India, see Swarupa Gupta, op. cit. However, among Serbs, Armenians, Sikhs, Arabs and the Ceylonese, demotic *ethnies* transformed into self-determining political nations.
18. James Mayall, 'Nationalism and the International Order', in Michael Leifer (ed.), *Asian Nationalism*, op. cit., p. 187.
19. Ibid., p. 188.
20. Ibid.
21. Stein Tonnesson and Hans Antlov (eds.), *Asian Forms of the Nation*, pp. 2, 29.
22. Ibid., pp. 22-40.
23. Stewart Gordon, *When Asia was the World*, New Haven and London: Yale University Press, 2008.
24. See Swarupa Gupta, op. cit. Also see Swarupa Gupta, '*Samaj*, *Jati* and *Desh*: Reflections on Nationhood in Bengal', *Studies in History*, New Series, vol. 23, no. 2, London, New York, Delhi, Singapore: Sage Publications, 2007, pp. 177-203.
25. See Rajat Kanta Ray, *The Felt Community*, op. cit.
26. Cf. Terry Eagleton (ed.), *Ideology*, Harlow, Essex: Longman Group UK Limited, 1994, p. 16.
27. The views of Rajat Kanta Ray, C.A. Bayly, Sugata Bose and Tim Harper are relevant in this context.
28. See Sugata Bose, *A Hundred Horizons: The Indian Ocean in the Age of Global Empire*, Boston: Harvard University Press, 2006.
29. See Stefan Tanaka, *Japan's Orient: Rendering Pasts into History*, Berkeley: University of California Press, 1993, mentioned by Prasenjit Duara, 'Post-colonial History', in Sarah Maza and Lloyd Kramer (eds.), *A Companion to Western Historical Thought*, Malden, Massachusetts: Blackwell, 2002, p. 420.
30. See Thomas Hodgkin, *Vietnam: The Revolutionary Path*, London: Macmillan, 1981, p. 166.
31. Eminent scholars such as C.A. Bayly and Rajat Kanta Ray have questioned the way in which the historiographical discourse of nationalism has been split into two disparate phases or periods (1) pre-colonial period when there were nestling bundles of communities with no strong sense of identity; and (2) the modern or colonial period when 'nationalism' was supposedly born, and flowed along a Western-derived, political trajectory. See C.A. Bayly, *Origins of Nationality in South Asia*; and Ray, *The Felt Community*, op. cit.
32. Partha Chatterjee claims that there was a sharp transformative leap from the pre- to the colonial period in terms of history writing. Earlier works—kingly chronicles such as *Rajabali* (1808)—sharply differed from Tarinicharan Chattopadhyay's *Bharatbarsher Itihas* (1876), in which history was no longer

interfused with myth (this was clearly not the case in reality, as many nationalist narratives of the late nineteenth century continued to mesh myth and source-critical fact in history writing), nor the play of divine will—but a struggle and contest for power. See Partha Chatterjee, *The Nation and its Fragments*, op. cit.

33. See Neil Lazarus, *Nationalism and Cultural Practice in the Post-colonial World*, Cambridge: Cambridge University Press, 1999, p. 11.
34. Edward Said, *Culture and Imperialism*, London: Chatto and Windus, 1993.
35. See Partha Chatterjee, *The Nation and its Fragments*, Princeton: Princeton University Press, 1993; *The Present History of West Bengal*, Delhi and New York: Oxford University Press, 1997; Nicholas Dirks (ed.), *Colonialism and Culture*, Ann Arbor: University of Michigan Press, 1992; Gyan Prakash (ed.), *After Colonialism: Imperial Histories and Postcolonial Displacements*, Princeton: Princeton University Press, 1995; M.L. Pratt, *Imperial Eyes: Travel Writing and Transculturation*, New York and London: Routledge, 1992. Also see Aijaz Ahmad's views on the politics of literary post-coloniality. See *In Theory*, London: Verso, 1992.
36. See Peter van der Veer and Carol Breckenridge, *Orientalism and the Postcolonial Predicament*, USA: University of Pennsylvania Press, 1993.
37. Homi K. Bhabha, *The Location of Culture*, London and New York: Routledge, 1994.
38. See Roy Starrs (ed.), *Nations under Siege: Globalization and Nationalism in Asia*, New York, Basingstoke: Palgrave, 2002.
39. L. Greenfeld, *Five Roads to Modernity*, Cambridge: Harvard University Press, 1993.
40. Walker Connor, *Ethnonationalism*, Princeton: Princeton University Press, 1994, Chapter 6.
41. Anderson, *Imagined Communities*, op. cit. and E. Gellner, *Nations and Nationalism*, Ithaca: Cornell University Press.
42. Modernity, like identity, history and nationhood does not have a fixed, West-centric connotation. It is more realistic to talk of multiple modernities, and to trace their intersections. Further, modernity or modernities, in whichever part of the world is incomplete without its seeming and oppositional 'other' tradition. These traditions themselves may have been modernized (cf. Rudolph and Rudolph, *The Modernity of Tradition*, Chicago: The University of Chicago Press, 1984), or they may still exist within interstices of modernity. They are not, especially in Asian countries, 'invented' whenever convenient; but they may be transformed and reified according to changing circumstances. To understand the dynamics of Asian modernity, one has to see how it is entangled with such reconfigured traditions.
43. See Clifford Geertz, *The Interpretation of Cultures*, London: Fontana Press, 1993; and Paul Brass, *Ethnicity and Nationalism*, Delhi: Sage, 1991.
44. See Richard Shusterman, 'Understanding the Self's Others', in Chhanda Gupta and D.P. Chattopadhyay (eds.), *Cultural Otherness and Beyond*, Leiden, Boston, Koln: E.J. Brill, 1998.
45. See Mrinalini Sinha, *Colonial Masculinity*, Manchester: Manchester University Press, 1995; and Indira Chowdhury-Sengupta, *The Frail Hero and the Virile History*, Delhi: Oxford University Press, 1998.
46. Okakura Tenshin's ideas and his interactions with Rabindranath Tagore are relevant in regard to details about pan-Asianism.

I. NATIONHOOD, PLACE AND HISTORY: SPECIFICITIES, GENERALITIES AND MEMORIALIZATIONS

2

Place and Difference: Reflections on Indian Identities and on Swedish Baptists during British Rule[1]

PETER ROBB

The links between identity and nation are neither straightforward nor stable. Accordingly the path from identity to nationalism may be complex and confusing—partly from the interplay between majoritarianism or dominance on one hand, and marginality, dissent or silence on the other; and partly because of the overlaps, interconnections and rivalries of human categories across localities, countries, regions and the world. These are confusions of place, meaning both allegiance and location. To them are added a paradox of difference, namely the part played in shaping identities at all levels by external or heterodox as well as common or standardizing influences.

The significance of place and the agency of difference set the agenda for this paper. I am not intending a philosophical or theoretical contribution,[2] but merely exploring the fact that all histories assume a place as their subject—the nation (for example) in regard to national history. The issue will be examined, after a more general discussion, through the example of a Baptist mission in north-east India. The paper accepts that, just as mental spaces are never without ideology, social spaces change according to the uses to which they are put and the relationships by which they are constituted.[3] I will offer some practical examples of the production of space through difference.

My case study and interpretation may seem to contradict the concepts of 'non-state places' and borderlands that have attracted much attention, as in the idea of 'Zomia' (including these Assamese hinterlands) discussed among others by Willem van Schendel and

in a recent book by James C. Scott. Their analysis emphasizes the intrinsic: ecology, for example, and a deliberate separation by hill-peoples. The cultural exclusivity of hills is well-documented, and so is the relationship between valleys (or plains), sedentary agriculture, irrigation, writing, and state-formation. But, as Scott makes clear, there is often a symbiosis of lowlands and hills, and hills and borderlands exist only *relatively*, not absolutely, outside states. Moreover, state authority may be avoided or excluded on the plains as well as in the mountains. Hence, I wish to recognize localized elements but at the same time remain sceptical about wholly autochthonous entities and histories.[4] Thereby the way is clear for a consideration of place and difference together.

Sanjib Baruah has blamed colonial mapping and perceptions for the supposed lack of affinity between plains and hills peoples in north-east India. He rightly notes, however, that a supposedly territorial indigeneity is being defended today by both centralizing governments and the local claimants of ethnic homelands. So territorial determinism persists, though the orthodoxy of indivisible sovereignty has disappeared from the legal textbooks. Baruah wishes instead for a common, objective citizenship by birth, descent or naturalization, based on given territory without internal boundaries, thus largely decoupling space from ethnicity—what might be called in more than one sense—an American ideal for India and the world.[5] But locality and particularity cannot simply be wished away by good intentions, nor even by national identities and modern communications. A common citizenship does not guarantee either multi-cultural harmony or homogeneity. States and nations, being constructed, make choices over time about the basis of their citizenship. On the one hand, they work with constants and survivals, and the great narratives of progress and identity. But also, on the other hand, they encounter local environments and heterodoxy, which in turn have their own constants, survivals and narratives.

THE IMPORTANCE OF PLACE

The issue of locality provides a commentary on the usual description of Indian nationalism. Westernized elites developed nationalist ideas, so the story goes, and eventually a new nation was born. As with other nations, India was constituted by defined groups and also individuals, who chose or were required to forge a nationality and a relationship with the state and its institutions. True, religious, social and ideological spheres were also organized, among Muslims,

Hindus, Dalits and others; and such sectional and communal parties contributed both to disunity and to alternative 'true' identities. But all shared the same generalizing, nationalist assumptions, and all in some sense invented their supposedly long cultural continuity and autonomy. Localities existed, but they were consistently and even forcibly submerged in these meta-narratives of identity, nationality and polity: so Bengali *bhadralok* Hindus praised Rajput heroism and became Indian nationalists. The strain of the process has been evident, for example, in the subdivision and re-organization of states, the creation of Bangladesh, and the Naxalite or north-eastern insurrections; but the nation supposedly remains supreme, in hearts and minds, and by force.

There are three main problems with such narratives, concerning the nature and role of place. Firstly, the story is inward-looking, when the experience was of global dialogue, not merely by way of casual comparisons but at its core. During British rule, India focused on a worldwide experience. At that time, a prevailing idea of the state developed from western Europe, where a few nascent polities survived more or less over centuries, and other nations were unified on historical, cultural, linguistic and/or political grounds. Later, more new states, including the post-colonial nations, were formed allegedly on the same basis. There was also a variant that was broadly imperial in origin and nature, as for the USA, Russia, or China, states based on annexation, conquest and settlement. The Indian subcontinent had had a long history of local or regional powers, local empires, and empires imposed by outsiders, and not much sense of a norm of being ruled by one's own kind, however, that is defined. Centralizing Mughal traditions were important in the eighteenth century and beyond, but the empire to back them up was imploding or under external attack, not least from 'Hindu' forces. Without British rule, then, the Indian subcontinent would have been likely to produce several nations, as in western Europe or Latin America. Instead, it became a few more or less unified states. British rule provided the conquests, infrastructure and some of the ideologies that prepared for modern India.

Secondly, and on the other hand, we should not think of British rule as something wholly European done to a pristine, essentially 'Indian' India. Of course, foreign rule was oppressive, both materially and psychologically. But the raj, building on the political and cultural complexity of pre-colonial ages, was also something done with India, and through Indians, and it helped produce what is 'India' today, which like all nations is a mixture of many things and continually changing.

More important, thirdly, any nation is made up of multiple identities that it must subsume. Dominant memories and narratives of civilizations and nations tend to forget these alternatives. They see, for example, the formation of the Indian nation, or the development of the Congress, as natural phenomena reflecting a given, all-encompassing unitary identity. Nationalist ideas may be very powerful, especially with modern media and communications. But iconic, localized memories too are continually experienced by and necessary to all peoples and political groups. People act in politics after defining their identities in a specific not a generic way; and their local or class stories do not *constitute* the mainstream, by amalgamation. The mainstream is made from elite, homogenizing perspectives; it is different from the sum of its parts, coalescing around a generalized place and a common imagined history. Nationality and nationalism require this dislocation even as they claim their homeland.

Historians too have to favour the general over the particular, interpreting evidence, searching for significance. Consider environmental arguments: many scholars (and rulers too) have explained India in terms of ecological zones.[6] Plains and passes, rivers and fords, and the uneven distribution of resources (soil, water, wood, livestock, and minerals) all have consequences in the patterns of land use and settlement, and in the generation and concentration of functions such as pilgrimage, trade, manufacture, or administration—even in the distances between centres of population. The cultural results are then evident, over long periods, as between sea- and land-oriented people, communities of the hills or plains, and agriculturists settled on irrigated lands or migrant pastoralists in the dry country. Local particularity is itself attributed to physical barriers, in the absence of strong centralizing forces, as we see in the famous resilience of the French *pays* and their dialects.[7] Despite chance and heterodoxy, we discover enduring cultural continuity in places and in groups, transmitted through language, institutions and technology.[8]

Ecology, material culture and human practice all then combine to define larger differences and grand narratives. Geographical imperatives, from Wittfögel's hydraulic civilization to Cunliffe's Atlantic seaboard,[9] are generalized to produce universal explanations of conditions and of change. We may cite Condorcet's social arithmetic, Comte's law of three stages, and Marx's laws of motion.[10] Evolution drives world and comparative history and the histories of commodities. Braudel's wonderful study of the limits of possibility in material life explains the changes between primitive subsistence, semi-monetized

markets, and developed capitalism.[11] His *Mediterranean World* exemplifies a vibrant tradition of geo-regional studies.[12] All these focus on great 'simplifications',[13] shared influences and experiences over wide regions and long-time spans. They also imply political agenda. Theories of progress were widely used to garnish worldwide European expansion. When Braudel wrote, people wished to confront both elitism and narrow, murderous nationalisms. Nowadays, cross-regional and global histories accompany worldwide interdependence and rapid communications.

Not only timely and pragmatic, theories of 'civilization' are universal. For example, in the juxtaposition of court and country, field and forest, at least in Eurasia, there is implied a direction of travel, despite elements of circularity, of ebb and flow. In South Asia as elsewhere, city cultures, based on the domestication of animals and crops and the management of people, water and soil, gave way to broader pastoral societies ranging with their herds over open spaces. In some places, they were succeeded in turn by territorial states and empires dependent on wide-scale agriculture, a transition also discernible between the Vedas and the Upanishads. Why, to take another example, is *Ramayana* so appealing over time and space? Apart from its drama, it deals in great archetypes, not only of good and evil, love and lust, freedom and captivity, but of the court contrasted with the forest, and kingly practice and filial duties, with exile and idyll; civil order is met with threat, negation and struggle, and also with alternative power—asceticism, the monkey realm, Ravana. In European myths and fairy stories too there is implied a memory of ever-extending frontiers and a retreat of difference, though they tell both of dangerous forests and of Arcadia, and thus are complicated and never value-free. Some of the folk tales derive from or have the same features as early Indian collections such as the third-century *Panchatantra* or the probably Persian *Book of Sindibad* or the *Arabian Nights*; they then appeared in Perrault, the brothers Grimm, and Hans Christian Anderson. Some, as also in Aesop's fox and grapes, or his wolves, lions, foxes and lambs, obviously juxtapose towns and farms with forest or wilderness. But, more generally, European collections (and inventions) of fairy tales, from the end of the seventeenth century to the nineteenth,[14] coincided with the impact of material and economic change. Over this period, European civilization encroached on so-called unpopulated lands (the plains of the Americas, Siberia and Australia for example), or on supposedly primitive peoples and unproductive economies, as if to fulfil the 'ancient' stories.

This linear narrative is like a single colour washing across a map. *Longue durée* processes explain how places are; they set parameters for action and ideas as much as for material culture and economic life. Agriculture extends over the forest; prevailing market systems and commoditization spread out and cover pre-existing modes of production and trade. Thus 'progress' expresses the superiority of order over lawlessness, contract over custom, organized religion over superstition, settled agriculture over hunting, manufacture over gathering, and so on. Then, in language, culture and society, there is replacement and standardization: whatever does not exist in the colonized space has to be created; that which exists is suborned. Such developments obviously contributed also to a modern political notion of place, as occurred in the Western European imagination but also among writers who from the late sixteenth century wrote histories of the Mughal empire as a spatial and social entity as well as a moral, geneological or chronological sequence. They implied a notion of causation and of human, not supernatural agency in accounting for events, and an elaboration of corporate identities and roles, for example in the coincidental codification of a Muslim order in India with other debates about conduct, religion and the state. Perhaps it related to rule by a 'heterogeneous professional immigrant *elite*'.[15]

In such ways, the nation too is one of the great simplifications; political progress is usually considered as a movement from one to another ideal type of state. In the first, rule is associated with a central place or zone. It may be progressively fragmented and delegated, in terms of space or function or both. At the peripheries, little kingdoms mimic the style and practice of the overlord, whereas within the centre, with a more complete control, the ruler typically assumes many roles (both landlord and law-giver, or religious head and commander-in-chief, for example). There is an impulse to expand from the heartlands, and this impulse tends to shape institutions as well as policy. Most operative identities, nonetheless, tend to be localized, of clan or tribe, and inherited or ascribed.

In the second ideal type, sovereignty is assumed to be even and objective across the realm. There are firm boundaries of jurisdiction, in both space and function. There are interiors and borderlands rather than peripheries. There are formal distinctions between public and private, and more identities may be generalized and more elective rather than ascribed. The state's functions ebb and flow, but there is an impulse to 'cultivate' an entire realm evenly, expressed through concepts such as improvement, responsibility, representation, common interests, and nationality, expressed not only politically and

strategically but in economic and social life. Where there are derogations or delegations they tend to be legal, bureaucratic and institutional rather than personal. Overall, we regard rule of the second kind as modern. It relates space to nationality, which it also frames. In the transition from the pre-modern to the modern, imperial systems subordinate smaller centres of power. A differentiation between central place and periphery is replaced by a universal sovereignty within borders. Ruler and subject are connected by (supposed) interest more than through destiny and dynasty.

Thus the imperial processes were not confined to excluding the external and the different, but also subverted the weak and destroyed much diversity within civilizations themselves. Ultimately engaged in the same project were the Mughal *pir* reclaiming the wetlands of eastern Bengal; minister Colbert (1619-83) with his maritime code and dream of trunk-roads criss-crossing France; the European settlers who tamed the pampas and dispossessed their peoples; the forest officers punishing informal local use of timber (a newly valuable and regulated resource); the schoolmasters drumming Shakespeare into young heads; and capitalists squeezing village labour into cities and factories. Within colonial India, some existing institutions were readily brought under the yoke. Borderlands were defined and confined. Some peoples could choose which larger entity they would merge into, but long-standing centres had little choice about where they belonged. Some lands lost their separate political identity, leaving behind cultural memories; where there were new administrative and political boundaries these tended to turn into social and cultural ones as well, through languages of education, media and government.

In modern times yet further homogenization occurred, because (like different classes of people) localities were seldom as much of the new mainstream as was supposed. In short, civilization and nation are centralizing, ordering, homogenizing concepts, hard to escape. Heterodoxy retreats.

Such processes are the building blocks of nations. So it was with 'Muslim' and 'Hindu' and 'the Congress'. Everywhere local and hidden worlds are being taken over by great forces of church, state and science, through print, travel and mass media, producing more integrated economic and social life. Frequently, there is violent repression and resistance, but mainly it is the winners' voices we hear. The mega-narratives assume relative homogeneity and overlook exceptions, and even chance and contingency. Therefore, modern nations contain common interests, technologies, laws, work and practices; common languages, memories, explanations and loyalties;

common activities and institutions, schools and armies, companies and bureaucracies, farms and fairs; shared consumption of goods, services and ideas. These do exist in reality as well as imagination.

However, in practice, there is no absolute divide between types of regime or society. Sovereignty is typically mixed, and relations among the powerful tend everywhere to be personal. Much diversity is never lost, and variations of jurisdiction within places and identities can always be seen, in the borders of active policy, as exclusions of various sorts by law, economic status, social standing, in private spheres or closed communities. Wilderness is not only associated with barbarism but also linked to harmony, social cohesion, and even original or better ways of life. Remorse and regret accompany progress. Places that are absorbed and 'lost' become sites of resistance; although to survive they must be organized using the tools of hegemony, such as generalized categories, convenient histories, and self-justifying ethics: in the Indian context the word *adivasi* or indigenous people sums up all three.

The national stories read unity back in time; but transitions and transformations are part of the remembered past. The stories are about fulfilment; and so they contain loss and resistance. Moreover, given that identities are fluid, the inheritances must be repeatedly renewed. Nations are defined continually by new standardizations that are always competing with the local, with the importance of place. Localities thus represent survivals and dissent, while being subject to incorporation and an overlay of national norms. Finally, however, a new focus on these variants does not really 'de-centre' the nation in the sense of ignoring its force, or denying influences across region or the globe. We should not replace evolution with stasis. Paradoxically, places develop their particularity in part through imported conditions and experiences, and the exchange of people and ideas, things taken out of their own place and transferred to another.

THE AGENCY OF DIFFERENCE

Outsiders matter to change. That is one way of considering colonial influence, a point I have made by stressing the diversity of colonial rulers and the contradictions of policy.[16] Here I turn to another example of outsiders at work: Christian missionaries, who were also an aspect of the supposed march of civilization already discussed. All advocates of change seek to convert others. Missionaries had to suppress their own sense of superiority—not always successfully—even though in essence that was the point of their mission. They

wished to provide an opportunity to others because what they offered they thought better; but they offered it to those who were potentially equal, as the message was for all; and once the converts espoused it, moreover, they became as one—supposedly members of a universal community. To compound the complexity, the missionaries acted by also concealing their purpose under cover of providing other public goods, demand or expectations for which they often generated: education, books, health care. There are obvious parallels with European political empire, both in the selfish motives for good works and in the unintended consequences.

The place of this study is a number of distinct small areas of different character and history,[17] all ostensibly covered by the Baptist mission to Assam that dated back to the 1830s. I shall take up a few aspects from about a hundred years later, among the Swedish Americans from Minnesota working under the auspices of the American Baptist Foreign Mission Society.[18] They failed to make any headway among the millions they regarded as bigoted Hindus and Muslims,[19] and had focused their activities on the borderlands—mostly the Garo hills and the Miri (Mising) and Naga territories to the west and southeast, and (from the 1890s) more precariously north of the Brahmaputra, amidst Kacharis and others. People from those areas living in the valley were also targeted, as were migrants to the tea gardens from Chhota Nagpur in east central India.[20] Swedish Christians, trained in America, working in British India, among hill-peoples, adjacent to Assam, seem as multi-layered in their marginality as can be imagined; but Christianity later played a significant part in the definition of these borderlands and peoples, and in the mediation of their identities within Assam and India. Here is yet another instance of the local and the specific in dialogue with a mainstream, as well as of the importance of external stimuli.

O.L. 'Dad' Swanson (b.1867) and his wife Grace, and J.E. Tanquist (b.1881) and his wife Mabel, and the next generation, Bengt and Edna Anderson and Reuben and Edna Holm, were leading Swedish Baptist missionaries of the early twentieth century. In the 1930s, times were hard financially, and there were doctrinal and personal disputes between modernists and traditionalists, the Swedes being of the latter persuasion. Nonetheless, by 1938, the Andersons alone had 144 churches with about 20,000 adherents.[21] There are 'bright, ambitious Christian young folks in all these hills around us', wrote Edna Forssell from the Jorhat Christian Hospital, while attending the Ao Naga Student Conference at the end of 1938.[22] The Baptists' main measure of success was the number of converts. Statistics about

printing and education came a close second, but were thought 'less romantic' and satisfying than Bible classes and Christian fellowship. The Andersons ran about sixty-five schools. Without Kohima school, it was said in 1934, 'we would have vastly smaller numbers of Christians in that whole part of the Naga hills'.[23] Missionaries also learnt and helped develop the local languages. Most became very proficient. In the 1930s, Swanson's preaching was said to be most effective in Assamese, which he had learnt forty years before.[24]

Medicine too was supported (meaning dispensaries, hospitals and general health care, as well as work among lepers), though financial and staffing problems limited the work. The first four nursing recruits (of 1934) graduated from Jorhat hospital in 1938. In Kohima, it was said, 'More sick people come all the time. High caste, out caste, Mohammedans, Christians in name and Christians who are real, hill people and plains tribes'. [25] Edna Forssell hoped many of the Hindu lepers among whom she worked would turn to Christ. In Jorhat, their leader, the year before an object of deep pity, his nose eaten away and infested by maggots, was now well-dressed and warm and 'sure of his message and of his Christ'. Indeed, Forssell found, among the lepers there were fine persons, 'with sensibilities as we have', who had held positions of responsibility, not the 'whining, begging type of derelict' she had supposed almost all lepers to be.[26]

Three short examples. First, Bengt Anderson, whose mission lasted with short interruptions from 1926 into the 1950s. He described his main work among Nagas as being 'to preach in the villages, meet with pastors and villages [*sic*] school teachers, supervise the hostel for Sema boys, and to arrange Bible conferences for five different areas'.[27] Anderson felt he could do little about the poverty of the people but claimed that 'the Baptist Mission was the first and for fifty years the only promoter of education for the Nagas', at a time when even British officials did not think they needed it. Schools were taught by converts, such as the first Naga graduate, Mayangnokcha, who headed the school in Impur.[28]

Secondly, we come to Joe Tanquist. He pressed the importance of printed scriptures, arguing that a translation of the gospels was needed wherever fifty Christians spoke a distinct language. Without this, conversions would fall by at least half. Moreover, the 'vigorous promotion of adult literacy' would not only satisfy the desire to read what had been made available, but also enable converts to become missionaries among their own people.[29] Between 1916 and 1928, Tanquist published at least ten books in four Naga languages—hymns, New Testament translations, *Pilgrim's Progress*.[30]

Finally, Reuben Holm. When he first arrived in Assam, he made a start at once by stopping his Ford motorcar in the street, and disposing of all his printed gospels—translations in Assamese, Hindu, Urdu, Bengali and Telugu. He sold them (albeit below cost) because things were valued the more for being bought, in his view. He then sang songs in English and his fledgling Assamese.[31] The production and distribution of texts continued to occupy him for the remainder of his mission. His fulfilment came in long journeys, over many days, hiking or on horseback and latterly by motorbike. He wrote eloquently of one trek through the Naga hills, conducting Bible classes amongst Lotha, Sema and Angami people who had seldom seen a European but who were willing to come dozens of miles to hear the gospel preached—54 miles (he claimed) in the case of one elderly couple, which was 'a good long walk to church'.[32] However, he also had a network of churches and schools. He managed to transfer one of sixteen village schools to the government in 1934, and found it hard to maintain the rest. But at the station school in Golaghat, the Holms had a hundred boys enrolled and about seventy attending, in five classes. They found the plains people too often uninterested so that many of the boys were supporting themselves and being taught free. Hill boys came too, to learn Assamese; some of them also were admitted free and even given food and clothing.[33]

What then was the impact of the local teachers and pastors, and the missionaries' texts and tours? (I am sure influence went both ways, as it did with colonial rule, but I am concerned with one-way traffic in this paper.) A set of farewell tributes to the Swansons in 1936 records their effect in the converts' own words. The couple reached out (these tributes said) to people on whom others looked down. They brought education to children from different groups—reading and writing and practical skills (ploughing, building and gardening) as well as Christianity. They taught the bad effect of opium and wine.[34] Most remembered was that Swanson had founded the Bible Conference in Golaghat, and Assam's first district Association, like the Indian National Congress, with an annual meeting, and that in 1914 he had set up the all-Assam Baptist Convention 'to bring unity to the whole of the work in Assam'.[35]

An exemplary convert, one of the minority ordained, was Tonaram Saikia, who had had decades of experience by the 1930s.[36] Many doctrinal and practical questions were brought to him. The Holms recorded a sample from Kacharis in 1934. Which is the true baptism, sprinkling or immersion? Should Baptists take and give communion with Lutherans? Why does the Baptist mission not pay

its village pastors? Why are there so many different missions? The questions moved across religion to social issues. What benefit is it for Christians to abide by the Christian Marriage Act of India? Must the marriage of a couple be registered if they do not wish it to be? Can a Christian have more than one wife? If a man leaves his wife and marries another, how long is it before he can be taken back by his church? Should there be a marriage price for girls?[37]

Each of these questions indicates an intervention by alternative ways of thinking, creating areas of contention and dynamism. One case, sent to Holm by Tonaram, concerned a gospel evangelist, who acquired a second wife, was spurned by the Christians, took a third wife, and ended up with three wives and their ten children all living together in the one household. Now, he was 'truly repentant', or at least willing to separate from the two later wives (while supporting them) but not to give up their children. Holm told him that he had no choice, and the children ought to be with their mothers, though he should provide for them and their education. Another case concerned a Hindu who had converted to Christianity and then reverted to Hinduism. He had sold his daughter to clear a debt. The creditor died and the man took back his daughter, but the creditor's mother was claiming her. What was Holm's advice? Of course, he read the man a lecture, told him that buying and selling children was illegal, and that he should be punished—not that he expected he would be.[38]

Girls as well as boys were targeted. The Tura Mission Middle English School, for example, had 200 enrolled in 1934. Hygiene classes by trained nurses proved popular, with the results to be seen in 'cleaner faces, hands, clothes, and combed hair'. Nearly sixty girls were being examined in sewing. In 1933 ten out of fifteen entrants had passed the Middle Scholarships examination. Three groups of Christian Endeavour were meeting every week, the intention being to develop 'girls who can be religious leaders'. Eight from the school had been baptized in October, along with twelve other girls.[39]

Wrote Wilbur Sorley, in the 1950s, echoing generations of Europeans and reformers, it is 'in the realm of a woman's life that the transforming power of the Gospel is particularly obvious'.[40] Assamese women, Hindu and Muslim, were mostly not permitted to appear in public, in markets for example, but Christian women went about freely. Bengali doctors supported the missions' medical work, but Ao women turned out to be able nurses; indigenous remedies dispensed by skilled women as well as men had been a feature of Naga life.[41] When the first conference of the Assam Students' Christian Movement was held in the Theological College at Cherrapunji in

1937, both men and women students were present; and, it was said, 'only those who have lived in India can appreciate the significance of that'.[42]

For the students at Cherrapunji, time was divided between discussion of Christian belief and witness, and the practicalities of village reconstruction: improving sanitation, water supply, and breeds of cattle and chickens; introducing primary education, and fighting superstition. The last was given an edge by news that the girls had lain awake all night in their dormitory for fear of a local snake god that had to be appeased by human sacrifice—cruel men were sent out to find victims and drain their blood, in return for large sums of money. Allegedly the practice still continued, even in these hills where the British government had its capital, and even though the Christian Khasis there were 'an enlightened people' who had had many advantages.[43]

On one hand, it was reported that, while 'dense ignorance and extreme poverty prevented the new members of the churches to do much for themselves', education was bearing fruit. Poor Christians could save enough to maintain their pastor—indeed none was provided without support. People were making intelligent use of their scant means and avoiding the wasteful brewing of rice beer. Even headhunters, those 'bloodthirsty enemies', were said to recognize the new power of the converts. In 1934, some 550 from the trans-frontier villages converted without any evangelical work, an unsown 'harvest without parallel' in the history of the mission.[44]

On the other hand, the fact that customs were attacked by the missionaries as by the British government did not mean that they vanished. Christian converts supposedly ate and distributed rice rather than turning it into beer for feast days and celebrations, but also those customs continued. Christians were not meant to pay a marriage price, among Nagas an important source of income for bride's families;[45] they were said to be taking the initiative to do away with it; but it remained a 'problem'. Holm preached against it vehemently whenever he had the chance, and extracted promises that it would stop, but 'old heathen customs' lingered on, disappearing and then reappearing. In one district, Holm blamed some 'few men who are stubborn and who do not seemingly have much of a hold on Christianity'.[46] As for headhunters, raids continued, from territories outside British control. Among Konyaks, the practice was said to have been stopped by government only in two villages where Christians had prepared the way. Missionaries were forbidden to visit or preach among these people, but a few Konyak boys had found their way to

Christian schools. One (who had wanted to continue his studies) was sent back to his people for the greater work of conversion. Seventy-one Konyaks were baptized in December 1934.[47] Elsewhere, among Semas, though warfare had been curbed, decorated posts still stood proudly in the villages, celebrating an earlier time with their scenes of hunting, feasting and sex; and war-drums were kept carefully as a relic of head-hunting days.[48]

A mixture of partial assimilation and outright opposition met the missionary efforts, as in most external intrusions on local custom. Certain Ao Naga Christians in government service were beginning to be open about their religion despite opposition;[49] but other elite Naga converts made sacrifices for their faith, being ousted from office and even from their villages.[50] In North Kamrup in 1934, a man named Khonda converted, with his family. They were to be baptized after their rice harvest. Before that, some fifteen Hindus came and beat Khonda and his wife until they fled, after which the mob plundered their property, pushed down some of the walls of their house and outbuildings, even digging up their vegetables. Holm, visiting the place, held a church service, played his mandolin, and spoke to some of the Hindus. Some said they were ashamed at what had been done. A complaint was made to the police who, once they found out that a *sahib* was interested, promised to do everything they could. The church in Gauhati provided money and clothes for Khonda and his family. Some time later the local preacher reported that all was quiet, and asked that someone be sent to officiate at the baptisms.[51]

The Holms also told the story of a school-boy, Puspa Chandra Das, from the heart of the valley, 'one of the most bigoted Hindu communities'. He was preaching Christianity but feared the persecution that would follow if he were baptized. Holm advised him to delay, and took the train with him to his home, telling everyone there about Christianity and that Pupsa Chandra was not being forced to convert. The boy's mother fell to the ground weeping: she would have to drive him from their home for committing the very worst of sins. Later, Pupsa sent Holm a card regretting that he could not be baptized. His schoolmasters and friends had prevented him by force; his brother had threatened suicide. 'The Hindu Society in our native land is very strong,' he wrote. 'The people think if a student goes away from among them the backbone of Hinduism will break'.[52]

'Perhaps', mused the Holms, a few days before this news, 'the outstanding reason why Christian work in the hill sections has progressed so far in advance over the plains is that the hill people are animists while the plains work has been among the Hindus with

their well established system of religion. The typical plains person also lacks that pep, open frankness and decisive action so readily seen among the hills people.'[53] A more pragmatic explanation was also offered. Some years before, during an uprising of the Kuki tribes, according to the Holms, the missionaries then present had helped with medical work. In recognition, a site was given for the mission, which it now occupied, and missionaries were permitted to work among the Tangkhul Nagas and Kukis. But they were forbidden to preach in Manipur where the people were 'strongly Hinduized'.[54]

Two final examples must suffice for evidence of the missionary influence on social and political life in these localities, and also for the complexity of this impact. First is Sarwan, an Anglican, headmaster of the Baptists' high school in Jorhat, who founded the Assam Chhotanagpuri Association, at a second attempt, in 1937. He described this as a lawful institution having the goodwill of the public, official and non-official, and of the Anglican, Lutheran and Catholic missions. Holm was opposed to it, and thought it typical of the man, who had earlier intervened in a heated dispute after the widower son of one Baptist family had run off with the daughter of another. Being of age, they gained the court's permission to marry. The boy's father consulted Sarwan, who helped him take a case to court against the young couple. As a result, the father spent much money, but the couple remained together. The missionaries taught that Christians ought not go to court against each other, and Holm told Sarwan that he should have referred the matter to their pastor.

Since then, Holm thought, Sarwan had tried to thwart the Baptists whenever possible, and the local missionaries in turn were planning to dismiss Sarwan from his post. Asked to support the new Association, therefore, Holm declined, on the grounds that its goal of social and moral uplift for the community was the Baptists' own aim—much of his work was among the Santhal migrants—and because, though all fifteen of Sarwan's officers were Christian, their manifesto made no mention of Jesus. The School Board required Sarwan to leave the school and the Jorhat compound by the end of the month. In response, he wrote to the Foreign Mission Society seeking to have Holm removed or at least barred from working with Chhotanagpuris. He stated that an American had no business interfering with the rights of a British subject, and claimed that Holm was paying his own people to go about spreading mischievous stories so as to discourage others from joining the Association.[55] The dispute played into earlier arguments between the Swedish Baptists, especially Holm, who were, they claimed, 'true to the faith', and the so-called Americans,

including members of the Foreign Mission Board, whom Holm considered 'definitely modernistic, and some who seemingly have no convictions at all'[56]—meaning in part that they wanted to spend more on education than evangelism. (At that time, J.C. Robbins, the 'modernist' or even 'heretical' secretary to the Board, also responsible for missionary placements, was said to have called Holm 'second-rate', and, through spite, to have conspired to refuse travel costs for the Bengt Andersons to return to Assam, preferring the 'modernist' Huttons. Such decisions, some claimed, were guided not by the Holy Spirit but by politics, meaning antagonism to the Swedes and their 'real' preaching of the Gospel, and a preference for social work that was ostensibly detached from evangelism.)[57]

Holm's view of Christians was as a single self-sufficient community, managing its own disputes; but the missions were inevitably involved in wider concerns. They sought land from government; they lived alongside non-Christians. Sarwan's Association was for Chhotanagpuris, people defined by outsiders, uprooted for the tea plantations; and it followed the pattern of organization and activities of the missionaries. It shared their aims too, as the Holms remarked. However, despite its Christian leadership, it turned in a secular direction, to areas of social improvement that the missionaries also espoused in order to attract converts.[58] Clearly, influence operated quite well even when the outsiders resisted its implications.

My second and last example is the family of Vichazelhu Iralu, Challie for short, who was an Angama Naga, educated at the American Baptist school in Kohima and St. Paul's College, an Anglican foundation, in Calcutta. Having completed his B.Sc. with financial support from a Baptist lady in New Jersey, he declared that he had long wanted to study medicine in the United States, and embarked on that enterprise with very limited funds but a guarantee from Ed Sorley, the missionary's brother, in Minnesota. Challie's father had been a Sub-Assistant Surgeon in government employ, who died in an accident; his mother was the daughter of early converts, nominally Christian and often showing 'much zeal for the Christian cause'. His maternal uncles were, it was said, 'agitators, trouble-makers and political revolutionaries'. In the late 1950s, his brother, Phizo, was a leader of the Naga opposition to the Indian government, claiming it had 'no right to rule over the always liberty-loving Nagas'. A reward was offered for his capture, dead or alive, and he fled from India. Another brother was in a Burmese jail on political charges. In America, Challie decided this was not the moment to take up an

offer of employment from the Christian Medical College in Vellore, in the present Tamil Nadu state in southern India. Even if not drawn into Naga nationalism, he thought, he would be hounded by the government.[59] Bengt Anderson later recalled that Prime Minister Nehru, speaking in Kohima in the 1950s, was said to have blamed missionaries for the unrest among Nagas.[60] In some ways, the missionaries *were* responsible.[61]

Social measures were regarded by them as means to the end of conversion, for the converts as much as the mission. Direct evangelism created real Christians instead of nominal converts. Therefore, much missionary influence was unintentional. Moreover, they undoubtedly had their share of racial arrogance and prejudice, though they realized that this could be a liability. The Tanquists' son, for example, recalled that as a child he played with 'the brown little boys of Christian families for they were cleaner than the non-Christian children, and there was not so much danger of getting skin diseases and various sicknesses from them, though my parents continually warned me not to touch their bodies or clothing'.[62] This world was glorious; its people not. The Holms remarked, fastidiously, that 'If one can look away from the sin, dirt and appalling spiritual dearth of the people, one can see a nature of real beauty, green in its verdure'.[63]

They made some accommodations and adaptations, but not very many.[64] Yet these fallable outsiders spent decades among the peoples of Assam's hills, working in local languages, and through local emissaries they had trained. More, they codified and standardized languages. Their residential schools helped to impart new customs and values and to promote solidarities where previously there had been none. They stressed Christian identity and community, linked to particular social practices or their avoidance.[65] But the same prescriptions might define other ethnicities and cultures which missionaries also helped label and define. By concentrating on the hill peoples, they contributed to those peoples' sense of separation from the plains. Certain places came to be identified with missionary activities and institutions. Churches, schools, meetings and associations provided a model of procedures and infrastructure for social and political organization. Finally, missionaries understood the importance of the state,[66] and positioned themselves and their converts accordingly. In these places, then, in ways prompted by the outsiders, local people began to define themselves, to organize, and to make new claims, in effect to nationality. The Christian population of

Assam's borderlands, and the Indian states of Meghalaya, Nagaland and Arunachal Pradesh, are now defined as peoples and places. Could they have merged instead into the mainstream, into the culture and language of the valley of the Brahmaputra? Or might they have retreated into long-term resistance, as dwellers of the forests and the margins have elsewhere, indeed nearby in the hills of Chittagong or of Burma/Myanmar? Nothing was a simple consequence of Christian missionary activities, but without them the localities' character and the content of these identities would clearly have been different.[67]

Where has our journey led? These stories attempt to flesh out the nature of a generally-accepted missionary influence, asking how and why change follows the migration of ideas and people. (The impact of migrants has something in common with the mark left by foreign rule, and with the consequences of significant innovation in material culture or production.) Our examples of such effects, in Nagaland, are part of the Indian national story, whatever the separatist aims of some peoples in this frontier region. The examples contain both intrinsic *and* outside influences. We see that the specifics of place are the bedrock of ineluctable conditions and memories, and also a challenge to generalization. Then we find that category requires difference, but that displacement is the price of standardization. Identity, obviously, is both formative and negative: what we are, as well as what we are not. It follows that category and difference, two sides of the one coin, are also important agents of change. I suggest that the usual emphasis on 'great' unifying evolutions (missionaries, say), rather than the 'minor' localizing continuities (here Nagas), derives from the static reification of both, and a failure to focus on their dynamic interplay. Instead, we may understand that places are made through the creation and re-creation of both specific and generic features, under both internal and external influence.

NOTES

1. The original version of this paper was written at the invitation of Concordia University (through Dr Rachel Berger), for a celebration of Professor John L. Hill on his retirement. The paper benefited from discussions with Sanghamitra Misra, working on a project on borderland identity sponsored jointly by the AHRC, ESRC and British Academy. See also note 18, below.
2. An overview, and a convenient example of thinking over recent decades, is Edward S. Casey, *The Fate of Place: A Philosophical History*, Berkeley: University of California Press, 1998. He notes that place, though ubiquitous to thinking, has, until recently, seldom been considered except as a 'modification' of space and a subordinate to time (p. x), perhaps in part because it is deemed irrelevant

to universals (p. xii). Note his discussion (pp. 40-2) of the distinction, in Plato, between *chora* and *topos* (space and place), which he sees as the basis of a long philosophical debate.

3. Henri Lefebvre, *The Production of Space*, tr. Donald Nicholson-Smith, Oxford: Basil Blackwell, 1991.
4. See James. C. Scott, '"Stilled to Silence at 500 Metres": Making Sense of Historical Change in Southeast Asia', *IIAS Newsletter* 49, Autumn 2008, pp.12-13; see Scott, *The Art of Not Being Governed: An Anarchist History of Upland Southeast Asia*, New Haven: Yale University Press, 2009.
5. Sanjib Baruah, 'Territoriality, Indigeneity and Rights in the North-East India', *Economic & Political Weekly*, vol. 43, no. 4, 22 March 2008. See also note 24, below.
6. See Christopher V. Hill, *South Asia: An Environmental History*, Santa Barbara: ABC-CLIO, 2008, passim; for example pp. 8-11, referring *inter alia* to B.S. Cohn's three general cultural zones (nuclear, route, relatively isolated) in his essay, 'Regions Subjective and Objective', in *An Anthropologist Among the Historians*, Delhi: Oxford University Press, 1987.
7. See Fernand Braudel, *L'Identité de la France* (1986), and that eloquent (if sometimes overwrought) evocation of the French *pays*, Graham Robb, *The Discovery of France*, London: Picador, 2007.
8. This is a larger subject than can be discussed here, as the phenomenon is to be found not only in every regional and national history, but also in most instances of cross-regional change: in the religious sphere, for example, in the Brahmanical adoption of local goddesses, the Christian adoption of local festivals and gods, the much-vaunted sectarian milieu of early Islam, the Persianate elements of shi'ism, the sufi approximations of bhakti for Indian proselytizing, the Christian missionary adaptations to caste and custom, the accommodations of Hinduism, Islam and Christianity with the Indian south and its forms of political authority, and so on.
9. Karl A. Wittfögel, *Oriental Despotism: A Comparative Study of Total Power,* New Haven: Yale University Press, 1957; Barry Cunliffe, *Facing the Ocean: The Atlantic and its Peoples 8000 BC–AD 1500,* Oxford: Oxford University Press, 2001. Casey, *The Fate of Place: A Philosophical History*, Berkeley: The University of California Press, pp. 301-8, discusses the conviction of Gilles Deleuze and Félix Guattari that 'where something is situated has everything to do with how it is structured' (emphasis removed). Casey refers to their contrasting 'nomadism' with 'settlement', and fringes with states, referring first to the central Asian steppes in 1227 [the death of Genghis Khan], and their suggestion, drawing on music and Pierre Boulez, that 'smooth' places encourage 'wandering and drifting between regions' while 'striated' places confine and shape the directions of travel. The ' "smooth" is a *nomos* [here a distributed model of law and custom, as opposed to *physis*, nature] whereas the striated always has a *logos*' [presumably meaning a particular discourse of rational order], and the 'fact that "all becoming [a key concept] occurs in smooth space" cannot conceal the equally important fact that "all progress is made by and in striated space"'; quoting G. Deleuze and F. Guattari, *A Thousand Plateaus*, 1980, pp. 478 and 486. Arguably, though the fit is far from exact (these 'smooth' places are heterogeneous, multiple and unobservable, allowing vagabondage and revolution), a parallel point is illustrated in this paper.

10. Condorcet's *Equisse d'un tableau historique des progrès de l'esprit humain* (1795) with its nine epochs from primitive nature to western Europe and beyond, applying mathematics and probability to analyze human behaviour; Comte's *Cours de philosophie positive* (1830-42) and other works, relating social and human development, from theological through metaphysical to positivist, scientific explanations; and Marx's *Das Kapital* (1867, 1873 and with Engels' editing on to 1890) on the evolutionary process of capitalism, based on the law of value, and through inherent contradictions giving way to socialism. See Casey, *The Fate of Place*, pp. xii-xiii, for comments on wider universalist aspirations, in mathematics and linguistics, on recent political reasons for shunning universals, and also on a recent 'active desire' for particularity. However, he remarks, modern rediscoveries of place regard it as being without formal structure of steadfast essence: they are about place 'at work', as an 'ingredient in something else' (history, nature, politics, imagination and so on). Though Foucault, for example, claimed that space and place are as ever-altering and inconstant as time (heterotopology), he did so (claims Casey) without really interrogating the concept of place, and while retaining 'universalist aspirations' (pp. 297-301).
11. Fernand Braudel, *Capitalism and Material Life, 1400-1800*, New York: Harper and Row, 1967, tr. Miriam Kochan, London: Weidenfeld and Nicolson, 1974.
12. Fernand Braudel, *The Mediterranean and the Mediterranean World in the Age of Philip II, 1949,* Berkeley: University of California Press, 1996.
13. Braudel, *Civilization and Capitalism*, Berkeley and Los Angeles: University of California Press, 1992, p. xiii, referring to three levels and spheres of life (material, economic and capitalist) that changed in their field of action.
14. On the fairy stories, see Iona and Peter Opie, *The Classic Fairy Tales*, London: Oxford University Press, 1974.
15. Peter Hardy, *The Muslims of British India*, Cambridge: Cambridge University Press, 1972, p. 11.
16. See most recently Peter Robb, *Empire, Identity and India*, vol. 1; *Liberalism, Modernity and the Nation*, vol. 2; and *Peasants, Political Economy and Law*, Delhi: Oxford University Press, 2007.
17. Udayon Misra, *The Periphery Strikes Back: Challenges to the Nation-State in Assam and Nagaland*, Shimla: IIAS, 2000 begins with this point; it also considers the extent to which different peoples gained 'meaningful space' within the new state of India (Ch. 1), though whether it is appropriate to call such peoples 'ethnicities' and 'nationalities' depends on the meanings given to those terms, and a recognition of the role, extent and limits of homogenizing forces. The British certainly sought to establish clear borders, and to extend their control by ordering the inhabitants as villagers, tribes and so on (see also Robb, *Liberalism,* Ch. 5). Inevitably these processes invested chosen groups with rights over specified lands, assumed ownership of resources such as trees, coals, or fish, and encouraged conflict between rivals over their exploitation. A forthcoming work by Bodhisattva Kar, *Accumulation of the Primitive: The North-Eastern Frontier of British India, 1790s-1930s*, discusses such issues and seems likely to deepen our understanding of this region's history. For example, examining the 'Inner Line' constituted by British administration to separate the plains and hills, and the assumed opposition between civilized cultivators and savage hillmen, Kar argues that such policy was qualified and affected by the mutual involvement of hills and plains, shown through tributes paid to hill chiefs (*posa*)

and various allowances for intermediaries, messengers and translators; there were also transitional processes whereby hillmen could become raiyats (rent-paying agriculturists).

18. I am drawing on papers that are deposited in the Bethel Seminary in St. Paul where many of the missionaries had trained. My research in this archive was supported by the British Academy and SOAS.
19. Edna and Reuben Holm (hereafter Holms) to the Swedish Baptist General Conference of America, 2 May 1933, Holm Papers, Bethel Seminary Archives, St Paul, Minnesota, hereafter B.S.
20. The Baptist General Conference took over the work in the north after 1946. See D. Coustan and M. Erikson (eds.), *Fifteen Eventful Years: A Survey of the Baptist General Conference, 1948-1960*, Chicago: Chicago University Press, 1961, pp. 84-100.
21. Among the Ao Nagas, Sangtams, Changs and Konyaks, there were 69 Baptist churches, claiming nearly 12,000 adherents, and 41 village schools that taught over 1,200 pupils; a new church had been built that year at Impur. Some 75 churches and 24 village schools served more than 8,000 Sema Nagas, that mission being centred on Kohima. Report for the year 1938 by Edna and Bengt Anderson, Anderson Papers, B.S.
22. Forssell to 'Friends', 17 January 1939, Holm Papers, B.S.
23. The school was then 'shaky' for want of money. Jonas Ahlquist to Hagstrom (his later son-in-law), 30 October 1934, Jonas A. Ahlquist papers, B.S. (Ahlquist died in a road accident, 12 March 1941.)
24. Holms to Hagstrom, 27 November 1932, Holm Papers, B.S.
25. Ahlquist to Hagstrom, 30 October 1934, loc. cit.
26. Edna Forssell to 'Friends in Christ', 17 January 1935, Holm Papers, B.S.
27. Rev. Bengt. T. Anderson, *We Lived in Nagaland: The Experiences of a Missionary Family* [1978], p. 17, B.S.
28. Ibid., pp. 18-20.
29. 'Mission Work among the Nagas', *The Standard*, official organ of the Swedish Baptist Conference, Chicago, Tanquist Papers, B.S.
30. In Angami, Sema, Kacha and Rengma Naga. See Tanquist Papers, B.S. Born in Sweden, he studied at the Bethel Seminary from 1904 to 1909 and sailed for Assam with his wife in 1912.
31. Holms to Esther [Sabel], 16 January 1933, Holm Papers, B.S. The incident was in Tezpur, which he thought, as a beautiful town on the north bank of the Brahmaputra, would be ideal for a mission station; it had only an Anglican who ministered to the Europeans and two Roman Catholic priests based there for their north bank activities. Tezpur was cosmopolitan, with Hindus and Muslims of all types, high-caste Assamese, merchants from all over India, coolies from the centre and south, and representatives of all the various tribes of the valley and hills. This meant, thought Holm, that no one group would become so bigoted and oppressive as to prevent the missionary work. As it happened he made his headquarters in Golaghat, further up the valley and across the river.
32. Extract enclosed with Holms to Esther [Sabel], 10 April 1933, Holm Papers, B.S.
33. Reuben Holm, 'Educational Report on the Golaghat Field, January-December 1934', Esther Sabel Correspondence, B.S.
34. Heathcare played its part. A Brahmin, Bhubonswar Sarma, recalled his being baptized after recovering from a serious illness during which he had dreamt of

Christ. Illness also led to the conversion of an Oriya, Premdas Urma. See note 35, below.

35. Note by Tonaram Saikia (translation provided in original), Farewell Letters for the Swansons, 1936, B.S. For others quoted above, from nearly 200, see ibid. The Convention met every two years, an opportunity for people from all parts to confer together. In 1934, its final church service ended with songs in each language represented: Kachari, Assamese, Garo, Mikir, Mundari, Doura, Ao Naga, Oriya, Karia, English and Swedish. Holm to 'Folks' (family members), 21 February 1934, Esther Sobel Correspondence, Holm Papers, B.S.
36. Reuben Holm to J.C. Robbins, Foreign Secretary, American Baptist Foreign Mission Society, New York, 16 July 1937, Holm Papers, B.S. He was converted by Swanson around 1904; see note 34, above. Though respected and experienced, when he was asked to take charge in North Lakhimpur, he did not want to leave Golaghat and felt his appointment would cause ill-feeling.
37. Holms to Esther [Sabel], 3 November 1934, Holm Papers, B.S. The bride price among Nagas was paid by the prospective son-in-law to her parents.
38. Holms to Esther [Sabel], 3 November 1934, Holm Papers, B.S. Daukow was the repentant evangelist.
39. Yearly report, Esther Sabel correspondence, Holm Papers, B.S. The School failed 15 of the 200 during the year to cut costs, and also considered closing their kindergarten. They did not, for fear that the Roman Catholics would be only too glad to mop up the pupils. Instead, the seventh class was suspended for a year. But things were not all bad. There was a better corps of teachers than ever in 1934, a good spirit among the pupils, and other girls were eager to join.
40. Explanations to accompany showing of black and white reel, Wilbur Sorley Papers, 1949-54, B.S.
41. Anderson, *We Lived in Nagaland*, p. 41.
42. Marion G. Burnham note, 25 October 1937, Victor Sword Papers, B.S.
43. Ibid.
44. Reports for the year 1938, Bengt Anderson Papers, B.S.
45. Anderson, *We Lived in Nagaland*, p.19.
46. Rengmai district; Holms to 'Folks', 10 July 1937, Holm Papers, B.S.
47. Edna Forssell to 'Friends in Christ', 13 January 1935, Holm Papers, B.S.
48. Anderson, *We Lived in Nagaland*, p. 22.
49. Edna Forssell to 'Friends in Christ', 17 January 1935, Holm Papers, B.S.
50. Anderson, *We Lived in Nagaland*, p. 21.
51. Holm to 'Folks', 21 February 1934, Esther Sobel correspondence, Holm papers, B.S. The mob was led by a man, Saiaram, who had persecuted the local preacher, Khogendra, a couple of years before. He slipped away before Holm arrived.
52. Edna and R. Holm to 'Folks' [family members], 25 March 1934, Holm Papers, B.S. The boy's village was Patacharutchi.
53. Holms to Esther [Sabel], 20 March 1934, Holm Papers, B.S.
54. Holms to 'Folks', 10 July 1934, Holm Papers, B.S.
55. Holm to Robbins, 16 July 1937, and to G.A. Hagstrom, President, Bethel Institute, St. Paul, 17 July 1937, Holm Papers, B.S. Sarwan, though an Anglican, had been kept on for want of alternatives. He had an M.A. Though doctrinally he was unsound, his character had been good in Holm's experience, though it was said that earlier he had been imprisoned in Chhota Nagpur for embezzlement while being employed in a government office. He had already appealed on this occasion to Lambert, Superintendent of Police in Jorhat, who had 'caused the

Christian people in the Naga Hillls . . . no end of trouble'. Holm and the School Board claimed to bear Sarwan no ill-will and to wish he 'could have listened to reason and saved his good name and career'.

56. Edna and Rube Holm to 'Lillian and Rube', 24 April 1933, Holms Papers, B.S.
57. Holm to Hagstrom, 7 June 1933, Holm Papers, B.S. A Commission of Laymen also visited Assam and criticized the work there from a similar perspective. Victor Sword note, Holm MSS, B.S. Closer ties with tea planters and European business interest had also been advocated by them and rejected by the missionaries in the field in the 1930s, as again in the 1950s.
58. So too the dispute with the modernists, Robbins and his colleague Padelford, and with the Laymen, had partly been about devoting more money and effort to education and reducing the subsidies for evangelical work, which was to Holm the heart of their mission. Holms to Esther [Sabel], 24 March 1933, Holm Papers, B.S.
59. Wilbur Sorley to 'Brother Erikson', 5 November 1958, Sorley Papers, B.S. On Angami Zapo Phizo (1900?-90), see Misra, *The Periphery Strikes Back,* pp. 33-5, 39, 41-2, 47-52, 55-6.
60. Anderson, *We Lived in Nagaland,* p. 75.
B.S. Reports of the accusation led the missionaries to bring court proceedings against the press. Later, legally cleared of the charge, the Andersons were not allowed visas to return to India. They had left because of the terminal illness of their son, Bruce, in the United States.
61. As Karen Ray remarked when this paper was read, 'A later Marxist rebel, coming to an agreement with the Indian government, was asked if his word could be trusted; he referred to Jesus (personal communication by Karen Ray, Concordia University conference).' My argument, however, is not that Christians as such were instrumental in all or any particular aspects of the political struggle. For example, though Naga revolutionaries in the National Socialist Council of Nagaland appealed to the twin causes of Nagaland and Christ, the leaders of the Ao-dominated Church had called for an accommodation with India; see Misra, *The Periphery Strikes Back*, pp. 51-2. The point is rather that broader changes were 'triggered' by Christian influence and conversion, as Misra notes (p. 54). Similar but wider influences lay behind the push for greater Assamese autonomy.
62. D.C. Tanquist, Autobiography, J.E. Tanquist Papers, B.S.
63. Holms to Hagstrom, 27 November 1932, Holms Papers, B.S.
64. Holm insisted on keeping to the rules. Approving the singing of Lotha planting songs with Christian words was about the limit of his accommodation to local customs. Holms to 'Folks', 7 December 1935, Holm Papers, B.S.
65. As John Hill remarked when this paper was read in Montreal, for Protestants their own families set an example.
66. Government patronage was important, and not only under the British. After independence, an extension of the Baptist hospital at Tezpur on land released by the Lutherans was supported by Assam's new government. The government's conditions had delayed the hospital building, but K.W. Hagstrom noted that there were advantages in working with the administration, so as to 'have the privilege of appealing to them if necessary', and that a 'wrong course of action'—such as depending on the tea planters—was liable to cause resentment. To seek 'the shelter of a European organization' would place them, said Hagstrom, in that category of 'independent foreigners' who trusted in 'a superior complex

that a white face is the best and most powerful'. Hagstrom to Danielson, 28 July 1949, Hagstrom Papers, B.S.

67. Misra, *The Periphery Strikes Back*, provides information about political events in aspects and periods not covered by this paper. Note, on the Naga Club that was calling for Naga autonomy in the 1920s, 'there was not much of political interaction between the tribes and the idea of a common approach to Naga issues was quite a new one'. The Naga National Council (1946), following separate Lotha and Ao Councils (1923 and 1928), thus marked a significant advance, based (Misra explains) on an incipient middle class, lessening inter-tribal rivalry, and emerging all-Naga consciousness, pp. 27-31.

3

Practices of Sovereignty, Practices of the Market: Writing Spatial Histories of North-Eastern India

SANGHAMITRA MISRA

The paper is an exploration in the histories of exchange, marketing practices, and trading networks in north-eastern India and its neighbourhood during the pre and early colonial periods. It is focused around Goalpara and its connections with the regions that surround it: the Eastern Duars, Cooch Behar, southern Himalayan foothills of Bhutan, southern Tibet, the north-eastern borders of Bengal and the western borders of Assam. The paper demonstrates that the histories of exchange and marketing practices in the region can also be located in another temporality, that of a rich connected history of this historically liminal and fluid space. Through the early 1800s and at least until the last decades of the nineteenth century, markets emerge as critical sites for recovering elements of this connected (and largely erased) history. Commercial transactions formed part of an extended social landscape in the region and through the pre- and into the early colonial, the history of trading was marked by cultural and political underpinnings that included notions of a sacred topography which bound the local polities of Tibet, Assam, Bhutan, Bijni and Sidli in various relationships of patrimony. The second half of the paper investigates the impact of colonial governmentality, particularly the colonial state's spatial strategies and its production of economically unified, bounded territorialized units, on the culture of trading in the region. As colonial institutions and ideologies of governance met the hierarchized and overlapping realms of multiple and shared sovereignty of Goalpara's zamindars, the Bhutan monarch, the Dalai Lama of Tibet, the Ahom ruler and various autonomous tributaries, practices of the market could no longer be represented as just one

more material instance of shared history. Rather, as some of the most visible sites for the production of indigenous, and now colonial, notions of space and power, they were inextricably entwined with this new history of contesting spatial practices that colonial intervention generated.

I

In the pre-colonial period and also into the early colonial, the several circuits of trade, pilgrimage and migration routes that intersected Bhutan, Tibet, Cooch Behar, Rangpur, of which Goalpara formed a part, and the Duars or the foothills of the Himalayas provided an enduring base for a connected history of the region. This was an area rich in ecological resources,[1] separating the towns and trading ports of western Assam and eastern Bengal from their markets inland, in Bhutan and Tibet, and the principal channel for trade between Tibet, China, Bhutan and Assam. Studying the region for its lateral connections,[2] the period emerges as one when its links with the imagined core of Indian history were less significant than those with other areas. These were clearly 'frontiers' only in the 'Indian' civilizational narrative.

From the late eighteenth century onwards, if not earlier, a considerable volume of trade was carried on in several of the weekly markets and fairs that were held along the foothills of the Duar area. In particular, the numerous fairs formed an important element in the trading network of the region. Some were also held in the plains of southern Goalpara and were connected to local shrines. Of these fairs, the ones held at Hajo, Kuriapara and Udalguri were among the best attended ones. The Kuriapara fair, held in the Duar by the same name on the borders of the Bhutan kingdom, was under the shared sovereignty of the states of Bhutan and Tibet, and was the principal channel for trade between Tibet, China, Bhutan and Assam. Francis Buchanan (quoted in Mackenzie 1884: 16) offers an interesting description of the fair:

> An annual event in which traders from all parts of Tibet, from Lhasa and places east, west and even north of it were present in the crowds, some of them clad in Chinese dresses, using Chinese implements and looking to all intents Chinese. Many have their families with them and carry their goods on sturdy ponies, of which some hundreds were brought down to the fair yearly. The annual caravan from Lhasa, carrying silver bullion to the amount of about one lakh rupees and a considerable quantity of rock salt halted at Chouna on the confines of the two states of Bhutan and Assam and carried back tussar cloth, iron, and lac from

Assam and otter skins, buffalo horns, pearls, and corals that were imported from Bengal.[3]

Mid-nineteenth-century colonial expeditions into Bhutan commented on the centrality of the Duars in the economy of Bhutan and described the region as forming 'the most valuable part of the Bhutan territory. Through them and from them are procured almost every article of consumption or luxury that the inhabitants of the hills possess. Their principal trade is with them' (Pemberton 1865: 17). Several mountain passes connected Bhutan with the plains of southern Goalpara and Bengal. The expeditions listed 'the numerous passes into Bootan along the frontier, some of which lead direct to the capital' and listed the 'Bijni, Buxa and Na Dooars among the principal Dooars or passes' (Eden 1865: 10). In his notes on his travels in the region, Ashley Eden observed that 'several of these routes connected northern Goalpara to Bhutan, including one which connected Bijni to Wandipur in Bhutan, and others which linked Bijni, Sidli, Bengtoli, Kachubari, Buro Bungloo, Dubleng, Cherrung to the capital of Bhutan' (ibid.). Through these passes flowed a trade in many articles. Woollen cloth, coarse cotton cloth, indigo, sandal, asafoetida, cloves, sugar, ghee and oil were brought up from the plains, while Tangun horses, blankets, walnuts, musk orange and cow tails from Bhutan were sold at the markets of Rangpur in the south (Bose 1865: 198).

In this trade through the markets of northern Goalpara and of the south, timber from the forests of the eastern Dooars was undoubtedly among the most important items. At the turn of the eighteenth century there was already a large timber trade in the region of the eastern Duars, much of which was not for local use, but largely for export to southern Bengal: 'the traders came with boats from Dhaka and Mymensingh during the rainy season to buy up timber in the Duars, on the borders of Garo Hills and up in Kamrup'.[4] Buchanan observed that 'Merchants of Goalpara usually export to the low country from the forests of Howraghat and Mechpara about 1500 canoes in the year . . . [T]he timber was floated down numerous rivers which included the Ai and the Manas, from the Dooar region and also from Nepal and Bhutan, towards the southern ports like Fakirgunj.'[5]

The timber was also tied into rafts and then floated down to the port of Narayangunj near Dhaka. The extensive sal forests in the Parbatjoar and Khuntaghat parganas were worked on by several duffadars and labourers, several of whom were from the neighbouring districts of Bengal and derived their livelihood solely from felling sal timber.[6] By the last decades of the nineteenth century, trade in timber

comprised the bulk of the trade exports from Goalpara to Bengal (Hunter 1879: 50). More than 600 boats came up every year from Serajgunj, Dhaka and other places in eastern Bengal for purchasing timber worth about £12,000.

Timber was only one of the several articles that linked this region to the other trading networks of eastern India in the pre-colonial period. A profitable trade in the region was in salt, for which southern Goalpara formed the transit point between Bengal and Assam. Some of the earliest references to the salt trade are in a historical narrative of seventeenth- and eighteenth-century Ahom rule. Compiled during the eighteenth century, the text reproduces the following response of the Ahom king, Raja Rudra Singha, to a request made by the Mughal *faujdar* at Rangamati for establishing commercial relations with the Ahoms in June 1793:

> Is it called trade if it is limited to a few maunds of salt from Bengal and the despatch of a few boats from our place? If the Nawab is intent on the establishment of commercial relations with us, he should send his merchants to Jugigopa and Goalpara, and our leading traders will proceed to Kandahar chokey with large quantities of valuable articles. If matters are arranged along this line, they acquire the status of haat-bat or trade.[7]

In the elaboration of marketing practices in the plains of southern Goalpara and in the hilly areas of the north, an implicit narrative is that of markets and expanding networks of trade acting as important transmitters of authority. Beginning with the late Mughal period, there was an increasing assertion of authority by zamindars and other local powers over trading practices and places of exchange in the region. This was evident in the exaction of several dues for passage at the *chokeys* or custom houses set up at several points along the chief waterways. Travelling along the western borders of Assam in the mid-eighteenth century, James Rennell observed several such *chokeys* along both banks of the Brahmaputra near Goalpara.

> The Assam country begins from the Bonaash [Manas] river on the north side of the Brahmaputra and one of their *Chokeys* is placed directly opposite Gwalpara . . . [F]rom the 2nd to the 6th of December we were employed in tracing the Brahmaputra from Gwalpara to the frontier of Assam on the southern side. We were not permitted to land on the northern side or the Assam side, all the way, there being several *Chokeys* placed.[8]

The rights to the collection of these dues were frequently hereditary and also an assertion of political rights. Colonial authorities noted, however, that:

> Several of the custom houses were also farmed out to the biggest bidder and the whole trade of the country [was] in fact monopolized by these individuals, who

> in terms of the treaty concluded in February, 1793 ought to leave only 10 per cent on exports and imports but in reality extort what they choose. (Hamilton, Symes, Canning, Cox et al. 1854: 102)

The *chokeys* on the Assam border were similarly regulated by the Ahom state with those custom houses 'towards the frontier of Bengal (being) farmed to two Rashi Barhmons, Komol and Parusuram . . . called Baruas (while) the chief custom house, Kandahar, usually called the Assam Chauki by the English, (was) situated at a place called Hadira in Pergunnah Bausi, nearly opposite Goalpara.'[9] The agent of the Assam government at Kandahar was the Duaria Baruah or the Kandahar Baruah who paid an annual rent of Rs. 90,000 and had the right to levy a rather moderate duty of 10 per cent on export and import. In practice, however, the 'custom has long been to leave this entirely to their discretion, and although there is no absolute law to prohibit the merchants from Bengal from carrying their goods to Jorhat or Guwahati . . . yet the Barua may be said to have complete monopoly and the whole trade passes through his hands.'[10]

> The Dooaria Baruahs realised the duty on all exports and imports. They received advances from the Bengal merchants for the delivery of Assam goods or accepted Bengal goods on credit. Goalpara on the south bank, Jugigopa and Rangamati on the north are the three eastern outposts of Bengal from where the merchants conducted their trade. (Martin 1976: 477)

This intervention by traditional political authorities in commercial exchanges persisted into the early decades of the nineteenth century. Buchanan noted with much dismay the various transit duties and the rights exercised by the zamindars and local chieftains during this period. These included the right 'to levying a share of all goods sold at the markets as well as transit duties on all goods carried from one place to another in the markets of southern Goalpara'. 'In some places', he added, 'it was even alleged that they granted small monopolies on several of the most important articles sold, such as cotton, salt and mustard seeds.'[11]

A particularly good example of marketplaces serving as 'an extension of a vision of patrimony' (Sen 1998: 6) in southern Goalpara was the weekly market on the borders of the Garo Hills. The Garo Hills were a key economic resource for the zamindars of Karaibari, Mechpara and Kalumalupara, who sustained themselves through relationships with the Garos, the locally dominant people who lived in the hilly regions surrounding their estates and carried on a flourishing trade in cotton with the inhabitants of these estates. Colonial records noted that large areas of surrounding woodland on

the fringes of these estates were eminently suited for the zamindars who 'held all the low country under the Garo Hills on that side . . . and as all the cotton, then the staple of the internal eastern trade, came from these hills, the Choudhuris had established at all the principal passes, haats or markets guarded by their burkandezes' (Mackenzie 1869: 21).

The taxes levied in these *haats* on both merchants from the plains and on the Garos formed one of the main sources of income of these choudhuris (ibid.). This conformed to similar practices in the late Mughal period, when in frontier areas, where the *mal* or the produce from the land was sparse, the greater proportion of the revenue came from the ability of the zamindars to extract a *sair* or commercial tax on all kinds of goods that passed through their territory. Thus, the zamindars of Goalpara,

> while paying a small tribute to the Mughal faujdar of Rangpur as acknowledgement of their loyalty, were to all intents and purposes independent. They were bound in fact merely to supply a certain number of elephants or a small quantity of *aghur*, a precious wood, to support for the maintenance of garrisons and the artillery park at Dhaka. Their estates were never subjected to land revenue assessment and they paid what they did pay from their sayer and not from the mal. The faujdar generally made advances on account of cotton to these great choudhuris, as the zamindars were called, and received from them yearly consignments of that article. (ibid.)

The revenue of several of the permanently settled estates of Goalpara was paid in cotton during the initial period of colonial rule as well, and the zamindars depended not only on taxes collected from the settled peasantry, but also on the resources garnered by raiding the neighbouring Garo Hills. The frequent raids by the zamindars of Karaibari and Shusang into the Garo areas, however, were not accompanied by an incorporation of these marginal areas into the territory of the chieftains. Occupation was only temporary, as when the zamindar of Karaibari built forts in the trading passes to assert control over the cotton trade, the aim of these attacks was to compel a weaker polity to submit its allegiance. The sovereignty and independence of the Garo chieftains were allowed to coexist with that of the other local chieftains. The Bemulwa or independent Garos, for instance, formed a significant proportion of the population of the Garo Hills and were responsible for several of the innumerable raids on the Goalpara plains.

What were later described in colonial records as 'stories of violence and murder by a few independent savages'[12] were often a means of asserting the shared rights of the communities over the resources of

the area as also of correcting the often unequal economic relationship conducted through the market. The Garos could hardly be defined as isolated communities defending themselves against an economically and politically more powerful civilization of the plains. Rather, through different strategies, of which frequent raids were the most visible, they routinely asserted their control over the resources of the region while continuing to retain their political and economic independence. The passage below illustrates the same:

> In those parts of Kalumalupara which border the hills, it is no uncommon practice with the Garos to enter the villages and make demands of pigs, goats, fowls, or any other articles . . . which the ryots are of course glad to comply. Such occurrences, if unaccompanied by homicide, are seldom reported to the police officer . . . when such acts become too frequent for endurance, they either desert the village and retire to some more secure spot or purchase the forbearance of the Garos by an additional donation (Matah) Matha Rakah, a species of blackmail, very generally paid by the ryots in remote situations in that pergunnah to the neighbouring Garo chief, for the preservation of their heads as the term denotes.[13]

Periodic looting and plunder of the estates continued through the nineteenth century, establishing the position of the Garo chieftains as tributaries who were autonomous and sovereign in their own right. In the winter of 1816, Garos living on the borders of the Mechpara zamindari estate carried out a violent attack that lasted for more than a month wherein 'they wounded the zamindar, massacred his servants besides several of the ryots and burnt and plundered his zamindari Kutcherry together with several villages situated in the same estate'.[14] The deployment of more troops by the Magistrate of Rangpur appeared to have little effect, for a report from the *daroga* of the Rangamati outpost stated that a burkandez had also been beheaded by the rebels.[15] Illicit duties imposed by the Mechpara zamindar on the cotton trade had evidently triggered off the immediate violence as the burning of the office records of the zamindar by the Garos was accompanied by the burning of the cotton that had been collected over five years in three or four adjoining villages.[16]

And finally, to return to the northern borders that this section began with, the relationship between trade and authority was one of immense significance in this area where exchanges in the marketplace were frequently the most visible articulation of local political powers. Contrary to what colonial records wrote, the region that later formed the northern part of the colonial district of Goalpara was neither an integrated part of the state of Bhutan, nor was it under the exclusive sovereignty of the chieftains of Bijni and Sidli. This was reflected in

the existence of shared rights of these powers over the resources of the area. The zamindars of the northern parts of this borderland, of the estates of Bijni and the Sidli, had a relationship of reciprocity with the Dharma Raja of Bhutan, wherein the zamindars sent up dried fish, endi silk and *salami* in return for Tangun horses and rights to the Cheerung forests.[17] The relationship, however, was not limited to reciprocity and in the region of the eastern Duars, and sovereignty and physical boundaries were frequently not conterminous. The Kuriapara Duar was under the occupation of the Bhutanese officials for eight months of the year while local powers claimed revenue during the rest of the year. The collection of tribute from the Duars could also be seasonal: in certain areas the soubah descended from the hills of Bhutan only 'when the cold air of December and January had rendered the region comparatively healthy'.[18] The kings of Bhutan were not the only claimant to such rights in this part of north-eastern India. In another example of overlapping territoriality that was extended across the physical space of the Tibetan plateau, the Ahom kings who were frequently in conflict with the state of Bhutan over the produce of the Duars also sent, however, an annual *peshkash* or tribute as an acknowledgement of the sovereignty of the Dalai Lama of Tibet over the region.[19]

The role of the market in enforcing indigenous notions of political space in the region was, therefore, of considerable significance. The *peshkash* paid by the Ahom king was offered at Chouna, a site for a market in the Eastern Duars, situated at a distance of a two-month journey from Lhasa[20] and from where the caravans left for the Tibetan capital. There were similar markets established at Gengushur, 4 miles away from Chouna. Prior to the occupation of the Duars, the Sath Rajas who were Bhutia chiefs who controlled the Kuriapara Duar and were considered subordinates of the Towang Raja, a tributary of Lhasa, paid their tribute through the purchase of cotton and other goods at the Udalguri fair, all of which were then sent to Lhasa and Towang.[21]

Evidently then, the pre-colonial history of western Assam and north Bengal (including parts of Bangladesh) is inseparable from the history of Bhutan and Tibet. Several of the fairs in the region of the eastern Duars appear to have been part of a larger sacred topographical space, with descriptions of the nature of trading in the Duar area suggesting that this region was perceived as part of the religious space of the sacred sovereign realm of the Bhutan monarch. The flow of pilgrims into the Duars and the plains below

were a significant accompaniment of the trade between the southern plains of the borderland and Tibet. Ethnographers and travellers to the region noted that 'the Bhutias considered the Dhurma Raja as their spiritual, incarnate deity, whose trade with inferior chiefs in the Dooar region was more in the nature of some Nuzzerana or offering from these chiefs'.[22] Religious motifs defined the relationship of submission between the rulers of Bijni and Sidli and the Dharma Raja of Bhutan. And finally, the town of Hajo was an 'important point in the sacred topography of the region . . . boast[ing] of a large establishment of priests [who were] attached to a temple, which [was], by the Bhutiahs and the Kampas, considered very sacred, and to which both these tribes, but specially the latter, resorted annually in large numbers'.[23]

II

With its extensive restructuring of the local spatial order, colonialism was a powerful disjuncture in the region. It began with the early characteristically hesitant interventions of the East India Company in the late eighteenth century and was replaced by a more confident state from the mid-nineteenth century onwards. Through its institutions of economic, administrative, and judicial control that included practices of mapping, classification through the census, surveys and measurement, the state realized its idea of a unified economic space. In several parts of the world, the restructuring of local spaces was almost irreconcilably linked to a larger process of creating homogenized global spaces forged by new sets of connections. In this part of the globe, however, colonization predominantly exemplified a fragmentation of the region into unambiguous, compact political units. By the last decades of that century, the state presented an absolute organization of space that was characterized by its frozen borders.[24] The tedious and complicated process of fixing territories with political boundaries that were previously continually negotiable, had begun simultaneously,[25] although the overlapping sovereignties of Bhutan, Bijni, Cooch Behar and smaller chieftainships (such as the Baikunthapur zamindar) would continue to be a source of considerable anxiety for colonial officials through much of the nineteenth century.

Nevertheless, an ideology of a unified territorialized entity was being realized, to be later claimed selectively by local collectivities, and stitched to an emerging entity called India. For administrative

units within this entity, spaces such as Bhutan, Tibet, Nepal and all the other places in between were firmly external to the new topography. The trajectory that would see their transformation from connected spaces into 'spaces that elude'[26] was now in place. Since there were no overlaps in territoriality allowed in a colonial spatial order, Cooch Behar, Goalpara, Garo Hills, the products of a 'cookie cutter' administrative imagination, were political units that could exist henceforth only as parts of this nationalized territory. That initial nationalist imaginings in colonial South Asia were 'crystallised around the notion of a territorially delimited economic collective, a national economy in the 1870s and 1880s',[27] only added to this production of a nation space.

In these now eastern borderlands of colonial India, agricultural expansion and an intensified collection of revenue helped stabilize local governance and the bounded unified economy that colonialism introduced. The aggressive sedenterization through the 'colonization of wastelands' scheme, the extension of colonial legality and the migration of over a million cultivators from the bordering districts of eastern Bengal into Goalpara (and also Cooch Behar) over just two decades of the twentieth century, dramatically altered the demographic composition of the region and the local economy and added to the economic surplus of the colonial state. It was the role of the market, however, in the production of these borderlands that offers crucial insights about the ways in which territory, economy and culture came to be imagined in this region after colonial intervention. In the section that follows, the paper looks at the transformation of the market and trading practices in the borderland into sites of political conflict between the colonial state and local powers and its effects on the regional polity and economy.

From the mid-nineteenth century onwards, changes in trading routes and in the geographical terrain of markets marked the beginning of processes that were to integrate Goalpara and the Duar region into the trading networks of eastern India, in particular of the province of Bengal. Over the eighteenth century, salt had emerged as the most important article in the trade between Assam and Bengal, with a vigorous trade being carried on through a few towns in Goalpara. Several European companies and individuals vied with one another for control over the market during this period and resisted the claims of local powers. Among these companies was the Society for Trade, established by Robert Clive for the sole purpose of trading in salt. The company was closed down in 1768 after the East India Company was

briefly deprived monopoly over the trade. Colonial records mention several individuals who participated in the salt trade from Goalpara of whom Daniel Raush and George Lear appear to have been the most prosperous. The former, according to these records, was a 'respectable Hanoverian and the principal merchant at Goalpara in 1769'.[28] The latter was an English merchant who resided in Rangpur and like Raush, had established an independent salt factory and salt emporiums in the town of Goalpara besides several warehouses at Dhaka.[29] Ganganarayan Roy, a Bengali salt merchant residing in Dhaka had also stationed his agent, Robert Bigger, at Jugigopa in the Goalpara district.[30]

The French East India Company also had a branch established in 1755 by Jean Baptiste Chevalier who was deputed from Chanderanagore on this project and had a salt factory at Goalpara. Until 1778, when they were recalled to Calcutta by the government, there were several French merchants at Goalpara, trading independently (S.K. Bhuyan, 1928: 3). The frequent skirmishes between these several trading groups required the intervention of the local powers who now 'negotiated disputes amongst the Europeans who [were] settled at Goalpara . . . to more effectually secure the peace of the country and to protect Assam from free booters . . . so that commerce may be carried out to the mutual advantage of both kingdoms.'[31]

The period also saw several officials of the East India Company struggling to gain exclusive rights over the sites of the production and distribution of salt. Hugh Baillie emerged as a persuasive representative of the Company's interests in the salt trade. In a memorial to the colonial administration in 1793, Baillie outlined the significance of this trade and Goalpara's position in it, while arguing persuasively for the appointment of an agent which would make way for a further control of the Company over the market (S.K. Bhuyan, 1949: 71). He argued that his experience as an agent of Clive's Society of Trade had allowed him 'the opportunity of acquiring a knowledge of the Company's business at Rungpore, and also of the interior parts of Bhutan and Assam, and the countries adjacent to Gualparah, which had never been explored by any European before' and offered to be a salaried agent of the Company, supervising the salt trade at Goalpara.[32] Baillie's appointment as the Superintendent of the Company at Goalpara in 1787 reflected the contradiction within the colonial political economy. An apparent freedom of trade coexisted with the need to control the market. By the end of the eighteenth century the Company was dealing in more than 100,000 maunds

of salt in the region, imported from Khulna and Dhaka in eastern Bengal through the towns of Goalpara and Jugigopa.

These trade links continued to be vibrant through the early decades of colonial rule, evident from the lists of commercial centres in Eastern Bengal in Francis Buchanan's writings on Goalpara. Buchanan suggests that the region of southern Goalpara and the eastern Duar area were integrated into the extensive trading circuits of Narayangunj, Serajgunj, Murshidabad and the Mughal port city of Dhaka. Connections existed through the waterways of the Brahmaputra and other smaller rivers like the Godadhor and the Gangadhar. These also linked Mymensingh in south-eastern Bengal to the external trading circuits of Bhutan and Tibet, the rest of Bengal, and the internal trade networks of Assam.[33] Buchanan noted that

> by far the greater part of the grain [from Goalpara] goes to Seerajgunj in the Moymonsingh district and to Narayangunj near Dhaka but a part also is sent to Murshidabad, Calcutta and the intermediate towns. The grain that is imported, chiefly mustard seeds, comes from Bhutan and from Bihar and from Assam. These areas were also the centres of the cattle trade . . . the greater part of which is exported to Seerajgunj and Narayangunj.[34]

Bhutan also exported horses, musk and paper to Murshidabad and Assam. Trade in several other products, including an illicit one in opium, linked Goalpara with the ports of eastern Bengal, while silk cloth from Murshidabad and cotton from Dhaka were imported into Assam from Rangpur and Goalpara.[35] The chief routes connecting Assam with Bengal passed through Goalpara. Accounts from the period suggest that there were three overland routes from Bengal to Assam:

> The first by Murshadabad, Mauldah [Malda], Dinagepore [Dinajpur], Rungpore and Goalpara. This is the line of the Calcutta dak but it is almost impassable during the rains. The second route is via Dhaka, Dumari, Pucuoloe, Jumalpore, Singimarry and Goalpara, also nearly impassable in the rains. The third passes by Sylhet, Chirra, Nunklow, Ranneygodown, Cannymook and Gohatti [Guwahati], but from its crossing over the Khasya hills, it is impracticable for any land carriage and beast of burden.[36]

Colonial records indicate that the bulk of the trade of Goalpara was now carried on directly with Calcutta. The principal exports were mustard seeds, silk cloth, timber, and cotton and lac obtained from the Garo Hills. The growth of several towns, including that of Dhubri, was also linked to their relative importance as transit points for the trade with Bengal.[37] See Table 3.1 for lists of articles which passed through the river ports of southern Goalpara, indicating the significance of the region in the trade between Bengal and Assam in the first half of that century.

Table 3.1: Trade between Bengal and Assam in the Early Nineteenth Century

Exports from Bengal in 1809	Rupees	Exports from Assam in 1809	Rupees
Salt, 35,000 maunds	1,92,500	Stick lac 10,000 maunds	35,000
Ghee, 1,000 maunds	1,600	Moonga silk	11,350
Fine pulse	800	Black pepper	500
Sugar	1,000	Long pepper	500
Stone beads	2,000	Cotton (with seed) 7,000 maunds	35,000
Coral	1,000		
Jewels and Pearls	5,000	Ivory	6,000
Spices	1,000	Bell metal vessels	1,500
Gold and silver cloth	1,000	Mustard seeds	20,000
Copper	4,800	Iron hoes	600
Red Lead	1,000	Slaves	2,000
English woollens	2,000		
Tafetas	2,000		
Satin	1,000		
Benarasi Khainkobs	500		
Muslin	10,000		
Shells	100		

Source: R.B. Pemberton's, 'Report on Bootan', in *Political Missions to Bhutan*, p. 82.

Anxious to promote a more regulated form of trade and commerce, the colonial state intervened in specific ways in the markets and marketing practices in the region. Significant among the administrative interventions was the prohibition of the exercise of indigenous privileges through local taxes and *chokeys*. These were seen as obstacles in the growth of free trade. Following the views of classical political economy proclaimed by the Company, Buchanan had perceived these practices as 'prejudicial to the public, by checking cultivation and commerce'.[38] He regarded the duties levied by the zamindar of Bijni on the transit and sale of goods as a 'gross usurpation' of the rights of the ordinary trader and merchant.[39] There was a gradual restriction and prohibition of local taxes and dues levied at markets, on ferries and, most importantly, by zamindars on the boat and timber trade. In March 1835, Kandahar *chokey*, which had been the most important site for the collection of dues by local rulers

during the Mughal imperium and even earlier, was closed.[40] The closure effected a sharp rise in the trade with Bengal, aided further by the introduction of regular river traffic on the Brahmaputra, the first steam-boat being put into service in 1847. By the second half of the nineteenth century, more changes in the trade with Bengal were in place. The growth of the tea industry in the province of Assam now replaced lac, cotton and ivory with tea (followed closely by jute and mustard) as the prime commodity of trade. The extension of tea cultivation in upper Assam and the operation of coal mines demanded an increase in the import of iron and steel needed for the laying of the railways, apart from the large influx of indentured labour from eastern and central India into the tea estates. By 1900, almost the entire trade of Assam was with Bengal, trade with regions other than Bengal amounting to less than one per cent.[41]

The growth in the Bengal trade was accompanied by a gradual decline in the trade with Bhutan. John Mcosh[42] observed that

> in former times, an extensive trade was carried out with Bhutan and there was established a well frequented mart at Seepotah but little of that traffic now exists. Colonial reports on trade from the 1870s attributed this decline to the absence of a good communication network.[43] There was a similar decline in the trade with Tibet, which had been lucrative . . . in the first decades of the nineteenth century, [and] amounted to more than two lakhs rupees [but] which has for many years discontinued.[44]

By the first decade of the twentieth century, British officials could dismiss this trans-frontier trade as 'of very little importance . . . the principal imports being rubber and the principal export, silk.'[45]

On the eastern side, the fairs held at Darrang, Udalguri and Kherkheria continued to have a considerable presence of traders from Bhutan as well as Tibet into the first decades of the twentieth century. Held during the winter months, between January and March, the principal articles of trade from Bhutan included ponies, lac, wax, blankets, musk, and from the British territories, yarn, piece goods, rice, brass and copper utensils, raw silk, iron bars, tobacco and areca nuts and dried fish. Until at least 1923-4, the fairs have a steady presence in colonial reports on trade with 'frontier tribes'.[46] Officials commented on the 'difficulty of getting reliable statistics', which they attributed variously to the nature of the trade itself (it comes down in driblets and it is almost impossible to check)[47] to the more obvious attribution of the absence of a certain notion of classification in the indigenous imagination. From 1916 onwards, a system of registration of the trade at Udalguri was effected and there are figures

for that year: Rs. 65,000 in imports and Rs. 40,000 in exports.[48] The registration evidently did not yield satisfactory statistics and officials worked to put in place a system that would help redirect local practices more firmly towards a colonial classificatory order. 'In the past statistics were collected by trade registrars who were stationed at fixed points on the border and any trader not passing their station was missed', reports the Deputy Commissioner of Darrang in 1924. 'Next year these registrars are to be abolished and details of trade will be collected from the headmen and principal traders'.[49]

Like the trade with Tibet, the trade with Bhutan too continued to record a steady decline. The trade statistics supplied by the *mauzadars* in the very next year showed a great decrease in the value of exports and imports.[50] By 1926, the economic significance of the trade at the fairs, never considerable in the records of the colonial state, had declined sufficiently for the entire system of registration of trade statistics to be discontinued.[51] Colonial officials attributed this variously to a 'decrease in the number of Bhutias who came down to Udalguri and Kherkheria' or on unreliable trade statistics.[52] These observations recur through the records of the next two decades, until 1935, when the Darranga fair with the Bhutias disappears altogether from the 1934-5 report. There is a simultaneous decline in the fair at Udalguri.

> The Udalguri fair is now of no importance. The ponies and sheep brought down were very poor in quality and sales were few. As I have reported previously, this fair has very nearly ceased to exist and I have proposed that the Udalguri outpost should be moved to Bhairabkund where it will be valuable. If this is done then the temporary Bhutia camp may also be sited near Bhairabkund.[53]

Among the possible explanations for the decline in trade with Bhutan, the most obvious would be the transformation of the resources of the region, particularly the rich forests of the Duars which were a reliable source of strong, durable timber such as sal that was of use in the expanding rail network in eastern India,[54] into raw products for the markets and industries of mainland Bengal and India. This was accompanied by the search for alternative, more profitable routes of trade with Tibet through Nepal. A lot of the trade with the Bhutanese moreover was conducted through everyday, unregulated forms of exchange across the hills. Official correspondence reported that 'the Bhutias, who are regarded as being under political control, gave little trouble but complaints were received of the Bhutias of Bhutan, who wander along this frontier in the cold weather', necessitating 'prompter measures in the British territory wherever reports of

offences are received, but unfortunately this is not always possible . . . patrols were sent out to Udalguri Post up to a distance of about 12 miles as a preventive measure and on one occasion succeeded on arresting some of these people who had been selling liquor.'[55]

Through a regulation of existing trade routes with Bengal and their improvement through a new infrastructure of roads and railways, combined with prohibitive restrictions on tolls levied by local powers and stricter controls at the borders, the colonial state ensured therefore a westward reorientation of the regional trade, ignoring routes and exchanges of pre-colonial times. On the southern borders of the Garo Hills and Goalpara, where there were more examples of the market emerging as a site for conflict between the British government and local rulers. Here the confrontation between notions of political space and trading rights was less masked, resulting in the colonial state using the market to effect changes not just in the trading practices of the region but in indigenous spatial and cultural practices as well. From the time of the Commissionership of David Scott, there are several voluminous records relating to the Garo tribes that argued for a legalizing of a separate administration for the Garos[56] and other 'hill communities', introducing in the process 'the master oppositional binary' in the colonial discourse in India—the hill-plain dichotomy.[57]

The weekly *haats* bordering the Garo Hills were as much about the demonstration of pre-colonial power hierarchies as they were about the richness of local cultural dynamics and imaginations of political space. Represented in official correspondence now only as places where the Garos were subjected to 'a constant succession of fraud and falsehood'[58] by the inhabitants of the plains, they helped produce a different spatial order altogether in which ethnic groups were fixed to particular physical spaces,[59] the 'correct' habitat for the Garos being the hills.

The relations between the zamindars and the hill tribes had been so undefined and fluctuating in their nature and so much influenced by local and accidental circumstances . . . there was considerable trouble fixing the principles by which they would be governed. The separation, however, of the hill tribes from the zamindars appeared to us as measures of the first necessity.[60]

Scott's proposals on the cotton trade between the Garos and the Goalpara zamindars returned the market as the site for effecting this separation. He

propose(d) to the government that the delivery of cotton should altogether be stopped and in lieu of this and the Kurm collections made in the northern

division, that a tax should be imposed upon the Garos of 5 Rupees per house of the 1st class and of 2 rupees on those of the lowest, that a deduction should be made from the gross proceeds of 25 per cent to provide for the expense of collecting the revenue. The collection should be conducted by a native officer. Garo sirdars should get a per cent for the trouble they had taken and also to make them more responsible.[61]

Other regulations included limiting the number of *haats* along the Garo-Goalpara border to twelve and curbing raids by Garos on the villages in the plains.[62] These measures were justified as part of the process of protecting the Garos from the zamindars of Goalpara who 'having been released from the responsibility of defending the country from the raids of the Garos could not be entitled to derive any profit from the lands over which they had exercised the right of property appertaining to the sovereign than those of mere land holders'.[63] Arguments for the introduction of a separate customary law, as distinct from the law in effect in the plains, accompanied these measures and Scott's proposal for the introduction of a system of police and criminal judicature among the population of 30,000 people that the Garos comprise of that was similar to 'the system pursued in Bhagalpur in regard to the people residing in the hills'[64] was adopted in the Resolutions of the Governor-General in Council. A narrative of civilization and morality that located the inhabitants of the hills/forests in the lowest rung of a temporal and spatial hierarchy neatly sealed this hill-plain binary and identified the ethnic inhabitants of mountainous regions in north-eastern India as the 'other' of a resurgent Indian civilization. As the Regulation X of 1822 (which separated the administration of the Garo Hills from that of Goalpara) noted in its objectives: 'To promote the desirable object of reclaiming these races to the habits of civilized life, it seems that a special plan for the administration of justice, of a kind adapted to their peculiar customs and prejudices, should be arranged.'[65]

Even while not changing structures in their entirety, therefore, colonial intervention through the market constituted a critically decisive shift in the region, replacing its connected history with a new set of spatial interactions that had at its core, the production of a national territoriality of colonial India. Goalpara was now a politically and economically demarcated entity, a unit of the colonial state, severed from all the several areas it had shared a pre-colonial connected history with. Reoriented from being a site for thriving commercial and cultural exchange between the northern polities of Bhutan and Tibet, and Assam and Bengal, into a hinterland of goods for the Bengal market, it is but obvious that this construction

of Goalpara was inextricably linked to the practices of the colonial spatial imagination and to the needs of an expanding market. In the spatial history of the region, this was a stage when it became part of a colonial borderland, an 'in between' space between the now two 'core' provinces of Bengal and Assam that does not get definitively absorbed into either of these 'civilizational spaces', and this had much to do with the shift in the nature of markets and trading practices, including the gradual erasure of previous cultural and political underpinnings. With the reorientation of the region's trade towards Bengal, a spatial restructuring was initiated by the colonial state that ensured that this borderland gradually came to constitute the frontiers of Assamese, and to an extent Bengali, identity, the focus on its still shifting boundaries and identities ensuring that it had only a minimal role in the discursive terrain of nationalist politics.[66] In short, the region became a good example of 'places that fell off the map' and through the cracks of the imagined history of nationalisms.[67]

NOTES

1. A report from an expedition prior to the British occupation of the Eastern Duars described the region as a 'narrow strip of land, ranging in breadth from 10 to 20 miles, which runs along the base of the lower range of the Bootan Hills from the Darjeeling district to the Frontier of Assam [and] extends from the Dhansiri river to the River Teesta on the west. The land within these limits is by nature singularly rich and fertile; it is formed of the richest black vegetable mould, is washed by many rivers, and has a southern slope from 1,500 feet to the level of the plains of Bengal.' (Ashley Eden, *Report on the State of Bootan and the Progress of the Mission of 1863-1864, Calcutta, 1865*, p. 2.) The thick forests of the Duars were also a reliable source of strong, durable timber, especially sal, a factor that was of considerable significance for the expanding rail network in eastern India and behind the colonial occupation of the area in 1866.
2. Sanjay Subrahmanyam, *Explorations in Connected History: From the Tagus to the Ganges,* Delhi: Oxford University Press, 2005, p. 11.
3. Ibid., p. 15.
4. Correspondence between the Deputy Commissioner of the Eastern Duars and the Commissioner of Cooch Behar, 10 May 1866, Goalpara Papers (henceforth GP), File no. 7, Assam State Archives, Guwahati.
5. The Buchanan Hamilton Papers, Book III, p. 207, Oriental and India Office Collection (henceforth OIOC). Buchanan noted: 'The merchants of Goalpara were the chief dealers in the timber trade and advanced at the rate of 1 Rupee for a pair of timbers, to be delivered at a place where they will float' (p. 215).
6. The Buchanan Hamilton Papers, Book III, p. 6, OIOC. Buchanan also mentions the 'joldhuyas', a group of about 30 families of the Rabha community living in the town of Goalpara, who cut timber and made furniture and were chiefly employed as wood cutters. (The Buchanan Hamilton Papers, Book V, p. 30, OIOC.)

7. *The Asam Buranji, from the earliest times to the Swargadeo Gadadhar Singha's recovery of Guahati from the Mughals in 1682. No. 6,* quoted in S.K. Bhuyan, *Anglo-Assamese Relations: 1771-1826,* Guwahati, 1949, p. 50.
8. James Rennell, November 1765, Extract from the *Memoirs of the Asiatic Society of Bengal*, vol. III, no. 3, pp. 95-248, 1910, in F.C. Hirst, F.C. and A.B. Smart, *A Brief History of the Surveys of Goalpara District*, Shillong, 1917, Appendix 1.
9. The Buchanan Hamilton Manuscripts, 'Nations Bordering Assam', Mss Eur D 76, p. 57, OIOC.
10. Ibid.
11. The Buchanan Hamilton Papers, Book V, p. 92, OIOC.
12. Letter from C.T. Metcalfe, Officiating Commissioner of the Cooch Behar Division to the Secretary to the Government of Bengal, June 1873, Government of Bengal Papers, 1873, OIOC.
13. Copy of a letter from David Scott to W.B. Bailey, the Acting Secretary to the Government in the Judicial Department, Extract Bengal Judicial Consultations, 16 February 1816, OIOC.
14. Copy of a letter from David Scott, the Magistrate of Rangpur, to W.B. Bailey, the Acting Secretary to the Government in the Judicial Department, 31 January 1816, Extract Bengal Judicial Consultations, 16 February 1816, OIOC.
15. 'Report from Mussiddin, the Daroga of Thanah Rangamati', enclosed in a letter from David Scott to W.B. Bailey, the Acting Secretary to the Government in the Judicial Department, 1 March 1816, Extract Bengal Judicial Consultations, 16 February 1816, OIOC.
16. The zamindar stated that he was returning from Mechpara after handing out *takavis* (advances) to the ryots, when he was attacked by the Garos. He was stabbed and had to flee for his life, while the 10 persons who were following him were beheaded by the Garos. The Garos carried away the Rs. 2,000 that the zamindar had with him after the collection of nankar rents, and the selling of cotton. . . . They also murdered several ryots and burnt the villages of Phoolpur and Gujeria. Since it was too dangerous for him to remain in his house, the zamindar was now living on a boat in the middle of the river. (Extract from a letter from Mahiram Choudhuri, the zamindar of Mechpara to Gurumohan Chacki and Hariprasad Vakeel, Board's Collection, 1818-20, OIOC.)
17. Translation of an undated sanad from the Deb Raja of Bhutan to Kumud Narayan of Bijni, GP File, no. 7, 1866-70, Assam State Archives, Guwahati.
18. Memorandum from C.T. Metcalfe, GP, July 1865, Assam State Archives, Guwahati.
19. 'An Account of the Kingdom of Assam', in *An Account of the Burman Empire and the Kingdom of Assam, Compiled from the Works and MS Documents of the Following Most Eminent Writers and Public Functionaries viz. Hamilton, Symes, Canning, Cox, Ley, Den, Morgan, Wade, Elliot &c*, Calcutta, 1854, p. 109.
20. Alexander Mackenzie, *History of the Relations of the Government with the Hill Tribes of the North East Frontier of Bengal*, Calcutta, 1884, p. 16.
21. Ibid.
22. William Griffiths, 'Journal of the Mission to Bootan', in *Political Missions to Bhutan, Comprising the Reports of Hon'ble Ashley Eden – 1864; Capt. R.B. Pemberton, 1837, 1838, with Dr. Griffiths's Journal and the Account by Baboo Kishen Kanta Bose,* Calcutta, 1865, p. 189.
23. Ibid., p. 125. Griffiths remarked that 'this pilgrimage [was] however connected more with trade than religion, for a fair [was] held in the same time. Coarse

woollen cloth and rock salt form[ed] the bulk of the goods which each pilgrim carries, no doubt as much for the sake of penance as for profit'. (Ibid.)

24. A large part of what later formed the district of Goalpara was already a part of British territory from the late eighteenth century. According to the terms of a treaty between the ruler of Cooch Behar and the East India Company in 1772, the former became a protectorate of the British government. The hilly Eastern Duars continued to be controlled by the Bhutan monarch until 1866, when they were ceded to British territory. This annexation also made Bhutan a separate, independent polity. The Garo Hills were constituted into a separate district by 1874, an enforced hill-plain dichotomy being the underlining notion of the bulky files that constituted the official discourses.
25. Letter from Major James Rennell, with one sketch map, dated December 1767, of Rangpur, Cooch Behar and Bhutan, Mss Eur F218/103, OIOC.
26. David Ludden, 'Where is Assam?: Using Geographical History to Locate Current Social Realities', *Himal South Asia*, November 2005.
27. Manu Goswami, 'From Swadeshi to Swaraj: Nation, Economy, Territory in Colonial South Asia, 1870 to 1907', *Comparative Studies in Society and History,* vol. 40, no. 4, p. 611.
28. *An Account of the Burman Empire*, p. 103.
29. Letter from George Lear to Warren Hastings, undated, Bengal Revenue Consultations, 23 January 1781, OIOC.
30. Bengal Revenue Consultations, 12 September 1780, OIOC.
31. Warren Hastings to the Asam Raja, 14 June 1780, *Calendar of Persian Correspondence*, vol. V, no. 1911.
32. Ibid.
33. Buchanan's list of the places with which Goalpara had commercial links included 'Serajgunj, a mart which seems to have arisen since the time of Major Rennell's survey and which is now a chief place of trade in Bengal, and stands on the Jhinayi river, Narayangunj, the port of Dhaka, Murshedabad and Calcutta.' (Buchanan Hamilton Papers, Book V, p. 5, OIOC.)
34. Ibid.
35. Ibid., p. 73.
36. R.B. Pemberton, 'Report on Bootan', in *Political Missions to Bhutan*, p. 9.
37. E.A. Gait, B.C. Allen and H.F. Howard, *Gazetteer of Bengal and North East India*, Shillong, 1905, p. 519.
38. The Buchanan Hamilton Papers, Book V, p. 92, OIOC.
39. Ibid.
40. H.K. Barpujari, *Assam in the Days of the Company 1826-1858*, Guwahati, 1963, p. 243.
41. H.K. Barpujari (ed.), *Comprehensive History of Assam*, vol. 4, Calcutta, 1992, p. 124.
42. John M'cosh, *Topography of Assam*, Calcutta, 1837, p. 66.
43. *Annual Report on the Trade between Assam and the Adjoining Foreign Countries*: various years beginning 1878.
44. Ibid.
45. B.C. Allen, Assam District Gazetteers, vol. III, *Goalpara,* Calcutta: Baptist Mission Press, 1905, p. 103.
46. *Annual Report on the Frontier Tribes of Assam: 1911-1924,* Shillong, OIOC.
47. *Annual Report on the Frontier Tribes of Assam, For the Year 1915-1916*, Shillong, 1916.

48. Ibid.
49. *Annual Report on the Frontier Tribes of Assam, For the Year 1923-1924*, Shillong, 1924.
50. *Annual Report on the Frontier Tribes of Assam, For the Year 1924-1925,* Shillong, 1925.
51. 'No trade statistics are now maintained in the locality': *Annual Report on the Frontier Tribes of Assam, For the Year 1925-1926,* Shillong, 1926.
52. *Annual Report on the Frontier Tribes of Assam, 1911-1912*, Shillong, 1912, OIOC.
53. *Annual Report on the Frontier Tribes of Assam, For the Year 1930-1931*, Shillong, 1931, OIOC. On the Udalguri fair: Much of the glory of this fair has departed during the last few years and this year the attendance was smaller owing it is said, to the superior attractions of Darjeeling and Kalimpong for the larger traders. (*Annual Report on the Frontier Tribes of Assam, For the Year 1928-1929*, Shillong, 1929, OIOC.)
54. Besides the belt of Terai forests at the foot of the Bhutan hills, there was a valuable tract of forests in the Gooma region of the Eastern Duars, stretching to the estate of Parbatjoar. Most of these forests were of sal trees, next only to teak in its durability, though more difficult to season.
55. *Annual Report on the Frontier Tribes of Assam, For the Year 1929-1930,* Shillong, 1930, OIOC.
56. These include several volumes of *The Board's Collection* in the OIOC.
57. Sanjib Baruah, 'Territoriality, Indigeneity and Rights in North-east India', *Economic and Political Weekly,* vol. 43, no. 12, 22 March 2008, p. 16.
58. Martin Montgomery, *The History, Antiquities and Topography and Statistics of Eastern India*, vol. 3, Collated from the original manuscripts of Buchanan Hamilton, Delhi, 1976; 1st pub. London, 1838, p. 686.
59. Baruah, 'Territoriality, Indigeneity and Rights', pp. 15-16.
60. Copy of a letter from David Scott, the Magistrate of Rangpur to W.B. Bayly, the Chief Secretary to the Government, enclosing the Report on the Garo Hills of 15 August 1818, The Board's Collection, 1825-26, OIOC.
61. Ibid.
62. David Scott's Report of the 20 August 1816, Bengal Criminal Judicial Consultations, 27 September 1816, File no. 47, OIOC.
63. Ibid.
64. David Scott's Report of the 16 April 1819 in Copy of a letter from David Scott, the Magistrate of Rangpur to W.B. Bayly, the Chief Secretary to the Government, enclosing the Report on the Garo Hills of 15 August 1818, OIOC. In the *Resolutions of the Governor General in Council* on the following year '(i)t was agreed that the General regulations should not extend to the Garos or other hill tribes . . . and that civil and criminal justice should be administered by the Commissioner under general rules and . . . founded on the usages, local prejudices and the habits of the people . . . measures of separating the zamindars from the hills tribes appeared necessary in as much as the latter had formed one chief cause of the acts of violence and revenge perpetrated by the Garos'. (*Resolutions of the Governor General in Council*, Board's Collection, 1825-26, OIOC.)
65. R. Clarke, *The Regulations of the Government of Fort William in Bengal, 1793-1853*, vol. II, London, 1854, p. 659. The introduction of a separate law was being proposed as an alternative to the use of military force against the Garos. Thus the Secretary of State observed that 'however necessary it may be to teach

the inhabitants of these wild districts that they are not inaccessible to the power of Government, it is very clear that we cannot hope to reclaim them from their savage habits, or to induce them to a higher stage of civilization by the mere display of military strength'. (Mackenzie, *History of the Relations with the Hill Tribes,* p. 24.)

66. The impact of the imposition of a hegemonic discourse of space and power by the colonial state and the accompanying erasure of local, more fluid spatial practices in areas which then came to constitute border areas has increasingly emerged as the central assumption of several works on the construction of colonial frontiers and borders. Rich reflections of such histories include Paul Nugent and A.I. Asiwaju (eds.), *African Boundaries, Barriers, Conduits and Opportunities,* London, 1996 and Thomas M. Wilson and Hastings Donnan (eds.), *Border Identities,* Cambridge, 1998.

67. The arguments offered by borderland studies, a rich and growing body of research that pushes for writing histories both outside and beyond the nation while raising related questions about the structuring of colonial knowledge and the historicity of spaces, offer an alternate conceptual location for studying local histories such as these, that have been the victims of much academic violence in the post-colonial histories.

4

Colonial Nostalgia as a Means of Resistance: Historical Discourses in Post-1997 Hong Kong

TZE-KI HON

In a crucial scene from *Infernal Affairs II* (2003), all the main characters of this Hong Kong crime-thriller undergo a transformation of identity at midnight of 1 July 1997. At 'point zero' in the transition from British Hong Kong to the Hong Kong Special Administrative Zone (HKSAZ), members of both the law enforcement agencies and the triad society have to clean the slate and start anew. On one side, the police have to replace their 'Crown Badges' with new insignia symbolizing their loyalty to the HKSAZ and the People's Republic of China and on the other hand, the leaders of the triad society (now dressed in tuxedos rather than rugged street wear) after toast to the dawn of a new era under the leadership of a charismatic triad boss. This change of identity also applies to the two duplicitous characters of the movie—the undercover police agent belonging to the triad society and the gangster who infiltrates the police. Young and aspiring, the two moles are promoted in their respective hierarchy of power. The undercover agent is recruited by the new triad boss to become an overlord of the underworld, while the gangster infiltrator is now a police inspector taking more responsibilities to combat crimes. Further away from their true identities but moving deeper into the targeted institutions they plan to subvert and supplant, the two moles become a pair of fierce opponents who clash publicly and violently in *Infernal Affairs I* and *Infernal Affairs III*.

As a metaphor for the Hong Kong transition, this important scene of *Infernal Affairs II* stresses the continuity of the colonial structure of power even after the departure of the British.[1] To be sure, externally the police wear a different insignia and the gangsters update their wardrobe. Yet, internally both sides still live in the same Manichaean

world where they are locked into the epic battle of good and evil. The same is true of the two moles. Hiding their true identities in order to achieve their goals of subversion, they continue to play the game of deceit and pretension. Despite the hyperbole about 'point zero', including the famous countdown of the 'Hong Kong Clock' in the Tiananmen Square,[2] *Infernal Affairs II* shows that the 1997 handover does not clean the slate or mark the beginning of a new era. The supposed triumph of national independence (signified by the removal of the 'Crown Badges' and the raising of the Chinese national flag) is just a ritual that does not bring about a fundamental change in government and society.[3] Similarly, the supposed awakening of the subjectivity of the colonized (symbolized by the fireworks and the toasting) turns out to be a façade to legitimize the *status quo*.[4]

By underscoring the persistence of the colonial structure of power, *Infernal Affairs II* raises questions about the nature of Hong Kong's post-coloniality. Is it a special type of national liberation that attempts to deal with the complex history of colonialism and the kaleidoscopic colonial ethos? Or is it an empty show that hides the continuation of the colonial structure despite the rhetoric of national independence? Or is it a complicated saga of collaboration and subversion (as the two moles in the movie represent) that goes beyond the conventional dichotomies between the colonizers and the colonized, the oppressors and the oppressed, the foreign occupiers and the resistance fighters? As Low Wing Sang has pointed out, the post-coloniality of Hong Kong deserves our special attention because it does not follow the usual pattern of decolonization and national liberation. Rather, it is shaped by 'collaborative colonialism' first practised by the British colonial rulers and now the Chinese leaders in Beijing.[5]

COLONIAL NOSTALGIA AS A MEANS OF RESISTANCE

In this article, I will examine the complexity of post-1997 Hong Kong by analysing the discourses on colonial Hong Kong. Since the mid-1980s, historical writings have been a site of contestation over the identity of the Hong Kong people. During the last five years leading to 1997, in particular, mainland Chinese historians published a large number of books and articles to retell the history of colonial Hong Kong.[6] In addition to educating mainland Chinese citizens about the significance of the return of Hong Kong, this outpouring of publications was aimed at the Hong Kong people, particularly the educated elite who saw the return of Hong Kong as the end of British

liberalism and the rule of law in the city-state. As John Carroll puts it, the publications were 'to shake loose Hong Kong Chinese from their identification with the colonial government and to construct a new identity with the motherland'.[7] This outpouring of publications, in turn, triggered an intense interest in colonial history among the Hong Kong cultural elite. In the name of writing a 'Hong Kong history for the Hong Kong people', local scholars produced their own version of colonial history. Thus, over the last two decades, two distinct views of colonial Hong Kong have emerged: the mainland Chinese view of the loss and recovery of an integral part of the nation, and the local Hong Kong historians' view of the blossoming of a cosmopolitan city-state that flourishes in global capitalism. Often presented in academic writings aiming at the educated readers, these conflicting narratives encapsulate two different visions of Hong Kong in its post-colonial age, and lend support to two opposing camps in post-1997 Hong Kong politics, the 'nationalists' (*qinzhong pai*) and the 'liberals' (*minzhu pai*).

From the perspective of post-colonial studies, it is intriguing that local Hong Kong historians vehemently affirm the contributions of the British colonial rule in developing a unique Hong Kong identity. In this case, we witness a peculiar practice of colonial nostalgia. Rather than the *ex-colonizers* remembering the colonial era to seek solace and satisfaction from the past, we find the *ex-colonized* engaged in colonial nostalgia to define their collective identity. Rather than a calculated move by former colonists to justify colonialism in the post-colonial age, we see the liberated locals remembering the colonial era to ward off the totalizing ethos of nationalism.

As a means to resist the totalizing ethos of nationalism, colonial nostalgia in post-colonial Hong Kong is important for two reasons. First, it is an avid affirmation of the fluidity and multiplicity of human identity. It shows human identity is indeed a 'contingent patchwork', as Yasmin Saikia describes, that is 'negotiated at many supportive and opposing levels'.[8] As such, the colonial nostalgia in post-1997 Hong Kong can be understood as a counter-narrative to the bounded nationalist history. Rather than focusing on the loss and recovery of the Chinese sovereignty in Hong Kong, local Hong Kong historians view the British colony as an immigrant city constantly searching for a new identity. Instead of stressing the cultural and economic ties to the motherland, they emphasize the diversity in the colonial outpost that welcomed investors, entrepreneurs, skilled professionals, and unskilled labours from all over the world.[9]

Second, this yearning for the colonial past in post-1997 Hong Kong challenges our concept of colonial nostalgia. Our 'anger' at colonial nostalgia (to use Renato Rosaldo's word) is a response to the continuing outpour of memoirs, movies, novels, and coffee table books about the former glory of colonial conquests.[10] Indeed, in our post-colonial age, these publications wrongly promote 'a mood of nostalgia [that] makes racial domination appear innocent and pure'.[11] Nevertheless, as Andrea Smith has demonstrated, some forms of colonial nostalgia (particularly those practised by misplaced ex-colonizers) are important in the politics of identity in the increasingly ethnically diverse European Union.[12] In cases where the ex-colonized practice colonial nostalgia, the situation is even more complicated. It may involve multiple colonization where the ex-colonized use colonial history to defend against new colonizers, be they foreigners or people of their own race.[13]

In what follows, I will examine colonial nostalgia as a means of resistance by comparing the 'official' and 'unofficial' narratives of two politically sensitive sites in Hong Kong: the Kowloon Walled City as a symbol of Chinese sovereignty, and the district of Causeway Bay as a site for conspicuous consumption and global capitalism.[14] In this comparison, I will highlight the double nature of post-colonial Hong Kong where de-colonization coincides with re-colonization, and national liberation conflicts with the demand for local autonomy. This duality, I argue, complicates the picture of Hong Kong's post-coloniality which does not fit the conventional narrative of decolonization and national liberation. At a time when the 'Manichaean structure of colonial society' based on race, skin colours and languages has been mutated into a global division of rich and poor, and possession and dispossession, the duality in post-colonial Hong Kong reveals the dangers of coupling nationalism with neocolonialism, which are subtle, self-righteous, and above all, seemingly benign.[15]

THE NARRATIVE OF NATIONAL LIBERATION

Shortly after the signing of the Sino-British Agreements on the future of Hong Kong in 1984, an outpouring of writings on the British colony began to appear on the mainland and in Hong Kong. It reached its climax in 1996—a year before the handover—when the Xinhua Book Company in Beijing published a series of monographs known as 'The Return of Hong Kong' (*Xianggang huigui*).[16] The goal of publishing these writings was to win the hearts and minds of the

seven million Hong Kong residents for the transfer of power in 1997. Hence, the main theme of these writings was to counter the narrative of colonial modernity that the British Hong Kong government had been promoting for decades. The narrative of colonial modernity included three parts: (1) Hong Kong was a barren rock until it became a crown colony in 1841; (2) the colonial government was benevolent and open-minded in treating the colony's residents, providing them with a refuge when China was in turmoil; (3) the colonial government made great efforts in building the infrastructure of the colony to smooth its transition from an entrepôt to an international financial centre.[17]

To counter this narrative of colonial modernity, mainland Chinese historians develop the narrative of national liberation. First, they emphasize the Chinese sovereignty over Hong Kong. In other words, the Chinese did not lose Hong Kong in 1841; they only ceded temporarily to the British the administration of Hong Kong. By stressing the Chinese sovereignty, mainland Chinese historians render the colonial government illegitimate, no matter how 'benevolent' or 'open-minded' it might have been. More important, they link the return of Hong Kong to 'the century-long quest of the Chinese people' for national recovery and national rejuvenation.[18] To drive home this point, Liu Shuyong (a leading mainland scholar of Hong Kong) opens his account of colonial Hong Kong with this succinct statement: 'Beginning in the 1840s, Hong Kong, a part of Chinese territory since ancient times, became a victim of Britain's persistent aggression against China.'[19] In one sentence Liu makes two important observations. He implies that as a part of the Chinese territory since time immemorial, Hong Kong must return to the motherland. Without doing so, the Chinese nation will not be complete. He also suggests that as a victim of Britain's aggression, Hong Kong must be saved. Winning it back becomes part of the nation's self-liberation from the dark history of Western imperialism.

Second, mainland Chinese historians reiterate the cultural, social, and economic links between Hong Kong and the mainland, particularly the adjacent Guangdong province from where most of Hong Kong residents originated. These links, invisible perhaps, show that Hong Kong was never 'a barren rock' but an integral part of southern China. By stressing these cross-border links, mainland Chinese historians partly nullify the 'colonial modernity' argument by emphasizing the 'China factor' in Hong Kong's splendid transformation into an international financial centre. Their argument for the 'China factor' is especially effective in reference to China's

role in facilitating Hong Kong's rapid economic growth during the 1980s and 1990s, when China (especially the Guangdong province) was opened to international trade and economic collaborations. In his account of colonial Hong Kong, Liu Shuyong puts special emphasis on this China-Hong Kong link:

> In the past century and more since Hong Kong became a commercial port, great changes have taken place in its economic developments. Since the 1960s, and particularly since China's introduction of the policies of reform and opening-up [from the late 1970s to the 1990s], there has emerged an economic upsurge in Hong Kong which has attracted worldwide attention, thus making Hong Kong one of the 'four little dragons' in Asia.[20]

Third, mainland Chinese historians harshly criticize the British colonial rulers for their monopoly of power. In emphasizing the colonists' monopoly of power, mainland Chinese historians employ the classic anti-colonial argument that Hong Kong was ruled by a Manichean structure based on race (Europeans *versus* Chinese), skin colour (white *versus* yellow), and language (English *versus* Chinese).[21] In Liu Shuyong's account, there is a lengthy summary of the political system of Hong Kong to underscore the dark side of the colonial rule:

> As the overwhelming majority of the people in Hong Kong were Chinese, the British government, fearing that the minority British nationals might not be able to subject the Chinese to their full control, adopted the system of a crown colony with centralized powers and rigid jurisdictional control in Hong Kong.[22]

For Liu, despite the splendid economic developments and the high standard of living in the colony, the Hong Kong people are denied their subjectivity and dignity due to the colonial rule. For this reason, Liu is not surprised to find that '[i]t has been the ardent desire of the Chinese people over the past 150 years and more to recover the Hong Kong region.'[23]

Taken together, these three points make the recovery of Hong Kong a perfect example of the Chinese government's campaign to unify the nation. Cast in the glow of anti-colonialism, national unification and national revival become mutually reinforcing. On the one hand, the country will not be strong until it is unified. On the other hand, the country will not be unified unless it shows its strength in making a bold move. In both ways, the recovery of Hong Kong exemplifies the inner logic of national unification and national rejuvenation. As a lost territory, the return of Hong Kong is a potent symbol of national unification after one and a half century of humiliation and defeats. As a victim of foreign aggressions, the return of Hong Kong to the motherland is a historic milestone marking a significant difference

between the current Chinese government and its predecessors, none of whom could bring Hong Kong back.

THE KOWLOON WALLED CITY

To the delight of mainland Chinese historians, there is one place in Hong Kong that symbolizes both the Chinese sovereignty over Hong Kong and the British aggressions in the colony. Located in the Kowloon Bay area (close to the former Kai-Tak Airport), the Kowloon Walled City is the site of a former military outpost of the Qing Dynasty (1644-1911). Covering an area of 6.5 acres, the military outpost was once a garrison town in the nineteenth century. Separated by the Victoria Harbour, the Kowloon Walled City was at the frontline of the Chinese defence against the British on Hong Kong Island. At its height, the military outpost was guided by 600 soldiers, and was equipped with cannons, watchtowers and gateways.[24] In addition to being a military post, the Kowloon Walled City also doubled as a symbol of Confucianism. Inside the garrison town, there was a school, the Longjin Communal School, aimed to 'strengthen the inhabitants' moral fibre against foreign decadence and materialism'.[25]

In 1899, the status of the walled city became ambiguous after the New Territories—an area north of Kowloon Bay and south of Shunzhen River—was leased to the British. Formerly a military post at the frontier between China and Britain, it was now deep in the British territory. To further complicate the matter, the Qing government refused to give up sovereignty over the walled city. In the Treaty of Beijing, the Qing government forced the British to accept a clause that allowed it to continue to exercise jurisdiction within the walled city.[26] Literally, the walled city became a Chinese territory inside the British colony, with a status equivalent, in today's international relations, to an embassy in a foreign country. For the British, the confusion lay in how to let the Qing government exercise jurisdiction over an area located in the heart of the expanded colony. To solve the problem, the British launched an attack at the walled city and drove away the Qing officials. From then on, the walled city existed in limbo when two governments claimed jurisdiction over it, but none was willing to assume administrative responsibility.

For mainland Chinese historians, the saga of the Kowloon Walled City is a 'microcosm of the history of British aggressions in China'.[27] First and foremost, it demonstrates that even if one were to accept the legality of the unequal treaties, the Chinese government would still have sovereignty over parts of Hong Kong. At the very least, as

spelled out in the 1899 Treaty of Beijing, the Chinese government would have undisputed sovereignty over the 6.4 acres of land marked by the former military outpost. At any time, the Chinese government could send officials and soldiers to enter the Kowloon Walled City.[28] More important, the saga of the Kowloon Walled City illustrates the British aggressions in China. A self-proclaimed law-binding nation, Britain violated the terms of the Treaty of Beijing by attacking the walled city. The violence shows the hideous goal of the British imperialists to subjugate and exploit China.[29]

As historical memory is selective, mainland Chinese historians avoid discussing the results of the legal ambiguity of the walled city. Being a place 'fallen between two stools' as Elizabeth Sinn describes it,[30] both the British Hong Kong government and the Chinese government (be it the Guomindang or the Chinese Communist Party) paid no attention to the location. Since World War II, the former walled city became an urban slum full of drug dealers, prostitutes and gangsters. Known to some as the 'City of Darkness', it was so packed with illegal buildings that no daylight penetrated into the houses.[31] For decades, particularly during the economic booms in the 1970s and 1980s, the 'City of Darkness' stood in stark contrast to the opulence and glamour of the 'Pearl of the Orient'.[32] To many Hong Kong residents, the 'Chinese territory' in the colony was a poor and lawless place, reaffirming their impression of the poverty and mismanagement of Mao's China. For them, the 'City of Darkness' provoked their fear of the mainland rather than reminding them of Chinese sovereignty.

For mainland Chinese historians, however, the saga of the Kowloon Walled City (minus the 'City of Darkness') is important for yet another reason. In 1995, based on a joint decision between the British and Chinese governments, the residents of the slum were removed and the illegal buildings were torn down. On the former site of the walled city rose a picturesque garden known as the 'Kowloon Walled City Park'. Inside the garden, a replica of the former Qing office was erected to symbolize the undisputed Chinese sovereignty over the walled city, and by extension, the entire of Hong Kong. Two of the original cannons were placed at the entrance of the garden, reminding visitors of the historical significance of the walled city in the Chinese resistance against foreign aggressions.[33] For mainland Chinese historians, the opening of the garden, two years ahead of the handover, signifies the closure of the history of colonial Hong Kong being a lost territory to foreign aggressors.[34]

HONG KONG HISTORY FOR THE HONG KONG PEOPLE

For many local Hong Kong historians, however, the 'national liberation' narrative is as unconvincing as the 'colonial modernity' narrative. It is particularly true to the Western educated, culturally hybrid, and professionally trained 'baby-boomers of post-war Hong Kong'. Born after 1949, the 'baby-boomers' are sons and daughters of Chinese immigrants who left China in the wake of the Chinese Communist Revolution.[35] They grew up in an environment where mainland China was considered a land of massive execution, famine and urban chaos. As youngsters, they witnessed first hand the horrors of revolutionary fanaticism of the Cultural Revolution when mainland supporters in Hong Kong organized riots in 1967 to topple the colonial government. Even in the 1970s, when travels and contacts were more frequent between the mainland and Hong Kong, they found out (sometimes in package tours, sometimes in solo travels) that mainland China was a lot poorer and undeveloped than Hong Kong.[36] All these preconceptions and personal discoveries affirmed that they were much better off to have been born and raised in British Hong Kong rather than in mainland China. Despite the well-known racism and prejudices in the 'Manichean division of the colonial society', they realized that they were given the opportunity to develop their professional careers and to have a higher standard of living. In this regard, the colonial 'objecthood', as Franz Fanon calls it, was a small price to pay in exchange for a cosmopolitan and affluent life.[37] In contrast, however, grandiose it might sound, national liberation did not make sense when it exacted the high price of poverty, ignorance and political oppression.

For the post-war baby-boomers, the harsh reality of 'national liberation' was vividly shown in two events: the negotiations of the Sino-British Agreement in 1984; and the Chinese crackdown on the pro-democratic protest in Tiananmen Square in 1989. In the former, the voice of the local Hong Kong people was deliberately ignored from the months-long negotiation that sealed the fate of British Hong Kong. Throughout the whole process, only the officials of the Beijing and London governments were involved in the negotiation, and no representative from the Hong Kong people was present in the closed-door meetings. To the baby-boomers, despite the pomp and circumstance in the announcement of the Sino-British Agreements, they knew there would be no change in their 'objecthood'. Their objecthood of colonialism would continue in the objecthood of

nationalism.[38] Worse still, the dark side of their new 'objecthood' was revealed in the horrifying events in 1989, when they saw from live TV news reports of how the Chinese government employed violent measures to forestall a peaceful pro-democratic demonstration. To show their support for their liberal-minded compatriots who asked for reforms in the communist system, more than a million Hong Kong residents (equivalent to one of six people living in the colony) took to the streets in the sizzling summer of 1989. No such massive demonstration had ever happened in the colony, and none had a strong and clear political message like this one. Ironically, the message was not aimed at the colonial government, but the colony's new rulers in Beijing. In the end, when the pro-democratic protest was violently crushed on 4 June by soldiers in tanks and armour vehicles, the baby-boomers (many of whom were leaders in government, business and cultural industry) realized that the objecthood of nationalism would be much more oppressive and dehumanizing than the objecthood of colonialism.

It was in this context of defending oneself against the objecthood of nationalism that local Hong Kong historians invested time and effort in writing the history of the colony. In promoting 'the history of Hong Kong for the Hong Kong people', the local Hong Kong historians developed a distinct view of colonial Hong Kong that challenged the 'national liberation' narrative of mainland Chinese historians.[39] Central to this style of history was an emphasis on 'the perspective of the Hong Kong people', namely, the complex human networks that developed in the colony, the fluidity of multi-ethnic and multi-national collaborations that linked the colony to other trading ports, and the vicissitudes of global capitalism that brought prosperity as well as challenges to the colony. From this perspective, Causeway Bay—a commercial and entertainment district on Hong Kong Island—was more representative of Hong Kong than the Kowloon Walled City.

A TALE OF TWO CITIES

In late nineteenth century, as British Hong Kong was expanding, Causeway Bay and Kowloon Bay (where the Kowloon Walled City was located) were the first two areas designed for urban and commercial development. Located on the opposite sides of the Victoria Harbour, both places provided new opportunities for growth outside the political centre of colonial Hong Kong: the Central District. East to the Central District on the Hong Kong Island, Causeway Bay

was particularly attractive to traders and businessmen because of its proximity to power holders and wealthy bankers. And the area was quickly developed into a commercial hub after the Jardine and Matheson Company built factories, warehouses and piers along the waterfront in the 1840s and 1850s.[40] By the same token, as part of the newly acquired land on the Kowloon Peninsula, Kowloon Bay was a prime location for urban development when wealthy Chinese settlers began to move to the colony. Realtors built elegant houses and apartment complexes on reclaimed land from the bay.[41] Known to the locals as the 'tale of two cities', Causeway Bay and Kowloon Bay were the two shining stars in the galaxy of a booming Hong Kong at the turn of the twentieth century.

But for historian Stephanie Po-yin Chung, the 'tale of two cities' is one-sided. 'Whereas the Kowloon Bay presents an image of an old man deep in the remembrance of the past,' Chung opines, 'Causeway Bay exults the pride and vitality of a young person constantly engaged in reinventing himself.'[42] The contrasts between the young and the old, forward looking and backward looking, living in the present and living in the past, are intentional. For Chung, despite the historical significance of the Kowloon Walled City and the nearby Song Emperor's Terrace,[43] Kowloon Bay is full of relics that allow educated elites from mainland China to inscribe their values and views into the history of Hong Kong. A prime example of this inscription is the couplet at the entrance of the Longjin Communal School inside the Kowloon Walled City. Making a poetic play on the name of the school, the author of the couplet described the transformation of a dragon (*long*) after being civilized, and the finding of a crossing (*jin*) after learning the Confucian doctrine. The target audience of the couplet, Chung stresses, was the villagers in the Kowloon Bay who were illiterate and uncultivated.[44] For the Qing officials stationed in the Kowloon Walled City, the villagers were 'savages' who had to be tamed, disciplined and civilized. They were the barbarians from within who posed as much danger to the safety of the Qing Dynasty as the British, the barbarians from without.

In contrast to the overly inscribed Kowloon Bay, Chung argues, Causeway Bay is lively and open for different interpretations. 'The story of Causeway Bay,' she writes, 'not only enriches the lore of the success of Hong Kong as the Pearl of the Orient, but also serves as a microcosm for the growth of the global consumer culture in [East] Asia.'[45] Shifting the focus from national history to global capitalism, Chung views Causeway Bay as a window into the metamorphosis of Hong Kong from a sleepy fisherman's village to a vibrant trading

and financial centre. To make her point, she adopts a motif from the 'colonial modernity' narrative, namely, Hong Kong was a 'barren rock' before 1841. Certainly, she knows that before the arrival of the British, Hong Kong had been part of the cultural, social and economic networks of southern China for centuries. But she argues that before being a British colony, Hong Kong was at best an island with only a few thousand villagers. Without the British takeover, it would not have undergone a paradigmatic change to become a hub of global capitalism.[46]

Paradoxically, in building her argument to link Hong Kong to global capitalism, Chung partly supports the 'colonial modernity' narrative. Yet, her support for colonial modernity is conditional. She supports it not because the colonists brought an efficient government and a Western urban infrastructure to the colony (as many British historians claim), but because they lifted Hong Kong from the Chinese network of trade and commerce, and repositioned it as an intermediary between the Sino-centric world and the Western world. Similar to Shanghai to the north and Singapore to the south, colonial Hong Kong was *in* East Asia but not *of* East Asia. In terms of location, Hong Kong was undoubtedly on the coast of South China Sea and linked to the Pearl River Delta. In terms of economic function, however, it was part of a global trading network, serving as a middle ground between Western and Chinese traders. In short, Hong Kong was reborn and reconstituted after the British takeover. It gained a new life as a link in the chain of trading ports to ferry capital, goods, and labour between the East and the West.[47]

Of course, Chung's argument is not new. By subsuming colonialism under global capitalism, Chung adopts the viewpoint of the world system theorists who see colonialism as a facilitating factor for the expansion of the Eurocentric network of trade and capital accumulation.[48] But what is significant about Chung's argument is that the paradigmatic change in Hong Kong allows her to make the case for a unique identity of the people in the colony. Stressing the cultural and psychological impact of global capitalism, Chung creates an image of the 'Hong Kong Person' (*Xianggang ren*) who has more in common with hybrid peoples in other trading ports than their compatriots on the mainland.

In two areas, particularly, Chung makes this 'Hong Kong Person' utterly unique. First, she points out that the settlers in Hong Kong were not all Chinese. On the contrary, Europeans, Indians, Persians, Jews, and others followed the British and settled in the colony. These foreign settlers and their offspring set up roadside stores, bazaars,

shops, and department stores that competed with (and in some cases, displaced) the indigenous Chinese rural markets. They formed their own communities that are still active.[49] More interesting still, even the Chinese residents in Hong Kong were not all local born or immigrants from the mainland. Chung stresses that many of the Chinese settlers were from Southeast Asia. The prime example of these Southeast Asian Chinese is Aw Poor Haw (1882-1954) and Aw Poor Par (1888-1944), the Burmese Chinese brothers who built a transnational enterprise of herbal trades and newspapers. Their elegant mansion, known as the Tiger Balm Garden, was once located on a hill overlooking Causeway Bay.[50] Thus, by stressing the multi-ethnicity of the Hong Kong people, Chung questions the basic assumption of the 'national liberation' narrative. How can the Chinese government speak of de-colonizing Hong Kong when the colonized are not all Chinese or sharing the value of mainland Chinese?

Second, Chung emphasizes the cut-throat competition of the capitalist system. Taking full advantage of Causeway Bay being a commercial and entertainment district, she traces the different waves of commerce and the various groups of winners and losers. She begins the story with the British dominance of the district in the mid-nineteenth century when the Jardine and Matheson Company built warehouses and factories on the waterfront. Then, she moves on to the dominance of Southeast Asian Chinese merchants who built splendid mansions and recreational parks during the early twentieth century. She continues the tale with the rise of Japanese investment in the 1980s and 1990s which turned Causeway Bay into a 'little Ginza'. Finally, she ends the story with the arrival of the American 'mall culture' which places shops, department stores and restaurants under one roof. In this story of fierce competition, Chung highlights the vicissitudes of capitalism where there is no permanent winner or loser. In each round of competition, she stresses, friends and foes change sides in response to the direction of the market. And in this fiercely competitive and highly tense environment, a unique Hong Kong identity is born.[51]

As a whole, Chung's account of a hybrid and complex Hong Kong exposes one major weakness of the 'national liberation' narrative: its reductionism. In presenting a simple picture of redemption and rejuvenation, the 'national liberation' narrative promotes the teleology of the nation state in its quest for liberation and independence. In its totalizing plot, the 'national liberation' narrative speaks for all Chinese as if they are the same, and it promotes a national goal as though every Chinese supports it. But, as Chung demonstrates, the

bounded nation state includes billions of people who have different backgrounds, personalities, career paths, and world-views. The 'national liberation' narrative is particularly inept in dealing with the racial and cultural hybridity in a cosmopolis like Hong Kong where people from various parts of the world meet and compete. By stressing uniformity and homogeneity, the 'national liberation' narrative does not come close to expressing the views and attitude of those who live in Hong Kong.

THE LIMITS OF COLONIAL NOSTALGIA

In presenting a saga of colonial Kong Kong as part of global capitalism, Chung creates a unique image of the 'Hong Kong Person' that fits the self-identity of the 'baby boomers'. Skilled in all kinds of trading (goods, services, realty, foreign exchanges, stocks), the 'Hong Kong Person' is *homo economicus* through and through. Growing up at a time when Hong Kong's economy was expanding by leaps and bounds, the 'baby boomers' tend to have an optimistic view of neo-liberal capitalism, namely, an economy driven solely by market. Despite the trials and tribulations of the global economy, they always find ways to land in a better job or move on to a new area of investment. In short, the 'Hong Kong Person' is full of confidence in his ability to master the game of capitalism and to adjust to the changing needs in the market. In contrast to their economic skills and versatility, the 'Hong Kong Person' is aloof and adrift in politics. They are used to being excluded from the political debates in the colony, and find themselves lucky for missing all the political campaigns in mainland China. As a group to whom 'nothing [politically] spectacular has happened' (as Chen Guanzhong aptly describes),[52] the 'Hong Kong Person' is politically dormant if not totally apolitical.

While this image of the 'Hong Kong Person' fits the self-image of the 'baby-boomers', it does not fit the more recent Hong Kong residents who grow up struggling with economic downturns in the late 1990s and the early 2010s. More important, after 1997, the demography of the former colony changes when many local residents go north to seek jobs and fortunes in the mainland, and many wealthy and well-connected mainlanders move south to take up high-pay jobs in the cosmopolis. Above all, the Beijing government keeps its promise to let 'the horses to continue to race and the dancers to continue to dance' in Hong Kong. Global capitalism, particularly in finance and real estate, continues to flourish in the former colony when the powerful state enterprises and wealthy businessmen in mainland China

keep pouring into the Hong Kong market. If indeed colonialism brought global capitalism to Hong Kong one and half century ago, the departure of the British colonists did not take it away with them. On the contrary, neo-liberal capitalism spread to China in stunning speed, and it pushed Hong Kong closer to the mainland when China became the engine of growth in the global market in the 2000s.

As a result, the *homo economicus* that Chung describes is no longer the hallmark of the 'Hong Kong Person'. It can be found everywhere in China in big and small cities. In an ironic twist, what began as a yearning for the colonial past to emphasize one's unique identity is now turned into an aspiration to join the present-day ultra-capitalistic China. Similar to the two moles in the trilogy of *Infernal Affairs*, the subverters always face the danger of being absorbed into the institution of power they want to supplant after spending a great deal of time in it.[53] As China is producing more and more *homo economicus* who are smarter and more efficient than many 'Hong Kong Persons', it is unclear how long the subverters can still hold on to the memory of the colonial past when it becomes increasingly irrelevant to the new generation of Hong Kong people.

NOTES

1. Crime-thriller movies made in Hong Kong before and after 1997 have been widely seen as metaphors for the Hong Kong transition. Luo Yongsheng (Low Wing Sang), in particular, uses the *Infernal Affairs I, II,* and *III* to discuss collaboration and subversion in post-Colonial Hong Kong. See *Zhimin wujian dao* (The Way of the Non-delineated Zones in Colonialism), Hong Kong: Oxford University Press, 2007, pp. 1-44.
2. In 1994, the Chinese government set up a giant clock in the Tiananmen Square for the countdown to the Hong Kong Handover. For the significance of the 'Hong Kong Clock' as a political metaphor, see Wu Hong, 'The Hong Kong Clock: Public Time-Telling and Political Time/Space', *Public Culture*, 9, 1997, pp. 329-54.
3. The continuation of the police force is one example of the persistence of the colonial system. On the transition of the former Royal Hong Kong Police to the police force of post-colonial Hong Kong, see Karen Fang, 'British Finest: The Royal Hong Kong Police', in Antoinette Burton (ed.), *After the Imperial Turn: Thinking With and Through the Nation*, Durham: Duke University Press, 2003, pp. 293-307.
4. On the continuity of the colonial policies in post-colonial Hong Kong, see Chen Guangzhong, *Xia yige shinian: Xianggang de guangrong shidai?* (The Next Decade: The Glorious Age of Hong Kong?), Hong Kong: Oxford University Press, 2008, pp. 49-73.
5. Law Wing-sang (Luo Yongsheng), *Collaborative Colonial Power: The Making of the Hong Kong Chinese,* Hong Kong: The Hong Kong University Press, 2009, pp. 1-6, 199-210.

6. For a list of books published by mainland Chinese historians in the mid-1990s, see Wang Hongzhi (Lawrence Wang-chi Wong), *Lishi de chenzhong: Cong Xianggang kan Zhongguo dalu de Xianggang shi lunshu* (The Heavy Burden of History: A Critical Review of the Mainland Studies of Hong Kong History from the Perspective of Hong Kong), Hong Kong: Oxford University Press, 2000, pp. 35-9. In addition to books, mainland Chinese mass media also produced large numbers of TV serials and movies to recount the colonial history of Hong Kong.
7. John M. Carroll, 'Colonial Hong Kong as a Cultural-Historical Place', *Modern Asian Studies*, vol. 40, no. 2, 2006, p. 518.
8. Yasmin Saikia, 'Religion, Nostalgia, and Memory: Making an Ancient and Recent Tai-Ahom Identity in Assam and Thailand', *The Journal of Asian Studies*, vol. 65, no. 1, February 2006, pp. 33-60.
9. For a summary of these two historical perspectives, see Lawrence Wang-chi Wong, 'Narrating Hong Kong History: A Critical Study of Mainland China's Historical Discourse from a Hong Kong Perspective', in Shi-Xu, Manfred Kienpointner and Jan Sevas (eds.), *Read the Cultural Other: Forms of Otherness in the Discourses of Hong Kong's Decolonization*, Berlin: Mouton de Gruyler, 2005, pp. 197-207.
10. Renato Rosaldo, *Culture & Truth: The Remaking of Social Analysis*, Boston: Beacon Press, 1989, p. 68. Note that in his critique of colonial nostalgia, Rosaldo uses the term 'imperial nostalgia'. But he basically refers to the remembering of the colonial rule.
11. Renato Rosaldo, *Culture & Truth,* 70. See also Laura Stoler and Karen Strassler, 'Casting for the Colonial: Memory Work in "New Order" Java', *Comparative Studies in Society and History*, January 2000, p. 4.
12. Andrew L. Smith, *Colonial Memory and Post-colonial Europe: Maltese Settlers in Algeria and France*, Bloomington: Indiana University Press, 2006, pp. 210-32.
13. Building on Benedict Anderson's concept of 'Creole Nationalism', Taiwanese historians view the Japanese colonial period as the beginning of Taiwan modernization, thereby envisioning a basis for forging a 'Taiwanese subjectivity' *vis-à-vis* the 'national unification' of mainland China. For 'Creole Nationalism', see Anderson, 'Western Nationalism and Eastern Nationalism: Is There a Difference that Matters', *New Left Review,* vol. 9, May-June 2001, pp. 31-42. For a discussion of the characteristics of Taiwanese nationalism, see Leo T.S. Ching, *Becoming "Japanese": Coloninal Taiwan and the Politics of Identity Formation*, Berkeley: University of California Press, pp. 51-88; Rwei-ren Wu, 'The Formosan Ideology: Oriental Colonialism and the Rise of Taiwanese Nationalism, 1895-1949', Ph.D. dissertation, University of Chicago, 2003, pp. 1-50, 384-425; Wang Chaohua, 'A Tale of Two Nationalisms', *New Left Review*, vol. 32, March-April 2005, pp. 83-103.
14. For a map of today's Hong Kong, see the interactive map on the website of Hong Kong Tourism Board at http://www.discoverhongkong.com/eng/trip-planner/hongkong-maps.html (accessed on 8/15/2010). For the location of the two sites, please use the 'search map' function on the webpage.
15. On the mutation of colonialism into Neo-colonialism in the age of global capitalism, see Homi K. Bhabha, 'Framing Fanon', in *The Wretched of the Earth*, New York: Grove Press, 1963, pp. vii-xlii. For another view of the mutation, see Azzedine Haddour, 'Foreword: Post-colonial Fanonism', in *The Fanon Reader*, London: Pluto Press, 2006, pp. vii-xxv. On the dangers of Neo-colonialism in the

age of global capitalism, see David Harvey, *Spaces of Neoliberalization: Towards a Theory of Uneven Geographical Development*, München: Franz Steiner Verlag, 2005.

16. The 'Return of Hong Kong' series include books that examine the history, economy and culture of Hong Kong. The book on the history of Hong Kong, *Xianggang de lishi* (History of Hong Kong) was written by Liu Shurong, a leading scholar of Hong Kong in mainland China. His book was later translated into English and was renamed as *An Outline History of Hong Kong*, which I will analyse in this article.
17. 'Hong Kong 1996', in Cheng Meibao and Zhao Yule (eds.), *Xianggang shi yanjiu lunzhu xuanji* (Selected Studies of Hong Kong History), Hong Kong: Hong Kong Open University Press, 1999, pp. 16-26. In their introduction, Cheng and Zhao point out some of the differences between the 'colonial modernity' narrative and the 'national liberation' narrative.
18. One of the dominant themes of modern Chinese historiography is recounting 'the century of humiliation' by foreign aggressors from 1840 to 1949. This theme of 'the century of humiliation' not only promotes anti-imperialist nationalism in China but also bolsters the legitimacy of the Chinese Communist Party as a nationalistic and modernizing force. For an analysis of this motif of 'the century of humiliation', see Peter Hays Gries, 'Narratives to Live By: The Century of Humiliation and Chinese National Identity Today', in Lionel M. Jensen and Timothy B. Weston (eds.), *China's Transformations: The Stories Beyond the Headlines*, Lanham: Rowman & Littlefield Publishers, Inc., 2007, pp. 112-28.
19. Liu Shuyong, *An Outline History of Hong Kong*, tr. Wang Wenjiong, Wang Minggu, Beijing: Foreign Language Press, 1997, p. ii.
20. Shuyong, *An Outline History of Hong Kong*, p. 127.
21. For an analysis of the Manichean structure of the colonial system, see Franz Fanon, *The Wretched of the Earth,* pp. 1-62; Albert Memmi, *The Colonized and the Colonizer*, expanded edition, Boston: Beacon Press, 1991.
22. Shuyong, *An Outline History of Hong Kong*, op. cit., p. 116.
23. Ibid., p. 169.
24. Elizabeth Sinn, 'Kowloon City and Early History', *Journal of the Royal Asiastic Society Hong Kong Branch,* vol. 27, 1987, pp. 31-3; Julia Wilkinson, 'A Chinese Magistrate's Fort', in Greg Girard and Ian Lambot, *City of Darkness: Life in Kowloon Walled City*, Haslemere, Surrey: Watermark Publications (UK) Limited, 1993, pp. 60-71.
25. Sinn, 'Kowloon City and Early History', op. cit., p. 32.
26. Ibid., pp. 35-6.
27. Liu Zehua, 'Jiulong chengzhai' (The Kowloon Walled City), in Jin Yingxi (ed.), *Xianggang shihua* (Accounts of Hong Kong History), Guangzhou: Guangdong renmin chubenshe, 1988, p. 104.
28. Zehua, 'Jiulong chengzhai', op. cit. p. 105.
29. Ibid.
30. 'Kowloon City and Early History', op. cit., p. 38.
31. The urban slum in the former walled city is well documented in pictures and videos. For pictures of the slum, see Greg Girard and Ian Lambot, *City of Darkness*. For a video of the urban slum, see http://www.youtube.com/watch?v=No_vQ8FiQiw (accessed on 8/15/2010).
32. The 'Pearl of the Orient' was a nickname given to Hong Kong in the 1960s and 1970s when the Hong Kong government promoted tourism.

33. For a description of the Kowloon Walled City Garden, see the news article from Leisure and Cultural Services Department of the HKSAZ: http://www.lcsd.gov.hk/parks/kwcp/en/index.php (accessed on 8/15/2010).
34. Shuyong, *An Outline History of Hong Kong*, pp. 69-74; Liu Shuyong (ed.), *Jianming Xianggang shi* (An Outline History of Hong Kong), new edition, Hong Kong: Sanlian Book Company, 2009, pp. 37-9.
35. Of course, grouping tens of thousands of peoples who were born in the late 1940s and the early 1950s is liable to overgeneralization. Yet, the category of 'post-war baby-boomers generation' is commonly used by scholars (particularly sociologists) in Hong Kong to discuss the distinctive expectations and behaviour of the cultural and political elites who are presently ruling Hong Kong. For a discussion of the importance of having the category of 'post-war baby-boomers', see Chen Guanzhong, *Wo zheyidai xianggangren* (My Generation of Hong Kong People), Hong Kong: Oxford University Press, 2005, pp. 3-25; Lü Dale, *Xianggang si dai ren* (Four Generations of Hong Kong People), Hong Kong: Jinyibu doumeiti youxiang gongsi, 2007.
36. For further discussion of the characteristics of the 'baby-boomers' or the 'Hong Kong Man', see Helen F. Siu, 'Remade in Hong Kong: Weaving into the Chinese Cultural Tapestry', in Tao Tao Liu and David Faure (eds.), *Unity and Diversity: Local Cultures and Identities in China*, Hong Kong: Hong Kong University Press, 1996, pp. 177-96.
37. For Franz Fanon, one of the characteristics of the colonial structure is to deny the subjectivity of the colonized, and he calls this mechanism of denial 'objecthood'. See Fanon, 'The Fact of Blackness', in *The Fanon Reader*, pp. 127-48.
38. Known as 'nostalgia cinema', movies made in Hong Kong during the late 1980s and early 1990s illustrate this frustration of being 'an orphan' in the realpolitik of Sino-British relations. See Natalia Chan Sui Hung, 'Rewriting History: Hong Kong Nostalgia Cinema and Its Social Practice', in Poshek Fu and David Desser (eds.), *The Cinema of Hong Kong: History, Arts, and Identity*, Cambridge: Cambridge University Press, 2000, pp. 252-72; Sheldan H. Liu, 'Filming Diaspora and Identity: Hong Kong and 1997,' in *The Cinema of Hong Kong*, pp. 273-313.
39. Cai Yongfeng (Tsai, Jung-fang) coined the term 'Xianggang ren zhi xianggang shi' (Hong Kong history for the Hong Kong people) to underscore the importance of capturing the local perspective. See *Xianggang ren zhi xianggang shi* (The Hong Kong history for the Hong Kong people), Hong Kong: Oxford University Press, 2001, pp. 1-14
40. Zhong Baoxian (Stephanie Po-yin Chung), *Shangcheng gushi: Tongluowan bainian bianqian* (The Tale of a Commercial City: A Century of Changes in Causeway Bay), Hong Kong: Zhonghua Book Company, 2009, pp. 70-4.
41. Song Xianlin, 'Jiulong Cheng dibiao zhi er: Qide Bin yu Qide feijichang de chongjian' (The Landmark of Kowloon City II: Kaitak Coast and the Rebuilding of Kaitak Airport), Zhong Baoxian (Stephenie Po-yin Chung) and Zhao Yule (eds.), *Jiulong Cheng* (Kowloon City), Hong Kong: Sanlian Book Company, 2001, pp. 143-206.
42. Zhong Baoxian, *Shangcheng gushi*, p. i.
43. For the significance of the Song Emperor's Terrace in the collective memories of the Hong Kong people, see my article 'A Rock, a Text, and a Tablet: The Making of the Song Emperor's Terrace as a *Lieu de Mémoire*, in Marc Andre Matten

(ed.), *Places of Memory in Modern China: History, Politics, and Identity*, Leiden: Brill (forthcoming).

44. Zhong Baoxian, 'Xulun: Songmo tiwang ruhe zhoujin Jiulong jindaishi?' (Introduction: How did the Emperors at the End of the [Southern] Song Enter into the History of Kowloon), *Jiulong Cheng*, pp. 28-9.
45. Zhong Baoxian, '*Shangcheng gushi*', p. 4.
46. Ibid., pp. 1-37.
47. Zhong Baoxian, *Shangcheng gushi*, p. 5.
48. Giovanni Arrighi, in particular, has pointed out the dual dialectic of space and capital in propelling the European colonial conquests. See Arrighi, *The Long Twentieth Century: Money, Power, and the Origins of Our Times*, London: Verso, 1994, pp. 1-84.
49. Zhong Baoxian, *Shangcheng gushi*, pp. 6-29.
50. Ibid., pp. 132-40.
51. Ibid., p. 32.
52. See Chen Guanzhong, *Wo zhe yi dai Xianggang ren* (My Generation of Hong Kong People), Hong Kong: Oxford University Press, 2005, p. 5.
53. In the movies, the two moles constantly suffer from depression and neurotic symptoms. The undercover police agent expresses his psychological anxiety by resorting to violence—the hallmark of gangsters. The gang infiltrator in the police expresses his psychological anxiety by aspiring to be a model policeman—the reverse of what he is supposed to do. In the end, the two moles embrace and excel in the institutions of power they want to subvert rather than succeeding in supplanting them.

II. NATIONALISM AND STATE-BUILDING

5

Insurgencies, Counter-Insurgencies and State-building in Asia: A Comparative Analysis

KAUSHIK ROY

INTRODUCTION

The late twentieth century is characterized by a proliferation of unconventional wars. The latter term refers to 'intra-state' rather than 'inter-state' wars. In recent times, the term 'insurgency' connotes 'an organized movement aimed at the overthrow of a constituted government through the use of subversion and armed conflict'.[1] Lieutenant Colonel Vivek Chadha of the Indian Army makes a distinction between terrorism and insurgency. In his framework, terrorist movements are based in urban areas whereas insurgencies establish their bases in rural areas and then graduate to the urban regions.[2] Chadha's definition is somewhat similar to that of James D. Fearon and David D. Laitin. According to them 'Insurgency is a technology of military conflict characterized by small, lightly armed bands practicing guerrilla warfare from rural base areas.'[3] Insurgencies include both guerrilla warfare as well as terrorism. This essay examines the rise of insurgency, responses by the polities (known as counter-insurgency or COIN), and its impact on state building in four regions of Asia: Iraq, Afghanistan, Kashmir and Nepal. Three of the above-mentioned regions experience 'Islamic' insurgency while the last region has recently undergone a Communist insurgency. While comparing and contrasting the four cases, this essay attempts to assess whether the Islamic insurgency differs from Communist insurgency and, further, if all the four insurgencies could be categorized as 'New Wars'.

NEW THEORIES OF INSURGENCIES

Several Western commentators claim that the new millennium is witnessing an evolving hybrid form of insurgency.[4] Mary Kaldor writes: '. . . during the 1980s and 1990s, a new type of organized violence has developed, especially in Africa and East Europe, which is one aspect of the current globalized era. I describe this type of violence as "new war".'[5] Similarly, retired British General Rupert Smith writes: '. . . we were now in a new era of conflict—in fact a new paradigm—which I define as "war amongst the people"; one in which political and military developments go hand in hand.'[6] In a somewhat similar vein, Peter H. Denton asserts: '. . . the psychology of all combatants is increasingly significant because warfare in the post-modern age inevitably involves whole populations and the leveraging of effects translates a local defeat or victory into something that affects a much larger group of people.'[7] Chadha also tows the same line. He writes: 'LICs (Low Intensity Conflicts) have generally remained a people-centric method of fighting.'[8] Smith continues that war amongst the people is mostly a tactical event with occasional forays at the theatre level. Most of the fights do not go to the strategic level. Some of the characteristic features of the war amongst the people are that they are mostly non-state wars, attritional in nature, and the media plays an important role in shaping the struggle.[9] Kaldor comments that these new wars cannot be categorized as private wars because the distinction between private and public is intermeshed with each other. The characteristics of the new wars are close intermeshing between war and organized crime. And though these wars are localized, they have transnational linkages. The new wars are also characterized by the impact of globalization. This is evident in the important role played by the international news reporters, mercenary troops, diaspora volunteers, non-governmental organizations, etc.[10] Further, in such conflicts and confrontations there is neither any clear-cut difference between war and peace, nor there is any predefined sequence between war and peace. Peace resolves conflicts but not necessarily the confrontations.[11]

Kaldor agrees that a Revolution in Military Affairs (RMA) has taken place. However, rather than in the field of technology, the revolution has occurred in the social relations of warfare.[12] Thus, Kaldor is reacting to the assertions of scholars like Eliot A. Cohen and others who argue that the RMA is centred around information technology.[13]

Robert M. Cassidy, an American Army officer, notes that since the Islamic insurgents are weak in the use of technology, they develop

and employ asymmetric warfare through ideas rather than through technology.[14] Smith, however, is unwilling to describe the new wars as asymmetric wars.[15] Smith has a valid point because inter-state war at times could be asymmetric war also if one of the polities enjoys qualitative technological or managerial superiority. However, this does not mean that the insurgents are oblivious to the importance of technology. Cassidy, like Kaldor, writes: 'Information technology and networking have enabled the linkage of a host of various insurgent movements and like minded organizations, including transnational criminal organizations that operate regionally and globally.'[16] According to one estimate, the Al-Qaeda which is encouraging insurgencies in Iraq, Afghanistan and Kashmir, is scattered among sixty to seventy countries. Michael C. Fowler writes that the collapse of Communism in the 1990s, resulted in the rise of 'weak states' in parts of eastern Europe and USSR. This has allowed the criminals to establish transnational linkages with the insurgents.[17]

Probably, the so-called new wars are not so new. Most of the above-mentioned scholars theorized on the basis of case studies of Yugoslavia and the Western experience in Iraq and Afghanistan. Our two case studies (Kashmir and Nepal) have more or less escaped their attention probably because the NATO and US forces are not deployed there. Even in the case of Iraq and Afghanistan, traditional elements of insurgency could be identified. Tony Balasevicius rightly says that Mao Tse-tung focused on controlling the people rather than merely possessing military capacity.[18] So, Mao could be categorized as the pioneer of the so-called 'war amongst the people'.

ORIGIN, EVOLUTION AND FEATURES OF INSURGENCIES

Havard Hegre, Tanja Ellingsen, Scott Gates and Nils Petter Gleditsch claim that semi-democracies (regimes intermediate between a democracy and an autocracy) exhibit a higher propensity for civil war than either democracies or autocracies.[19] As regards our case studies, Nepal before the outbreak of the Maoist insurgency was a classic case of being a semi-democracy. Halvard Buhaug and Scott Gates write that civil wars are of various types. And they could be categorized on the basis of their objectives. For instance, a war over control of a state will be different from a war of secession.[20] In our case, the Maoist insurgency in Nepal is a classic case of war over control of the country, while Kashmir is essentially a case of secessionism.

Monica Duffy Toft claims that the percentage of civil wars in which religion (especially Islam) has become a central issue, has increased over time. Further, the religious civil wars are much more destructive

than wars fought over other issues. Toft continues that religious civil wars last longer and result in more combatant and especially non-combatant deaths. Toft's points that while nationalism by nature tends to be a local issue, religion (especially Christianity and Islam) tends to be transnational,[21] also applies to the case of trans-national Marxist insurgencies.

Fearon and Laitin comment that a region with a lower per capita income favours the techniques of insurgency because recruiting younger men as insurgents is far easier when the economic alternatives are worse.[22] This assertion, to an extent, applies to the case of Nepal. However, instead of an economic reductionist formula, Bishwa Nath Tiwari comes up with a multi-causal framework. He writes that the probability of conflict is high when the level of poverty and malnutrition is high. However, conflict is not only due to economic reasons but also due to social and ethnic factors. Inequalities in the level of development and poverty increase the likelihood of conflict and once the conflict is initiated with political leaders or conflict entrepreneurs, the intensity of conflict is guided more by the social variables rather than the economic variables.[23] A more focused approach on organizational issues is taken by Thomas A. Marks. He asserts that neither ideology nor ethnic or national issues cause insurgency. Rather, the principal causative factor is the breakdown of negotiated relationship between the leaders and the followers.[24] Though Tiwari has formulated his model keeping Nepal in mind, it could be used for analysing insurgencies outside Nepal too. Now, let us look at the origin of insurgency in our four case studies.

IRAQ

As the Saddam Hussein regime collapsed during the Second Gulf War and the Coalition troops entered Iraq, the population of south Iraq did not rebel against Saddam Hussein's authority and welcome the Coalition force as liberators.[25] The US-led Coalition force over-estimated the level of popular support they would get from the Iraqis. Insurgency broke out in May 2003. The support base of the insurgency is the Sunni Arab community and some Sunni Turks. Together these two communities constitute some 20 per cent of Iraq's population. Political, economic and cultural marginalization of the Sunni Arabs in post-Saddam Iraq pushed this community towards insurgency. The domination of the Sunni Arabs started in the mid-nineteenth century with the Ottoman rule in Mesopotamia. In 1921, the British institutionalized Sunni Arab ascendancy in Mesopotamia.

Saddam Hussein's rule (1968-2003) further institutionalized Sunni Arab domination. Especially, the coercive apparatus of the Ba'thist regime was dependent on the Sunni Arabs. Now, under the Coalition rule, the Sunni Arabs lost all power, privileges and identity. On 24 May 2003, Paul Bremer, the American proconsul in Iraq, dissolved the armed forces of Saddam Hussein and the jobless and identityless former Sunni Arab soldiers and officers took to insurgency.[26] Ahmed S. Hashim notes: 'The Sunni Arabs no longer define Iraq, and that coupled with what they perceive as their deliberate marginalization, has presented them with a deep identity crisis. . . . People also fight not only to maintain or advance things they value materially, but also for a set of *nonmaterial* value that are subsumed under the rubric of identity.'[27]

Some of the insurgent factions in Iraq have at least nominal linkages with the Al-Qaeda and employ suicide *mujahidins* from Saudi Arabia, Sudan, Yemen and Chechnya.[28] Most of the insurgents equipped themselves by looting the Iraqi government's arsenals in the immediate chaotic aftermath of the Second Gulf War. Weapons abandoned in the battlefield by the defeated Iraqi Army also passed into the hands of the insurgents.[29]

AFGHANISTAN

In the 1980s, the Soviets in Afghanistan were opposed by a transnational force of guerrillas. The estimated number of *mujahidins* who fought the Soviets and later constituted the base of Bin Laden's support comprised 5,000 Saudis, 3,000 Yemenis, 2,800 Algerians, 2,000 Egyptians, 400 Tunisians, 350 Iraqis, 200 Libyans and dozens of Jordanians.[30] The expulsion of the Soviets was followed by the rise of the Taliban in Afghanistan. *Talib* is an Arabic word. Its literal meaning is one who is seeking something for himself. It is derived from the word *talab*, meaning desire. *Taliban* is the plural of *talib*. In Pushto, the word *taliban* denotes students studying in *deeni madrasas*. Most of the Taliban personnel are Sunnis who followed the Hanafi *fiqah* and belong to the Qadiriya *silsila* of the famous Sufi saint Abdul-Qadir Al-Gilani of Baghdad. The Talibans are mostly Pushtuns and the Pushtuns have dominated Afghanistan from the mid-eighteenth century onwards under the auspices of the warlord Ahmad Shah Abdali. The Pushtuns comprise some 43 per cent of the population. They dominate the eastern provinces of Afghanistan. Large pockets of Pushtuns are also present in the northern provinces amidst the Uzbeks, Tajiks and Turkomans.[31] The Taliban military

organization comprised about 3,000 hardcore personnel and another 8,000 who joined after 1995 and about 12,000 foreign volunteers. In addition, various warlords and tribal chiefs controlled about 25,000 armed men of doubtful loyalty. In 2001, Afghanistan was a country which had experienced civil war for the last two and a half decades and its Gross National Product was US $5 billion, most of which was raised by smuggling and drug trade.[32] The financial muscle of the rebels in Afghanistan comes mostly from trade in heroin. In 1998, 1 kg of heroin with 90 per cent purity fetched a price of $60,000 in the USA.[33]

KASHMIR

About two-thirds of Kashmir is under India's control and the rest is under Pakistan. The region under Pakistan is called *Azad* (independent) Kashmir by the Pakistanis and India calls it Pakistan Occupied Kashmir (hereafter POK).[34] The Indian strategic analyst K. Santhanam rightly points out that the non-state actors cannot function without support from a state. In Kashmir's case, support of Pakistan to the insurgents is extremely important.[35] The Pakistan Army and especially the Inter-Services Intelligence (ISI) have been supporting the insurgents from the mid-1980s with money, equipment and training. The objective is to exhaust India by giving a 'thousand cuts' with the aid of the insurgents.[36] Pakistan's strategy is to give moral and material assistance to groups like Hizb-ul-Mujahidin which aim at secession of Kashmir from India through armed struggle and then merger with Pakistan. There are other groups/organizations like the Jammu and Kashmir Liberation Front, etc., which want only an independent Kashmir.[37] The transnational connection is also apparent in the Kashmir case. The Al-Qaeda connects sub-national organizations with a trans-national network.[38] Osama bin Laden declared a *jihad* in Kashmir in 1989 and extended support to the Harkat-ul-Mujahideen (HKUM), Harkat-ul-Jihad-Islami (HUJI), Harkat-ul-Ansar (HUA), Lashkar-e-Toiba (LET) and Jaish-e-Mohammed (JEM) *tanzeems* (militant outfits).[39]

Certain internal factors also resulted in the spurt of insurgency in Jammu & Kashmir from 1989 onwards. Political mismanagement by the Indian state encouraged the rise in insurgency. To cite an example, the Jammu and Kashmir National Conference party (JKNC) entered into an alliance with the Indian National Congress (INC) and the 1987 election was marked by intimidation of political opponents, voter fraud and ballot irregularities. The Muslim United Front, an agglomeration of local political parties opposed to the JKNC-INC

alliance, resorted to armed violence.[40] After the rise of sectarian violence in Assam, the refugee Bangladeshi *maulvis* went to Kashmir and contributed to the rise of fundamentalism in the latter region.[41]

NEPAL

A popular uprising in 1990 forced the king to allow a multi-party system to replace the non-party Panchayat System imposed in 1962. Nepal became a democracy in 1990. The Communist Party of Nepal-Maoist (CPN-M), which participated in the general election in 1991 and in local election in 1992, resorted to armed conflicts in February 1996.[42] Hegre, Ellingsen, Gates and Gleditsch rightly say that autocratic countries do not become mature consolidated democracies overnight. They usually go through a rocky transition, in which mass politics mixes with authoritarian elite politics in a volatile way. Political change deconsolidates political institutions and heightens the risk of civil war. When authoritarianism collapses and is followed by ineffectual efforts to establish democracy, the interim period of relative anarchy is ripe for ethnological or ideological leaders who want to organize rebellion.[43] In Nepal's case, that leader happened to be Pushpa Kamal Dahal alias Prachanda.

On 13 February 1996, the CPN-M launched the *janayuddha* (people's war).[44] Its leader Prachanda (literal meaning 'furious') reformed the views of the Marxist leaders like Nirmal Lama and M.B. Singh by proposing that the army is the principal form of organization and war is the principal form of struggle.[45] This is known as the Prachanda path. Anup K. Pahari claims that this strand in Prachanda path is akin to Mao's dictum: 'without a people's army, the people have nothing'.[46]

The Maoists conceived their armed violence against the state as a sort of *dharmayuddha* (just/righteous war). The violence they resorted to was detached and positive, for the well-being of the community and in reaction to the corruption, inefficiency and misrule of the rich against the poor.[47] The social fabric of Nepal to a great extent was responsible for the outbreak of the Maoist insurgency. The Brahmins, Chhetris and the Newars constitute 37.5 per cent of the population but they used to hold a disproportionate share in politics, administration and education. These three groups control over 80 per cent of the leadership positions in important areas of governance.[48]

Madhav Joshi says that the feudal land tenure system persisted in Nepal in favour of a coalition between the king, *ranas* and the military bureaucratic machinery. And the coalition of political parties also

derived substantial support from the landed elites. The rural people were alienated from the benefit of a market economy as a liberal market was not fully functional in the rural villages which further strengthened the patron-client relationship between the landed elites and the rural people.[49] Avidit Acharya reminds us that simple economic analysis would not explain the rise of Maoist insurgency in Nepal. The insurgency started from the two districts of Rolpa and Rukum. Inequality in landownership is lowest in these two districts. However, these two districts are also without good communication links. This aided the insurgents to hide from the government's forces. Acharya claims that the political difference between the royalists or the centrist or liberals on the one hand and the ultra-radical left on the other was the principal factor behind the origin of the Maoist insurgency. Acharya accuses the history of ultra-left activism as the main motor behind the Maoist insurgency.[50]

Kristine Eck writes that by linking the villagers' disaffection with their daily lives to the larger problems in the political system, the CPN-M was able to exploit grievances for the purpose of rebel recruitment. The significance of indoctrination was considered more *vis-à-vis* training and acquisition of arms.[51] Since 1996, Maoist cultural troupes travelled through the country and enacted for the villagers colourful politico-cultural programmes. The first cultural battalion known as the Madhya Samana Battalion 6 was formed in October 2006. It includes the four cultural companies of Central Nepal: Sen Chyang Cultural Company, Anekot Cultural Company, Shiv Sharada Cultural Company and Chunu Shilpa Cultural Company. The battalion is under the cultural section of the party named Akhil Nepal Jan Sanskritik Mahasangh (All Nepal People's Cultural Federation). During public programmes, the cultural activists attempted to win the people's support for the revolution. The Maoist cultural activists produce both literary works including magazines, poems, dramas, novels and performance art such as dance, theatre, songs that circulate through tapes. Cultural programmes are used for fund raising. The CPN-M has a Youth Communist League (YCL). The YCL is also an organ for recruiting and training young men even under 18 years of age. The YCL also collected tax from private schools. This tax was used to fund indoctrination and also to further Maoist propaganda campaigns about establishing people's education (an equitable educational system) for all.[52] Due to these organizational innovations, the Maoist insurgency in Nepal is more or less successful without any significant external support.

COUNTER-INSURGENCIES AND STATE-BUILDING

Buhaug and Gates make an important point when they say that rough terrain is ideal for guerrilla warfare and difficult for a government army to control. Mountain areas give advantage to the rebel troops, allow them to expand their bases and forests provide cover against detection and aerial attacks.[53] It is to be noted that in 1927, Mao established his base in the mountainous areas of Jiangxi.[54] Afghanistan, Kashmir and Nepal fit the above-mentioned scenario. The Maoist rebellion which broke out in Peru in 1980 started from the remote mountainous wasteland region of Ayacucho.[55] The importance of geography is challenged by Tony Balasevicius and Bernd Horn. They claim that rather than physical geography, the cultural mosaic of the operational area is more important for both the 'rebels' and the COIN forces.[56]

The insurgents mostly attack soft targets, i.e. those with low degrees of survivability and low abilities to defend against violence.[57] Stathis N. Kalyvas writes: '. . . violence is primarily a resource rather than the final product; it is intended to shape the behaviour of a targeted audience by altering the expected value of particular actions.'[58] Islamic insurgents resort to suicide terrorisms. The suicide bombings, writes Denton, unless used for directed assassinations are used for leverage purposes in a global political context, especially in the psychological plane.[59] One scholar is of the view that due to the prevalence of 'post-heroic' mentality, the Western soldiers are no more willing to die. Sacrifice of life in war is more considered an ideal rather than commonplace reality in the Western societies.[60] And this might have an adverse effect on the global war on terror. This is not a problem in case of India which commands huge demographic resources and the concept of life is regarded as quite cheap due to extensive poverty and underemployment.

Fowler writes that compared to the armies of the polities, the insurgents use 'flat organization'. It means there are very few layers of bureaucracy between the decision makers at the top and insurgents at the bottom. In such an organization, orders can be passed quickly and actions can be taken rapidly.[61] Eliot A. Cohen argues that the present-day world is experiencing an RMA centring round information technology. Cohen, like Fowler, claims that like the corporate houses, the military organization should also get rid of the intermediate layers in the bureaucracy in order to make them more agile.[62] Fowler comments: 'To counter global insurgency, faster-moving forces are needed. They should be smaller than traditional

size units . . . "flatter" command structure than is currently used. . . . Forces should be able to operate autonomously in a network because they may have to combat a foe who is similarly dispersed.'[63] Cassidy notes that the employment of indigenous forces is a necessity if the US wants to pacify Iraq and Afghanistan.[64] As we will see in the sub-sections below, this proposition is followed both in the case of Afghanistan and Iraq.

David P. Fidler notes that the COIN doctrines of both the USA and India have certain similarities. For instance, both the *Counterinsurgency Field Manual* (US Army and Marine Corps 2007) and the *Doctrine for Sub-Conventional Operations* (Indian Army 2006) focus that COIN operations have to be undertaken with full respect to human rights.[65] Thomas R. Mockaitis writes that the basic principles of COIN strategy remain valid for today's terrorism as when practitioners worked them out to root out the communist insurgency 50 years ago. Intelligence remains the key to victory in COIN operations. Garnering accurate and timely information requires winning the trust of the general population who supports the insurgents tacitly or actively. Trust and cooperation depend in turn on recognizing and as far as possible addressing the real needs and legitimate grievances on which the insurgency feeds. Good intelligence allows the security forces to use force against the terrorists in a limited and focused manner so as not to further alienate the general population. This strategy is described as 'winning hearts and minds'.[66] Winning hearts and minds also require use of indigenous forces to the greatest possible amount. Dipankar Banerjee asserts that from studying the Malayan Campaign, the Indian Army learnt the objective of winning the 'hearts and minds'. In Banerjee's formula, this means that the focus of COIN operations should be the population rather than the insurgent forces. Unconsciously, here Banerjee comes very close to Smith's concept of war amongst the people. Banerjee continues that without support from the populace an insurgency cannot continue. And without winning the people, an insurgency cannot be defeated. The role of the armed forces is to limit the violence of the insurgents and to allow space for the political process to resolve the issue.[67] Colonel Bhaskar Sarkar of the Indian Army accepts that acquisition of intelligence from the local people of the disturbed areas is a must if success is to be obtained.[68] Amnesty programmes are promoted frequently by the political actors to encourage defection of the insurgents and reward civilians who defect and cooperate with the COIN forces.[69]

Sumit Ganguly and Fidler accept that small unit tactics worked better for Indian COIN efforts than fire and manoeuvre tactics by large-scale troop concentrations.[70] In 2007, the US Marine Corps noted that success in the tactical plane did not guarantee overall success. Further, use of excessive force is unproductive.[71] Sarkar accepts that COIN operations are going to be attritional. There is no shortcut to victory. He notes that the objectives of the COIN forces should be to eliminate the insurgents and to respect and help the people inhabiting the disturbed zones. Sarkar continues that at the tactical level, the COIN forces (especially the army units) should get rid of their heavy weapons. The focus should be to organize elite commando units. At best, the COIN forces should operate at company size. The COIN forces should be familiarized with the local terrain, customs and traditions of the people of that region, etc.[72] Let us shift the focus to COIN operations in the four regions that are discussed in this paper.

IRAQ

Urban operations in Basra comprised aggressive patrolling and use of checkpoints.[73] In 2005, suicide terrorism reached an unprecedented level in Iraq. Most of the suicide bombers were foreigners. George Michael and Joseph Scolnick claim that in reality it shows the despair of the insurgents. They argue that suicide bombings should be used sparingly for its symbolic effect. However, regular use of suicide bombings inured the observers both inside and outside the Muslim community about its shock effect. Further, suicide terrorism also resulted in death of many civilian casualties. And non-combat casualties also caused grievances among the Muslim civilians and alienated them from the insurgents.[74]

Lieutenant-Colonel Tim Collins commanded the British Special Forces in Iraq in 2003. He notes in his autobiography: '. . . how we had developed a good rapport with the townsfolk'.[75] Collins admits: '. . . the difficulty of policing a region where cultures are different and the language barrier extreme'.[76] Collins notes: '. . . in the US military there was no culture of engagement with the local population'.[77] The US reservists enjoyed torturing the prisoners at Abu Gharib Prison near Baghdad.[78]

Warren Chin warns that the Americans rely too much on firepower aiming to annihilate the enemy rather than getting concerned with peacekeeping. Indiscriminate and intense cordon and sweep

operations result in the detention of several thousand innocent Iraqis which further alienate them from the Coalition forces. In 2007, the US had 140,000 troops and between May 2003 and March 2006, the US force had suffered 2,500 killed and 19,000 wounded.[79] So, the Americans are now relying more and more on indigenous auxiliaries. In 2009, the new Iraqi Army' strength was 130,000 men and the Iraqi police had 190,000 personnel.[80]

AFGHANISTAN

Intelligence is vital for the COIN forces. This in turn requires access to the population (an important feature of the war amongst the people or successful guerrilla warfare). The *mujahidin*'s control of the population enabled them to develop an extensive network of observers and messengers throughout the country which enabled them to maintain continuous watch over the Soviet movements in the 1980s.[81] Emily Spencer and Horn rightly note that winning hearts and minds requires an understanding of the host society. In Afghanistan, which is largely rural, xenophobic and tribal, the cultural divide between 'us' (Western peacekeeping force) and 'them' (Afghans) is huge. It requires empathy on part of the COIN forces.[82]

COIN strategy includes both military and non-military elements. The military in several cases is used not to annihilate but to deter the insurgents and if possible to encourage them to change sides. One view which is emerging among the American policy makers is that instead of brute force, the US should depend on diplomacy. In other words, the US should encourage the Taliban commanders to defect and join the US-NATO project of reconstructing post-Taliban Afghanistan. Those Taliban commanders who would join the West would be considered as 'Good' Taliban and those who would oppose the West should be branded as the 'Bad' Taliban.[83]

Initially, the anti-Taliban militias gathered under the Ministry of Defence as the Afghan Military Forces (AMF). However, they were of little use in hunting down the remnants of the Taliban. Then, the Coalition relied on smaller militias extracted from the AMF known as Afghan Security Forces (ASF). They were trained by the Coalition forces. A single battalion was trained by the British in February-April 2002 to become Afghanistan's National Guard. Recruitment in the Afghan National Army (ANA) started in May 2002. The objective was that gradually the international trainers would be replaced by Afghan trainers. Battalions were trained in a basic course of ten weeks and establishment of a full-fledged disciplined unit was

supposed to take six months.[84] In 2003, the Afghan security forces numbered only 6,000 soldiers. Their number increased to 25,000 in 2005, about 36,000 in 2006, again 50,000 in 2007 and finally 58,000 in 2008. In 2009, fatalities among the Afghan security forces exceeded 1,000 per year.[85]

In 2009, US President Barack Obama ordered deployment of 21,000 US troops in Afghanistan. Soon, there will be 55,000 American soldiers in Afghanistan.[86] In the same year, it was decided to increase the size of ANA from 57,000 to 82,000 men.[87] In 2009, there were about 60,000 Western troops and 140,000 Afghan security forces in Afghanistan. And during the same period, there were about 700,000 soldiers and police (plus 100,000 volunteers) in smaller and less populous Iraq. The population of Afghanistan according to the 1973 census was 18,293,800.[88] The troop strength in both these countries is an indicator that in Western strategy, Iraq at present is more important than Afghanistan.

KASHMIR

Between 1990 and 1995, the number of *tanzeems* in Kashmir rose from 12 to more than 50.[89] Let us have a look at the organizational strength of two *tanzeems* which are operating in this region at the beginning of the new millennium. The Al Barq was formed in 1990. Its headquarter is at Srinagar and its strength is 350 (including 20 foreigners). Its objective is liberation of Kashmir through armed struggle and establishment of Islamic rule. This outfit possesses about 100 AK-47 rifles and gets financial support from ISI through *hawala* transactions. A smaller outfit is the Al Fateh Force. It came into existence during February 1994 and its headquarter is at Bandipur in Baramulla district. The objective of this group is merger of Jammu & Kashmir with Pakistan.[90] In the 1990s, the insurgents conducted select killings of prominent Hindus in the Kashmir Valley in order to encourage exodus of the Hindus from Jammu & Kashmir. The Lashkar-e-Toiba's strategy is to eliminate the pro-peace leaders and to conduct *fidayeen* (suicide) attacks.[91]

General Shankar Roychowdhury, who became the Chief of Army Staff of India in 1994 notes in his memoirs:

> In Kashmir, the Indian Army was deployed in two separate but closely interlinked conflicts. One flickered along and across the LoC involving exchanges of intense artillery, missile, mortar and automatic fire between the regular armies of India and Pakistan along with almost daily clashes between our border patrols and mujahideen attempting to infiltrate into the Valley. The other was the

counterinsurgency and counter-terrorism in the hinterland of the Valley against militant Islamic tanzeems and their overground organizations.[92]

The Indian COIN forces use *ikhwans* (captured militants). They worked with the security forces against their former compatriots. In response to criticism of human abuse perpetrated by the COIN forces, Prime Minister Narasimha Rao created the National Human Rights Commission in 1993. This body brought the operations of armed forces under greater scrutiny.[93] In the long run, monitoring of COIN operations by this autonomous body added legitimacy to India's COIN operations.

NEPAL

Between 1996 and 2006, the Maoist conflict resulted in 13,000 casualties in Nepal. The CPN-M had a few dozen fighters in 1996 in its army known as the People's Liberation Army (PLA). By November 2006, when the Comprehensive Peace Agreement was signed, the CPN-M had about 30,000 fighters. Like the African guerrillas, the Maoists also abducted children (especially teenagers) in order to form child soldiers. The armed personnel were taught how to ambush security forces and techniques of making grenades, etc.[94] On 26 November 2001, the Royal Nepal Army (RNA) was deployed against the Maoists.[95] The PLA was divided into two divisions, seven brigades, and 19 battalions. In addition to the PLA, the Maoists also controlled a 50,000 strong militia. The PLA was never able to win against the RNA in any conventional confrontation. After March 2005, the RNA was mostly engaged in suppressing opposition to King Gyanendra's 1 February 2005 coup rather than in fighting the Maoists. The Maoists then collaborated with the democratic political forces in order to topple the king. And after the February 2005 royal coup, the UK government suspended its planned package of 1.3 million sterling pounds military aid which included provision of equipments such as night flying helicopters, bomb disposal equipment, etc. The CPN-M joined the parliament in 2007 and is leading a coalition government from August 2008. Its combatants and arms are in the cantonments under United Nations Mission in Nepal.[96]

However, the Maoist supremacy started crumbling soon. On 16 January 2007, the Madhesi People's Rights Forum exhibited both violent and non-violent protests against the Maoists. And Madhesi opposition to the CPN-M is growing. The term Madhesi applies to the people living in the Tarai region. The Madhesis spread over

20 districts constitute 33 per cent of Nepal's total population. The Madhesi population comprised various groups: indigenous groups like Tharus, Hindu communities settled there and businessmen of Indian origin like the Marwaris, Sikhs, Muslims, etc.[97]

CONCLUSION

The features of both insurgencies and COIN operations include elements traditional and new. The Islamic insurgents in Iraq, Afghanistan and in Kashmir are conducting terrorist strikes. Such attacks could be categorized as sub-conventional attacks. Suicide bombers are common in both Iraq and Kashmir. In contrast, the Maoists in Nepal have been able to transform themselves into a sort of conventional army capable of fighting with the RNA. The Maoist insurgency in Nepal which developed without any significant transnational connections was similar to many Communist insurgencies which erupted in Asia during the Cold War. There is a basic difference in the COIN operations conducted by the US and Coalition forces and the Indian Army. While the Indian Army is fighting the 'rebels' within its own country, the COIN operations of the US and Coalition forces are overseas in nature, i.e. they are fighting the 'rebels' in foreign countries. Nevertheless, there are certain similarities in the COIN operations of the Indian Army and the US-Coalition forces. The Coalition's use of the 'Good Taliban' is somewhat similar to the Indian Army's use of *ikhwans* in Kashmir. Again, both the US led Coalition's COIN force as well as the Indian Army engaged in COIN duties follow winning the 'hearts and minds' of the people technique. However, it would be too early to assert that the new millennium belongs to the insurgents. The CPN-M came to power in Nepal not through military victory but through political compromise by reaching an agreement with the 'bourgeois' political parties of Nepal. Despite large-scale disturbances, the insurgents in Kashmir are in a no-win situation. And in Sri Lanka, the government force has been able to annihilate the LTTE. However, that is a different story.

NOTES

1. Emily Spencer and Bernd Horn, 'Introduction', in Spencer (ed.), *The Difficult War: Perspectives on Insurgency and Special Operations Forces,* Ontario: Dundurn Press, 2009, p. 13.
2. Lieutenant-Colonel Vivek Chadha, *Low Intensity Conflicts in India: An Analysis,* Delhi: Sage, 2005, p. 25.

3. James D. Fearon and David D. Laitin, 'Ethnicity, Insurgency, and Civil War', *American Political Science Review* (hereafter *APSR*), vol. 97, no. 1, 2003, p. 75.
4. Robert M. Cassidy, *Counterinsurgency and the Global War on Terror: Military Culture and Irregular War*, Westport, Conecticut: Praeger, 2006, p. vii; Herfried Munkler, 'The Wars of the 21st Century', *International Review of the Red Cross*, vol. 85, no. 849, 2003, p. 9.
5. Mary Kaldor, *New and Old Wars: Organized Violence in a Global Era*, 1999; rpt., Dehradun: Natraj, 2005, p. 1.
6. Rupert Smith, *The Utility of Force: The Art of War in the Modern World*, 2005, rpt., London: Penguin, 2006, p. xiii.
7. Peter H. Denton, 'The End of Asymmetry: Force Disparity and the Aims of War', in Spencer (ed.), *The Difficult War*, op. cit., p. 47.
8. Chadha, *Low Intensity Conflicts in India*, p. 21. Chadha uses the term Low-Intensity Conflict (LIC) while referring to insurgencies. The term LIC was invented during the Cold War era to designate Communist insurgencies.
9. Smith, *Utility of Force*, op. cit., pp. 16-17.
10. Kaldor, *New and Old Wars*, op. cit., pp. 2, 4.
11. Smith, *Utility of Force*, op. cit., pp. 16-17.
12. Kaldor, *New and Old Wars*, op. cit., p. 3.
13. To be fair to Cohen, he accepts that to implement a successful RMA, a country needs to gel rapid technological changes with political purpose. Eliot A. Cohen, 'A Revolution in Warfare', *Foreign Affairs*, vol. 75, no. 2, 1996, p. 51.
14. Cassidy, *Counterinsurgency and the Global War on Terror*, op. cit., pp. 10-11.
15. Smith, *Utility of Force*, op. cit., p. 3.
16. Cassidy, *Counterinsurgency and the Global War on Terror*, op. cit., p. 13.
17. Michael C. Fowler, *Amateur Soldiers, Global Wars: Insurgency and Modern Conflict*, Westport, Connecticut: Praeger, 2005, pp. 30, 56.
18. Tony Balasevicius, 'Mao Zedong' and the People's War', in Spencer (ed.), *The Difficult War*, op. cit., p. 25.
19. Havard Hegre, Tanja Ellingsen, Scott Gates and Nils Petter Gleditsch, 'Towards a Democratic Civil Peace? Democracy, Political Change, and Civil War, 1816-1992', *APSR*, vol. 95, no. 1, 2001, p. 33.
20. Halvard Buhaug and Scott Gates, 'The Geography of Civil War', *Journal of Peace Research*, vol. 39, no. 4, 2002, p. 418.
21. Monica Duffy Toft, 'Getting Religion? The Puzzling Case of Islam and Civil War', *International Security*, vol. 31, no. 4, 2007, pp. 98, 101, 103.
22. Fearon and Laitin, 'Ethnicity, Insurgency, and Civil War', op. cit., p. 80.
23. Bishwa Nath Tiwari, 'An Assessment of the Causes of Conflict in Nepal', in Mahendra Lawoti and Anup K. Pahari (eds.), *The Maoist Insurgency in Nepal: Revolution in the Twenty-First Century*, Oxon: Routledge, 2010, p. 253.
24. Thomas A. Marks, 'Ideology of Insurgency: New Ethnic Focus or Old Cold War Distortions?', *Small Wars and Insurgencies*, vol. 15, no. 1, 2004, pp. 109, 112.
25. Alice Hills, 'Basra and the Referent Points of Twofold War', *Small Wars and Insurgencies*, vol. 14, no. 3, 2003, p. 31.
26. Ahmed S. Hashim, *Insurgency and Counter-Insurgency in Iraq*, London: C. Hurst, 2006, pp. 59, 60-7, 92-5.
27. Italics in original. Hashim, *Insurgency and Counter-Insurgency in Iraq*, op. cit., p. 67.
28. Cassidy, *Counterinsurgency and the Global War on Terror*, p. 2.
29. Tim Collins, *Rules of Engagement: A Life in Conflict*, London: Headline, 2005, pp. 271, 295.

30. Thomas R. Mockaitis, 'Winning Hearts and Minds in the "War on Terrorism"', *Small Wars and Insurgencies*, vol. 14, no. 1, 2003, p. 26.
31. Kamal Matinuddin, *The Taliban Phenomenon: Afghanistan 1994-97, with an Afterword Covering Major Events Since 1997*, Karachi: Oxford University Press, 1997, pp. 12, 27-8.
32. Warren Chin, 'Operation "Enduring Freedom": A Victory for a Conventional Force Fighting an Unconventional War', *Small Wars and Insurgencies*, vol. 14, no. 1, 2003, pp. 61, 66.
33. Imtiaz Ahmed, 'Contemporary Terrorism', in Vice-Admiral K.K. Nayyar and Jorg Schultz (eds.), *South Asia Post 9/11: Searching for Stability*, Delhi: Rupa, 2003, p. 52.
34. V.G. Patankar, 'Insurgency, Proxy War, and Terrorism in Kashmir', in Sumit Ganguly and David P. Fidler (eds.), *India and Counterinsurgency: Lessons Learned*, Oxon: Routledge, 2009, p. 66.
35. K. Santhanam, 'Sources of Terror: India', in Nayyar and Schultz (eds.), *South Asia Post 9/11*, p. 34.
36. Amelie Blom, 'A Patron-Client Perspective on Militia-State Relations: The Case of the Hizb-ul-Mujahidin of Kashmir', in Laurent Gayer and Christophe Jaffrelot (eds.), *Armed Militias of South Asia: Fundamentalists, Maoists and Separatists*, Delhi: Foundation, 2009, pp. 136-7.
37. Patankar, 'Insurgency, Proxy War, and Terrorism in Kashmir', op. cit., p. 68.
38. Claudia Haydt, '"New" Terrorism: Guidelines for Security Forces', in Nayyar and Schultz (eds.), *South Asia Post 9/11*, p. 15.
39. K. Santhanam, Sreedhar, Sudhir Saxena and Manish, *Jihadis in Jammu and Kashmir: A Portrait Gallery*, Delhi: IDSA and Sage, 2003, p. 25.
40. Sumit Ganguly, 'Slow Learning: Lessons from India's Counterinsurgency Operations in Kashmir', in Ganguly and Fidler (ed.), *India and Counterinsurgency*, op. cit., p. 79.
41. Chadha, *Low Intensity Conflicts in India*, op. cit., p. 115.
42. Mahendra Lawoti, 'Evolution and Growth of the Maoist Insurgency in Nepal', and Madhav Joshi, 'Between Clientelistic Dependency and Liberal Market Economy: Rural Support for the Maoist Insurgency in Nepal', in Lawoti and Pahari (eds.), *Maoist Insurgency in Nepal*, pp. 3, 92.
43. Hegre, Ellingsen, Gates and Gleditsch, 'Towards a Democratic Civil Peace?', p. 34.
44. Prakash Nepali and Phanindra Subba, 'Civil-Military Relations and the Maoist Insurgency in Nepal', *Small Wars and Insurgencies*, vol. 16, no. 1, 1983, p. 84.
45. Marie Lecomte-Tilouine, 'Fighting with Ideas: Maoist and Popular Conceptions of the Nepalese People's War', in Gayer and Jaffrelot (eds.), *Armed Militias of South Asia*, p. 65.
46. Quoted from Anup K. Pahari, 'Unequal Rebellions: The Continuum of "People's War" in Nepal and India', in Lawoti and Pahari (eds.), *Maoist Insurgency in Nepal*, p. 198.
47. Lecomte-Tilouine, 'Fighting with Ideas: Maoists and Popular Conceptions of the Nepalese People's War', in Gayer and Jaffrelot (eds.), *Armed Militias of South Asia*, op. cit., pp. 67-8.
48. Ram S. Mahat, 'Democracy in a Plural Society', in Nayyar and Schultz (eds.), *South Asia Post 9/11*, op. cit., p. 90.
49. Joshi, 'Between Clientelistic Dependency and Liberal Market Economy', in Lawoti and Pahari (eds.), *Maoist Insurgency in Nepal*, p. 93.

50. Avidit Acharya, 'The Maoist Insurgency and the Political Economy of Violence', in Lawoti and Pahari (eds.), *Maoist Insurgency in Nepal*, op. cit., pp. 263-80.
51. Kristine Eck, 'Recruiting Rebels: Indoctrination and Political Education in Nepal', in Lawoti and Pahari (eds.), *Maoist Insurgency in Nepal*, op. cit., p. 34.
52. Monica Mottin, 'Catchy Melodies and Clenched Fists: Performance as Politics in Maoist Cultural Programme', and Amanda Snellinger, 'The Repertoire of Scientific Organization: Ideology, Identity and the Maoist Student Union', in Lawoti and Pahari (eds.), *Maoist Insurgency in Nepal*, op. cit., pp. 52-3, 88.
53. Buhaug and Gates, 'Geography of Civil War', op. cit., p. 422.
54. Balasevicius, 'Mao Zedong and the People's War', in Spencer (ed.), *The Difficult War*, op. cit., p. 30.
55. Marks, 'Ideology of Insurgency: New Ethnic Focus or Old Cold War Distortions?', p. 118.
56. Tony Balasevicius and Bernd Horn, 'Intelligence and its application to Irregular Warfare', in Spencer (ed.), *The Difficult War*, op. cit., p. 57.
57. Fowler, *Amateur Soldiers, Global Wars*, op. cit., p. 59.
58. Stathis N. Kalyvas, 'The Paradox of Terrorism in Civil War', *Journal of Ethics*, vol. 8, 2004, p. 100.
59. Denton, 'The End of Asymmetry: Force Disparity and the Aims of War', in Spencer (ed.), *The Difficult War*, op. cit., p. 47.
60. Munkler, 'Wars of the 21st Century', op. cit., pp. 9-10.
61. Fowler, *Amateur Soldiers, Global Wars*, op. cit., p. 9.
62. Cohen, 'A Revolution in Warfare', op. cit., p. 48.
63. Fowler, *Amateur Soldiers, Global Wars*, op. cit., p. 55.
64. Cassidy, *Counterinsurgency and the Global War on Terror*, p. 20.
65. David P. Fidler, 'The Indian Doctrine for Sub-Conventional Operations: Reflections from a US Counterinsurgency Perspective', in Ganguly and Fidler (eds.), *India and Counterinsurgency*, p. 215.
66. Mockaitis, 'Winning Hearts and Minds in the "War on Terrorism"', p. 21.
67. Dipankar Banerjee, 'The Indian Army's Counterinsurgency Doctrine', in Ganguly and Fidler (eds.), *India and Counterinsurgency*, op. cit., pp. 194, 197.
68. Colonel Bhaskar Sarkar, *Tackling Insurgency and Terrorism: Blueprint for Action*, Delhi: Vision, 1998, p. 125.
69. Kalyvas, 'The Paradox of Terrorism in Civil War', op. cit., p. 99.
70. Ganguly and Fidler, 'Conclusion', in Ganguly and Fidler (eds.), *India and Counterinsurgency*, p. 227.
71. Fidler, 'The Indian *Doctrine for Sub-Conventional Operations*: Reflections from a US Counterinsurgency Perspective', in Ganguly and Fidler (eds.), *India and Counterinsurgency*, op. cit., p. 212.
72. Sarkar, *Tackling Insurgency and Terrorism*, op. cit., pp. 102, 111, 122-3.
73. Hills, 'Basra and the Referent Points of Twofold War', op. cit., p. 30.
74. George Michael and Joseph Scolnick, 'The Strategic Limits of Suicide Terrorism in Iraq', *Small Wars and Insurgencies*, vol. 17, no. 2, 2006, pp. 116-17.
75. Collins, *Rules of Engagement*, op. cit., p. 225.
76. Ibid., p. 264.
77. Ibid., p. 355.
78. Ibid.
79. Warren Chin, 'Examining the Application of British Counterinsurgency Doctrine by the American Army in Iraq', *Small Wars and Insurgencies*, vol. 18, no. 1, 2007, pp. 1, 3-4.

80. Allan Orr, 'Recasting Afghan Strategy', *Small Wars and Insurgencies*, vol. 20, no. 1, 2009, p. 88.
81. Balasevicius and Horn, 'Intelligence and its Application to Irregular Warfare', in Spencer (ed.), *The Difficult War*, op. cit., p. 56.
82. Spencer and Horn, 'Introduction', in Spencer (ed.), *The Difficult War*, op. cit., p. 13.
83. Fotini Christia and Michael Semple, 'Flipping the Taliban: How to Win in Afghanistan', *Foreign Affairs*, July-August 2009, p. 37.
84. Antonio Giustozzi, 'Auxiliary Force or National Army? Afghanistan's "ANA" and the Counter-Insurgency Effort, 2002-2006', *Small Wars and Insurgencies*, vol. 18, no. 1, 2007, pp. 47-8.
85. Michael O'Hanlon, 'Toward Reconciliation in Afghanistan', *Washington Quarterly*, vol. 32, no. 2, 2009, p. 140.
86. Christia and Semple, 'Flipping the Taliban: How to Win in Afghanistan', p. 34.
87. Orr, 'Recasting Afghan Strategy', p. 88.
88. O'Hanlon, 'Towards Reconciliation in Afghanistan', p. 141; Matinuddin, *The Taliban Phenomenon*, op. cit., p. 27.
89. Blom, 'A Patron-Client Perspective on Militia-State Relations', in Gayer and Jaffrelot (eds.), *Armed Militias of South Asia*, op. cit., p. 135.
90. Santhanam et al., *Jihadis in Jammu and Kashmir*, op. cit., pp. 55, 57, 61-2.
91. Chadha, *Low Intensity Conflicts in India*, op. cit., pp. 127, 159.
92. Shankar Roychowdhury, *Officially at Peace: Reflections on the Army and its Role in Troubled Times*, Delhi: Viking, 2002, p. 44.
93. Sumit Ganguly, 'Lessons from India's Counterinsurgency Operations in Kashmir', in Ganguly and Fidler (eds.), *India and Counterinsurgency*, op. cit., pp. 81, 83.
94. Eck, 'Recruiting Rebels', Marie Lecomte-Tilouine, 'Political Change and Cultural Revolution in a Maoist Model Village, Mid-Western Nepal', and Mahendra Lawoti, 'Ethnic Dimensions of the Maoist Insurgencies', in Lawoti and Pahari (eds.), *Maoist Insurgency in Nepal*, op. cit., pp. 33, 120, 124, 131, 139.
95. Nepali and Subba, 'Civil-Military Relations and the Maoist Insurgency', op. cit., p. 95.
96. Mahendra Lawoti, 'Ethnic Dimensions of the Maoist Insurgencies: Indigenous Groups' Participation and Insurgency Trajectories in Nepal, Peru, and India', Ashok K. Mehta and Mahendra Lawoti, 'Military Dimensions of the "People's War": Insurgency and Counter-Insurgency in Nepal', Pahari, 'Unequal Rebellions', and Bishnu Raj Upreti, 'External Engagement in Nepal's Armed Conflict', in Lawoti and Pahari (eds.), *Maoist Insurgency in Nepal*, op. cit., pp. 138, 176, 178, 199, 223, 228.
97. Pramod K. Kantha, 'Maoist-Madhesi Dynamics and Nepal's Peace Process', in Lawoti and Pahari (eds.), *Maoist Insurgency in Nepal*, pp. 156-8.

6

Ethnicity and State-building in Afghanistan

ARPITA BASU ROY

Afghanistan is a cultural mosaic with multiple ethnicities, primarily trans-national. Ethnic arguments have increasingly been deployed in political agitations and there has been a visible tendency towards ethnicization of the conflict. At the same time, the national idea has remained weak and underdeveloped, lacking appeal or influence, except in a small and unrepresentative educated urban, literate class. In the post-2001 phase, it is imperative that the process of nation-building, democratization and institution-building have to be explored and understood through the lens of the societal cleavages that exist in Afghan society. After a discussion on the contribution of political science to the question of ethnicity and nationalism and exploration of the cultural mosaic of Afghanistan, the paper explores the context where the defeat of the Taliban in 2001 was a new opportunity to create an ethnically inclusive state. State-building refers to the reconstruction of governmental institutions and structures, including a constitution, often after a major political upheaval. The paper explores whether constitutional provisions guaranteed under the Constitution of Afghanistan, 2004, assumes significance and whether the state is equipped to pursue policies of religious, linguistic and cultural unity. In Afghanistan both processes require and are affected by constitutional crafting in a post-conflict situation. Literature relating to such crafting has distinguished between seeking to manage or to eliminate ethnic differences. By way of conclusion, the paper argues that it would be surprising if a strong nation in the Western sense did emerge as the country remains fragmented along ethnic, religious and ideological lines and geographical/topographical constraints. I argue that ethnic plurality, the root cause of endemic conflict in the country, can be tackled by a political accommodation

in the form of a federal structure that strikes a balance between the requirements of a strong centre and the demand of the provincial autonomy.

POLITICAL SCIENCE'S CONTRIBUTION TO THE QUESTION OF ETHNICITY AND NATIONALISM

James G. Kellas points out that the subject of nationalism and ethnicity is to be found in at least ten disciplines in Western academic writing.[1] These disciplines range from socio-biology to political science, and cover the most primordial aspects through to the most overtly political. The distinctive contribution of political science relates to nationalist political behaviour and conflict resolution. Political scientists are not concerned as are philosophers or sociologists with the ideology of nationalism, nor do they specialize in its historical origins. The focus is on contemporary political demands such as secession, autonomy and rights, and they seek possible solutions to national/ethnic conflict through strategies of political accommodation such as 'constitutional engineering'.[2]

The contribution of political science to the containment and/or resolution of extreme political conflicts deriving from nationalism and ethnicity are primarily two. First is *consociational democracy* and the second is *political accommodation strategies* based on breaking down ethnic solidarities. Two political scientists are exemplars of each type—the Dutch political scientist Arend Lijphart and the American political scientist Donald L. Horowitz.[3] These two political scientists' work is particularly relevant to multinational or multiethnic states characterized by 'cultural pluralism'. Consociational democracy was an inductive theory based on the political arrangements found in the four countries of Europe in 1960s—the Netherlands, Belgium, Switzerland, and Austria. Consociationalism had four features: (1) a Grand Coalition of the segments in the central government; (2) a veto power in the government for segments when their interests are at stake; (3) a proportional share of offices and expenditures for each segment; and (4) autonomy for each segment in managing its own affairs (especially education, language rights, broadcasting). This blueprint or a variant of it is to be found repeatedly in constitutions of 'divided societies'. Lijphart, himself a Dutch, knew from the experience of the Netherlands that this kind of democracy was stable, while many other segmented societies were marked by civil wars and violence. However, the consociational model failed to produce the results that were expected. In his 1977 book, *Democracy*

in Plural Societies, he applied the model to non-European cases such as Canada, Israel, Lebanon, Malaysia, Cyprus, Nigeria, Indonesia, and Uruguay, and extended the European cases to Northern Ireland. By the 1980s it was evident that the model was not working or had not been applied to these countries. Even his four classic cases of the Netherlands, Belgium, Switzerland and Austria were failing to live up to the expectations which signalled that a less rigid blueprint with perhaps some different strategies altogether, need to be applied. This is where Donald Horowitz has made a major contribution to the subject.

Unlike Lijphart, Horowitz's aim is to produce a constitution which will overcome these divisions by breaking them into smaller units, and to provide incentives for ethnic cooperation, not only at the level of 'elite accommodation' but at the grassroots electoral level as well. Thus, stability would come not only from the top-down (initiative of the leaders) but also from the bottom-up (the act of voting). In the consociational scheme, voters voted only for their segmental parties, and grassroots electoral behaviour was stable and entirely along ethnic lines. Thus he sees 'constitutional engineering' for divided societies in a completely different light and emphasizes the choosing of an electoral system to break down ethnic voting solidarities. In his 700-page long work he criticizes consociational democracy for its rigidity since the same constitutional arrangements would have different consequences in different circumstances. It would be wrong to say that Horowitz provides an entirely non-consociational model. He does not recognize the complexity of the segmentation and breaks it down further through complicated constitutional and electoral arrangements, which he calls 'mechanisms of conflict resolution'.

Political science has thus engaged in at least two types of constitutional engineering for deeply divided societies. There have certainly been relevant success in conflict resolution, and the four classic consociational cases in Europe are encouraging. In time, their example may be followed elsewhere, but the conditions for success are not well-established in political science as yet, although much work is being done on the subject.

AFGHANISTAN'S DIVIDED SOCIETY: THE IDEA OF A NATION

Ethnic diversity is thus extremely prominent whereas it is more homogeneous along religious or sectarian lines—99 per cent of the population happens to be Muslims, 80 per cent of whom are

Sunnis. The national and patriotic idea has remained weak and underdeveloped in Afghanistan, lacking appeal or influence except in a small and unrepresentative educated, urban, literate class, whose members are often in important respects culturally cut-off from the mass of rural or tribal population. Afghanistan's rural population lived for most part in remote rural areas and usually had restricted horizons and limited political consciousness. Afghanistan has never been a nation in the sense of a common people with a shared destiny, but rather a collection of disparate groups joined together by the vagaries of geopolitics. It has been recounted in several scholarly works, how Afghanistan emerged as a state built around the Pashtun tribal structure.[4] The Saddozai Popolzai clans of the Durrani tribes formed a great Pashtun confederation and carved out an empire between India and Persia in the mid-eighteenth century. They were followed by the Mohammadzai Barakzai clans, also belonging to the Durrani tribes, in 1818, but it lacked internal cohesion.[5]

Antony Hyman argues that nationalism could not exert its peculiar ideological appeal until the majority of Afghanistan's population was integrated into the collective life of the society.[6] Although modernization of Afghan society had made considerable progress from the 1950s, its impact was restricted almost entirely to the educated elite of Kabul. Even this small educated class was itself deeply divided along ethnic lines, between Pashtuns and non-Pashtuns, bitterly resenting the virtual monopoly of power and pretensions of the Pashtun elite. In Kabul and the few other large towns, the elite and urban middle class were subject to a process of Persianization of speech and culture.[7]

Despite gaps in the relatively liberal city and the conservative-minded countryside, the political system of Afghanistan has been dominated by a tribal aristocracy. The place of the Mohammadzai family as Emirs and later, kings of Afghanistan, was crucial to the development of nationalism as the monarch was often regarded as a key factor in personifying and in the imbibing of national feeling. For example, Zahir Shah (from 1933 until 1973) was successful in unifying the millions of urban educated as well as rural poor and thus demonstrated the intimate linkage between 'modernization, nationalism and the institutions of the monarchy'.[8] There is an inherent sense of the essence of their common culture based on religion and other cultural practices, which has sustained Afghanistan through years of conflict and displacement. A sense of national identity does exist, elements of divisiveness notwithstanding.[9] These resilient

communities are strong and quick to recover from any crisis with the ability to withstand hardships, and this is definitely of enormous value in the country's post-war reconstruction.

FAMILY/KINSHIP /*QAWM* RELATIONS

Afghanistan is essentially a patrilineal society, Afghans generally identify themselves as part of an extended patrilineal family where the sons inherit the property of the father and continue to work on it in common. Affinal kinship relations are, on the other hand, important mechanisms for mobilizing allies. But in societies where polygamy is practised, it can create tremendous complexities. The ideal form of marriage includes arrangements where agnatic cousins marry their children to each other or exchange sisters whereby bride wealth remains within the lineage and also strengthens relations between the families.[10]

An Afghan's honour requires him to defend and control those elements collectively known as *namus*: *zan, zar,* and *zamin* (woman, gold and land). *Zamin* includes both land owned by the family and the homeland of a broader kinship group referring to tribe or lineage. Men thus see women as the repository of their honour. The social customs through which male control is expressed are *pardah* and *chadri*. Some women especially in the Islamic movement, contest the reading of these customs as signs of male domination and reinterpret them as signs of female self-determination within Islam.[11]

The family in Afghanistan shades off into larger groupings and other components of identity based on kinship, commonly known as *qawm*. It is common to describe this phenomenon by calling Afghanistan a tribal society. *Qawm* is sometimes translated as tribe, but in reality refers to any form of solidarity or *asabiyya*. *Qawm* identity might be based on kinship, residence or occupation. Afghans are conscious of belonging to a larger entity which takes the form of more or less endogenous community or solidarity group (the *qawm*), whether its sociological base is either the tribe, clan, professional group (*qawm* of the mullah or barbers), caste (*bari* or *nuristani*), religious group (*sayyad*), ethnic group (*munjani*), village community or simply an extended family.[12] While the state claims authority over society within a territory, a *qawm* claims jurisdiction over a set of persons bound by kinship relations.[13] The geographical barrier set by the Hindu Kush Mountains created a barrier between Kabul and the rural areas and retarded the development of centralized political

institutions, which could only expand in power at the expense of local loyalties.[14] Inter-*qawm* rivalry over various issues was common. Local conflict was/is a major concern for most local Afghans faced with informal and formal governance structures which struggle to find equitable and suitable resolutions as a result of the conflict and associated social changes.[15] Conflicts over access to, or control of, land and water represent nearly half of the conflicts, followed by conflicts related to weddings/marriages, divorces and domestic violence.[16]

ETHNIC MOSAIC

The several ethnic groups of Afghanistan (Pashtuns, Tajiks, Hazaras, Uzbeks, Turkmans, Baluchis, Pashais, Nuristanis, Aymaqs Qirghiz, Qizilbash, Gujurs, Brahuis and even Arabs) speak different languages. Besides Pashto (used by the Pashtuns) and Dari (Afghan Persian) which are official languages, Uzbeki, Turkmen, Pashai, Nuristani and Pamiri (Alsana) are also spoken by the corresponding ethnic groups. The 1964 Constitution of Afghanistan, introduced with the 'New Democracy', named two official languages, Pashto and Dari, the latter name given to Afghan Farsi or Persian.[17] However, Dari remained the *lingua franca* of the country as a whole. Language was to remain a deeply contentious and divisive issue. An official drive to make Pashto more viable as a national language by creating one standard language instead of numerous regional dialects led to the creation in 1937 of a Pashto Academy known as the Pashto Tolaney.[18] But the state-led drive failed to make Pashto, in any real sense, a competitor to Persian. Another reason for Pashto failing to rise up to the standards of Dari lay in the fact that not only was it difficult to learn compared to the simplicity of Persian (Dari) grammar, but there was also a general animosity felt against the Pashtun political dominance and a clear sense of cultural superiority expressed by members of the Tajik, Turkic and other non-Pashtun groups. Repeated attempts by the state to foster the growth and spread of Pashto, however abjectly failed.[19]

Afghanistan has often been described as a tribal confederation, comprising multi-racial groups and nationalities. The dominant group, both in economic and numerical terms, as said, comprises the Pashtuns. Concentrated in the South and the South-East, but settled in most regions, the Pashtuns constitute around 38 per cent of the total Afghan population. The Tajiks, the second largest nationality, is estimated to constitute 25 per cent of the total population and is concentrated around Kabul, the Panjsher Valley and the Badakhshan

province.[20] Apart from these two nationalities there are a large number of smaller groups such as the Hazaras (19 per cent), Uzbeks (6 per cent), other minor ethnic groups like Aimaqs, Farsiwans, Heratis, Turkmens, Brahuis, Baluchs and Nuristanis (around 12 per cent).[21] Among the tribally organized communities are the Pashtuns, Hazaras, Aimaqs, Nuristanis and the Baluchs. The non-tribal communities include the mountain Tajiks, Uzbeks, Turkmen, Farsiwans and Kohistanis. All these groups maintain their own distinctive culture and sense of identity.[22]

The trans-border connectivity and linkages established mainly due to shared ethnicities across border and cross-border movements form a distinctive feature and help in creating social networks. Afghanistan is truly wedged between cultural boundaries, creating puzzle-like cultural patterns that defy simple definitions. For example, the largest ethnolinguistic group in the country is also known as the Pushtuns, Pakhtuns, or Pathans. It is worth noting that while there are nearly eight million Pashtuns in eastern and southern Afghanistan, there are twice as many in neighbouring Pakistan, linking these two countries. The Taliban are predominantly Pashtun, which explains, in part, the support from many Pakistanis across the border. In terms of religion, most Pashtuns are Sunnite Muslims, but it should not be assumed that all Pashtuns are as fundamentalist as the Taliban in their views of Islam.

The second largest ethnic group in the country is the Tajiks, accounting for about 25 per cent of the population. Like the Pashtuns, they speak an Indo-European language, Dari, an eastern dialect of Farsi (Persian or Iranian). Overall, about half of all Afghans speak Dari according to the Central Intelligence Agency (2001). Tajiks, for example, share millions of ethnic brethren in neighbouring Tajikistan, Uzbekistan, and China. Within Afghanistan, Tajiks are concentrated in the north-eastern part of the country, and in certain pockets in the west. They are reported to comprise an important part of groups which had challenged the Taliban rule. Although Tajiks are Sunnite Muslims, they are generally considered to be less fundamentalist and conservative than the Taliban government.

A third important group in the country is the Hazara, who inhabit much of the central part of the country. Numbering in the millions, and accounting for just fewer than 20 per cent of the population, Hazaras speak Dari like the Tajiks and other groups. Most Hazaras are Shi'ite muslims, which along with other cultural differences had put them at odds with the Taliban. Persecutions of Hazara within Afghanistan have caused a great deal of concern within Iran. The

1998 massacre in the city of Mazari-i-Sharif of hundreds of Shi'ites, pushed Iran and Afghanistan to the brink of war. The major other ethnic groups in Afghanistan include the Nuristani, Turkmen, Uzbek, Kirghiz, Chahar Aimak, Brahui, and Baloch groups. The Turkmen, Uzbek, and Kirghiz (Kyrgyz) groups share cultural areas with majority groups in neighbouring Turkmenistan, Uzbekistan, and China. In general, they are later settlers than other groups in the country and possess distinct cultural differences. They all speak Turkic languages that are different than the Indo-European tongues spoken by the Pashtuns, Tajiks, Hazaras, and the like. Islam is a unifying feature to some degree, but these Central Asian minorities often have considerable disagreements with Pashtun fundamentalism. Uzbeks alone account for about 6 per cent of the population.[23]

The Aimak of Western Afghanistan are notable because they are probably of Mongolian origin, a reminder of past invasions. They have Mongoloid features and live in dwellings similar to those found among groups in Mongolia and Western China (*Britannica*: 2001). Despite their eastern Asian origins, however, they speak the Farsi dialect of Dari. Finally, the Baloch (Baluchi) and Brahui groups live in a large area that includes parts of southern Afghanistan, Iran, and Pakistan. Known as Balochistan (or Baluchistan), this dry, isolated region prompts many to live as nomadic shepherds. This isolation has also spawned distrust of the central authority, and the Baloch have periodically made attempts to gain greater autonomy from the governments of Pakistan, Afghanistan, and Iran. Most Baloch are Sunni Muslims and speak an Indo-European language that is somewhat related to Kurdish. They number about 250,000 in Afghanistan alone, and nearly 8 million across the region. The Brahui are a smaller group of about 2 million speaking a language that is Dravidian in origin, a language family that dominates in southern India, and which includes Tamil and Telugu. Because of its isolation from languages of the same family, and owing to the fact that it is not a written language, Brahuis have borrowed many words from other languages and bilingualism is common (*Ethnologue*: 2000).

ISLAM AND OTHER RELIGIOUS IDENTITIES

Islam in Afghanistan is part of an entire civilization and the source of universal values and ethics that give life a transcendent meaning.[24]Apart from tens of thousands of Hindus and Sikhs, and a small minority of Armenian Christians and Jews in the major cities,

all other Afghans are Muslims. Muslims are roughly 99 per cent of the total population, and around 85 per cent of them are Sunnis of the Hanafi School. Most of the rest, including the Hazaras, the Qizilbash and some Farsiwan, are Imami (Twelver) Shi'as, as are the Wakhis of the Wakhan Corridor.

In any review of nationalism in Afghanistan, it is important to study the role of Islam in Afghan society as legitimizer of authority, and at times of rebellion too—under successive rulers. Although from outside Afghanistan may appear as a remarkably homogeneous group, even if they did form a distinct social group, there is a basic divide between the Sunni Muslim majority following the Hanafi rite, and substantial Shi'a Muslim minorities—mainly Imami Shi'a (Twelvers), but also Ismailis. The Sufi *tariqas* and their *pirs* (hereditary saints) have and retain till today a wide following, and tribal custom is more important in many spheres of life than Shari'a law.[25] In principle, the Shi'a faith is more unified and hierarchical than Sunnism. Religious dignitaries among the Shi'as enjoy extremely high prestige and influence because they either claim descent from the Prophet (Saddad) and/or because of their reputation for learning or pilgrimage to holy shrines like Mashhad, Nejaf and Kerbala.[26]

Islam has, however, served at times as a unifying force against foreign, non-Muslim invaders, but it has never been cohesive enough to unite all the Pashtuns and other ethnicities of Afghanistan. Some scholars regard pan-Islamism as an attractive ideology, stronger at times with anti-colonialist fervour. The contemporary phenomenon of 'political Islam' in Afghanistan arguably has a basis in the traditional role of Sufism and the influence in society of the most prominent *pirs,* together with the constant allure for the Afghans, of the concept of jihad and martyrdom. Afghanistan's contemporary Islamic movement has cohered around a new Islamic paradigm focusing on the concept of the state and legitimacy of power.[27]

POLITICAL ACCOMMODATION IN THE POST-2001 PERIOD

Historically speaking, Afghanistan's diversity has also not been reflected in its governing institutions. It was in fact the Pashtuns who had dominated Afghanistan in all governing institutions and this was evident in government appointments and official histories, which tended to erase the contribution of the non-Pashtun groups in the country. The exclusionary policies were further continued by the Taliban from 1996-2001.

In his description of the exclusionary policies pursued by the Pashtuns, Sharani paints a bleak picture. The demarcation of the borders of Afghanistan as part of the Great Game by Britain during the reign of Emir Abdur Rahman (1880-1901) laid the foundation for the troubled status of Afghanistan as a modern nation state. He writes:

> Backed by Britain, Emir Abdur Rahman terrorized the people within these freshly marked borders. He and his Muhammadzai/Durrani *Pashtun* clan hailed from Kandahar, the recent spiritual headquarter of the Taliban, as well as the home of Hamid Karzai, the leader of the current U.S. installed Interim Administration in Afghanistan. The *Pashtun* in this southWestern area of Afghanistan belong to different tribes than those living further east along the borders with Pakistan. After decimating the leadership of the eastern Ghilzai *Pashtun* tribes whom he did not trust, Emir Abdur Rahman moved against the *Hazaras* in the center of the country. The *Hazaras* resisted Abdur Rahman's conquest (as they also recently opposed the Taliban invasions) of their territory and, as a result, were subjected to extremely harsh punishments: entire villages were massacred, people were skinned alive, and women and children were enslaved. A particularly gruesome form of torture perpetrated against the *Hazara* people was to form a rim of dough around the shaven heads of men so that boiling oil could be poured on them to fry their brains. Stories of such atrocities remain a permanent part of public memories in this area of the country and are still in circulation (see Mousavi: 1997). Emir Abdur Rahman employed violence and torture in his rampages of conquest and subjugation of all of the peoples within his designated domain. In the east, where the inhabitants were not Muslims (Kafiristan), he forcibly converted them and renamed the area Nooristan (Land of Light). The same brutalities were used in subjugating Uzbek, Turkmen, Tajik, and other ethnic communities in the northern region. Throughout the entire country dur-ing the 21 years of his reign, people were brutally terrorized into submission. Emir Abdur Rahman created a relatively strong centralized state through the use of such tactics, by advocating a conservative and xenophobic interpretation of Islamic ideology, and by the liberal use of foreign money and weapons. Indeed, Emir Abdur Rahman-nick-named by his British colonial masters, the 'Iron Emir' for his cruel two-decade-long rule, laid the foundation for an ill-suited centralized state structure that lasted for most of the 20th century. The Iron Emir was intensely suspicious of his citizens, especially of those *Pashtun* who did not belong to his own clan or tribe and the non-*Pashtun* groups in the center and northern regions of the country. In order to insure his sovereignty over the non-*Pashtun* peoples in the north and central regions of the country, Emir Abdur Rahman mobilized large groups of Durrani *Pashtun* nomads from the south to occupy large areas of pastureland in central Afghanistan belonging to *Hazaras* (see Ferdinand: 1962; Kakar: 1979; Mousavi: 2000). He also resettled tens of thousands of *Pashtun* tribesmen from the south in the strategic parts of Afghan Turkistan along the borders with Central Asian Khanates under czarist Russian control (Tapper: 1973). By doing so, he laid the ground for the enforcement of century-long policies that were nothing but a crude form of internal colonialism run by the ruling clique in Afghanistan.[28]

The *Pashtun* exclusionary policies continued until the fall of the Taliban in 2001. Persecution intensified under the Taliban regime (1996-2001), as its soldiers advanced into Afghanistan's north and the Hazarajat. In 1998, in retaliation for war crimes committed by the United Front against Taliban soldiers and targeted because of their Shiite faith, the Taliban slaughtered approximately 2000 Hazaras in Mazar-e Sharif. Civilians were killed in residential areas and market places, some dying from having their throats slit. The Taliban governor Mullah Manon Niazi had publicly incited the attack, preaching: 'Hazaras are not Muslim. You can kill them. It is not a sin.' Highlighting the driving ethnic and religious nature of the attack, Hazaras were reportedly warned to take lessons from their own history, and to either convert, flee or be killed. Hundreds fled the terror of Mazar-e Sharif. Massacres continued, with Taliban soldiers rounding up civilians in the Yakaolang district in 2001, publicly executing at least 170, many of whom were Hazaras.[29]

Having reflected upon the societal cleavages and traditional Pashtun dominance in Afghan politics and the persecution perpetrated on the other ethnic groups, it is worth noting that the main institutional choices arising from these categories relevant to Afghanistan in post-2001 phase concerned whether the country should become a federation or a unitary state, whether it should be presidential or parliamentary democracy, and whether consociational forms of power-sharing in elected and non-elected institutions of the state should be adopted.

A significant feature of Afghan politics is that it has not suffered from a secessionist movement. This is perhaps because a consciousness for a nation state did not matter for the people whose identity revolved around their *qawm*. But as Barnett Rubin notes, ethnic politicians from different groups advocated different views of how to constitute the Afghan nation after the fall of the Taliban in 2001. The Afghan constitution of 2004 was produced after extensive deliberations and bargaining.[30] The Constitutional Commission published the results of its deliberations in November 2003 after extensive, albeit secretive, discussions.[31] In December 2003, the Constitutional *Loya Jirga* (Grand Assembly) was given an opportunity to debate the constitutions' provisions and make amendments before the final draft was agreed upon in January 2004. The central debates related to the powers of the presidency, the issue of national language, the role of the king, human rights and the role of Islam. Significantly, the changes made in the CLJ 'were almost entirely determined by the northern (ethnic)

block' that helped the Americans topple the Taliban. Afghanistan's Constitutional *Loya Jirga* promulgated a new Afghan constitution and ratified it early in the New Year on 4 January 2004.[32]

MAJOR DEBATES

One of the major debates in the constitution-making process in Afghanistan was whether 'ethnicity' should be formally recognized within institutions of the state.[33] There is no correct answer as to whether formal recognition is successful in ensuring political stability in ethnically divided societies. Some scholars like Brian Barry have argued that this type of recognition perpetuates and hardens identities, undermines a sense of national identity, and makes conflict more likely in both the short and long term.[34] In contrast, supporters of recognizing diversity such as Brendan O Leary argue that a hard confrontation with reality forces certain options on decision makers in deeply divided societies.[35] They argue that communities will be insecure without this recognition, thus leading to a further politicization of identities and potentially escalating tensions. In addition, if we accept that individuals possess more than one identity, recognition does not automatically cause conflict because different identities will be more prominent at different points in time. Although differences existed between the various ethnic communities, a coalition of ethnic groups seeking to limit the perceived danger of Pashtun dominance emerged during these deliberations. Pashtun 'centralizers' were opposed by those arguing that an ostensibly 'non-ethnic' position actually served the interests of the largest groups. Such debates and deliberations were an essential feature of the political process in the 2000s and had enormous significance 'for the future of inter-ethnic relations between Pashtuns and non-Pashtuns'. This was a result of years of Pashtun domination of the state and their persecution of other ethnic groups like the Hazaras, Tajiks and the Uzbeks which contributed to this antipathy.

Certain international actors played a very significant role in this constitution-making process, either directly or through Afghans like Karzai who were aware of the parameters within which they were acting, concerning the role of Islam in the constitution and Washington's desire for a strong presidential system. A significant role was played by Special Presidential Envoy and former US Ambassador to Afghanistan Zalmay Khalilzad and by UN Special Representative Lakhdar Brahimi after 40 per cent of the delegates

to the CLJ boycotted the proceedings in early January 2004. They played an instrumental role in bringing the process back on track after serious disagreements emerged between the different communities.

After the removal of Taliban from power, academic discussions on the appropriateness of federalism for post-conflict Afghanistan proliferated. Federal forms of government have been criticized in divided societies because of the belief that federal autonomy is likely to increase pressures for secession, increase feeling for separateness, and give groups the resources with which to mobilize against the centre. However, if federation has failed in this multi-ethnic society, so have other forms of government. Federal forms of government differ according to many criteria, including level of centralization, the number of federal units, and whether they are majoritarian or consociational. Therefore to 'blame' federal forms of government for divisive tendencies would be erroneous. What needs to be thought out in relation to the country's ethnic demography is vital in this equation.

Many regarded post-Taliban Afghanistan as 'a perfect candidate for federalism' while others argued that it would be a 'recipe for disintegration'.[36] Demands for a parliamentary federation were made especially from the Uzbek community led by General Abdul Rashid Dostum and the Hazaras led by Karim Khalili. These communities were small but sufficiently territorially concentrated for federalist arrangements to afford protection from central government in which they would most likely have only minimal representation.

In contrast, Pashtun representatives argued that a federal constitution would result in the division of the country, given the fiefdoms controlled by regional warlords. This also fitted with their demand for a presidential system. Pashtuns are particularly concentrated in the southern and south-eastern part of the country but they also live in several other provinces of the country. Probably they feared that federation would further divide their community and empower the Tajiks. On the other hand, the Tajiks, since they are less territorially concentrated than either the Uzbeks or the Hazaras, were also not demanding a federal structure or territorial autonomy. Rather they were focussing on power-sharing in the central state. Thus the centralizers eventually won this argument and Article 1 of the Afghan Constitution specifically states that 'Afghanistan shall be an Islamic Republic, independent, unitary and indivisible state'.

Thus Afghanistan is not only a unitary system but also *de jure* is very highly centralized. While Kabul's writ does not extend throughout the country and therefore it may not result in *de-facto* centralization, any

perception of an ethnically dominated centre discriminating against territorially concentrated ethnic groups will inevitably lead to major disaffection and potential tension. This is where the importance of representation rights lie. Without guaranteed representation in central government institutions, certain communities maybe excluded. Guaranteed representation also poses the problem of determining appropriate quotas for the different communities. The call for meritocracy in appointment to non-elected state institutions such as the bureaucracy is a laudable one as it has the advantage of selecting the best candidates. However, it may reinforce historical ethnic domination of a particular community if certain communities have not benefited from the same opportunities like education that other communities have enjoyed.[37]

There is also a long-standing debate existing over whether presidential or parliamentary systems are best suited for ethnically divided societies. Some argue that presidential systems in general 'cannot compare with the advantages of a truly collective and inclusive executive'.[38] This is primarily because presidential systems tend to be zero-sum games in that there can be only one winner from one community. In contrast, a parliamentary system can include members of various ethnic communities, and electoral mechanisms exist to facilitate the election of a president who is acceptable to most of the communities in the country.[39] In the case of Afghanistan, the United States of America as well as the Pashtuns favoured a Presidential system due to the perceived need of a 'strong man' to lead Afghanistan. In fact, Karzai at that point of time threatened that he would only stand in future presidential elections if the *Loya Jirga* approves the strong presidential system. The CLJ was in fact split along ethnic lines on this issue, with Tajiks, Uzbeks and Hazaras opposed to the adoption of a strong Presidency, fearing it would exclude them from power.

Political Scientist Will Kymlicka also talks about polyethnic rights while discussing and distinguishing several different types of political recognition.[40] Polyethnic rights happen to be the weakest form of recognition and are not dependent on a community being territorially concentrated. These rights include the right to retain personal laws for ethnic communities such as marriage laws, and the recognition of different languages for use in government institutions. These types of rights remain controversial. Although giving legal recognition and rights to a community's culture, language or religion gives them security, it can also set them in opposition to other identities. Despite the rejection of formal self-governing and representation rights

in the Afghan constitution and the removal of the word ethnicity from its preamble, a significant change was made in the recognition of polyethnic rights. Ahmed Rashid describes it as 'the single most important development in the Loya Jirga and the most surprising'.[41] Article 16 retained Pashto and Dari as official languages—a status that both have enjoyed since the constitution of 1923 but provided that 'in areas where the majority of the people speak in any one of the Uzbeki, Turkmeni, Pachaie, Nuristani, Baluchi or Pamiri—any of the aforementioned languages, in addition to Pashto and Dari, shall be the third official language, the usage of which shall be regulated by law'. This sends a potentially strong signal of the state's commitment to these language communities. In fact, the recognition of polyethnic rights in terms of language policy, has conferred a sense of perceived worth by the central government to Afghanistan's various linguistic communities, as well as offering them access to power, especially at the local level.

A strong argument in favour of incorporating the tremendous strengths of a re-emergent civil society into a new community rule-based state structure has been given by M. Nazif Shahrani.[42] He considers this as the only feasible road to face national challenges. He also argues that a constitutional guarantee of the rights of community self-governance at the local, district, provincial, and regional levels throughout the country, allowing local communities to run their own civil, judicial, security and educational administrations and also to maintain law and order with the help of a community police force is necessary. In some Islamic religious thoughts, the *Shura* (council or the *Jirga* in pashto) is considered the ideal model for governance. Such local governing bodies have also functioned as advisory councils formed to solve conflicts, resolve disputes, or deliberate on decisions affecting the community. Such councils comprise those whose opinions, negotiating skills, and knowledge of tribal and/or religious law are respected, usually including elders, religious authorities and local influentials. The *Shura* can deal with problems or disputes that arise within the community and also may deal with division of labour or resources where communal issues are concerned.[43] Though from outside such a system appears exploitative and corrupt, yet it gives the people access to justice which they otherwise do not get. Though the system is not democratic, the institutions are representative of the local population and hence a critical resource for political and physical reconstruction. The tradition of *Loya Jirga* has been utilized in Afghanistan in the post-Taliban period to establish the transitional government.

CONCLUSION

Thus the 2004 Constitution guaranteed a unitary state with a Presidential form of government and guaranteed polyethnic language rights to ethnic minorities. I argue that centralization without power-sharing at the centre in ethnically divided societies has the potential to alienate ethnic communities, especially if they are potentially concentrated like the Hazaras and Uzbeks of Afghanistan. Although it is understandable that in the immediate aftermath of the fall of the Taliban, holding the country together by diluting ethnicities became imperative, and Karzai emerged as the binding figure in Afghan politics, yet with time, granting more federal powers to the provincial centres becomes a logical and pertinent need. Moreover a few key players like Karzai have been instrumental in the operation of these institutions since 2001 but with Karzai becoming politically weakened since the 2004 election, it is highly questionable whether these mechanisms will survive Karzai. Therefore formal institutional arrangements for ethnic coalitions are imperative.

Some scholars have made the case for consociationalism. Scholars like Amin Saikal advocate that Afghans can benefit from the experiences of countries which have derived the benefits from consociationalism like Austria, Switzerland and Columbia by modifying some aspects of the model in light of Afghan conditions, and by guarding against known causes of failure. The mutual veto, for instance, will have to be limited somehow in order to prevent certain groups from abusing it and endangering stability. The actual workings of the veto mechanism, moreover, must be carefully designed to avoid deepening social cleavages or hindering the growth of broad social and economic interactions among microsocieties.[44] Ethnic plurality, the root cause of endemic conflict in the country, can be tackled by a political accommodation in the form of a federal structure that strikes a harmonious balance between requirements of a strong centre and demands of the provincial autonomy. Rights of ethnic groups are more easily affirmed through federal arrangements.

Transition from conflict to peace is unlikely to be a smooth process and the goals of state-building will ultimately be achieved by reconstruction and reconciliation that are geared towards social and institutional structures that can be mobilized to prevent future conflicts. It must involve the transformation of the institutions, networks and incentive systems: nationally, regionally, and locally, that caused and perpetuate the conflict system in Afghanistan into a cohesive framework.[45] The necessity of incorporating such socio-

political subsystems into the greater system is a major challenge of this highly divided ethnic society, known as Afghanistan.

NOTES

1. James G. Kellas, *The Politics of Nationalism and Ethnicity*, Basingstoke: Macmillan, 1991, pp. 171-3.
2. James G. Kellas, 'Nationalism and Ethnic Conflict: The Contribution of Political Science to Political Accommodation', *Studies in East European Thought*, vol. 46, nos. 1/2, Special Issue: Nationalism and Social Science, June 1994, pp. 105-17.
3. The main works mentioned here are Arend Lijphart, *Democracy in Plural Societies: A Comparative Exploration*, New Haven and London: Yale University Press, 1977; *Democracies: Patterns of Majoritarian and Consensus Government in Twenty-One Countries*, New Haven and London: Yale University Press, 1984; Donald L. Horowitz, *Ethnic Groups in Conflict*, Berkeley: University of California Press, 1985; and *A Democratic South Africa?: Constitutional Engineering in a Divided Society*, Berkeley: University of California Press, 1991.
4. Ashraf Ghani, 'Islam and State-building in Afghanistan', *Modern Asian Studies*, vol. 12, no. 2, 1978, pp. 269-84 and Olivier Roy, *Afghanistan: From Holy War to Civil War*, Princeton: Darwin Press, 1995.
5. Larry Goodson, 'The Fragmentation of Culture in Afghanistan', *Alif: Journal of Comparative Poetics*, no. 18, Post-Colonial Discourse in South Asia, 1998, p. 271.
6. Antony Hyman, 'Nationalism in Afghanistan', in *International Journal of Middle East Studies*, vol. 34, no. 2, Special Issue: Nationalism and the Colonial Legacy in the Middle East and Central Asia, May 2002, pp. 299-315.
7. Frederick Barth (ed.), *Pathan Identity and its Maintenance in Ethnic Groups and Boundaries*, Boston: Little Brown, 1969.
8. Hyman, 'Nationalism in Afghanistan', op. cit., p. 300.
9. Nancy Hatch Dupree, 'Cultural Heritage and National Identity in Afghanistan', *Third World Quarterly*, vol. 23, no. 5, October 2002, pp. 977-89.
10. Barnett R. Rubin, *The Fragmentation of Afghanistan: State Formation and Collapse in the International System*, New Haven and London: Yale University Press, 1995, pp. 23-4.
11. Ibid., p. 24.
12. Olivier Roy, *Islam and Resistance in Afghanistan*, Cambridge: Cambridge University Press, 1986, p. 12.
13. Rob Hager, 'State, Tribe and Empire in Afghan Inter-Polity Relations', in Richard Tapper (ed.), *The Conflict of Tribe and State in Iran and Afghanistan*, London and Canberra: Croom Helm, St. Martin's Press, 1983.
14. Larry Goodson, 'The Fragmentation of Culture in Afghanistan', *Alif: Journal of Comparative Poetics*, no. 18, Post-Colonial Discourse in South Asia, 1998, pp. 269-89.
15. Christian Dennys and Idrees Zaman, 'Trends in Local Afghan Conflicts', Synthesis Paper, Cooperation for Peace and Unity (CPAU), Publication, June 2009.
16. Ibid.
17. The name 'Dari' has been adopted and insisted on as a correct term essentially to differentiate the Afghan form of Persian from that of Iran.

18. Hyman, 'Nationalism in Afghanistan', op. cit., p. 300.
19. Ibid., p. 301.
20. Estimates for ethnic groups vary. The *CIA 2001* puts the figures as follows: Pashtun: 42 per cent; Tajik: 27 per cent; Hazara: 9 per cent; Uzbek: 9 per cent; Aimak: 4 per cent; Turkmen: 3 per cent; Baloch: 2 per cent; other: 4 per cent.
21. Anthony Hyman, *Afghanistan under Soviet Domination, 1964-83*, London: Macmillan, 1984.
22. Arpita Basu Roy, *Afghanistan: Towards a Viable State*, Delhi and London: Hope India and Greenwich Millenium, 2002, p. 13.
23. *CIA World Factbook.*
24. Barnett R. Rubin, *The Fragmentation of Afghanistan*, New Haven and London: Yale University Press, 1995, pp. 38-9.
25. Hyman, 'Nationalism in Afghanistan', op. cit., p. 311.
26. Asta Olesen, *Islam and Politics in Afghanistan*, Surrey: Curzon, 1995, pp. 53-4.
27. Ibid., pp. 227-55.
28. Nazif M. Shahrani, 'War, Factionalism, and the State in Afghanistan', *American Anthropologist*, New Series, vol. 104, no. 3, September 2002, pp. 715-22.
29. Denise Phillips, 'Hazaras' Persecution Worsens: Will the New Government Show Leadership by lifting the Suspension on Afghani Asylum Claims?', in *Australian Policy and History*, < http://www.aph.org.au/files/articles/hazarasPersecution.htm, > , accessed 8 October 2010.
30. Barnett Rubin, 'Crafting a Constitution for Afghanistan', *Journal of Democracy*, vol. 15, no. 3, July 2004, p. 11.
31. The Constitutional Commission was a large body of 35 members who reviewed the text. They also consulted a few international experts and the government's National Security Council.
32. Larry P. Goodson, 'Afghanistan in 2003: The Taliban Resurface and a New Constitution is Born', *Asian Survey*, vol. 44, no. 1, January-February 2004, pp. 14-22.
33. Some of the major debates covered in this section have been also discussed in: Katharine Adeney, 'Constitutional Design and the Political Salience of "Community" Identity in Afghanistan: Prospects for the Emergence of Ethnic Conflicts in the Post-Taliban Era', *Asian Survey*, vol. 48, no. 4, July-August 2008, pp. 535-57.
34. Brian Barry, 'Political Accomodation and Consociational Democracy', *British Journal of Political Science*, vol. 5, no. 4, October 1975, pp. 477-505.
35. Brendan O'Leary, 'Debating Consociational Politics: Normative and Explanatory Arguments', in Si Noel (ed.), *From Power Sharing to Democracy: Post Conflict Institutions in Ethnically Divided Societies*, Montreal: McGill-Queen's University Press, 2005, p. 9.
36. For example, David Cameron argued in favour of federation in Afghanistan while Omar Zakhilwal argues the opposite ('Forum on Federations: What's New in Federalism Worldwide'), Special Issue on Afghanistan, Ottawa, 2001, www.forumoffederations.org
37. Katherine Adeney, 'Constitutional Design and the Political Salience of "Community" Identity in Afghanistan: Prospects for the Emergence of Ethnic Conflicts in the Post-Taliban Era', *Asian Survey*, vol. 48, no. 4, July-August 2008, pp. 535-57.
38. Arend Lijphart, 'Constitutional Choices for New Democracies', in Larry Diamond and Marc Plattner (eds.), *The Global Resurgence of Democracy*, Baltimore: John Hopkins University Press, 1996, p. 171.

39. Donald Horowitz, *Ethnic Groups in Conflict,* Berkeley: University of California Press, 1985, p. 636.
40. Will Kymlika, *Multicultural Citizenship: A Liberal Theory of Minority Rights*, Oxford: Clarendon Press, 1995, pp. 26-33.
41. Ahmed Rashid, 'Lessons from Loya Jirga for Pakistan', *The Nation* (Pakistan), 12 January 2004.
42. M. Nazif Sharani, 'The Future of the State and the Structure of Community Governance in Afghanistan', in William Maley (ed.), *Fundamentalism Reborn?*, London: Hurst & Company, pp. 240-1.
43. Alexander Their and Jarat Chopra, 'Political and Institutional Reconstruction in Afghanistan', in *Third World Quarterly*, vol. 23, no. 5, 2002, pp. 896-7.
44. Amin Saikal, 'Afghanistan: A New Approach', *Journal of Democracy*, vol. 3, no. 2, April 1992, pp. 95-104.
45. B. Rubin, A Ghani, W. Maley, A. Rashid and O. Roy, 'Afghanistan: Reconstruction and Peacemaking in a Regional Framework', Berne Centre for Peacebuilding, Swiss Peace Foundation, 2001.

III. CULTURAL NATIONHOOD: ETHNICITY AND LINGUISTIC IDENTITY

7

Indian Anthropology and the Construction of 'Tribal Ethnicity' before Independence

DANIEL J. RYCROFT

During the pre-Independence decades of the twentieth century, the concept of 'race' was nationalized in India. In view of the connectedness between anthropological knowledge and cultural policy, the question emerges of how exponents of Indian anthropology reformulated 'race' within a nationally relevant racial studies framework. My paper aims to trace how the relational concepts of 'tribe' and ethnic diversity were reconfigured within a new sociological, rather than colonialist, discourse of race, thereby setting out the terms for a national science. By questioning how and why researchers dispensed with the idea of the 'aboriginal' before 1947, the counter-ideological background of both Indian anthropology, and the closely related field of Tribal studies, will become clear. The paper focuses on the work of Brajendra Nath Seal, Sarat Chandra Roy and Dhirendra Nath Majumdar, who were the main exponents of this emerging discipline.[1]

CONCEPTUAL OVERVIEW

The parameters and overlaps between physical and cultural anthropology in India may be questioned according to shifts in the relationship between the subject and object of representation throughout the early to mid-twentieth century.[2] Recognition of the contribution of Indian anthropology to racial studies may inform a historical critique of Tribal studies in India.[3] Approaching the 'concept of race' through the anthropological representation of 'racial formations'—especially in the contested milieu of high imperialism and national

collectivization in India—demands a critical re-assessment of those concepts that supported the racial studies framework, notably tribal ethnicity, and thereby articulated the 'racial subject'.[4] Beyond this, the discursive interplay between ideas of race, tribe, ethnicity and nationality may be ascertained.[5] During the early to mid-twentieth century, there was little certainty or agreement between exponents of racial and ethnic studies in India about the legitimacy and/or accuracy of pre-existing ethnological parameters. The emerging discipline of Indian anthropology was therefore marked by an interventionist modality to re-define, re-legitimate and re-substantiate the terms of study, so that imperialist baggage might be off-loaded.[6] Race and related concepts were re-made to accord with the values and ethics of the new nation.

Since its inception, the field of anthropology in India has been organized into physical and cultural sectors.[7] In the pre-Independence phase, most exponents combined physical and cultural approaches leading to the production of a discourse that may be analysed according to the biases given either to racial typology or ethnographic/cultural representation, as well as to either anthropometric or Sanskritic sources.[8] Yet to set these strands apart may be to misread the symbiosis, in terms of anthropological methodology, between each of these elements. Not until Indian anthropology had defined its own institutional basis at the time of national independence did clear lines of demarcation identify the parameters of physical anthropology *vis-à-vis* cultural anthropology and sociology. For anthropological historians, the analytical impact of the blurred boundaries between these different approaches to the study of humanity and human heritage in India is that the cultural ethnographies brought new significations to the interpretation of ethnicity. These harmonized the imperatives, trajectories, patterns and processes of national decolonization, raising possibilities for inter-subjective 'self-awareness' (*vis-à-vis* the new constellations of race, ethnicity and nationality) amongst the Indian anthropological community.[9] These were harnessed as the institutions of Tribal studies, Indian anthropology, and Indian sociology defined new directions and faced ongoing challenges after Independence with respect to their 'regional distinctiveness and delimitation'.[10]

PROBLEMATIZING RACE IN INDIA

Racial studies in India—or India's raciology—had a rich intellectual genealogy in the pre-Independence decades. At the outset, however,

my enquiry will focus on the late 1930s and 1940s in order to encounter key themes, which will then be explored historically. An influential researcher in this pedagogic field was Dhirendra Nath Majumdar, a Bengali anthropologist based at Lucknow University (in present-day Uttar Pradesh), who had spent long periods in the 1930s researching the interface and divergence between categories of tribe and race in northern and central India.[11] By 1939, he had become President of the Anthropology Section of the Indian Science Congress and in the 1940s he produced two decisive texts that engaged both physical and cultural anthropology. *The Fortunes of Primitive Tribes*, published in 1944, presented his work as superintendent of the 1941 census of the United Provinces.[12] It comprised four ethnographic case studies and two theoretical chapters, which set out debates that have been widely taken up since independence.[13] Supported by the Government of the United Provinces, his ethnographic survey may be read in terms of the hegemonic Tribal studies approach that I have analysed elsewhere.[14] His *Racial Problems in Asia* (1947), however, is more introductory in its scope and therefore suits the terms of this phase of my analysis.[15]

DHIRENDRA NATH MAJUMDAR AND RACIOLOGY

To counteract contemporary global experiences of race-as-conflict, and the administrative application of this model within India,[16] Majumdar presented India's own racial history within a patterning of social diversity, which signified harmony.[17] Setting out a binary framework of 'indigenous' and 'invading' races that, following centuries of inter-cultural cooperation, could be negated and reproduced in terms of a diverse civilizational heritage, the 'problems' that Majumdar referred to in his title were more of the analytical, rather than the social, variety. Unlike Grigson's 'aboriginal problem' that re-oriented the engagement between anthropologists, Adivasis (or India's indigenous and tribal peoples), and the national public,[18] Majumdar's 'problem' referred to the pedagogical predicament of race, as it was encountered in the colonial and national anthropologies of India. As such, it contributed to an emergent anti-racist agenda, which has a largely unacknowledged intellectual genealogy. As an exemplar of both physical and cultural approaches, Majumdar did not aim to consider biometric abstractions and cultural realities in independent terms. Rather, he attempted to construct an interpretative framework within which the problematic of race could be made an integral feature of national identity.

As such, his approach resonated with his intellectual forebears, notably Brajendra Nath Seal (1911) and Sarat Chandra Roy (1920). It is apt to speak of this resonance as an *anthropological heritage* that correlated—in axiological terms—with the civilizational and human diversities that were under consideration.[19] Hence the subject-object relationship, between the anthropologist and diverse fields of study, became aligned with the nation's 'cultural pluralism'.[20] In this way, the Indian anthropologist was able both to define the terms of the new science, and also to explore his own subjectivity in relation to the 'social patterning' being debated.[21] Ethnic and cultural *diversity*, one might say, had subsumed ethnic and cultural *difference*, engendering the conditions for the internalization of the national ideology of unity-in-diversity within anthropology.

I would contend that this positional anthropology was a defining feature of Tribal studies in pre-Independence and post-colonial India. A critical deconstruction of this field's institutional, intellectual and political contours remains outside the scope of this article. I contend, however, that the inter-subjective positioning of the author or researcher, in relation to India's civilizational and human heritages, made it possible for the anthropological community to sustain a cosmopolitan and multi-vocal narrative that interweaved strands of scientific modernity, cultural nationalism and primitivism. The inclusion of debates on tribal identities and racial formations within such discourses meant that concepts of 'tribe', 'primitive tribe' and 'race' would circulate and gain renewed currency in both academic and wider political milieus.[22] Defining the features of this new cultural matrix remains a critical task for those attentive to the integrationist and assimilatory tendencies of Indian anthropology, and Tribal studies in particular. Such approaches cannot dismiss the national narrative, for it was via the notion of 'civilizational diversity',[23] and the anthropological community's articulation of this, that the reification of 'tribal India' became meaningful after Independence.

For Majumdar, the idea of Adivasi (as 'aboriginal') heritage as distinct from tribal heritage was a non-starter. Even though he was content to use terms such as 'indigenous' race, and 'aboriginal' populations, it was the idea of cultural continuity—between tribal and non-tribal peoples, and/or between primitive and non-primitive groups, throughout the length and breadth of India—that enabled him to relate histories of acculturation and 'tribal absorption' into caste society to both an integrationist anthropological method and to an adaptationist ideology.[24] The relevance of this 'culture complex' to contemporary Indian sociology and raciology meant that descendants

of the so-called aboriginal populations could not be considered as distinct from the national majority.[25] There are numerous key issues at stake in this model. Post-Independence attempts to fashion national integration, between the Scheduled Tribes and the rest of society, presupposed the historic marginalization of the 'aboriginal' populations and their descendants and pertained directly to Dhirendra Nath Majumdar's model.[26] In Majumdar's model, there could be no distinct aboriginal heritage to speak of, because over centuries it had been superseded either by the assimilation of aboriginals or by new tribal, and inter-tribal, communities. The concept of tribal ethnicity thereby assumed great efficacy here as a means to displace colonialist concepts of isolated, marginal, aboriginal or 'primitive' tribes.[27]

Envisioned in both ethnic and cultural terms, for Majumdar and his contemporaries the assimilatory process brought to the foreground the idea of cultural inter-dependence, which dispensed with the imperialist fictions of isolated races. For Majumdar, this model did not presuppose cultural homogeneity, either across regions or between non-tribal and tribal populations (whose physiognomies supposedly revealed aboriginal racial characteristics, to either a greater or a lesser extent). Rather, it signified that India's civilizational heritage, whilst witnessing socio-political discrepancies, rationalized these according to Indo-centric notions of centre and periphery, thereby defining a conceptual space for the analytic of 'tribes in transition'.[28] Majumdar argued, therefore, that the uneven cultural and socio-political predicaments of tribes in India should not be envisaged as inter-racial conflict. Rather, he maintained that cultural inter-dependence '. . . has softened and stifled antagonism, and every social group in India shares in some form or other the cultural heritage of India.'[29] Majumdar's inclusive heritage paradigm accommodated the tribal on terms that privileged the national and the anthropological, and disavowed the widespread history of Adivasi antagonism in the colonial period.[30] Beyond this disavowal, the concepts of the aboriginal and the tribal were set at odds with each other, fragmenting Adivasi subjectivity in ways that have made it difficult for the post-colonial Adivasi movement to gain recognition as 'indigenous' rather than as tribal in India.[31]

CREATING A CONCEPTUAL SPACE: BETWEEN 'THE ABORIGINAL' AND 'THE TRIBAL'

In India's early raciology, 'the aboriginal' signalled an abstract non-Aryan and non-Dravidian racial entity. This could only be

accommodated, therefore, in narratives that either dwelt on India's ancient past or ignored histories of inter-ethnic contact. Such representations held sway in colonialist accounts of aboriginal tribes in India, who were apprehended as relics of a primitive age. This colonial primitivism had many administrative and anthropological consequences.[32] Yet national anthropologists subscribed neither to the history nor to the image of disaggregation. As noted, the concept of tribal India invoked a 'continuity of culture', thereby making the notion of aboriginal distinctiveness irrelevant to India's ethnographic and political present. Through this nationalist approach to anthropology in India, a chasm between the aboriginal and the tribal was opened up. The inter-cultural or transitional tribal signified civilizational distance from the isolated aboriginal of the past, and hence became connotative of a synchronous national-tribal present.

In this milieu, Indian anthropologists were able to develop a 'coeval' imaginary that disrupted dominant notions of tribal antiquity and cultural insularity.[33] As such, the processes and patterns of historical transformation—of aboriginals into tribals—required definition and substantiation. The related project, of finding conceptual pathways to cross between the abstract racial classifications of pre-Dravidian 'aboriginals', etc., and the cultural anthropology of the tribal, generated a complex interface between anthropometric and ethnographic representations in the pre-Independence phase. Sarat Chandra Roy was one of the most influential contributors to this reformulated racial formation. Speaking as President of the Indian Science Congress, in February 1921, he set out a complex agenda for 'Indian anthropology'.[34] Cognisant of the role of mid- to late-nineteenth century ethnological surveys—as embodied by the likes of Captain Sherwill and Colonel Dalton—in making tribal peoples visible to the colonialist administration and orientalist academia,[35] Roy urged his contemporaries to identify and transcend the hermeneutic and analytical limitations of these works.[36] He conceptualized a modified field of 'Indian ethnography', which could realize 'mutual relations', between 'better sifted facts' and the ethnographer.[37]

Having already touched on the relevance of Majumdar's inter-racial thesis to Tribal studies, it is important to consider the terms of his intellectual heritage within 'Indian ethnography', as these invariably informed his engagement with the problem of race. If critiqued, this genealogy would unravel to reveal a host of engaging intellectual exchanges between colonialist knowledge and anthropological decolonization, between racial pasts and new ethnographic tropes, and between empirical research and anti-racist agendas. My aim is not to

unravel the patterning of this intellectual heritage to the extent that anthropological pasts in India, whether colonial or national, might be uniformly condemned as oppressive. Rather it is deemed more purposeful and suggestive to critique India's anthropological heritage from nuanced historical vantage points, each highlighting specific contests over political, cultural and intellectual representation. In recognition of Majumdar's representation of, and positioning within, the Indian anthropological matrix, I turn to Brajendra Nath Seal's much earlier intervention on the meaning of race, tribe and nation.

ANTHROPOLOGICAL INTEGRATION AND NATIONAL MODERNITY

How did original exponents of an Indian anthropology contest, internalize and transform the colonial concepts of race and tribe? A key figure in this assessment is Brajendra Nath Seal, a political philosopher who built a foundation for subsequent attempts to re-invent these dominant concepts in anthropological research and writing. I will take Seal's article 'Meaning of Race, Tribe, Nation' (1911) as setting out possible trajectories for India's nascent anthropological heritage.[38] Was the historical assimilation of some aboriginal populations—whose descendants would become recognized in the national constitution as Scheduled Castes, following their colonial representation as 'depressed classes'—an inevitable future for less integrated tribal peoples? Was the assimilation or the subordination of tribes by Hindu upper castes a threat to the dynamic participation of tribes within India's cultural and human heritage? This kind of subordination was, of course, what some administrators and anthropologists in India came to contest as the 'aboriginal problem'.[39] So how did the terms of this protectionist approach, which seemingly set tribals and Hindus as distinct communities, resonate against the 'continuity of culture' paradigm?[40]

Keeping such questions in mind, I will assess how Seal articulated an intellectual context for social science in India that would be taken up and reproduced in discourses of national self-empowerment and local self-government. I aim to trace how the approaches devised within the new 'Indian anthropology' enabled practitioners constantly to re-route their enquiries across these inter-penetrating fields. Challenging the epistemological authority of colonial anthropology, their work created possibilities for the re-connection of physical and cultural anthropology. These routes cleared the ground for the future presence of anthropology in statist programmes of tribal

integration and development,[41] which aimed to foster economic and ideological synergy between tribal customary institutions—as well as other facets of tribal authenticity—and the independent nation. The anthropological observation, documentation and articulation of integrated (rather than assimilated or absorbed) tribes, and their cultural heritage and contemporary predicament, therefore became politically relevant.

Seal emphasized the potential role of the tribal *panchayat* (five-member village council) within patterns of political and cultural de-colonization. His approach was retraced and elaborated within the new 'Indian ethnography' in the pre-Independence phase. For example, contemporary sociologists such as Radha Kamal Mookerji provided important re-assessments of the 'race elements' pertaining to 'aboriginals', namely their '. . . very elaborate system of agrarian distribution and settlement, tribal government and centralised control.'[42] Even as the titles of the *panchayat* members were borrowed from Hindu caste society (such as Raja, Thakur, Dewan, Pande, etc.) the 'indigenous' village organization of Santal, Ho, Munda, Oraon, Bhil, and Maria Gond communities in central and eastern India demonstrated the historical 'survival' of 'vital institutions'.[43] Prefiguring later ethnographic and administrative approaches that delineated and celebrated tribal difference, Mookerji interpreted this vitality as an elementary aspect of 'indigenous tribal organisation',[44] thereby paving a pathway towards the anthropological realization of an ideal concept: the integrated tribal community.

This ideal type was in touch with other aspects of Indian civilization and society, yet not subjugated by these, and whilst being somewhat removed from the imaginary centre, in spatial and ideological terms, was not isolated or marginal. The 'corporate spirit' and 'autonomous social and economic management' of tribal villages therefore acquired a new discursive presence.[45] I contend that this *panchayat*-oriented discourse, of tribal power, discipline and organization, became part of a modernist anti-colonial academic project. As such, it fashioned a cosmopolitan space for the representation of tribal ethnicity, which has been recovered by subalternist historians and exponents of Tribal studies in divergent ways after Independence.[46] Exchanged between practitioners of Indian ethnography and related disciplines, re-interpretations of tribal participation in the democratic heritage of India assumed contemporary relevance and political efficacy. This was because the history of tribal 'resistance' (versus the oppression of dominant groups) became appropriable and readable as a new signifier of national heritage.[47] It was the task of the newly fashioned

fieldworkers of Indian anthropology to make both the tribal particulars and the national frameworks legible and, more importantly, mutual or interdependent. Brajendra Nath Seal began this work in 1911.

'RACIAL COSMOPOLITANISM' AND THE MEANING OF TRIBE AND NATION

Seal's tract 'Meaning of Race, Tribe, Nation' (1911) opened the panel on the Fundamental Considerations for Papers on Inter-racial Problems, at the Universal Races Congress in London, 1911.[48] I assess the work as an opening gambit in an emergent dialogue between Indian anthropology, global modernity and Adivasi/tribal political heritage. In terms of Adivasi subjectivity, it is noteworthy that the presentation focused on continuity—between race and ethnicity, between tribal organization and nation state, and between cultural heritage and citizenship—rather than on disjuncture (as may have been the case had Adivasi assertion and colonial counter-insurgency been addressed). As such, Seal brought the 'tangled skein' of ethnography and indigeneity in India into another ongoing dialogue: between Indian nationalists, British colonialists, and contemporary advocates of a world against imperial oppression. As a doctoral graduate in History, Seal later became professor of Philosophy at Calcutta University, from 1912-20. A member of the Brahmo-Samaj, he advised eminent thinkers, such as Rabindranath Tagore, on the politics and sociology of national de-colonization and interacted with colleagues, such as Sarat Chandra Roy, on the future of anthropology. As evident in Seal's talk, he was committed to the application of physical and cultural anthropology in India's national movement. It is therefore important to question how Seal negotiated and transformed the terms of race, tribe and nation into workable prospects for an Indian anthropology.

> A scientific study of the constituent elements and the composition of races and peoples, of their origin and development, and of the forces that govern these will alone point the way to a settlement of the inter-racial claims and conflicts on a sound progressive basis ... [to inform] the scope and methods of social legislation in every modern state.[49]

It is clear from this quotation that Seal was intent on bringing the concept of race into the politics of nationhood and internationalism. Mindful of India's racial, ethnic and cultural diversity, Seal's vision was one of social unity, which might be achieved through a scientific and anti-imperialist investigation of difference. It presumed that the ability of the future nation to respond to the ethno-cultural make-up of

particular regions, and to create a framework of unity for all citizens, irrespective of ethnic identity or histories of caste domination, hinged on the knowledge of India's anthropologists. Whilst the presence of race in Seal's enquiry echoed a dominant discourse of imperialism, it is important to reassess how both his tract and its recovery in subsequent anthropological policies purported to an anti-racial agenda. In this anthropological movement for intellectual *swaraj* or self-rule,[50] the relatedness of concepts of ethnicity and nationhood were made paramount.

Seal used the concept of race to annotate India's human and civilizational diversity through the ages. It could, therefore, be readable and reproducible (by anti-racist anthropologists) within a narrative of change: 'A synthetic view of Race is possible only when we consider it not as a static but as a dynamic entity.'[51] Seal's re-conceptualization of race, in the face of colonialist attempts to racialize and classify India for administrative purposes, focused less on the isolation of 'permanent physical types' within physical anthropology, and more on the 'geographical zones of ethnic culture'.[52] Cultural ethnology gained at least an equal footing to physical anthropology. At the time of Seal's presentation, colonial primitivism dominated the anthropological outlook, to the extent that tribal India was, in Seal's mind at least, falsely excluded from the national self-representation of human and cultural heritages. Although, following its spatial turn, the culture-zones model of ethnicity is now widely considered problematic within social anthropology, in Seal's vision it enabled the notion of race to become historically active, as '. . . plastic, fluent, growing, with energies not exhausting but superimposing layer upon layer like the earth, its scene, still subject to the primal forces that have built up the bed-rocks in their order of sequence and distribution.'[53] The impact of Seal's racial imaginary, which combined geological stability and Hindu metaphors of earthly power (*shakti*), became evident in the approaches adopted by later Indian anthropologists, such as Govind Sadashiv Ghurye (1932) and D.N. Majumdar (1947), who used comparable notions of racial dynamism to critique colonial interpretations of caste and tribal systems as distinct. So how would the concept of tribe, used by colonial anthropologists to classify India's racial map and to codify India's population through the decennial censuses, also become a key feature of a new national science?

In the first instance, Seal deployed the idea of endogamous tribal peoples to uphold the idea of distinct 'ethnic cultural units', which indicated part of the history of human evolution in India.[54] Beyond

the idea of tribe, Seal also applied the terminology of cultural unit to classes, peoples, and historical nationalities. Such an approach corresponded closely with romantic and primordial accounts of '*ethnies*', which have been critiqued by some theorists of nationalism.[55] According to Seal, it was the task of Indian physical anthropologists to trace the 'peculiar characters' of each unit.[56] Although such a project chimed with Euro-centric ethnology, it is important to recognize the intellectual and historical implications of Seal's advocacy of national agency. Given the proximity of these approaches to imperial visions and representations, it may be difficult at first to broach the relevance of physical anthropology either to an anti-racist agenda or to any inter-racial model, as later espoused by D.N. Majumdar. But in fact, Seal moved away from fixed definitions of racial identity, to put forward a model of fluid core-periphery types. Within the model, race was not defined according to abstract physiognomic traits but posited—according to India's cultural heritage discourse—in relational terms, as a continual flux or flow between ideal (core) and real (periphery) types.[57] By implication, being an idealized abstraction, no distinct race could exist as such in India. Rather, certain racial groups were perceived to exist according to their relative proximity to, or distance from, these ideal types (such as the 'Aryan' or the 'Dravidian'). Seal suggested that the core-periphery model might allow physical anthropologists to grasp India's 'racial cosmopolitanism', and therefore to reject imperial theories of racial hierarchy or racial distinctiveness between tribal ethnicities, and more generally between 'tribes' and 'castes'.[58] As such, he articulated an image of politico-racical realism, which was nation-centric and raised possibilities for intellectual de-colonization. It also weaved 'the periphery' into the textures of national heritage and national modernity. The ramifications of this approach were evident in the way Seal also addressed the topic of cultural identity in modern India as an ongoing process of exchange between the 'cultural race' (tradition, ethnicity, the rural, etc.) and the 'national race' (modernity, nationality, the industrial, etc.).[59]

Of critical significance to my inquiry, Seal used the concept of national race to imagine the future of India's own nation state, and create a pattern of centralized and de-centralized governance that could sustain India's de-colonization according to the cultural identities of different regions and peoples. The 'cultural' and 'national' aspects of Seal's racial theory therefore remained on an equal footing. For Seal, this composite system of governance enabled the interpenetration of ancient customs (cultural race) and

modern laws (national race), in a manner that would be taken up by administrative and sociological exponents of Panchayati Raj during the later parts of the twentieth century.[60] One may also speculate that Seal's delineation of a symbiosis between the ethnic and the political, may have informed R.K. Mookerji's celebration of tribal cultural resistance, India's indigenous heritage and political survival, as well as D.N. Majumdar's re-configuration of the tribal, *vis-à-vis* both the aboriginal and the national. Seal's vision revealed an early commitment, in terms of the national imaginary, to a dual framework of government. This framework created potential channels of inter-dependence between the state and the community. It became a key task for later practitioners of Indian anthropology to recognize and harness the methodological relevance of these channels, and Seal's notion of 'racial cosmopolitanism' more generally.

Despite its problematic raciological terminology, Seal's conceptualization of a future system of dual governance shows his commitment to India's cultural de-colonization, and his willingness not to marginalize tribal peoples. The *swadeshi* (politico-cultural self-reliance) ideology is clearly evident in his vision of the unity and diversity of India's future constitution: 'The sphere and scope of the State legislation within the social personality is bound to tolerate and respect the personality of its members in their activities to realize their own schemes of values and ends.'[61] Through the decentralization of India, Seal set out the terms for the harmonization of statehood and personhood. Although there was in Seal's imagined governance an over-determination of cultural diversity and an idealization (bordering on fetishization) of state power, Seal's willingness to decolonize the terms of anthropology in India is testament to the partial success of the Universal Races Congress to re-situate the parameters of race, against imperialism. That Seal's vision corresponds to shifts in later anthropological practice and policy reveals the discursive power of his intervention.

This concluded with a celebration of the concept of 'universal humanity' and of international co-partnerships, within the orbit of the Universal Races Congress and the pages of an (unrealized) International Journal of Comparative Civilizations. In this newly connected regional-national-international context, the core/periphery model of racial types was reformulated to heighten anthropological knowledge and understanding of tribal ethnicities in India. The possibilities for convergence and divergence between (a) India's diverse human/cultural heritages, (b) the Indian ethnographic

present, and (c) the political future, merited close consideration and some closure. Such were the axiological and intellectual directives for Indian anthropology, which the likes of S.C. Roy, D.N. Majumdar, and their contemporaries attempted to realize.

PHYSICAL ANTHROPOLOGY AND TRIBAL ETHNICITY

Sarat Chandra Roy, author of numerous influential ethnographies of 'tribal' subjects, was the leading exponent of Indian anthropology in the early twentieth century. A contemporary of the polymath Seal, Roy first worked as a lawyer in Ranchi (capital of present-day State of Jharkhand), before becoming anthropologically engaged on issues of tribal ethnicity, cultural heritage and social justice in Chhota Nagpur (Jharkhand). He aimed to generate amongst the colonial administrators, and other agents of political and academic power, awareness of tribal custom and of the possibilities for a national anthropology. He used his lecture series at Patna University in 1920 to define the terms of India's anthropological future. His talks accompanied the birth of anthropology as an independent discipline in India, at the University of Calcutta. Indeed, Roy himself coined the term 'Indian anthropology' during this lecture series,[62] which set out the need for a new intellectual apparatus to consider the ethnography of India.

The series, entitled 'Principles and Methods of Physical Anthropology', summarized those anthropological theories, such as evolution and racial classification, that Roy considered should find their application in India. The series was followed by another batch of lectures on 'Types of Cultural Theory'. These encompassed the comparative method, statistics and adhesions, anthropo-geography, culture areas, the sociological mind, and convergence, and were published in an early volume of *Man in India*.[63] The extent to which anthropologists took ownership of the field of physical and cultural anthropology was a measure, as perceived alike by colonial administrators and Indian elites, of India's ability to govern itself. This comprehensive engagement revealed the extension of the burgeoning modernist/rationalist consciousness amongst India's intelligentsia into the domain of anthropology, and had a significant effect on approaches to national governance, development and cultural policy after Independence. It would therefore be misguided to critique the presence of race in Indian anthropological science and policy as a direct extension or derivative of colonialism. Rather,

this may be considered as one aspect of colonial modernity, and/or of colonial governance, which would be transformed and re-applied to suit the demands of national heritage, national modernity and national institutional values.

It is necessary to probe how Roy identified the principles of physical anthropology and made them relevant to the Indian context. The treatise consists of transcripts of six lectures, presented between January and March 1920, and allowed Roy to situate himself within an anthropological/administrative/national milieu embodied by the likes of Edward Gait and B.N. Seal. Before the first lecture, Gait introduced 'The Scope, Divisions and Methods of Anthropology and Man's Place in Nature' by emphasizing the dominant model of Aryan racial advancement *versus* tribal primitivism.[64] Holding sway in most colonial approaches to race in India, Gait's binary model served to locate Roy's expertise within the specific demographic context of the Chhota Nagpur region. Chhota Nagpur was a major sub-division of the colonial province of Bengal, Bihar and Orissa and, being the site of numerous anti-colonial rebellions, has since become synonymous with the spatial politics of the Adivasi movement.[65] Yet according to early twentieth-century administrators and anthropologists, Chhota Nagpur was represented as a site of Aryan and pre-Aryan co-habitation. It became a region that could encode, via the anthropological internalization of Indo-centric (or Aryo-centric) notions of self and other, both the civilizational difference between the primitive and the non-primitive and the national narrative of unity-in-diversity.[66] In Seal's terms, these could be represented according to the core-periphery model of the national/cultural race, as either more marginal (primitive) or less marginal (non-primitive), respectively. The possible lines of demarcation between Aryan and non-Aryan types, and between the tribal and non-tribal populations, therefore became pertinent topics for Roy's research, as well as for census reports and other related enquiries.

I contend that through his construction of new terms, methods and visions for 'Indian anthropology', Roy contributed to the de-binarization of the Aryan/non-Aryan model, not just in relation to Chhota Nagpur, but on a more national basis. An effect of the binary model, which Roy addressed, was to group all non-Aryan races, peoples, cultures, and languages under the umbrella heading of 'Dravidian'. In the early twentieth century, colonial administrators and related ethnologists construed the Dravidian entity as a counterpoint to the Aryan domination of India. In this model, which would be contested during the 1920s-40s, all aboriginal and tribal peoples

were initially viewed as Dravidian. This binary framework was applied, for example, by Hira Lal in his research article on 'The Aborigines of Central India' (1922). In this milieu, 'the Dravidian' became synonymous with the parameters of Indian ethnology: 'The question of the origin and ancient distribution of the Dravidian race belongs to the domain of anthropology, and of anthropology alone [*vis-à-vis* philology].'[67] Within these parameters, Indian ethnologists increasingly attempted to reify 'aboriginal' types and drew up related categories, notably the 'pre-Dravidians', and the 'Mundas' (or 'Kols'),[68] which would find their way into colonial and national administrative purviews following the Census of India in 1931.

Focusing on 'primitive tribes' this critical event provided a new counter-ideological context for the symbiosis of physical and cultural anthropology, as advocated by D.N. Majumdar. The problematic colonialist bias of the 1931 census—the segregation of aboriginal communities, in conceptual terms, from the rest of rural Indian civilization—also engendered new approaches and definitions of tribal integration and national cultural heritage amongst Indian anthropologists.[69] I acknowledge that these merit analysis in their own right, on account of their own historicity. Suffice to say, after the 1931 census, Roy explored key areas of India's burgeoning raciology, such as the 'pre-Dravidian', and made more widely applied notions, namely the 'proto-Australoid', relevant to the analysis of aboriginal India.[70] This created a archaeo-anthropological imaginary, in which various 'submerged' types, such as the 'Negritic' or the 'Negroid', could be assessed as being autochthonous and evident, for example, in the physiognomies of Kadar and Irula people in southern India.[71] Perceptions of this racial substratum shaped the construction of a detailed taxonomical structure, which was imaginatively mapped onto India's human heritage. This mapping distinguished (i) the submerged strata from (ii) the 'pre-Dravidian' and (iii) the 'Munda' or 'Kolarian' tribal groups, and thus disrupted the Aryan/Dravidian dichotomy. The 'pre-Dravidian' and 'Munda' lineages were conceptualized as extensions of various early proto-Australoid populations, whose ancestors had retained or lost tribal modes of organization, tribal ethnicity, and tribal languages, etc., to varying extents through the ages, according to their geographical, social and political conditioning.[72]

Against this backdrop, Indian anthropologists became interested in the representation of tribal ethnicity, and its relationship to national ethnic diversity. By paying attention to the constantly shifting configurations of ethnic identity in India, Roy tentatively set out the

terms for a 'human heritage' discourse in India,[73] which retains some visibility in Indian anthropology still today.[74] This discourse was characterized by the presence of either (a) more unified, or (b) more fragmented ethnic and social groups, who became recognizable through their various 'grades and types of moral and material culture'.[75] Roy aimed to situate new meanings for contested terms, such as aboriginal, tribe, primitive, etc., within an array of unstable and interacting analytical frameworks. These encompassed histories of assimilation and non-assimilation (between tribal and Hindu caste groups), polar notions of savagery versus 'historic civilization', and cultural transformations across and between cultural 'strata'.[76] This analytical range ensured their applicability in disparate regions, localities and historical contexts. In this milieu, Roy made subtle but important distinctions between so-called primitive tribal groups and (non-primitive) dominant tribes. In the jargon of subsequent Tribal studies, the non-primitive tribes demonstrated high levels of 'tribal integration' (in a manner that corresponded with Mookerji's representation of 'vital' political institutions), and hence these became paradigmatic: meaning that they would define developmental and welfare policies that attempted to harmonize national and tribal values, and hence fabricate new foundations for tribal citizenship as well as national integration.

For Roy, the teleological notion of cultural development underpinned his engagement with dominant anthropological concepts and with more locally mediated cultural forms, allowing his observations to be attentive to multiple influences, from indigenous, to organic, to borrowed, and to modern forms: '. . . the same cultural features may not always have developed from the same causes.'[77] In view of this sense of inter-cultural exchange—mediated by histories of group migration, inter-marriage, and religious conversion, as well as colonization and industrialization—it was clearly unworkable for Indian anthropologists to essentialize different ethnicities.

'PRIMITIVE' AND NON-PRIMITIVE TRIBES

Having already dealt with his recasting of race, it is now worthwhile to assess Roy's construction of primitivism as pertaining to India's tribal peoples. A key point, which would have ramifications in the early phase of Indian anthropology covered by this paper, is that of a socio-spatial as well as ideological distinction between the so-called hill or forest-based 'primitive tribes' and more settled tribal

agriculturalists. The identity of the so-called primitive tribes was characterized by geo-cultural isolation, non-engagement with dominant economies, and a low status within an imagined culture strata pertaining to low levels of human-racial-cultural evolution.[78] Typically the non-primitive tribes would be characterized as having a close cultural and economic interaction with dominant groups, and therefore be more centrally positioned within the core-periphery imaginary (a location that, in the parallel imperial discourse, was annotated as more 'advanced' in terms of culture history). The spatial and occupational predicaments of tribes were clearly just as important, for the rendering and interpretation of their ethnicity, as somatic characteristics were.

For Roy, the region of Bihar and Orissa could be mapped meaningfully as an anthropological treasure trove '. . . in which we [Indian anthropologists] may study in situ the various stages in the slow and laborious evolution of human culture.'[79] The construction of a national subjectivity is crucial here, one that could relate closely both to the cosmopolitan anthropological world and to the particular tribal milieus. Internalizing the concepts of racial and cultural primitivism set out by colonial anthropologists, Roy began to situate the various tribes according to what at first glance might be defined as an imperial transition narrative: from migratory to settled lifestyles, and from forest-based to agricultural livelihoods. The communities of Hill Korwa, Hill Kharia, Birhor, Savara, Birjia, Maler, Paharia, etc., were confined to the primitive tribe status whilst 'Slightly above them rank those aboriginal tribes of Chhota Nagpur and Orissa like the Mundas, Santals, the Bhumij, the Hos and Oraons who although they have settled down into regular agriculturalists still retain their totemistic social organization, animistic religion and other primitive institutions.'[80] There is no doubt that the imperial ideology of transforming tribal peoples into agricultural producers provided Roy and his contemporaries with an ideological premise through which to set up distinct culture 'strata'.[81] He could thereby organize non-primitive and primitive tribal types, on terms that made the core-periphery model of national heritage relevant.

Yet to dismiss the distinction of tribes into primitive and non-primitive types as an imperial device would be to misinterpret the meaning of primitivism within India's intellectual decolonization. Emphasizing inter-cultural contact and cultural transformation, rather than fixed cultural or ethnic identities (in any given layer of the culture strata), Roy's approach crucially focused on the

spaces of indeterminacy between the layers of the culture-strata model, rather than on the strata themselves.[82] This more fluid re-conceptualization could be applied at different points historically and geographically, and account for various reconfigurations of ethnicity, according to changes in the racial, linguistic, religious, structural or behavioural composition of any given tribal grouping. Following Seal, Roy's vision emphasized the shifting make-up of ethnic and cultural groups in relation to national modernity. Thus practitioners of Indian cultural anthropology came to engage with disparate aspects of tribal ethnicity.

CONCLUSION

Following Roy, critical attention may be drawn towards the presence of a cosmopolitan imaginary in the works and world-views of the exponents of Indian anthropology as discussed above. Brajendra Nath Seal's pivotal presence and articulation of 'racial cosmopolitanism' at the Universal Races Congress may usefully be re-assessed as a means to substantiate Holton's notion of plural cosmopolitanisms, with a view to re-evaluating the interconnections between 'race' as a mobile analytical category and cultures of de-colonization. By re-visiting Roy's delineation of Indian anthropology, the interfaces between, on the one hand, the world/cosmos (and attendant processes of global modernity, imperialism and de-colonization, etc.) and, on the other, polity/political philosophy (and related signifiers of national heritage and community) may be comprehended in terms of anthropological intervention and conceptual repositioning. Writing in response to Seal's exegesis in 1911, and against Euro-centric notions of universalist cosmopolitanism that have previously been critiqued as 'narrow and provincial' by S.K. Nandi,[83] and have informed the analytical standpoint of Dipesh Chakrabarty,[84] Holton has recently framed the question of multiple cosmopolitanisms thus: 'If the development of cosmopolitanism is far more than the historical sociology of the West, then what other cosmopolitan configurations have emerged, and how do these render distinctions between the West and its Others incoherent, or at best a partial way of understanding the global cultural dynamics?'[85]

By re-tracing the intellectual and political parameters of raciology in pre-Independence India, tribal ethnicity may therefore be read simultaneously: (1) as a site of worldly objectivism, that is to say as an anthropological or scientific ontology, which could be re-theorized and approached according to national values; and (2) as an efficacious

political trope that imbricated 'the national' and 'the tribal' into a mutual relationship, of a kind that also defined the symbiosis of 'the universal' and 'the particular' (within emergent cosmopolitanisms). Contesting imperialist framings of 'the aboriginal' in India, Seal and Roy provided Dhirendra Nath Majumdar with the necessary counter-ideological moorings to re-inscribe the terms through which race could be comprehended in the mid-twentieth century. It is either a testament to his anthropological authority, or to the rhetorical power of the national constitution and the institutional presence of the Anthropological Survey of India, that the field of Tribal studies still abounds with tracts that reproduce discourses of ethnic diversity and national/tribal integration, and yet leave unresolved the historical problematic of how the overlaps between 'the cosmo' and 'the politan' are engendered and reproduced. In re-appraising how concepts pertaining to tribal ethnicity were negotiated before Independence, critical attention can be directed to the question of how, as embodiments of 'new cosmopolitanism',[86] Seal and his anthropological followers fashioned a critical space in which to re-map, as unified, the contours of the tribal and the national.

NOTES

1. I am very appreciative of Sangeeta Dasgupta (Jawaharlal Nehru University) and N.K. Das (Anthropological Survey of India) for their insightful comments on an earlier version of this paper.
2. G. Sarana, 'Indian Anthropology: Retrospect and Prospect', in I.J.S. Bansal and P. Singhal (eds.), *Anthropology in Indian Context*, Delhi: Today and Tomorrow's Printers and Publishers, 1983, pp. 71-84.
3. D.J. Rycroft and S. Dasgupta, 'Indigenous Pasts and the Politics of Belonging', in D.J. Rycroft and S. Dasgupta (eds.), *The Politics of Belonging in India: Becoming Adivasi*, London: Routledge, pp. 1-13.
4. Peter Robb (ed.), *The Concept of Race in South Asia*, Delhi: Oxford University Press, 1995; M. Omi and H. Winant (eds.), *Racial Formation in the United States*, London: Routledge, 1994; D.T. Goldberg, *Racist Culture: Philosophy and the Politics of Meaning*, Malden: Blackwell, 1993.
5. T.K. Oommen, *Alien Concepts and South Asian Reality: Responses and Reformulations*, Delhi: Sage, 1995, pp. 214-35.
6. T.N. Madan, *Pathways: Approaches to the Study of Society in India*, Delhi: Oxford University Press, 1994, p. 138; P. Uberoi, S. Deshpande and N. Sundar, 'Introduction', in P. Uberoi et al. (eds.), *Anthropology in the East: Founders of Sociology and Anthropology*, Delhi: Permanent Black, 2007, pp. 9-10.
7. S.C. Roy, *Principles and Methods of Physical Anthropology*, Patna: Government Printing, 1920; B. Singh, 'Anthropology: Physical and Cultural', in Bansal and Singhal (eds.), *Anthropology in Indian Context*, op. cit., pp. 31-8.

8. L.P. Vidyarthi and B.K. Rai, 'History of Indian Anthropology', in L.P. Vidyarthi and B.K. Rai (eds.), *The Tribal Culture of India*, Delhi: Concept Publishing, 1977, pp. 25-37.
9. Madan, *Pathways*, op. cit., p. 135.
10. Vidyarthi and Rai, 'History', op. cit., p. 37.
11. D.N. Majumdar, 'Tribal Cultures and Acculturation', *Man in India*, vol. 19, nos. 2-3, 1939, pp. 99-173.
12. D.N. Majumdar, *The Fortunes of Primitive Tribes*, Lucknow: Universal Publishers, 1944.
13. See, for example, B.C. Mamoria, *Tribal Demography in India*, Allahabad: Kitab Mahal, 1957.
14. Rycroft and Dasgupta, 'Indigenous Pasts'.
15. D.N. Majumdar, *Racial Problems in Asia*, Delhi: Indian Council of World Affairs, 1947.
16. See, for example, J.H. Hutton, 'The Possible Effects on the Primitive Tribes of India of the Proposals Made by the Simon Commission', Transcript, J.H. Hutton Collection, Centre for South Asian Studies, University of Cambridge, *c.* 1930; J.H. Hutton, 'Anthropology and India', in *The Shaping of Indian Science: 1914-1947* (1935), Indian Science Congress Association, Hyderabad: Universities Press, 2003, pp. 339-54.
17. Majumdar, *Racial Problems*, op. cit., p. 20.
18. W.V. Grigson, 'The Aboriginal in Future India', *Journal of the Royal Anthropological Institute of Great Britain and Ireland*, vol. 74, nos. 1-2, 1944, pp. 33-41; also see Rycroft, 'India's Adivasis' op. cit.
19. Also see Uberoi et al., 'Introduction', op. cit., p. 21.
20. N.K. Das, 'Identity Politics, Cultural Pluralism and the State in South Asia: An Anthropological Reappraisal', in N.K. Das and V.R. Rao (eds.), *Identity, Cultural Pluralism and the State: South Asia in Perspective*, Delhi: Macmillan, 2009, pp. 22-76.
21. Majumdar, *Racial Problems*, op. cit., p. 20.
22. For a more recent example, see P.P. Majumdar et al., 'Anthropometric Variation in India: A Statistical Appraisal', *Current Anthropology*, vol. 31, no. 1, 1990, pp. 94-103.
23. Quoting S.C. Roy, 'Caste, Race and Religion in India', *Man in India*, vol. 17, no. 3, 1937, p. 148.
24. Majumdar, 'Tribal Cultures', op. cit., pp. 99-103.
25. Majumdar, *Racial Problems*, op. cit., p. 20.
26. Vidyarthi and Rai, 'History', op. cit., p. 70.
27. Rycroft, 'India's Adivasis', op. cit.
28. Madan, *Pathways*, op. cit., p. 26.
29. Majumdar, *Racial Problems*, op. cit., p. 20.
30. See D.J. Rycroft, 'Beyond Resistance: Idioms and Memories of Insurgency in the Adivasi Movement, Jharkhand State, Eastern India', in S. Das Gupta and R.S. Basu (eds.), *Voices from the Margins: Aspects of Adivasi History in Colonial and Post Colonial India*, Delhi: Primus Books, 2011, pp. 257-76.
31. W. Fernandes, 'Indian Tribals and the Search for an Indigenous Identity', in A.K. Singh and M.K. Jabbi (eds.), *Tribals in India: Development, Deprivation and Discontent*, Delhi: Har-Anand, 1997, pp. 62-79.

32. See, for example, C. von Furer-Haimendorf, 'Problems and Prospects of Indian Anthropology', *Man in India*, vol. 29, nos. 3-4, 1949, pp. 147-68; Grigson, 'The Aboriginal'; P.P. Majumdar et al., 'Anthropometric Variation', op. cit.
33. Uberoi et al., 'Introduction', op. cit., p. 43; see also Das, 'Identity Politics', op. cit.
34. S.C. Roy, 'Anthropological Research in India', *Man in India*, vol. 1, no. 1, 1921, pp. 11-56.
35. Roy, 'Anthropological Research', op. cit., p. 13; see also D.J. Rycroft, *Representing Rebellion: Visual Aspects of Counter-insurgency in Colonial India*, Delhi: Oxford University Press, 2006.
36. Roy, 'Anthropological Research', op. cit., p. 29.
37. Ibid, p. 43.
38. B.N. Seal, 'Meaning of Race, Tribe, Nation', in G. Spiller (ed.), *Papers on Inter-racial Problems*, London: P.S. King, 1911, pp. 1-13.
39. Rycroft, 'India's Adivasis', op. cit.
40. Also see Das, 'Identity Politics', op. cit.
41. See Sarana, 'Indian Anthropology', op. cit.
42. R.K. Mookerji, 'Race Elements in the Indian Village Constitution', *Man in India*, vol. 3, nos. 1-2, 1923, pp. 1-2.
43. Ibid., pp. 2-5, 19-23.
44. Ibid., p. 12.
45. Ibid., p. 10.
46. Rycroft and Dasgupta, 'Indigenous Pasts', op. cit.
47. Mookerji, 'Race Elements', op. cit., p. 8.
48. Seal, 'Meaning of Race', op. cit., see also R.J. Holton, 'Cosmopolitanism or Cosmopolitanisms?: The Universal Races Congress of 1911', *Global Networks*, vol. 2, no. 2, 2002, pp. 153-70.
49. Seal, 'Meaning of Race', op. cit., p. 1.
50. Madan, *Pathways*, p. 138; see also Uberoi et al., 'Introduction', op. cit., p. 17.
51. Seal, 'Meaning of Race', op. cit., p. 2.
52. Ibid., p. 1.
53. Ibid., p. 2.
54. Ibid., p. 3.
55. See Das, 'Identity Politics', op. cit.
56. Seal, 'Meaning of Race', op. cit., p. 3.
57. Ibid., p. 4.
58. Ibid., p. 6.
59. Ibid., pp. 9-11.
60. See B. Mundu, *Indigenous Traditional Administrative Systems: The Case of Adivasis of Jharkhand Homeland*, Saarbrucken: VDM, 2009; Rycroft, 'Beyond Resistance', op. cit.,
61. Seal, 'Meaning of Race', op. cit., p. 12.
62. Roy, *Principles and Methods*, p. 16.
63. See S.C. Roy, 'Types of Cultural Theory', *Man in India*, vol. 1, no. 3, 1921a, pp. 210-61.
64. Roy, *Principles and Methods*, p. 1.
65. For various assessments, see S.C. Roy, 'An Indian Outlook on Anthropology', *Man*, vol. 38, 1938, pp. 146-50; S.C. Roy, 'The Aborigines of Chota Nagpur: Their Proper Status in the Reformed Constitution', *Man in India*, vol. 26,

no. 2, 1946, pp. 120-36; Rycroft, *Representing Rebellion*; Mundu, Indigenous Traditional Administrative Systems; Rycroft, 'Revisioning Birsa Munda', Rycroft, 'Beyond Resistance', op. cit.

66. See, for example, Roy, 'Indian Outlook'.
67. Hira Lal, 'The Aborigines of Central India', *Man in India*, vol. 2, 1922, p. 13.
68. Ibid., p. 14.
69. Roy, 'Caste, Race and Religion', op. cit.; Roy, 'Indian Outlook', op. cit.; Majumdar, 'Tribal Cultures'.
70. Roy, 'Caste, Race and Religion', op. cit., p. 147.
71. Ibid., see also Ananda Krishna L. Iyer, 'A Short Note on the Physical Anthropology of the Kadars of the Cochin Hills, and Their Present Social and Economic Condition', *Man in India*, vol. 3, nos. 1-2, 1923, pp. 29-35.
72. Roy, 'Caste, Race and Religion', op. cit., p. 147.
73. Roy, *Principles and Methods*, op. cit., p. 4.
74. See D. Balsubramanian and N. Appaji Rao (eds.), *The Indian Human Heritage*, Hyderabad: Universities Press, 1998.
75. Roy, op. cit., p. 4.
76. Ibid., pp. 4-5.
77. Ibid., p. 7.
78. Ibid., p. 4.
79. Ibid.
80. Ibid., pp. 4-5.
81. Ibid., p. 5.
82. Ibid.
83. S.K. Nandi, 'Studies in the Aesthetics of Brajendra Nath Seal', *Journal of Aesthetics and Art Criticism*, vol. 24, no. 1, 1965, p. 53.
84. D. Chakrabarty, *Provincializing Europe: Postcolonial Thought and Historical Difference*, Princeton: Princeton University Press, 2000, pp. 4-5.
85. Holton, 'Cosmopolitanisms', op. cit., p. 156.
86. Ibid., p. 153.

REFERENCES

Aiyer, S.S.K., 'The Future of Anthropology', *Man in India*, vol. 6, nos. 2-3, 1926, pp. 182-6.

Balsubramanian, D. and N. Appaji Rao (eds.), *The Indian Human Heritage*, Hyderabad: Universities Press, 1998.

Chakrabarty, D., *Provincializing Europe: Postcolonial Thought and Historical Difference*, Princeton: Princeton University Press, 2000.

Das, N.K., 'Identity Politics, Cultural Pluralism and the State in South Asia: An Anthropological Reappraisal', in *Identity, Cultural Pluralism and the State: South Asia in Perspective*, ed. N.K. Das and V.R. Rao, Delhi: Macmillan, 2009, pp. 22-76.

Fernandes, W., 'Indian Tribals and the Search for an Indigenous Identity', in *Tribals in India: Development, Deprivation and Discontent*, ed. A.K. Singh and M.K. Jabbi, Delhi: Har-Anand Publications, 1997, pp. 62-79.

Furer-Haimendorf, C. von, 'Problems and Prospects of Indian Anthropology', *Man in India*, vol. 29, nos. 3-4, 1949, pp. 147-68.

Ghurye, G.S. *Caste and Race in India*, Mumbai: Popular Prakashan, 2004 (1932).

Goldberg, D.T., *Racist Culture: Philosophy and the Politics of Meaning*, Malden: Blackwell, 1993.

Grigson, W.V. 'The Aboriginal in Future India', *Journal of the Royal Anthropological Institute of Great Britain and Ireland*, vol. 74, nos. 1-2, 1944, pp. 33-41.

Hira Lal, 'The Aborigines of Central India', *Man in India*, vol. 2, 1922, pp. 12-32.

Hira Lal, 'Baiga', *Man in India*, vol. 4, nos. 3-4, 1924, pp. 273-6.

Holton, R.J., 'Cosmopolitanism or Cosmopolitanisms?: The Universal Races Congress of 1911', *Global Networks*, vol. 2, no. 2, 2002, pp. 153-70.

Hutton, J.H., 'The Possible Effects on the Primitive Tribes of India of the Proposals made by the Simon Commission', Transcript, J.H. Hutton Collection, Centre for South Asian Studies, University of Cambridge, *c.* 1930.

———, 'Anthropology and India', in *The Shaping of Indian Science: 1914-1947*, Indian Science Congress Association, Hyderabad: Universities Press, 2003 (1935), pp. 339-54.

Iyer, Ananda Krishna L., 'A Short Note on the Physical Anthropology of the Kadars of the Cochin Hills, and Their Present Social and Economic Condition', *Man in India*, vol. 3, nos. 1-2, 1923, pp. 29-35.

———, 'Anthropology of the Kanikars', *Man in India*, vol. 8, nos. 1-2, 1928, pp. 21-2.

Madan, T.N., *Pathways: Approaches to the Study of Society in India*, Delhi: Oxford University Press, 1994.

Majumdar, D.N., 'Tribal Cultures and Acculturation', *Man in India*, vol. 19, nos. 2-3, 1939, pp. 99-173.

———, *The Fortunes of Primitive Tribes*, Lucknow: Universal Publishers, 1944.

———, *Racial Problems in Asia*, Delhi: Indian Council of World Affairs, 1947.

Majumdar, P.P. et al., 'Anthropometric Variation in India: A Statistical Appraisal', *Current Anthropology*, vol. 31, no. 1, 1990, pp. 94-103.

Mamoria, B.C., *Tribal Demography in India*, Allahabad: Kitab Mahal, 1957.

Mookerji, R.K., 'Race Elements in the Indian Village Constitution', *Man in India*, vol. 3, nos. 1-2, 1923, pp. 1-28.

Mundu, B., *Indigenous Traditional Administrative Systems: The Case of Adivasis of Jharkhand Homeland*, Saarbrucken: VDM, 2009.

Nandi, S.K., 'Studies in the Aesthetics of Brajendra Nath Seal', *Journal of Aesthetics and Art Criticism*, vol. 24, no. 1, 1965, pp. 53-8.

Omi, M. and H. Winant (eds.), *Racial Formation in the United States*, London: Routledge, 1994.

Oommen, T.K., *Alien Concepts and South Asian Reality: Responses and Reformulations*, Delhi: Sage, 1995.

Robb, P., (ed.), *The Concept of Race in South Asia*, Delhi: Oxford University Press, 1995.

Roy, S.C., *Principles and Methods of Physical Anthropology*, Patna: Government Printing, 1920.

———, 'Anthropological Research in India', *Man in India*, vol. 1, no. 1, 1921, pp. 11-56.

———, 'Types of Cultural Theory', *Man in India*, vol. 1, no. 3, 1921a, pp. 210-61.

———, 'Caste, Race and Religion in India', *Man in India*, vol. 17, no. 3, 1937, pp. 147-76.

———, 'An Indian Outlook on Anthropology', *Man*, vol. 38, 1938, pp. 146-50.

———, 'The Aborigines of Chota Nagpur: Their Proper Status in the Reformed Constitution', *Man in India*, vol. 26, no. 2, 1946, pp. 120-36.

Rycroft, D.J., *Representing Rebellion: Visual Aspects of Counter-insurgency in Colonial India*, Delhi: Oxford University Press, 2006.

———, 'Revisioning Birsa Munda: Visual Constructions of the "*Vanavasi*" in Jharkhand', in *Identity, Cultural Pluralism and the State: South Asia in Perspective*, ed. N.K. Das and V.R. Rao, Delhi: Macmillan, 2009, pp. 261-80.

———, 'Beyond Resistance: Idioms and Memories of Insurgency in the Adivasi Movement, Jharkhand State, Eastern India', in *Voices from the Margins: Aspects of Adivasi History in Colonial and Post Colonial India*, ed. S. Das Gupta and R.S. Basu, 2011, Delhi: Prinks Books, pp. 257-76.

Rycroft, D.J. and S. Dasgupta, 'Indigenous Pasts and the Politics of Belonging', in *The Politics of Belonging in India: Becoming Adivasi*, ed. D.J. Rycroft and S. Dasgupta, Routledge (forthcoming).

Sarana, G., 'Indian Anthropology: Retrospect and Prospect', in *Anthropology in Indian Context*, ed. I.J.S. Bansal and P. Singhal, Delhi: Today and Tomorrow's Printers and Publishers, 1983, pp. 71-84.

Seal, B.N., 'Meaning of Race, Tribe, Nation', in *Papers on Inter-racial Problems*, ed. G. Spiller, London: P.S. King, 1911, pp. 1-13.

Singh, B., 'Anthropology: Physical and Cultural', in *Anthropology in Indian Context*, ed. I.J.S. Bansal and P. Singhal, Delhi: Today and Tomorrow's Printers and Publishers, 1983, pp. 31-8.

Uberoi, P., S. Deshpande and N. Sundar, 'Introduction', in *Anthropology in the East: Founders of Sociology and Anthropology*, ed. P. Uberoi et al., Delhi: Permanent Black, 2007, pp. 1-63.

Vidyarthi, L.P. and B.K. Rai, 'History of Indian Anthropology', in *The Tribal Culture of India*, ed. L.P. Vidyarthi and B.K. Rai, Delhi: Concept, 1977, pp. 3-24.

8

Identity Image(s) and Actualities of the Bhoti Language Movement in Post-Colonial India

BUDDHADEV BHATTACHARYA

The right of language is a basic cultural right of the people and linked with their economy, culture, and social system. The UNESCO recognizes the status of a language spoken by a group or a community as an equality right whether it has a script or not.[1] Strikingly, the Bhoti language spoken by a sizeable Bhotia Himalayan community with their separate script has not yet been included in the Eighth Schedule of the Indian Constitution. In a nation marked by great socio-cultural and linguistic diversity, such a glossing over/non-recognition goes against the structural process of the Indian Republic.

THE BHOTI IDENTITY IMAGE

The problems in this respect are as follows:

1. The case of entering 'Bhoti' in the Eighth Schedule of the Constitution of India has been omitted since its framing. The reasons for such omission are not known. Is it a case of gross negligence in respect to a minority community?[2]
2. The Bhoti-speaking communities are scattered across the Indian Himalayas, from the POK (Pakistan occupied Kashmir) up to Arunachal Pradesh in multiple pockets. Despite minor variations in the spoken language, the language structure as written among the speakers is one and the same.
3. The Bhoti speakers are Indian nationals with voting rights and are directly involved in the Indian democratic political framework.
4. The Bhoti-speaking communities in the Indian Himalayas are to be found in Ladakh, Himachal Pradesh, Uttarakhand, the Terai belt

of the Shivalik region, West Bengal (Darjeeling district), Sikkim and Arunachal Pradesh. Apart from that, a sizeable number of Bhotias/Bhote, in Nepal from Mustang up to the foothills of Uttar Pradesh and Bihar have been residing there for centuries.

5. People who speak Bhoti belong to different religions such as Buddhism, Islam and Christianity. They may be labelled as indigenous in the sense of having an agro-pastoral livelihood in general, and mercantile trade professions in particular.
6. At the state level, Bhoti has been nomenclaturally different, and that makes it problematic for consolidating dialectical diversity as a unitary language in the Indian Constitution (n.6, Appendix).
7. In the language Census Records of India (1961), separate local naming was evident. For instance, *Dazong ka* has been entered in Sikkim; Bhotia/Bhutia/Bhote is entered Mon pa in Darjeeling district of West Bengal; Khamba, Manba and Mon pa are entered in Arunachal Pradesh; Khunm, Bhoti, Lahuli and Spiti languages in Himachal Pradesh; and Budi/Ladakhi in Ladakh under Jammu & Kashmir, etc. (D.D. Sharma).[3]

SIGNIFICANT ISSUES AMONG/CONCERNING THE BHOTI LANGUAGE SPEAKERS

In the contemporary scenario, Bhoti language speakers are ignored, and excluded from mainstream politics. The question arises: why did the framers of the Indian Constitution not include this language in the Eighth Schedule of the Indian Constitution? The structure of the language was derived from Sanskrit by the seventh century AD in the line of the Trans-Himalayan Literary Language of Tibet with five vowels and thirty consonants. The Bhoti script is an offshoot of the Indian Brahmi script as Pandit Rahul Sankrityayan determined (*Purātattva Nibandhāvali*, 1941).[4]

It has a rich literature in different fields; such as Medicine, Architecture, Astrology, Music, Arts, Dance, Drama, Yoga, Philosophy, Tantric Literature and Grammar. The collection of Buddha's teachings 'Tripitaka' that comprises 108 volumes, and the Tantras are also available in the Bhoti language. It is surprising that despite this rich genealogy and literary heritage, which some other languages in the Eighth Schedule do not have, the Bhoti language has been excluded.[5]

As a person moves into Indian Himalayas from the East trijunction corner mark, where Myanmar, China and India meet (28.2 E and 96.5 N) towards the Western Himalayas up to PoK, one

may encounter a sizeable number of Bhoti-speaking Indian nationals. During the British period, G.A. Grierson, in his Linguistic Study of India (LSI), had referred to speakers of Tibeto-Himalayan languages in classified nomenclatural rubrics such as Tibeto-Burmese group, Tibeto-Nepali and Western Himalayan group. In terms of territorial residence, the Bhoti-speaking Himalayan groups belonging to three sectors of the Indian Himalayas are:

1. The Bhoti-speaking group of the Western Himalayas belonging to the north-western corner of Ladakh and Arunachal Pradesh.
2. A group residing in the middle sector, which is bilingual.
3. Bhoti-speaking groups belonging to the vast area of the Indian Himalayas in the eastern sector, from Indo-Nepal Himalayas up to the north-eastern corner of Arunachal Pradesh (Appendix).[6]

Five states, including Jammu & Kashmir, Sikkim, West Bengal, Himachal Pradesh and Arunachal Pradesh have recognized the Bhoti language. Different schools, colleges and universities throughout the world are imparting education in this language. All India Radio Leh, Shimla, Gangtok, Karshang, Darjeeling, Tawang and Delhi broadcast news in the Bhoti language. More than ten newspapers and magazines are available in the Bhoti language and nearly 7,000 monasteries of the Himalayan region follow this language in their practices and operations.[7]

Further, in the eyes of civil and criminal law of the land (with the exception of personal laws), Bhoti citizens are equal. Non-inclusion of Bhoti language is another form of punishment, which seems flagrant, especially as the community has not indulged in illegal or untoward actions.

Article 29 of the Indian Constitution deals with the 'Protection of interests of minorities'. It states that 'any section of the Citizens residing in the territory of India or any part thereof having a distinct language, script or culture of its own shall have the right to conserve the same'. The non-recognition of the Bhoti language is a violation of the minority rights; therefore it has undermined and violated the spirit of Article 29 of the Indian Constitution.

STATUS OF THE BHOTI SPEAKERS

The Indian Himalayas horizontally cover a vast area containing numerous ethnic groups of multiple indigenous origins. During the British rule the Himalayan people belonging to diverse ethnicities

were assimilated in three different sectors. The British took care of the Tibetan group of the Himalayas by giving them separate names. For instance Mon pas who belong to the sloping belt of the Eastern Himalayas possessed a separate speech from the migrated Sar duk pa(ms) of Eastern Bhutan. Similarly the Membas and the Khamber use a separate diction other than She duk pas. While they justify their group identity, they do not object belonging to the Tibeto-Burmese Bodic language. In this regard, S.K. Chatterjee points out their link to the Bodic languages of the Eastern Himalayas on account of their settlement within their boundaries. They constitute an example of 'Natural Nationalism' in India since 1959-60.

Since the middle of the first millennium, occasional migration in the Indian Himalayas from Burma (present Myanmar), in particular Arakan and mid-Burma and south-west Tibet occurred a number of times. In medieval India, the Muslim rulers did not oppose their entrance into those remote areas. Their settlement in those regions had been approved by the local *Gāragirdās* by the then system of *Pāttā*. So far as the Mon pas are concerned, the Towang Monasteries had been built on the remote grassy slopes and dales by the Mon pas who had a mobile merchandise system stretching to Kamrup and Hajo. The latter was a big market up to the British period during which the traders from Arakan (Myanmar) Kham pa, Mon pa, Duk pa (Bhutanese) and Sarthan Chinese lo used to meet and exchange their commodities. Their commercial language developed in the course of their journey. The Towang was built as a resort for travellers from the north-east, from Bhutan's Mdo khams.

The middle sector of the Indian Himalayas with a higher elevation than that of the eastern sector is primarily a pastoral sector, with trade opportunities for traders belonging to Uttar Kashi, Garhwal and Nainital. The market centres were important for both money-lenders of southern Tibet, Nepal on the one hand and the pilgrims to Mansarovar and Kailash from Uttar Kashi through Pithoragarh, in addition to the Nepal route. The merchant groups from Pithoragarh and the adjacent areas who became familiar with the southern Tibetan and the central Tibetan dialects, spoke Garhwali and Kumaoni fluently. On the other hand, central Tibetan dialect was regarded as the standard Tibetan language till 1959.

PROCESSING AT THE PARLIAMENTARY LEVELS

Language is not only a medium of communication, but also reflects the history, culture, relationships, system of governance, ecology,

religion, politics, etc. Bhoti is a systematic, scientific, culturally and intellectually rich language. In a country like India, the richness of the language hardly matters, because the protection and preservation of the sanctity of the language is more an arbitrary or number game.

The low representation of the Himalayan region in the Indian parliament is a major constraint for strong advocation of reforms in policy. Even the handful of representatives from this region are mostly scattered and unorganized in different directions. The Himalayan people are not only geographically scattered, but also politically unorganized. On 12 December 2005, the trans-Himalayan Parliamentary Forum submitted a memorandum to the Home Minister of India for the inclusion of the Bhoti language in the Eighth Schedule. The memorandum was signed by eight members of parliament from the trans-Himalayan region. On 25 September 2003, the Himalayan Buddhist Cultural Association submitted a memorandum to the prime minister of India for the inclusion of the Bhoti language in the Eighth Schedule. Again on 21 February 1995, eighty-one members of parliament from different political parties made a formal request to the prime minister to introduce a bill in the parliament to include Bhoti language in the Eighth Schedule of the Constitution. On 22 May 1995, approximately 49 members of parliament belonging to different political parties submitted another memorandum to then prime minister of India. Shri Virbhadra Singh, chief minister Himachal Pradesh, T.K. Lochen Rinpoche, former member of the Minority Commission, Lama Chosphel Zotpa, member of the Minority Commission and many other concerned individuals and institutions became consistently engaged in this movement for the inclusion of Bhoti language in the Eighth Schedule.

A sizeable number of Bhoti speakers reside in the Himachal Pradesh, west of the Kumaaun hills from Kal pa, in Rampur Bushahr up to the boundary line. Among them, inhabitants of Lahul, Spiti and upper Kinnaur deserve special mention for their identity awareness. And that might be significant for Dejong state government. Bhoti language in local nomenclature '*Dejong ke*' is one of the state languages of Sikkim. Above that, they have devised a distinct language modality to distinguish themselves from the Rong Community (Lepcha).[8]

UNITY AND DIVERSITY

The Constitution of India is not rigid, and it has no fixed number of languages to be included in the Eighth Schedule. Many languages have been included in the Eighth Schedule of the Constitution

after India's Independence. Many of these languages were found neither numerically stronger, nor grammatically richer than Bhoti. Assamese, Sindhi, Nepali, Konkani, Manipuri, Kashmiri, Sanskrit (1991 census), for instance, have lesser number of speakers than the Bhoti-speaking populace, but Bhoti has unfortunately not been included in the Eighth Schedule. This remains a conundrum. Bhoti is a language of the masses. It is a language of the people who have struggled for centuries. It is regarded as a language of the Himalayans, that blessed and bestowed the world with wisdom and prosperity. Also considered as a language of the saints and poets, it treasured the beauties of the nature. Today this language is struggling for its identity in a country which is considered to be the world's largest democracy and proclaims 'Unity in Diversity' as its foundational essence.[9]

After India's Independence, the destiny of the people living in the Himalayas was decided by the people who were mostly alien and ignorant about the realities and life-conditions of the Himalayas. Time and again the plains' friendly developmental policies and programmes were imported and imposed in the Himalayas. Such policies and programmes have broken down the indigenous system of economy, culture, ecology, employment and language. The inappropriate and irrelevant intervention has not only made them confused and frustrated, but also created an inferiority complex about their own culture, identity and language. They have been displaced from their own lands and villages. Family values and co-operative social systems have broken down. The narrow outlook and prejudiced attitude of the outsider policy makers, coupled with difficult accessibility have resulted in consistent marginalization of the region by the governments, media and donor agencies. Not including Bhoti language in the Eighth Schedule of the Constitution is clear evidence of the government's discrimination against three million people of the Himalayas, for whom this language is an integral part of their existence and mental and material universe. For them, it is not a mere language, but a way of life that propels progress in harmony with nature. Non-inclusion of the Bhoti language in the Eighth Schedule is the source of alienation, violence, social discord, intellectual dependency and cultural degradation. Today the Indian Constitution recognizes 22 languages in the Eighth Schedule. The criteria of recognition or non-recognition of the languages in the Eighth Schedule seem completely arbitrary and political.

IDENTITY MOVEMENT

A new movement thus started since the last quarter of the twentieth century in spite of including Bhotia and the Tibetan under the Scheduled Tribes in the Republic of India. This inclusion has been widely popularized in the broad trans-Bhotia region, referring to the issue as an Indian National Tribes' question. This has particular significance for the Bhoti-speaking people residing in the greater Himalayas up to the Duars, and in places such as Pashighat in Arunachal and Phuntholin. Similarly, the Tibetans as included in the Eighth Schedule Tribes, and include all the Tibeto-Mongoloid and the Tibeto-Burmese speakers under one category. The language awareness thus prompted the Bhotis and the Tibetan to articulate their language identity/unity.

Identity is not always theoretical but applied. In respect to the Tibet, language becomes primary and art becomes secondary. In the material culture of the Tribes of India under the Scheduled category, there is a claim that they are distinct from the mainstream in spite of being a minority. The solidarity of the mainstream should be dependent on the recognition of identity of the minority community in a multi-ethnic, multi-lingual, multi-ritual or multi-behavioural country. Hence, the identity image is subjective, while the identity depicted in arts and crafts, indigenous designs, indigenous dance, music, etc., reflects the unity of a particular community as a whole.[10] Evidently it is not a pseudo-political movement, but a movement for human identity, and human rights, which should be acknowledged by the national authority. The Bhoti movement opens new vistas for cultural expression through the unique literature, education, and art belonging to the Bhoti people.

NOTES

1. Matthias Koenig (Editor-in-Chief) and Eda Derhemi (Guest Editor), *International Journal on Multicultural Societies (IJMS)*, vol. 4, no. 2, 2002; *The Impact of Government Policies on Territorially Based Ethnic or Nationalist Movements*, Paul de Guchteneire, Laponce, 1987; De Swaan, 1993, 2001.
2. 17 September 2006, it was printed in the *The Times of Tibet*:
   'It is difficult to wake up a giant elephant which is intentionally pretending to be sleeping. All these efforts are of no use, when the Government of India is neither concerned nor interested in the promotion and development of language and culture of the Himalayas. The continued negligence and alienation of the Himalayan people in the mainstream may compel them to demand for greater political autonomy in the form of Statehoods and Union Territories. If the

Government of India sincerely and honestly wants to unite and strengthen the whole country, including the peace-loving and vulnerable communities of the Himalayan region, it should not hesitate to include the Bhoti language in the Eighth Schedule of the Indian Constitution, so that the people in the Himalayas can also be proud of their own language; our students can also appear in the Civil Service Examination with their mother tongue as an optional paper, our members of Parliament can also represent us in a more effective way by addressing our problems and aspirations in our own mother tongue; more research and development work can be feasible, with adequate government's support and the benefits are many more if it included in the Eighth Schedule.'

3. D.D. Sharma, *A Comparative Grammar of Tibeto-Himalayan Languages,* THE *TIBET JOURNAL*, vol. XXIV, no. 1, spring 1999.
4. Pandit Rahul Sankrityayan, *Purātattva Nibandhāvali* (New Leaders of New India), in Hindi, Allahabad, 1941.
5. Some Dimensions of Bhoti Literature in India (subject-wise distribution):

Arts and crafts

Rang re'i dbyangs kyi ide mig dar zhabs—'Jams dpal skal ldan, Kalimpong, W. B., India, 1973; *Lha ldan rva mo che jo bo'i sku tshab dkar chag*—Thub bstan rin po che, Va na legs bshad gter mdzod par khang, Sarnath, Varanasi, U.P., India.

Astro-Medicine

Bod kyi rig pa'i sman rdzas dpe ris gsal ba'i me long—Amchi Dawa (Sman rtsis khang, Gangchen Kyishong, Dharmsala, H.P., India); *Gso dpyad kyi don*—(Bon po text) authorship is ascribed to Gshen rab mi che (Occhaghat, H.P., India).

BIBLIOGRAPHICAL WORKS

BUDDHIST

'jam dpal sa skya Pandita chen po kun dga' rgyal mtshan dpal bzang po'i rnam par that pa (Sa skya pa'i mtho rim slob grwa, U.P. India).

Rgyal dbang 'brug chen bzhi pa kun mkhyen pad ma dkar po'i gsung byin rlabs can (Gangchen Khyishong, Dharamsala, H.P., India).

Grub thob brgyad cu rtsa bzhi rnam thar-Ngag dbang kun dga' bsod nams & 'jam Am yes zhabs (Sakya Cebtre, Dehradun, U.P., India, 1985).

Mkhyen brtse'i rnam har-Kong sprul yon tan rgya mtsho, Delhi, India.

Doctrinal works

BUDDHISM

Rigs lan slob gnyer khang gi ngo sprod-'gan 'jing blo bzang rgya mtsho (Rigs lam slob gnyer khang, Dharamsala, H.P., India, 1981).

Legs bshad blo gsar mig 'byed ('phag yul Dha sa shes rig par khang, Dharmsala, H.P., India, 1963).

Ri dwags kyi gtam nges 'byung gi pho nya (Darjeeling, W.B., India, 1963).

Lugs zung gi bslab bya Mu thi la'i phreng ba (Pub. Rdor gling Rang dbang par khang Darjeeling, W.B., India, 1960).

Gsung 'bum – Bdud ljoms Rin po che (1904-87), Manali, H.P., India.

CHRISTIANITY *ye shu'i chos bshad pa*

Sdig pa nas thar ba'i lam (Scripture, Gift Mission Ecclesiastical Hall, London, S.W. I, England).

ECOLOGICAL RESPONSIBILITY

Smad bcud rten 'byung 'drel ba'i gdams ngag nyung nu'I tshings bead du bslebs pa-Ta lai bla ma skye phreng bcju bzhi pa (Sa skya'i dge slong bstan 'dzin rgya mtsho, Delhi, India, 1993).

EPIC STUDIES & LITERARY CRITICISM

Gsham yul na bshad pa'i Ke sar gyi sgrung collected by A.H. Francke (Asiatic Society, Calcutta, India, 1905-41).

Rgyan gyi bstan scos me long gi 'grel chen – Blo gsar byung ba rol pa'i dga tshal (Namgyal Institute of Tibetology, Gangtok, Sikkim, India, 1968).

FOLK SONGS

La dwags kyi yul kyi (Art, Culture & Language Akademi, Leh, Ladakh, India, 1992).

GEOGRAPHICAL TEXTS

Gangs ljongs dbus gtsang gnas bskor lam yig nor bu zla shel gyi se mo do – Ka thog si tu chos kyi rgya mtsho (1880-1925), Sungs rab gnyam so rgyun 'phel par khang (Palampur, H.P., India).

GRAMMATICAL EXPLANATION & LINGUISTICS

Sgra yi don sdeb snang gsal sgron me: Zhang Zhung smar yig che bzi Ka dp'o (Delhi, India, 1965).

Padmo rnam par 'byed pa'i legs bshad nyin byed kyi snang ba-Dge 'dun sbyin pa (Mon gho 'bras blo gling gtsug lag gter ndzad 'phrul par khang, Mundgod, Karnataka, India).

HIPPOLOGY & VETERINARY MEDICINE

Glud dang bzang nan rtog tshul dang (Rampur Bushahr, Kinnaur, Himachal Pradesh, India, 1934).

HISTORICAL & EPIGRAPHIC WORKS

Deb ther dkar po (Hokhang House recension) (Pub., Rdo gling rang dbang par khang, Darjeeling, W.B., India).

Ma bcos dngos 'brel brjod pa dus kyi sbrang char-Gdong thog pa'i rgyal mtshan (Delhi, India, 1974).

La dwags-Saphud Thub bstan dpal (Sle, Ladakh, India, 1983).

La dwags rgyal rabs chi med gter – Yoseb Gergan (Leh, Ladakh, 1976).

INTERNATIONAL AFFAIRS & INTERNAL ADMINISTRATION

Mes rgyal 'dzugs bskrun (Pub, Krung dbyang gsar 'gyur Calcutta, India).

Skyabs mgon chon pos mi mang la rtsal ba'i bka' slob dag (Publisher: Rdor gling rang dbang par khang, Darjeeling, India, 1968).

Mnyal 'brel rgyal tshogs su phebs mi don gcod thun mong gi las bsdoms bsnyan zhu'i ngo bsdus-(Rdo gling rang dbang par khang, Darjeeling, India, 1960).

MENTAL SCIENCE & MEDITATION THERAPY

Gsung 'bum-Kun mkhyen 'jigs med gling pa. (ed. Sonam T. Kazi, Gangtok, India, 1972).

MUSIC & ORCHESTRA

Mchag gyur gling pa'i dbyang yig (1829-70)—*Tshangs chen rdo rje'i rgyud mang* (in Rtsa gsum sgrub skor gces btus Delhi, India, 1979).

Poems & Lyrics

Legs par bshad pa chu'i bstan bcos lugs gnyis rlabs 'phren brgya ldan-Gun than dkon mchog bstan pa'i sgron me (1762-1823 AD, Dbus bod kyi gtsug lag slob gnyer khang, Sarnath, Varanasi, U.P., India, 1991).

Lho yig tshigs bead ('bras gzhung shes rig deb tsom sgrigs khang, Gangtok, Sikkim, India, 1985).

Gang ri'i brtes dung-Gcod pa Don grum & Chab 'gag rdo rje tshe ring (Gan su'u mi rigs dpe skrun khang, India, 1996).

Kun gsal me long-'Gong sa' bcu gsum pa (Ka sbug 'Phags-Bod nang pa'i rig gnas slob gnyer khang, Kalimpong, Darjeeling, W.B., India, 1966).

Non-metrical Prose Compositions

Lho yig tshing lhug ('bras ljongs shes rig deb tsom sgrigs khang, Gangtok, Sikkim, India, 1985).

Ngo tshar dad pa'i rol mtsho-Mi fam chi med grub pa (Ka thong Rig dzing chen po'i Gsung 'bum (Dalhousie, H.P., India, 1976).

Kong sprul yon tan gya mtshos gangs can gyi ljongs su rgyal bstan ris gnad gcig tu bsgrub pa'i tshul la dpyad-Ri mgul spul sku (Sikkim National Presss, Gangtok, Sikkim, India, 1962).

Kha che pha lu'i 'jig rten las 'bras rtsi lugs kyi bslab bya (Lithograph edn. Tibetan Printing Press, Dharamsala, H.P., India).

Tibetan Translation Works (from Sanskrit, Pali, Hindi, Bengali, Arabic, English texts)

Chos kyi tshigs su bcad pa (Dhamapada in Pali, Dge 'dun chos 'phel, Sikkim Durbar Press, Gangtok, Sikkim, India, 1946).

Snyan ngag bsdus pa (Select poems pf Rabindra Nath Tagore; from Bengali), tr. S.K. Pathak, Delhi, India, 1961.

Ra bin dra na th Tha kor gyis mdzad pa'i glu thal sbyar ma (Gitanjali of Rabindra Nah Tagore), tr. Dngos grub (Bod Kyi khang, Delhi, India, 1983).

Ra bin dra na tha kur mchog gis Sangs rgyas dang nang ba'i lugs skor-Sgang tog rgya gar gzhungs spel las khungs (Gangtok, Sikkim, India, 1960).

Ra bin dra na tha Te gor brtsom pa'i lzos gar Gar (Pujarini) mkhan ma'i mchod pa Rgya gzhung sbrel las khungs, Gangtok, Sikkim, India, 1960).

Biblical

Dam pa'i gsung rab: Zhal chad gsar ba'i mdo rnams (Rgya gar dang se nga la'i gsung rab dar bar mjed pa'i gshes gnyen lhan rgya, Bangalore, India, 1960).

Zhal chad suga phyi gnyis kyi mdo (The Bible Society of India, Bangalore, India, 1968).

Islamic

The Qurran (Tibetan translation partially done (City Masjid, Sle Ladwags, India).

Miscellaneous

Dga' bya zla zer (Sanskrit text *Laghu Siddhanta Kaumudi* (Varadaraja, Mchog sbyin rgyal po), tr. Blo bzang nor bu (Va na legs gter mdzod khang, Sarnath, Varanasi, U.P., India, 1989).

Pha yis rang hi bu mo la sphrings pa'i 'phin tshogs (Letter to his daughter)-*Paind Ja 'jo har lal Neh rus brtsam pa* (Rgya gar gzhung gi gsar spel las kungs, Gangtok, 'bras ljoings, Sikkim, India, 1960).

6. APPENDIX

Locality	Ethnic Group
WESTERN SECTOR	
Baltistan, north-western Kashmir having Gilgit valley as an important seat	Balti, Niya
Jozila to Drass towards Eastern Purik	Purik district from the Nubra inhabitants (Spurigs/spu'I rgyal ?)
North Kashmir Jozila to Upper region of Ladakh	Ladakhi consisting of several sub-groups excluding Dog pa.
Jammu & Kashmir	The people of Nubra holds separate language identity from that of the Leh tahsil.
Lahul (Lha yul/Lhya hul, i.e. Lahaula)	The inhabitants claim a separate identity though Kinship descended from a fraction of Ladakhi Mon pa. Loke the Gahri the Pattani, the Tinanni speakers.
Spiti	Ethnic identity differs from the Ladakhi with the speech affinity of Purik and with Nyamkat 'bru (za) skad.
Upper Kinnaur (Kinnara) (north-west of Rikangfu and Kalpa up to Jang thang and above) Nyamkat	Broad name of Kinnori with distinct ethnic feature from the Lower Kinnaur—people of Rampur, Bushahr with a probable connection to Guge?
MIDDLE SECTOR	
Tehri Garhwal Bhotia Mahal Uttar Pradesh/Uttaranchal Upper region of Uttar Kashi Neelam	Marcha, Tolcha, Garhwali Bhotia, Jad, Bhoti.
Pithoragarh Bhotia Mahal	Bhoti probably migrated from Upper Eastern Nepal and Guge for trade and cattle grazing.
EASTERN SECTOR	
West Bengal, Darjeeling district extending up to north-western borders of Nepal	Toto Bhotia, Sher pa (having kinship with the Sharpas of Nepal) ; different ethnic groups Kagate (Yulmo), the Tamang, etc.
Sikkim	Bhotias claiming separate identity as De(n) Jong pa, east-west and north having (rus) plurality.

Arunachal Pradesh Kameng district and the area bordering Bhutan in the west	The Mon pa. Sardugpan, Duk pa settled from 'brug yul. A few Lhopa families settled from Lho Kha (south Tibet).
North-eastern part of Indian China border	Kham ba and Mem ba groups migrated from eastern Tibet Kham and a few Lho pa, families of Lhoka.

7. Family-wise grouping of the 122 scheduled and non-scheduled languages, 2011

Language families	Number of languages	Persons who returned the languages as their mother tongue	Percentage to total population
1	2	3	4
1. Indo-European (a) Indo-Aryan	21	790,627,060	76.87
(b) Iranian	2	22,774	00.00
(c) Germanic	1	226,449	00.02
2. Dravidian	17	214,172,874	20.82
3. Austro-Asiatic	14	11,442,029	01.11
4. Tibeto-Burmese	66	10,305,026	01.00
5. Semito-Hamitic	1	51,728	00.01
Total	122	1,026,847,940*	99.83*

* Out of the total population of 1,028,610,328 for India, the balance of 1,762,388 (0.17 per cent) speakers are 'Total of Other languages' other than Scheduled and Non-Scheduled languages. The total population excludes the figures of Paomata, Mao Maram and Purul Subdivision in Manipur.

The names of the 122 Scheduled and non-Scheduled languages falling in the above five language families are given below with the Scheduled Languages denoted as (S). Of the 22 Scheduled Languages, 15 fall in the Indo-Aryan branch of the Indo-European family, 1 in Austro-Asiatic family, 4 in the Dravidian family and 2 in the Tibeto-Burmese family.

(A) INDO-EUROPEAN

(a) INDO-ARYAN

1. Assamese(s), 2. Bengali(s), 3. Bhili/Bhilodi, 4. Bishnupuriya, 5. Dogri(s) 6. Gujarati(s), 7. Halabi, 8. Hindi(s), 9. Kashmiri(s), 10. Khandeshi, 11. Konkani(s), 12. Lahnda, 13. Maithili(s), 14. Marathi(s), 15. Nepali(s), 16. Oriya(s), 17. Punjabi(s), 18. Sanskrit(s), 19. Shina, 20. Sindhi(s), 21. Urdu(s).

(b) IRANIAN

1. Afghani/Kabuli/Pashto, 2. Persian.

(c) GERMANIC

1. English.

(B) DRAVIDIAN

1. Coorgi/Kodagu, 2. Gondi, 3. Jatapu, 4. Kannada(s), 5. Khond/Kondh, 6. Kisan, 7. Kolami, 8. Konda, 9. Koya, 10. Kui, 11. Kurukh/Oraon, 12. Malayalam(s), 13. Malto, 14. Parji, 15. Tamil(s), 16. Telugu(s), 17. Tulu.

(C) AUSTRO-ASIATIC

1. Bhumij, 2. Gadaba, 3. Ho, 4. Juang, 5. Kharia, 6. Khasi, 7. Koda/Kora, 8. Korku, 9. Korwa, 10. Munda, 11. Mundari, 12. Nicobarese, 13. Santali(s), 14. Savara.

(D) TIBETO-BURMESE

1. Adi, 2. Anal, 3. Angami, 4. Ao, 5. Balti, 6. Bhotia, 7. Bodo(s), 8. Chakesang, 9. Chakru/Chokri, 10. Chang, 11. Deori, 12. Dimasa, 13. Gangte, 14. Garo, 15. Halam, 16. Hmar, 17. Kabui, 18. Karbi/Mikir, 19. Khezha, 20. Khiemnungan, 21. Kinnauri, 22. Koch, 23. Kom, 24. Konyak, 25. Kuki, 26. Ladakhi, 27. Lahauli, 28. Lakher, 29. Lalung, 30. Lepcha, 31. Liangmei, 32. Limbu, 33. Lotha, 34. Lushai/Mizo, 35. Manipuri(s), 36. Maram, 37. Maring, 38. Miri/Mishing, 39. Mishmi, 40. Mogh, 41. Monpa, 42. Nissi/Dafla, 43. Nocte, 44. Paite, 45. Pawi, 46. Phom, 47. Pochury, 48. Rabha, 49. Rai, 50. Rengma, 51. Sangtam, 52. Sema, 53. Sherpa, 54. Simte, 55. Tamang, 56. Tangkhul, 57. Tangsa, 58. Thado, 59. Tibetan, 60. Tripuri, 61. Vaiphei, 62. Wancho, 63. Yimchungre, 64. Zeliang, 65. Zemi, 66. Zou.

(E) SEMITO-HAMITIC

Arabic

The Indo-Aryan languages are spoken by the maximum number of speakers, followed in the descending order by the Dravidian, Austro-Asiatic, and Sino-Tibetan (Tibeto-Burman) languages.

Twenty-two Indian languages: Assamese, Bengali, Bodo, Dogri, Gujarati, Hindi, Kashmiri, Kannada, Konkani, Maithili, Malayalam, Manipuri, Marathi, Nepali, Oriya, Punjabi, Sanskrit, Santali, Sindhi, Tamil, Tel-ugu, and Urdu are included in the Eighth Schedule. Among these two languages, Sanskrit and Tamil are assigned the status of Classical languages.

Indian multilingualism is unique in many respects—it has naturally evolved and is coupled with the multilingualism evolving through schooling.

Indian population in 1991 exhibited 19.4 per cent of bilingualism and 7.2 per cent of trilingual, so that the total percentage of 'Native Languages' is at about 127 per cent.

8. *Bodo, Dogri, Maithili* and *Santali* have been included as Scheduled languages from 2001 Census following the 100th Amendment of the Constitution of India. Konkani, Manipuri and Nepali are appearing as Scheduled languages since 1991 following the 73rd Amendment of the Constitution of India.

   The change in Hindi percentage in 1991 from the published percentage in 1991 is due to exclusion of Maithili from Hindi.

9. Stanzin Dawa, *Arguments for including Bhoti Language in the 8th Schedule of the Indian Constitution*. From *The Times of Tibet*, 17 September 2006.

   'In the era of globalization and vastly more efficient communication networks, languages die more frequently than they are born. The stronger language

eliminate the weaker ones, sometime violently but more often peacefully as a result of people shifting to a language with a greater purchasing power, whether the purchase is of economic, political or cultural goods (Bourdieu 1991; Krauss 1992; Grin 1994; Breton 1999; Nettle and Romaine 2000; Crystal 2000). The prediction that most of the existing 7,000 odd languages spoken today in the world will disappear and that relatively few will be born (7,000 is the upper estimate given by Ferguson in 1964 and Grimes in 1998). India as a state is an assimilators and protectors of languages. It tend to weaken if not destroy the languages of the minority internally while protecting their own dominant languages on the national and international scene. Globalization may well weaken the state in the economic field, but if that weakening increases the sense of insecurity of a language community, globalization will then, very likely, strengthen the state in its role of protector of language and culture.'

10. Keeping this into consideration the Government of India should include the Bhoti language in the Eighth Schedule for the security and promotion of Bhoti language, culture, identity and dignity. Gautama the Buddha says, 'There is nothing permanent in this world except change itself'.

IV. NATIONALISMS IN EURASIA

9

Shifting Perceptions in Buryat Identity

SUCHANDANA CHATTERJEE

INTRODUCTION

In the emergent discourse about Asiatic Russia as an interactive space, the regional specificities of Buryatia, an east Siberian republic of the Russian Federation with its idyllic Lake Baikal surroundings, have attracted attention. The region appears to be calm compared to the other chaotic post-Soviet borderlands. Conventionally regarded as a region with Mongolian orientation, Buryatia experienced a quiet transition from an autonomous Soviet Socialist republic (territorially demarcated in stages in 1923, 1937 and 1958) to an independent republic of the Russian Federation in 1992. Retrospective analyses about Buryatia's connected histories indicate renewal of interest in the region's Mongol heritage, Buddhist spirituality, a Tsarist colonial setting and nationalist awakening. After the Soviet disintegration, the initial emphasis was on Buryatia as a re-ethnicized region, but with some disclaimers. Buryatia's ethnic cohesiveness seems unusual and here is a distinct case which did not experience ethnic 'backlash' that was so common in Central Asia and the Caucasus. A mild approach towards Buryat nationalism has been replaced by assertions about a Buryat intellectual milieu that took shape in the early decades of the twentieth century when intellectuals like Bazar Baradin, Gombozhob Tsybikov and Mikhail Bogdanov expressed their views *for* Buryat-Mongol national culture, Buryat education and language and *against* imperial projects like land distribution. These agendas are extremely appealing to the new generation of Buryat scholars who tend to reflect on the intellectual maturity of their predecessors. Their assessments suggest that the Buryat intellectuals were not mute observers of the reform process that began in 1905 with Stolypin's agrarian reforms.

In Buryatia, there are echoes of the debates about the evolution of nationalist thought in the colonial world.[1]

The negative image of Buryatia as isolated and marginalized gave way to positive images about Buryatia as a cosmopolitan space. Colonial trajectories about a centralized set-up and the post-colonial hypotheses about borderland identities have been supplemented with topics like 'integration' that suggest a reconstitution of centre-periphery relationships. The analysis is about the instruments of integration of Asiatic nationalities of Siberia and the Far East during the early decades of the twentieth century. The complexity of the integration process and the inner strains of a nationalist movement have also been indicated.

According to the new assessments, multi-ethnicity is a manageable affair in Buryatia primarily because integration is the dominant element in Buryatia's political culture.[2] One feature of integration is Russian-Buryat bonding despite divergent urbanization patterns and divergent use of language (as majority of the people living in the urban areas speak Russian even though there is a preferential and selective use of Buryat as a dialect of the Mongol language).[3]

The Buryat-Russian relationship is not only a matter of psychological bonding due to long-established links with Russia but also due to economic and social reasons as Buryats want better benefits like good education and employment opportunities in Moscow. So there is an image of Buryatia as an interactive and inter-ethnic space that is not detached from its Russian environment. In Buryatia, there is hardly any difficulty in being Buryat and Russian at the same time. Due to co-habitation and co-existence over centuries, the two ethnic groups have remained cohesive.

This essay tries to integrate different perceptions of Buryat identity including, a trans-national ethnic Mongol identity that idealizes a Mongol 'pax', a nationalist identity that owes allegiance to the ideological positions of Buryat intellectuals of the colonial era, a spiritualized Buddhist identity that takes the form of a generalized aesthetic creative force, and some hybrid sentiments that sanctify Buryat culture.[4] What is somewhat lacking is a comprehensive analysis of the Soviet period, although the capital, Ulan Ude became the showpiece of Soviet urban development during the 1960s-80s.[5] However, there are nostalgic feelings for the 'radiant past' and these are mostly connected to World War II when young Buryat-Mongols with Cossack traditions were recruited for military service.[6] Literary writers of the Soviet period like Namzhil Baldano (1907-84) also

feature prominently in the revivalist discourse that pays homage to the writer and his compositions that dealt with the humaneness of Buryat folklore and Buryat epics (*Geser*).[7] However, these are reflections and personal narratives of the Soviet past[8] rather than comprehensive accounts of a Soviet professional space.

ETHNICITY

There is a common perception about the inner and outer world of the Mongols. The Mongol domain stretches from Mongolia all through Inner Asia that includes Buryatia's linguistic groups dispersed over territories of the Baikal region, Tibet and some portions of Central Asia. On the whole, the pan-Mongol rhetoric is dominant. But there are various shades and opinions that look beyond the prism of Chingizid statehood or a pan-Mongol affiliation. For instance, the Buryat *mentalite* is expressed through such self-definitions as 'We-Buryats'.[9] Such reassessments are growing in number, but there is an overall consensus about the Mongol ethos.

But revisionists have modified the hypothesis of ethnicity by identifying parameters that are specific to the Buryat case. According to recent analysis, ethnicity is the backbone of political culture that has grown and survived in Buryatia. Modifying the hypothesis of group distinctiveness based on culture and descent, the new argument projects *survival* of minority and marginal groups which, despite centralization, have not disappeared.

In contemporary Buryat ethnicity discourse, what is projected is the adaptability of the Buryat *ethnos* to its environment. The Buryat community was after all a compact unit that was not static, but dynamic in nature. On the whole, there seems to a superstratum of Mongol-speaking Buryats concentrated in the Lake Baikal region who were integrated into the colonial system, as well as a substratum of Turkic-speaking Buryats like the Tungus tribes who remained outside the tribute-paying mechanism of the colonizers.[10] There was an attempt by Russian imperial administrators to implement a system of governance to the region through ethnic generalization. The Mongol communities were bound together as an ethno-linguistic group with a shamanist spiritual culture and shared Mongol genealogies that made them constituent units of an ethnic Mongol stock. They were integrated into the East Siberian governor *generalate*; and Irkutsk, Verkhoudinsk (now Ulan Ude) and Kyakhta prospered as economic centres.

The cultural variation of the Buryats who lived on the western and eastern sides of the Baikal was not taken into consideration in the strict sense during the Soviet period. The Buryats ideologically belonged to the Mongol commonwealth and were framed as a territorial unit (BMASSR or the Buryat-Mongol Autonomous Soviet Socialist Republic) with well-defined territorial identity units like the Aga autonomous *okrug* (district), and the Ust-Ordinskii *okrug* (that had a high density of Buryat population) within the Irkutskaya and Chita *oblasts*. In a phased way, the territoriality of the Buryats was altered in accordance to historical considerations, as well as Mongol genetic ties. In the 1950s, the Mongol component was removed from the ethnonym 'Buryat-Mongol', and the republic was renamed as Buryat ASSR. According to Tatyana Skrynnikova and Darima Amongolova, this is an example of ethnic manoeuvring. This ethno-political strategy was revived in the 1990s with the creation of a Buryat Republic and 'historical ties' were injected into the post-Soviet ethnicity rhetoric. Referring to re-ethnicization in Buryatia, these scholars have pointed to the politicization of historical memory and the adoption and deletion of the ethnonym 'Buryat-Mongol' for very limited purposes.[11] Social polarization became more intense after 2005 when President Putin issued decrees on *ukrupnenie* (merging) on grounds of regional consolidation.[12] Merging of the two Buryat districts of Ust Orda and Aginsky with Irkutsk's Olkhon district has created discontent not only about Moscow's authoritarian stance but also about the logistics of the arrangement, and its direct impact on Buryatia's ethnic culture. Revisionist writers argue that there were extreme territorial, economic and ethnic asymmetries.[13] They feel that the mergers have resulted in the deletion of autonomous *oblasts* due to their incorporation into the wealthy Russianized environment of the Irkutsk and Transbaikal *oblasts*.

Recently, there have been further shifts in the ethnicity discourse. Usually there is consensus about inter-ethnic bonding between the Buryats and the Russians. But this parameter is questioned from the standpoint of rural-urban relationships in Buryatia. Alternative versions suggest that there are multilayered responses among urban Buryats. So to consider them solely as an ethnic group is not justified. The Buryats in urban centres are more influenced by personal and individual affiliations rather than group interests.[14] Surveys reveal a disproportionate ratio between Buryat and Russian students, professional groups and technical trainees. So, an urbanized culture tends to be centred in Ulan Ude, and there seem to be different responses to the ethnicity marker. Pavel Vernavsky notes that the

practice of increasing one's social status through education is the answer to the negative effects of globalization. So, in Vernavsky's opinion, in contemporary Buryatia, there is a marked use of ethnic social practices, and ethnicity has evolved as *individual social strategy* (rather than group interest), and is oriented towards improving social status through education. What is addressed more frequently is 'the urban phenomenon of Ulan Ude' and various methods of personal adaptation explain the socialization process in contemporary Buryatia.[15]

1905 AND ITS AFTERMATH: THE SHAPING OF REGIONAL ALTERNATIVES

The shaping of an urban mood in different historical contexts has also assumed importance. The focus is on the regional settings—Siberian and Buryat.

The Siberian Setting

In post-Soviet reckonings of the colonial past, the subject of imperial encounters has acquired a new dimension. The ideal regional setting that was well suited for imperialist action is focused upon. In the 1890s, there was a perfect atmosphere for intellectual development. The completion of the Trans-Siberian Railway and the Chinese Eastern Railway in 1903 resulted in an exalted image of Russia in Far Eastern affairs. Siberia was now beginning to feel the influence of economic development and also faced the complications of Far Eastern politics as Cossack regiments of the Russian army held firm ground there, and as the main group of settler population, interfered in the conditions in Siberia and the Far East. After the 1905 Revolution, political activism became more intense with demands for self-government through a Siberian Regional Duma. The momentum for action came from this regional union that demanded equal re-presentation with the central government in regard to colonization laws pertaining to water and land rights, local finances, local communications, mines, etc. The regulation of relations between Siberia and European Russia became the governing principle of constitutional reforms after 1905. The introduction of private landed property in the eastern regions was recognized as an urgent task in the overall scheme of empire-building. Landownership in Siberia by private peasant settlers was a crucial component of the internal colonization system. To the patriots in Siberia, this was a method of

assimilation that would make the Cossack or Russian peasants private landowners while the indigenous people would become the landless people in a gigantic expanse of state-owned land that actually went to the private proprietors in service of His Majesty's government. Land usage by non-indigenous peasant agricultural farmers became a contentious issue as the non-Russian population like the Buryats in Eastern Siberia and the Kazakhs in the Steppe region made appeals to government bodies to protect the cultural prestige and dignity of their right to land ownership.

After 1905, there were other issues that aroused nationalist forces in Siberia. The separatist, autonomist, regionalist groups became less cohesive after the Revolution and the Civil War. After 1917, a series of resolutions on the Siberian question surfaced. The *oblastniki,* fearing the danger of elimination, worked on the model of an autonomous Siberian regional government. The regional alternatives created more polarization during the Civil War period.

The Buryat Setting

The Buryat-regions in the Irkutsk province and the Transbaikal district were responsive to the *zemstvo* (local council) model, but they soon got sidelined as they collaborated with the adherents of pan-Mongolism and the Japanese militarists who actively collaborated with ataman M.G. Semyonov. In the Civil War period, 'White Siberia' was the cradle of all sorts of group interests, and Buryat autonomy with Mongolian orientation was slowly entering the turbulent scene. To renegotiate their economic position *vis-à-vis* their Russian competitors, the Buryats demanded a provincial directorate and *aimaks* and *khoshuns* became the model units for provincial restructuring. The *zemstvo* was regarded as a platform for direct participation of the people in political and economic affairs of the region, especially those pertaining to education, health care and communication. But all these measures proved futile during the Civil War period especially because most of these groups were engaged in military and political alliances in some form or the other. The issues of landownership and cultural representation of the Buryats and the formation of the Buryat-Mongol Autonomous *oblast* within the Far Eastern Republic and the RSFSR were problematical.[16]

So, Buryat activism started taking shape after 1905. Buryat autonomists started gravitating towards Social Revolutionaries looking for solutions that prescribed an evolutionary path rather than a drastic imposition of 'new order'. They were mostly intellectuals

who spent their early years in a typical Mongol setting and who understood the folklore, superstitions, and ways of life of their people. Most of them were trained by the University of St. Petersburg where they cooperated with Russian orientalists and travelled widely in Siberia, Central Asia and European Russia and sometimes in Western Europe. But they strongly reacted to Russian expansionism into Buryat territory especially after the land laws of the 1900s. Combined with this was Russia's Far Eastern debacle in Japan, and the new threats from Manchuria and China that impacted the intellectuals, who responded to the local dynamics in Outer Mongolia centring Urga, which was close to the Russian border.

Mikhail Bogdanov (1878-1917) was one such leader with revolutionary orientation. Bogdanov was sentimental about Buryat culture but was also adaptive to the novel and avant-garde changes that had occurred in the Buryat surroundings. Like another intellectual Tsyben Zhamtsarano (1880-1940), Bogdanov favoured the Buryats' cultural self-determination and his linguistic preference was Mongol, and he opted for the Mongol alphabet. He was emphatic about the Buryats' Mongol history. But he was mainly a proponent of land reform and stressed protection of Buryat land from Russian encroachment and argued for the continuation of tribal ownership—a proposal that reflected local resentment of imperial government's land laws. Bogdanov's engagement in land debates was analysed in biographical commentaries on his work and activities in the journal *Zhizn Buryatii.* As a *Buryatoved*, he wrote extensively on the social structure of the Irkutsk Buryats, their tribal groupings and subdivisions comprising the Ekhirits, Bulagats and Khoris. He was a specialist of Buryat ethnography and wrote about the Buryats of the Angara and Yenisei basins, their spiritual culture, (i.e. shamanism) and several rituals and practices (e.g. *zegetei aba*).[17] But as a city-bred Buryat (based in Irkutsk) he was adaptive to Western ideas. Bogdanov had immense fan-following primarily because of his external contacts. As a Social Revolutionary, he went to Berlin to study from where he moved to Zurich. By 1905, he returned to Russia and led a congress of Buryats in Irkutsk. From 1907 onwards, his articles were published in the journal *Sibirskie Voprosy* where he indicated his independent line of action as a 'Mongolophile'. He formulated a plan for Mongolian self-government within the Russian empire. During the Civil War that spread to Siberia, he led a group of 2000 Buryats to Barga in Manchuria where he became a victim of Kolchak's White Army general, Semyonov. In contemporary Buryatia, Bogdanov is the icon of Buryat cosmopolitanism.

Bogdanov's contemporaries were Gombozhob Tsybikov (1873-1930), Bazar Baradin (1878-1937), Tsyben Zhamtsarano (1880-1940), and Petr Badmaev (1841-1920) who were trained by the Buddhological school in Russia as fieldworkers in the eastern borderlands. The articulation of a Buryat alternative through this Buddhological school is another component of Buryatness.

BURYAT BUDDHISM

Buddhism, officially recognized by the 1940s, was firmly entrenched in Gusino Ozero, south-east of Lake Baikal and close to the Mongolian/Chinese border which became a Lama stronghold, and had strong ties with Gomang College, Drepung University in Lhasa, Tibet. Buddhism in Buryatia strengthened as a cultural influence in the realm of literacy and education, and expanded as an art form. An indigenous ecclesiastical structure, the Buryat National Buddhist Church under the patronage and administrative control of Russian officials came into being. A network of monasteries was set up in the regions west and east of Lake Baikal during the period 1850-1920.

At the turn of the twentieth century, the surroundings of Lake Baikal became the centrestage of Buryat autonomists who were engaged in the transportation of alternative ideas to the Far Eastern sector. They responded to the new ideological approach to the study of ancient Buddhist texts based on the living oral traditions of Buddhism that were articulated by Oldenburg and Scherbatsky in St. Petersburg. Such approaches questioned the traditional European philological method in interpreting old Buddhist texts and relied on the interpretations of the Buddhist Lamas to facilitate such ground knowledge and understanding. So, the emphasis, from the end of the 1890s, was on the interpretations of the eastern educators and their ideas of their own cultures. Their choice fell on Gombozhab Tsybikov (1873-1930), Bazar Baradin and Tsyben Zhamtsarano, who became future leaders of the Buryat autonomy movement after 1905 and participated in 'nationalist reconstruction' of the Soviet state in the 1920s. These Buryats came to study at the Oriental Faculty at St. Petersburg to acquire elite jobs in imperial service or in the diplomatic department. But their mentors in St. Petersburg viewed that their students' future lay elsewhere. They were offered special training for their research trips to Tibet which was closed to European scholars at that time. Their data was very useful in terms of the descriptions as well as their interpretations. Tsybikov and

Baradin were the duo who reported to their Tsarist mentors about the state of Tibetan affairs.

Gombozhab Tsybikov came from a poor nomadic Buryat family, but his father decided to educate his younger son. He graduated from Chita *gimnaziia* and studied medicine in Tomsk University. His mentor there was Petr Badmaev who advised him to quit medicine and come to St. Petersburg to pursue oriental studies and diplomacy. After graduation, Tsybikov spent some time doing field research on land management in Transbaikalia after which he was picked up for service for the Russian Geographical Society which sponsored his expedition to Tibet. The trip was undertaken in three years: from 1899 to 1902. In Tibet, he played a double or even triple role—as a fellow traveller and travel companion of the Buryat pilgrims, a dedicated fieldworker of the Imperial Russian Geographical Society taking unusual risks and as a Russian secret agent whose goal was to gather geographical information about the political and socio-economic situation in Tibet. He was also a Buryat nationalist who became a member of the Buryat intellectual circles who would later utilize his position as a veteran field worker to advance the Buryat cause in the post-revolutionary years. On his return to Russia, Tsybikov presented a talk about his expedition at the Russian Geographical Society. His field notes entitled *Buddhist-palomnik u sviatyn' Tibeta* was published in 1918 and re-published from Novosibirsk in 1991.[18] He is considered to be the first scholar-traveller from the Russian empire who managed to penetrate Tibet in the late nineteenth century. His trip went unnoticed in the West until the British (Francis Younghusband's) invasion of Tibet that opened up a Pandora's box about clandestine links among interventionists centring Tibet and the role of secret agents in this imperial 'game' for gaining access to the borderlands.[19]

Tsybikov's entry into the Tibetan scene was reported in a series of English-language publications. There was a report of his journey in *Izvestiya IRGO* in 1903 that was translated and published in *The Geographical Journal* in 1904.[20] The report says that after his year-long stay in Lhasa, when he collected valuable books by lama scholars on philology, astronomy, medicine, history and *hu-rums* (incantations), Tsybikov travelled to the high passes of Central Tibet, dotted with monasteries like Sera, Amdo, Daibun and Galdan. He reported on populous trade centres like Shigatse, Gyangtse and Lhasa, and the settlements of foreigners and traders of Indian origin. What is most striking is the indifferent and often critical tenor of Tsybikov's des-

criptions of Tibetan sacred places. He seems to be satirical, very typically reflecting the austere mind of a tutored disciple, trained by his imperial Russian scholarly environment to be indifferent and/ or condescending especially when he described the ruling class, the nobility and the social stratification in Tibet, the austerity of Buddhist monastical order, the norms of Buddhist scholasticism (evident in the granting of degrees like the *lharampa* from Gandan monastery, and so much valued in Amdo, Mongolia and Buryatia), etc. Despite his sceptic tone, Tsybikov made a noteworthy contribution because he described/commented upon the socio-economic scenario—his topics ranged from the status of women in society, to every detail of the Buddhist pantheon, the biographies of the lamas and the role of monasteries as repositories not only of faith and worship, but also of literary texts, manuscripts, art, xylographs and architecture. So, Tsybikov covered a huge gap in the West's oriental knowledge about religion and tradition. His travelogue opened up a new field of Tibetan studies in the field of fine art and aestheticism. Through his analyses, he had deconstructed Tibet and had unravelled the mysteries of old Tibet as he passed through the Buddhist pilgrimage route from Chita via the Mongolian grasslands, the Gobi, Tsaidam and Lhasa. A cross-section of the same route was followed from the Indian side by Nicholas Roerich, the Russian painter in the 1920s.

The second explorer to Tibet was Bazar Baradin. Under the direction and training of Scherbatsky and Oldenburg, he was sent on a one-year field visit to the monasteries of Amdo and Kumbum (which were also visited by Tsybikov on his way to Lhasa). He then undertook a second trip to Central Tibet. Unlike Tsybikov who was not happy with the institution of Buddhism as a religious faith and criticized the rigidity of the practitioners, Baradin was more sympathetic towards Buddhism as a social institution. He made a detailed sketch of the monastic establishment in Labran. His biggest contribution is his travel account of the pilgrimage route which is of enormous ethnographic value given the range of themes he covered. It is Baradin's analysis of Buddhist philosophy that is of rare aesthetic value. In fact, Baradin's work, published in 1926, is a worthy contribution to the realm of Tibetan studies because it disengages or dissociates Buddhism from the world of religion *per se*, and establishes Buddhology as a tradition that is represented through Buddhist texts and Buddhist art forms, rather than blind/ mundane practices. In his work, the monastery forms an ideal museum containing rare and precious artefacts. So, Baradin's fascination for, and interest in Buddhism lay in its scholastic and artistic traits, and the monastic

habitat where the living experiences of the monks are especially significant. He describes the monasteries as communities where various ethnic groups come and live together. The language in each monastery is different too, i.e. there is a mix of diverse Mongolian and Tibetan dialects. To Baradin, Tibetan monasteries were idyllic cosmopolitan centres. They were convergence-centres of people belonging to different nationalities. There is a basic continuity of the monastic tradition in the Asiatic landscape beyond the Himalayas, he argues. He considers that the monks have been exemplars of energy and endurance over generations. This (the ideological and cultural rendezvous, and the life-work of religious worshippers) forms a basic tradition which contextually transcends cultures. He was fascinated by the multicultural notion of Buddhism, which may form a reference point for other kinds of links (ideological, religious, cultural, and historical) between various Asian countries and regions. To Baradin, Tibetan Buddhism represents an *Asian tradition* that has its own specificities. Baradin recreated the Eurasian imaginary originating from one single cosmos. He was the field worker with qualities of 'selective participant observation' while Tsybikov was the critical observer and intruder who reported on the internal conditions of Tibet to the Russian government. What is striking, however, is a specific form of internally-differentiated, complex Asianism articulated by these intellectuals. There was a blend of pan-Mongolism and pan-Buddhism in Buryat intellectualism with nerve-centres in Mongolia and Tibet.

SECRET DIPLOMACY

A different trajectory is the story of secret diplomacy that revolves round the secret missions in Tibet. The widest coverage relates to Agvan Dorjiev, the thirteenth Dalai Lama's Buryat emissary to Tibet, who is rumoured to be actively involved in a parallel diplomatic engagement, i.e. Russian military preparations in Tibet. The interplay of local factors with imperial motivations is not a new subject of study. The refreshing novelty relates to the Buryat connection, and the intriguing regional politics of Inner Asia centring Tibet. What has also assumed focus is the wide gamut of trans-national networks based on the lamas' contacts. Nikolai Kuleshov gives an account of the lamas' political influence in the region.

Kuleshov's central character is Dorjiev (1854-1938) who received his training in philosophy and was selected by high-ranking Buddhists for further training in Mongolia and Lhasa.[21] In 1880, at the age of

26, Dorjiev landed in Lhasa and earned the respect of his seniors. He became the philosophy teacher of the thirteenth Dalai Lama, Thubten Gyatso and dedicated himself to the protection of his student. The Russian government acknowledged Buryatia's autonomy claims, especially in religious affairs. The Buryats' engagement in all Russian affairs was evident. The lama's influence and role in Inner Asian affairs cannot be denied especially because of the existence of scholar-networks in the monasteries of Buryatia, Kalmykia and Mongolia. On the whole, there could have been a linkage of interests that actually brought Dorjiev into the limelight. Dorjiev's role has been conventionally assessed from this viewpoint of regional awakening. But Dorjiev was not only close to the Russian government, but also had a special standing in the Tibetan court. This made him a central figure in Inner Asia's Buddhist world. He represented a distinct case of the scholar lamas' engagement in regional geopolitics.

In the entire spectrum of opposing political ideologies that emerged in Buryatia during the Civil War period, Buddhism expressed itself as an ethical variant. For example, the aim of a 'pure land' of Lubsan Sandan Tsydenov was to establish a Buddhist *sangha* in Buryatia outside the established monastic communities of Sera, Drepung or Gomang in Lhasa. The interest in Buddhist destiny leads to introspection about the 'social order' that emerged almost on a global scale in the post-First World War period. Ideas of regeneration and reincarnation became popular in France, Poland and Estonia, as in Buryatia.

Tsydenov's project has aroused great enthusiasm in academic circles that are keen to explore the ruptures rather than highlight Dorjiev's game plan of idealizing a monolithic Buddhist community belonging to the Dalai Lama tradition in Russia. In an attempt to resurrect the nationalist groups of Buryatia, scholars have not only dealt with the story of Stalinist repression of the *datsans* in the 1920s (that erased Gusino Ozero from public memory), but have also analysed the nature of resilience among these marginalized or under-represented confessional groups in the erstwhile Buryat Autonomous Republic and the present-day Republic of Buryatia.[22] The lamaist ideology, the deliberations in the Buryat-Mongol bureau of the Russian Communist Party (Bolshevik) during the 1920s, and the idealization of a theocratic state by Buryatia's Buddhist intellectuals, reflect a repertoire of regional sentiments and the foundations of alternative thought about Buryatia's future that have found a new status in the contemporary revivalist discourse in Buryatia.

CONCLUSION

In contemporary Buryatia, parallel discourses question colonial trajectories and socialist hypotheses about territoriality, ethnicity, religion and history. The new perspectives have dealt with Buryat activism in the pre-1917 period as a special category. The philosophy and role of the lama scholars unravel a lesser known aspect of Buryatia, that of a reformist milieu which is juxtaposed to the monolithic sacred space centred in Tibet. This perspective questions the notional allegiance to Tibetan Buddhism. The ruptures indicate that the concept of Buddhist allegiance was not static but in constant flux, and impacted upon local and regional cultures of trans-Asiatic Himalayan region, uniting the Tibetan, Indic, Chinese, Mongolian and Buryat spiritual worlds.

Anya Bernstein's critique of a universal Buddhist model may be juxtaposed to this notional concept of Buddhism as a uniting force.[23] According to Bernstein, the Buryats adhered to a different model—that which downplayed internationalist Tibetan Buddhist ties and asserted itself as an independent Buddhist model.

There also seem to be different opinions about Buryat intellectualism. On the one hand, the idea of Buryat nationalism as an alternative to the Soviet model gained ground.[24] Speaking of a later phase of their ideological orientation and activism, Pavel Vernavskii pointed out the differences between the 'old school' of Buryat Bolsheviks and the 'new school' of Buryat nationalists, indicating two different versions of the nationalist project in Buryatia.[25] There are indications of dissenting voices among Buryat intellectuals. Dina Amongolova argues that despite the preponderance of a modernization programme in Buryatia during the 1920s, there were several issue-based debates among Buryat intellectuals. Debates centred round autonomy as a model in Eastern Siberia, and the roles played by the Buryats, Mongolians and the Tibetans became a contested terrain during the Civil War period.[26] Such varying positions lead us to ponder about the diverse images of Buryatness—whether it means their historical preferences for a pan-Mongol space, or a rejuvenated Buryat ethnic feeling, or Buryat nostalgia about a national culture that was suppressed in the 1930s, or mixed sentiments of a post-Soviet generation that are evident in responses towards social adaptation. New perspectives about colonial and post-colonial settings have also added an extra dimension to Buryatness.

NOTES

1. D.D. Amongolova, E. Ye. Elaeva, T.D. Skrynnikova (eds.), *Buryatskaia ethnichnost' v kontekste sotsiokulturnoi modernizatsii*, Irkutsk: Radian, 2005.
2. Discussed in Olaf Leisse and Utta Kristin Leisse, 'A Siberian Challenge: Dealing with Multi-ethnicity in the Republic of Buryatia', *Nationalities Papers*, vol. 35, no. 4, September 2007.
3. Scholars have referred to the language and ethnicity links in Buryatia. Buryat as minority language is preserved in combination with Russian making many Buryats bilingual persons with dual identities, a feature which is very typical of a multi-ethnic state like Russia. The Buryat language has a more symbolic, unifying value, and even if it is not strictly used in the official sense, that does not affect ethnic identity. The Buryat case demonstrates that survival is possible by preserving one's own ethnic identity, i.e. the Buryat-Mongol identity. See Erjen Khilkhanova and Dorji Khilkhanov, 'The Changing Dynamics of Language and Ethnic Identity Link by Russian Minorities: The Buryat Case Study', *Journal of Eurasian Research,* vol. 2, no. 1, Winter 2003.
4. Eleanor Peers, 'Representations of the Buryat in Political and Popular Newspaper Discourse: The Sanctification of Buryat Culture', *Inner Asia*, vol. 11, no. 1, 2009.
5. Balzhan Zhimbiev, *History of the Urbanization of a Siberian City: Ulan Ude*, Cambridge: The White Horse Press, 2000.
6. Interaction with Olga Buraeva, Institute of Mongolian, Buddhist and Tibetan Studies, Ulan Ude, July 2010.
7. Marina Baldano, 'Istoriya svozdaniya svobodnovo varianta eposa "Geser" v kontekste proekta natsieststrotel'stvo', in Anita Sengupta and Suchandana Chatterjee (eds.), *Eurasian Perspectives-in Search of Alternatives,* Delhi: Shipra Publishers, 2010. Also see Marina Baldano, 'The National Regimes of Russia in Search of their Indigenous History', in *Writing History in Eurasia: The Soviet State and After*, Kolkata: Towards Freedom, 2010.
8. *Etnokulturnoe I folklornoe nasledie Mongolskikh narodov v kontekste istorii I sovremennosti*, Ulan Ude: Institute Mongolovedeniya, Buddologii I Tibetologii SO RAN, Buryat National Centre, 2008. Reiterated in 'Narratives of Social Change in Rural Buryatia, Russia' thesis of Luis Ortis Echevarria, Department of Anthropology, Georgia State University, 2010.
9. See 'Conclusion' of L.L. Abaeva and B.V. Bazarov in L.L. Abaeva and H.L. Zhukovskaia (eds.), *Buryaty*, Moscow: Nauka, 2004, p. 588.
10. During the thirteenth to the seventeenth century, the Baikal region became the contact zone between Siberian taiga people and the steppe people of Central Asia, where complex interactions between different tribes took place. So, the Baikal region was simultaneously co-habited by the Turkic, Mongol and Tungus tribes. The expansion of Mongol rule resulted in the assimilation of Buryat tribes who along with the Barga, were tribute-paying tribes who moved out from Barguzin valley and fled back to Aga and Nerchinsk, and finally settled down on both sides of Lake Baikal, that became separated from Mongolia in the seventeenth century. From the thirteenth to the seventeenth century, the Buryats' assimilation by Chingiz Khan's son Jochi became the deciding factor in the region's history. The pre-eminence of a supra-ethnic Mongol stock was fairly established. The Turkic tribal groups were either

pushed back from the Baikal region (the Tofalars and the Yakuts for instance) towards the upper reaches of the Oka River and the Lena basin, or were assimilated by the Buryats and other western Mongol groups (Ekenats, Segenuts, Dzhungars). There are therefore manifestations of internal displacement as some of the Turkic subgroups residing in the Uigur Kaganate from the eighth to the twelfth century, were displaced from the Baikal region by the Mongol tribes like the Buryats.

11. Tatyana Skrynnikova and Darima Amogolonova, 'Discourse on Ethnicity in Post-Soviet Buryatia', *Central Eurasian Studies Review,* vol. 5, no. 2, Summer 2006.
12. Comment by Matthew Derrick, 'The Merging of Russia's Regions as Applied Nationality Policy: A Suggested Rationale', *Caucasian Review of International Affairs,* vol. 3, no. 3, Summer 2009.
13. A series of writings indicate the tone of dissent. Andrey Makarychev, 'New Challenges to Russian Federalism'. [http://ceres.geogetown.edu/esp/ponarsmemos/page/78412.html]; Gary N. Wilson, 'Abandoning the Nest: Regional Mergers and their Impact on the Russian North', *Polar Geography,* vol. 27, no. 3, 2003; Fatma Asli Kelkitli, 'Russian Foreign Policy in South Caucasus under Putin', *Perceptions,* Winter 2008.
14. Pavel Vernavsky, 'Etnichnost' I individual'nye strategii osvoeniya obrazovatel'novo prostranstvo (na primere respubliki Buryatii), in www.innerasia.ru.
15. Young Buryat girls commonly use the Russian name *Sveta,* apparently to help them connect themselves to the Russian-speaking milieu in Ulan Ude. See Anna Yuerevna Buyanova, 'The Adaptation of Young Rural Buryats to Ulan Ude's Urban and Educational Space', *Inner Asia,* vol. 11, no. 1, 2009.
16. Dina A. Amanzholova, 'The Movement for Siberian Regional and National Autonomy in the Early 1920s', *Sibirica,* vol. 3, no. 1, 2003.
17. Details in *Ocherki Buryat-Mongolskovo Naroda,* Ulan Ude: Izdatel'stvo Buryatskovo Gosuniversiteta, 2008.
18. G.Ts. Tsybikov, 'Buddist palomnik u sviatyn' Tibeta', in *Izbrannye Trudy v dvukh tomakh, Tom I,* Novosibirsk: Nauka, Sibirskoe Otdelenie, 1991.
19. The espionage missions of interventionists like Ekai Kawaguchi and Sarat Chandra Das may be mentioned here.
20. Tsybikoff, 'Journey to Lhasa', *The Geographical Journal,* vol. 23, no. 1, January 1904.
21. Nikolai S. Kuleshov, 'Agvan Dorjiev: The Dalai Lama's Ambassador', *Asian Affairs,* vol. 23, no. 1, 1992; Nikolai S. Kuleshov, *Russia's Tibet File: The Unknown Pages in the History of Tibet's Independence,* Delhi: Library of Tibetan Works and Archives, 1996.
22. L.V. Kuras, I.S. Tsyrempilova, 'Religioznye konfessi v Buryat-Mongolskoi ASSR v 20-30 gody XX veka', in *Konfessii Narodov Sibiri v nachale XVII-nachale XX veka (Materialy vseRossiskoiNauchnoi Konferentsii, 3-4 Fevralya 2005),* Irkutsk: Anons, 2005.
23. Anya Bernstein, 'Pilgrims, Fieldworkers and Secret Agents-Buryat Buddhologists and the Eurasian Imaginary', www.princeton.edu/ ~ restudy/soyuz_papers/Bernstein.pdf. Republished as 'Pilgrims, Fieldworkers and Secret Agents-Buryat Buddhologists and the history of a Eurasian Imaginary', in *Inner Asia,* vol. 1, no. 1, 2009.

24. The advocates of cultural self-determination belonged to the Mongol ethnic stock, spoke Russian fluently, had excellent education in the University of St. Petersburg where they cooperated with Russian orientalists and also travelled extensively in Siberia, Central Asia, European Russia and Western Europe. Their influence extended beyond the borders of their homeland to Outer Mongolia and Tibet, and to smaller areas of Manchuria and Uriankhai territory. These intellectuals interacted regularly as they travelled between St. Petersburg and the Baikal region and communicated with each other on aspects related to Tibetan and Lamaist studies. Robert Rupen emphasizes the activities of the indigenous leadership in Buryatia and the 'progressive' view of an earlier generation of Buryat intellectuals. See Robert Rupen, 'The Buryat Intelligentsia', *The Far Eastern Quarterly*, vol. 15, no. 3, May 1956.
25. Pavel Vernavskii, 'Granitsy sovetskoi buryatskoi natsii-"natsional'no-kuturnoe strotel'stvo" v Buryatii v 1926-1929 gody v proektakh natsional'noi intelligentsii I natsional-bolshevikov', *Ab Imperio*, vol. 1, 2003.
26. Dina A. Amanzhalova, 'The Movement for Siberian Regional and National Autonomy in the Early 1920s', *Sibirica,* vol. 3, no. 1, April 2003.

10

Modernity and Denial: The Case of the Kurds in Turkey

ANITA SENGUPTA

In recent times, with its policies of a 'democratic opening', the Justice and Development Party (*Adalet ve Kalkinma Partisi*, AKP), government in Turkey, has embarked upon an enterprise that will attempt a rethinking on a number of issues, including the dilemma of establishing a secure foundation for the state in a setting of societal heterogeneity and particularly the state's policy towards the Kurds or the *Kurt Sorunu*. This is part of the broader rethinking on the Kemalist modernity project which was oriented towards a particular vision of a 'modern' Turkish state which had attempted the transformation of a multicultural multilingual society into a nation 'happy to call itself Turkish'.[1] The aim of 'Turkish' modernity was to create a Turkey that conformed to the principles of 'advanced civilization' where attachment to 'traditional' issues like religiosity and ethnicity were perceived as irrational.[2] The Kemalists wanted to see Turkey transformed into a modern nation state which, in the words of Kemal would 'live as an advanced and civilized nation in the midst of contemporary civilization'.[3] Such a nation would have to be secular and rational, emphasizing science and modern education in order to create a modern industrial economy. Kemalism ascribed to the classical tenets of modernity which is generally conceptualized as a process where reason is the driving force of progress or in the words of Habermas, a process which sought 'a rational reorganization of everyday social life'.[4] The attempt was to transcend the monarchical and imperial structures of the Ottoman society and replace them with rational bureaucratic institutions under the rule of law within a nation state. However, it has been argued, the insistence on modernization proved to be an ideological handicap both from a conceptual as well as a pragmatic point of view.[5]

It is now argued that the republican project of building a 'nation state' and making a 'new nation' out of the remains of the Ottoman Empire was an example of top-down modernization. These were not carried out in a 'democratic' regime but by a single party government through 'revolutionary' means. Democracy, with its elementary mechanisms and institutions, began in 1950, which is described by many Kemalists as the era of 'counter revolution'. Such post-Kemalist criticisms of Turkey's modernization process are not uncommon.[6] Since the 1990s post-modern critiques of Kemalist modernity have been particularly visible in Turkish politics, it has been argued that one way to explain the ideological problems confronted by the People's Republican Party (*Cumhuriyet Halk Partisi*, CHP) created by Kemal and by the centre-left as a whole can be explained in terms of a crisis of Turkish modernity or Turkey's modernization project.[7] The centre-left continuously re-emphasized classical Kemalist modernity and took a dismissive and hostile approach to alternative conceptions of modernity. This was highlighted in their reflections on Islam and the Kurdish question. Of course, part of the problem lay with the notion of modernity itself and the idea that there are certain goals and values that could be considered 'universal'. And part of it was because 'modernity' in the Kemalist lexicon meant an erasure of the Ottoman past and all its features in the course of installation of a secular 'modern' state. Subsequently, societal complexities have questioned the unilinear path to modernity and in the Turkish context, since the 1990s a plethora of movements have provided alternatives or even rejected the validity of the Kemalist modernization project. Such criticism has been both at the state-structural level as well as the level of the individual. At the state-structural level a group of intellectuals referred to as the 'Second Republicans' are in agreement that Kemalist modernization measures are obsolete, based on the view that the structures and institutions of Kemalist Turkey are alien to Turkish culture.

On the other hand, there have also been debates on whether the Kurdish people could have been included within the new stage of Turkish modernization by addressing Kurdish claims in ethnic-cultural, national, political and socio-economic areas without undermining social harmony and territorial integrity.[8] Andrew Mango argues strongly against the opinion that it was the Kemalist failure to accommodate Kurdish nationalism that led to the alienation and subsequent dissident movements among the Kurds.[9] He argues that Kurdish nationalism could not have been accommodated without endangering law and order and the construction of the modern

state. Kurdish nationalism first appeared among malcontents among the feudal leadership of the fragmented Kurdish tribal society. It was inseparable from the threat to law and order that the tribes had always posed. The Kemalists sought to solve it by co-opting part of the feudal leadership in order to isolate the malcontents and by modern development of the area. Mango goes on to argue that the Kemalists are also accused of exacerbating the Kurdish problem by disestablishing Islam and then by using force to subdue Kurdish disaffection. But, he argues, the disestablishment of Islam was a precondition to the country's modernization process, irrespective of its effects on the Kurdish society. In any case, there is broad agreement on the fact that the Kurdish question is closely connected to the Turkish question, to the question of how a more inclusive formulation of 'Turkishness' can be adopted. The Turkish perception of social-political diversity is still affected by the so-called 'Sevres syndrome', which refers to the dominant ways in which Turks interpret how they lost their Empire and came to the brink of colonization in the early twentieth century. These interpretations attribute the Ottoman meltdown to the unbridled spiralling of hostile minority nationalisms that foreign powers fostered and liberal Ottoman-Turkish elites endorsed. This has inculcated scepticism towards minority movements.

While taking note of the plethora of debates on the viability of the Kemalist project, this article will focus on how the transformation of the traditional Ottoman cosmopolitan ethos in the course of a project of creating a 'modern' Turkey leads to denial of diversity within the state and subsequent attempts at neutralizing heterogeneity through an examination of the 'Kurdish question'. It will also examine a critical rethinking of this project of modernity in recent times. This rethinking has sought to come to terms with the cultural plurality of a society that had traditionally imbibed within itself varied groups with multiple religious and ethnic identities. Sponsored by a government whose own 'Islamic' background remains an anathema to the Kemalists it has brought to the forefront, policies of assimilation that fell short of transforming a majority of Kurds into 'Turks'. It has been suggested that just as the first modernizers of the Ottoman Empire, the *Tanzimat* reformers, attempted to forestall the collapse of the state by incorporating Christian minorities as equal citizens, the AKP government is planning an 'opening' that seeks to bring to an end the Kurdish question by setting the stage for the assertion of societal autonomy.[10] It has been noted that the conflict between the 'old Turkey' represented by the Kemalist establishment and the 'new

Turkey' represented by civil society has to be resolved through the establishment of a more inclusive social contract that addresses the cultural diversity of Turkish society. Here, it has been argued, that a neo-Ottoman ethos would be more pluralistic and cosmopolitan. It is undeniable that compared to the Ottoman system, Kemalism was essentially exclusivist and attempted to create a uniform Turkish citizen, which resulted in the denial of Turkey's 'true' cosmopolitan identity.

This article is an attempt to deal with how 'modernity', and in this specific case, the establishment of a 'modern' nation state does not entail solutions for 'traditional' elements like ethnicity within society, elements that had in fact been neutralized by inclusion within more 'traditional' systems. In fact, it was the creation of a 'Turkish' identity and the non-recognition or 'denial' of the existence of other communities/identities along with a denial of the 'pre-modern'/Ottoman past of Turkey that leads to the creation of the 'other' within society. It is interesting that this 'other', which in this case is the Kurdish population of Turkey, also imbibes within itself various cleavages. It is not uncommon to come across a Kurd who considers himself to be a member of a particular tribe, holds Kurdish ethnic identity, but also feels himsef to be a Turkish citizen. In certain instances there are also elements of this 'other' who sympathize with the majority cause and in fact the ideologue of the new Republic, Ziya Gokalp, had eastern Anatolian origins. In a way this is inevitable and in many ways a universal process. However, in the Turkish case, there are certain peculiarities. Given the process of the emergence of the state it was the intensity of focus on secularism as well as non-recognition or denial of the existence of groups other than the 'Turk' that becomes significant. Here one would have to keep in mind not just the complex mosaic of people who constituted the new state but also the fact that a pan-Turkic thinking was also in existence at this time influenced by men who were more often than not from outside the boundaries of Anatolia. It is also important that the debate on identity is as vibrant today as it was in the 1920s and 1930s. The article does not focus on the radicalization of the Kurdish problem but its continuing existence over the years as Republican Turkey attempts to come to terms with its multi-cultural and multi-ethnic heritage. It also does not take into account the plethora of opinions within the Kurdish society relating to assimilation. This article therefore begins with an examination of the multi-cultural ethos of Ottoman society and how it was transformed in the years immediately after the establishment of the Republic.

TRANSFORMING A MULTI-CULTURAL SOCIETY

The imperial Ottoman system had been open to outsiders and had refashioned multilinguistic and multi-religious populations into Ottomanist provincial societies during the last centuries of the Ottoman Empire. Under the Ottoman Empire, nationalities were defined in terms of religious affiliation rather than ethnicity. Diverse peoples of Turkic, Lazi, Kurdish, Greek and Armenian backgrounds came to form an entirely new kind of society as they participated in Ottoman military and religious institutions. It was only in the late nineteenth and early twentieth centuries when the non-Muslims as well as non-Turkish Muslims began clamouring for independence and the Ottoman Empire became a hotbed of nationalist uprisings, that the notion of Turkishness assumed political relevance. It is now argued that in actuality the transformation of various groups who constituted the Ottoman world into ethno-national communities developed through different stages of development among the Turkic groups themselves and finally culminated in the emergence of 'Turkishness' and Turkism in the Ottoman Empire.

Although the founders of the Ottoman Empire had consisted of tribal groups, merchant craftsmen, and Sufis, mostly Turkish in origin, the state did display conscious awareness of its ethnicity. Eventually the Empire also included several major ethnic communities. Among them, including the Greeks, Serbians, Bulgarians, and Arabs, collective myths of common ancestry, historical memories of statehood, elements of common culture, an idea of a specific homeland and a sense of group solidarity developed. The Turkic groups of Kazan, Crimea and Azerbaijan likewise constituted ethnic communities not very different from those of the non-Turks in the Ottoman Empire. The Muslims of Russia, consequently played an important role in defining the developing ethno-national identity and nationalist ideology of the Ottoman Turks, just as they, in turn were profoundly influenced by the modernization movement and the education system of the Ottoman Empire. The impact of pan-Islamism and pan-Turkism of Russia's Turkic peoples and vice versa is therefore significant. In fact, Kemal Karpat argues that the concept of some sort of Muslim union emerged mainly as a reaction to Russia's occupation of Central Asia.[11] The genesis of Turkish nationalism was thus a multifaceted process occurring in several stages.

Attempts at modernization, in fact, has had a long tradition in the region. Throughout the nineteenth century the Ottoman society had made various attempts at modernization. The foundations of

the *Tanzimat* reform period (1839-76) had been laid by Sultans Abdulmejid I (1839-61) and Abdulaziz (1861-76) in response to Western pressure.[12] Since the *Gulhane Imperial Edict* of 1839, important changes had been carried out within the military organization, state administration and law and education systems.[13] Despite the fact that the traditional sultanate remained intact at the beginning of the twentieth century, important steps had been taken in the direction of forming a modern centralized state. This structure, on which the Turkish nationalists built the modern republic during the 1920s, was very different from the one prevalent at the beginning of the reform period. Modernizing reforms also meant that the Ottoman society drew closer to the West. Another effect was that the role played by religion in different fields of social and political life was reduced. The growing Western influence and the process of secularization were issues of fundamental concern. Moreover, as the Ottomans were repeatedly losing territory to peoples' struggling for national independence (the Greeks, Serbs, the Bulgarians, etc.), the question of a political identity of the Turkish-speaking Muslim Ottomans also had to be answered. All these problems were often discussed in terms of civilization. The questions that were raised were related to which civilization the Turks belonged, and to which civilization they wanted to belong to in the future. Islam had left its mark. However, there were questions about its future prospects. The division of the Islamic world presented a crisis, and the question was whether any reunification or revitalization of its powers would be possible in the future. The Islamic world was also confronted with the Western world with its capacity for rapid modernization that was more dynamic in terms of economic development, military technology and scientific achievements.

During the Ottoman centuries, majority of the Kurds lived in south-eastern Anatolia and Mesopotamia, and were part of the Sunni majority of a cosmopolitan Muslim empire. The Ottoman Sultans pragmatically recognized that the mountainous geography of the region coupled with the deep rooted tribal authority of Kurdish emirates would present major obstacles for the establishment of direct rule from Istanbul. Also, imposing central taxation and imperial conscription on these lands bordering the Persian territories ran the risk of losing the support of Kurdish emirates that could then forge an alliance with the Safavid dynasty. Geography and strategic considerations therefore restrained the Ottoman coercion of the Kurdish provinces. The Kurdish provinces therefore enjoyed a status of semi-autonomy until the early decades of the nineteenth century.

During the decades of Ottoman decline, Kurdish nationalism did not present a major threat. Not just the deep rooted tribal rivalries of Kurdish society but also the partition of Kurdish provinces between Safavid and Ottoman empires have been identified as reasons as to why the sense of Kurdish unity and national identity developed much later than Turkish, Persian or Arab nationalism. Beyond tribal identities and imperial manipulations, the Kurds also remained divided along sectarian and linguistic lines.[14]

From about the mid-nineteenth century, faced with challenges to its authority from various quarters, the Ottoman state attempted reassertion of control and started the elimination of the Kurdish emirs who were increasingly being perceived as subversive. The region witnessed an unprecedented military confrontation which gained further momentum after the declaration of the Tanzimat centralist reforms in 1838. By 1850 Ottoman forces had managed to eradicate most of the Kurdish emirates. The eradication of the emirates in the 1850s destroyed the dominant administrative organization in Ottoman Kurdistan. With their ability to mediate between tribes, the emirs constituted the critical organizational bonds that loosely united the Kurdish tribes into confederations. In their absence, regional governors appointed by the Ottoman central authority proved unable to restore law and order in the Kurdish provinces. In this situation, Naqshbandi and Kadiri *sheikhs,* as the only figures whose influence exceeded the limits of the tribes, expanded their networks and gradually assumed greater political influence in the region. The political ascendancy of the *sheikhs* in Ottoman Kurdistan coincided with the pan Islamist reign of Sultan Abdulhamid II (1876-1908) and this played a crucial role in the reconciliation of Ottoman and Kurdish interests. It also gave the Sultan an opportunity to channellize Kurdish belligerence against Armenian agitators and Christian missionaries operating in eastern Anatolia. As part of his pan-Islamist project, Abdulhamid also inculcated certain Kurdish and political leaders within the Ottoman system. In 1890 he also created the *Hamidiye* regiments, a Kurdish cavalry force modelled after the Russian Cossack troops.

In Istanbul the Abdulhamid years were characterized by suppression of political opposition and censorship of the press. It was in this political atmosphere that a Kurdish intelligentsia emerged, composed mostly of sons of exiled Kurdish emirs. Like the nationalist literati of the other Ottoman ethnic groups, they were also involved in journalism and politics and launched clandestine political organizations. For instance in 1898 Mithat Bedir Khan began publishing

the first Kurdish language journal, *Kurdistan.*[15] Yet there were also a substantial number of assimilated Kurdish students who refused to adopt ethnic Kurdish nationalism as a political ideology. Instead they joined constitutional opposition movements that operated as secret societies within the military and political academies of Istanbul. For instance, Abdullah Cevdet and Ishak Sukurti were both born in Kurdish provinces and educated in the Military Medical School in Istanbul and became founder members of the Committee of Union and Progress. Another student of eastern Anatolian origin who was to become the most influential ideologue of the Unionist movement was Ziya Gokalp. In fact, some of the most important ideologues of the Unionist movement were of Kurdish origin, and sympathetic to the successful assimilation of the educated Kurds within the Ottoman intelligentsia.

In Turkey the *Tanzimat* reforms were combined with the ideas of Ziya Gokalp in the perception of what the modern state would be like. As a member of the Committee of Union and Progress, Gokalp had a significant influence on the development of Kemalist mindset. It has been argued that this was particularly true of his conceptualization of how society should be organized.[16] Gokalp saw *Tanzimat* reformist ideas as the acceptance and domination of the Empire by Western norms, ignoring native culture, which he believed was the binding element of a healthy and ethical society. On the other hand, he argued that all ideals and aspirations, personal or societal, should be subservient to the well-being and interest of the Turkish state, which was culturally defined in terms of commonalities of language, feelings, aspirations and education, steering clear of any notion of ethnic and geographical identities. Having perceived common culture as the essence of 'Turkishness', Gokalp believed that all interests in society should unite to achieve this. Religion was seen as an important element, as an aid to societal solidarity.

In fact, the question of the changing role of Islam in a world challenged by modernization and secularization had been on the agenda of Ottoman intellectuals ever since the middle of the nineteenth century. The Young Ottoman Society founded by intellectuals and professionals in Istanbul in 1865, was indicative of such activities. However, due to the authoritarian character of the Ottoman regime, open debate remained limited. The period leading up to the First Constitutional Period (1876-8) signified a short-lived exception. The Second Constitutional Period, following the Young Turk Revolution in 1908, was more promising. To begin with, the leaders of the

Committee of Union and Progress, had no objection to criticism as long as it was not directed against their own immediate actions and policies. This period therefore represented an unprecedented upsurge of open public debate. However, due to internal conflicts, the 1908 revolution could not live up to the heightened public expectation. The liberal faction of the Young Turks was sidelined and there emerged a proclivity for nationalist authoritarianism in the wake of the Bulgarian declaration of independence and the Austrian annexation of Bosnia Herzegovina. There was increasing realization that without a strong centrist state the Ottoman empire would disintegrate. Therefore all nationalist organizations, including Kurdish ones, were shut down and had to go underground. Repeated attacks against the new regime forced the Committee of Union and Progress to move away from power for a short period in 1912. By staging a coup in 1913, they retrieved political control. Thereafter the Committee, under the leadership of Enver, Talat and Cemal held on to power till they escaped to Odessa after the Mudros armistice in 1918.[17]

Starting from the early 1920s when the Turkish state emerged as the Ottoman empire's successor, the men who had led the military campaign against the Greeks were concerned with the creation of a state based on a different set of principles. Believing that they had 'to create a modern, therefore western state in Turkey', Kemal and his followers, mainly former military officers, were eager to announce to the people and the world community that the old system of arbitrary relations between the ruling elite (*askeri*) and the *rea'ya*, the tax paying subjects of the empire who were excluded from politics, would be abolished. In its place, the Western idea of citizenship would be firmly established as the new principle responsible for regulating the relationship between the elected, constitutionally limited rulers and 'the people'.[18] Kemal Karpat, however, argues that the evolution of events revealed that the transformation of the *rea'ya* into the people as sovereign was not the highest priority of the reformers.[19] Aware of Turkey's weak military and financial condition and the limited appeal of its pro-Western ideas to the uneducated rural and religion-oriented population, they concentrated their attention on the construction and function of the country's political institutions. A 'socialist democracy' was proposed which would be supportive of individual and associational pluralism, guaranteeing full expressional rights. The adoption of *halkcilik* or populism was a reflection of Gokalpian influence. With this in mind, six principles or guidelines

were put in place; republicanism (*cumhuriyetcilik*), secularism (*laiklik*), nationalism (*milliyetcilik*), populism (*halkcilik*), statism (*devletcilik*), and revolutionary-reformism (*inkilapcilik*). These guidelines were incorporated into the programme of the Republican Peoples' Party (CHP) in 1931 and its constitution in 1937. It is in this background of transformation of a multi-cultural society that the Kurdish question will be examined.

THE 'KURDISH' QUESTION IN REPUBLICAN TURKEY

The world's 35 million Kurds are often described as the biggest ethnic group without a state. Since the Allies dropped their pledge of a Kurdish state made after the World War I the Kurds have been divided among four countries, Turkey, Syria, Iran and Iraq.[20] At the heart of Turkey's Kurdish issue is the question of the identity of the nation. Ataturk noted 'The people of Turkey that has founded the Turkish Republic is called the Turkish nation.' Accordingly, the Turkish Constitution states that everyone tied by citizenship to the Turkish state is a Turk. Defenders of the Kemalist model note that this was not supposed to carry any ethnic connotations and a Turk so defined could be Kurdish, Bosnian, Albanian, Circassian or of any other nationality. From the onset the Ataturk also made it clear that he was seeking statehood for the multicultural entity of Anatolia, heir to the Ottoman state, and he did not emphasize ethnic Turkishness as the basis of the new nation.[21] In fact, the Ataturk clearly stated that autonomy would be granted in provinces inhabited by the Kurds. His stance helped him gain the support of the Kurds and other minority groups in Anatolia. Despite the fact that the Treaty of Sevres offered the Kurds the prospect of establishing a homeland and gaining self-rule, most of the Kurdish tribes and notables sided with the new Turkish government created in Ankara in 1920. This multicultural sense of solidarity fuelled the national liberation movement and carried it to victory. The founders of the Republic, well aware of the multicultural nature of their society, chose to call their new state the Republic of Turkey, referring to the geographical region in which all the peoples of Turkey lived rather than to name it after the dominant ethnic group. The same political consciousness was reflected in their choice of a name for the state's highest decision-making organ, the Grand National Assembly of Turkey. However, the Treaty of Lausanne also ensured that the status and rights of Turkey's minorities came to be based on religion rather than ethnicity. Therefore along the lines

of the Ottoman *millet* system, the new Turkish Republic did not recognize any of the Muslim ethnic groups as constituting a minority. As a result only the Jewish, Armenian, and Greek communities came to be considered as official minorities.

The pluralist ethos of the Ottoman past was repudiated in the nationalist drive for homogeneity. In fact, from 1923 onwards, the state refused to acknowledge the existence of the Kurds and until the 1990s they were known as 'Mountain Turks'. There were several reasons for this. First, sizeable Ottoman minorities had been removed from the new Republic. Most Armenian populations had been deported to areas outside the Republic after World War I and the Greek population of Anatolia had been exchanged for the Muslim population of Greece. In 1925, when Turkey engaged in a struggle with Britain to regain control over the oil rich regions of what is now northern Iraq, a major Kurdish rebellion erupted in south-eastern Turkey. While to an extent the Turkish view that the Kurds were instigated by the British was true, it was also a fact that the rebellion was a reaction to the encroachment of the new government on the autonomous power of the local Kurdish elite. Since the inclusion of the Kurdish areas in the Ottoman Empire in the fifteenth and sixteenth centuries, Ottoman sultans had granted considerable autonomy to the Kurdish local leaders in return for their allegiance to the state. With the ruling elite establishing principles of governance that were secular, Western, progressive, and centralist, and Kurdish elites viewing the new Republican regime as a threat to their historical rights and privileges, the potential for conflict emerged. Also unlike the other dispersed Muslim minorities of Anatolia who had come from the Balkans or the Caucasus, the Kurdish communities were indigenous people and felt threatened by the wave of Turkish nationalism. The abolition of the Caliphate in 1924 similarly created a legitimacy crisis for the government in Ankara in the Kurdish provinces, especially among the Naqshbandi *sheikhs*. Therefore while the story of assimilation of the Balkan and Caucasian minorities was voluntary, the Kurdish story of assimilation was one of resistance during the 1920s and 1930s. The Sheik Said rebellion was the most significant of the rebellions during this period. However, like all the other rebellions that occurred in the early years, it lacked cohesiveness. Sheikh Said's supporters mostly came from the Zaza-speaking Sunni tribes who received no support from the neighbouring Alevites or Kurmanji-speaking Sunni communities. The religious dimension of the Kurdish discontent strengthened

Ankara's determination to crush all kinds of Islamic opposition. Soon after the Sheikh Said uprising, the government banned all Sufi brotherhoods, shrines, lodges and schools.

With the declaration of the Republic, the newly-born state took an increasingly modernist and secularist character which was accompanied by a series of social and political reforms. This process included a redefinition of the national identity with an emphasis on territoriality rather than religion. For the founders of the Turkish Republic, the European, and in particular, the French experience of the past century was central to their project. The 1924 Constitution defined a 'Turk' as anyone living within the boundaries of Turkey and attached to Turkey by bonds of citizenship. Legally the state would be indifferent to a citizen's religious or ethnic identity. Yet, from the very beginning it was clear that in practice, matters would evolve differently. The indication of this divergence appeared during the assembly debates on citizenship when a member of the Assembly remarked with striking frankness that the legal definition was fine but the 'real' citizens of Turkey were the Hanafi Muslims who spoke Turkish. Such a definition risked leaving out not only the Kurds, who did not speak any Turkish and belonged to the Shafi branch of Sunni Islam, outside the definition of 'real' citizenship in the new Turkish republic, but also Arabs, and Alevis. The portrayal of Kurds as an ethnic community with the right to self-rule changed in 1924 when a new Constitution replaced the 1921 Constitution. Article 88 of the 1924 Constitution stated: 'The people of Turkey regardless of their religion and race would, in terms of citizenship, be called Turkish.' [22]

As Mesut Yegen notes, a first reading of this text seems to suggest that 'Turkishness' designed by Turkish citizenship is defined in political terms: it refers not only to those who reside on Turkish territory but also those who do not have a Turkish ethnic origin, yet reside on Turkish territory.[23] This has prompted the postulation that Turkish citizenship has nothing to do with real or assumed ethnic descent, and that it is expansionist and inclusive: rather than exclusivist and differentialist. However, Yegen argues that the wording itself indicates that there is a more authentic Turkishness considered by the state which is not based just on citizenship but on ethnic terms. While the 1924 Constitution still recognized the existence of various ethnic groups in Turkey, it also stated that no special rights of any kind would be granted to these communities. This was spelled out in the new Constitution and continues to be a matter of debate even today.

> Our state is a nation state. It is not a multi-national state. The state does not recognize any nation other than the Turks. There are other people who come from different races (ethnic groups) and who should have equal rights within the country. Yet it is not possible to give rights to these people according to their racial (ethnic) status.[24]

In other words by 1924, the Turkish Republic began to perceive the Kurds as an ethnic community with no group rights. In the eyes of the Turkish state, Kurds, just like any other citizen of the Republic, had become Turks. There were no more Kurds or any other ethnic groups as an ethnic political community but simply Turkish citizens. Henceforth, references to the 'peoples of Turkey' were abandoned completely. With the exception of Istanbul's non-Muslim citizens (whose minority rights were guaranteed by the Treaty of Lausanne), all other citizens of Turkey had to adopt a Turkish identity. Bosnians, Albanians, Georgians, Laze, Circassians and other non-Turkish Muslims living in Turkey accepted Turkishness and became assimilated.

By contrast, the Kurds, cut-off from the rest of the country by their remote location in the mountainous south-eastern regions, divided along tribal lines, and economically dependent on local landed elites, remained largely unaffected by the new regime's policies of assimilation and modernization. Kurdish unrest and occasional rebellion throughout the 1930s was dealt with in an authoritarian manner with little regard to the human and consensual dimension of politics. The establishment in Turkey began to perceive Kurdish resistance/Kurdish question not as an ethno-political question but as one of reactionary politics, tribal resistance and regional backwardness. The resisters were not perceived as Kurds, but as *tribes*, *bandits* and *sheikhs*—as embodying all the evils of Turkey's pre-modern past, and therefore as elements that had to be denied existence within the 'modern' secular state. However, Kurds were also perceived as 'prospective' Turks and a series of assimilatory measures were undertaken. These were neither voluntary nor spontaneous. Plans by the Eastern Region Reform Commission included settling Turkish-speaking immigrants into the lands inhabited by the Kurds, prohibition of speaking Kurdish in public, increasing state sponsored education, teaching Turkish to women and ensuring that soldiers recruited from the Kurdish region spent their military service in other regions.[25] Rebellions also resulted in the deportation of Kurdish groups from their ancestral lands in south-eastern Turkey to the western provinces. Later, the hardships associated with subsistence farming also drove the Kurds to the west especially

after the 1950s. In 1965, roughly 65 per cent of Turkey's Kurds lived in the south-east. This number has since diminished substantially. Reliable numbers of Kurds living in Turkey are difficult to estimate particularly since the government is reluctant to count minorities. According to the 1965 national census, the last to reveal the breakdown of the population by mother tongue, Kurdish speakers numbered 2.37 million.[26] However, current estimates note that the Kurds constitute about 18 per cent of the population of Turkey which is approximately 14 million.

The political leadership that emerged after the War of Independence was also radically secularist. Of all the different opinions relating to identification of civilizations, the most radically Western conception became the prevailing one. Part of the reason was the war itself. The victory of the Turkish army was because of those sections of the army that had the best training according to modern standards had succeeded in taking control. The officers trained in military colleges based on the Western model were naturally more inclined to modern and European values than were other groups. Ever since the Balkan Wars, the political power had been in the hands of the military leaders. Mustafa Kemal emerged out of the War of Independence as a very successful commander, and as he belonged to the more radical Westernizers, this partly explains the directions that were carried out in the judicial system, in education, in the script, and in headgear and clothing. While the 1924 Constitution had stated that the 'religion of the Turkish state is Islam' this clause was deleted in an amendment made in 1928. To stress the secular character of the state even more strongly, the principle of secularism was added to the Constitution in 1937.

Similarly, a programme was initiated by the Kemalists for the reformation of religious practices. A commission was set up with instructions to purify, simplify and intellectualize mosque services. A very significant part of this process was language. Turkish was to be the language of all ritual worship. As part of this, traditional religious schools in Kurdish regions, which were instrumental in reproducing Kurdish cultural practices and values, were closed down. In fact, authorities succeeded in making Turkish the language for the call for prayers, thereby enforcing the unpopular inhibition against Arabic until the political liberalization in 1950. In November 1925, all male Turks were compelled to abandon the *fez* and wear in its place a hat with a brim, thereby ending social and religious distinctions which had been obvious from a person's headgear. This was followed by the introduction of a new

calendar. Until 1917 the Turks had used three different methods of dating; the lunar Islamic system which began with year one in AD 622 when Prophet Muhammad migrated from Mecca to Medina; the modified Julian calendar with a thirteen day difference with the Western Gregorian; and the Gregorian calendar which was used for official purposes. In March 1917, the Unionists introduced a modified Gregorian calendar with the traditional years retained. The Kemalists ended the confusion by adopting the Gregorian calendar which went into effect on 1 January 1926.[27] The Islamic way of keeping time with the new day beginning with the evening prayer made way for the international clock. These changes were made to facilitate communication with the outside world, especially regarding business matters. For the same reason, in 1935, Sunday was made the weekly holiday bringing the Turkish working week in line with the West. These standardizations were aimed at further reducing societal plurality.

The Arabic script was replaced by the Latin in the writing of Turkish. The Arabic-Persian letters had come to be seen as unsuitable for writing Turkish and considered to be the cause of the low level of literacy of the Turks. Reformers had considered simplifying the alphabet so as to make Turkish easier to read and write. Enver Pasha who had become Minister of War in 1914, produced an alphabet to increase literacy in the army. But few had considered abolishing the script and replacing it with a new one. By the early 1920s, however, there was a precedent when in 1924, the Soviet government decided to replace Arabic letters with Latin in the Turkic republics. The matter was debated in Turkey, throughout the 1920s. As a trial, Western numerals replaced Arabic numerals in May 1928. On 1 November 1928, the parliament passed a law introducing the new Turkish alphabet which was to be used in all publications from the beginning of New Year. The Constitution prohibited teaching any language other than Turkish as a mother tongue. This prevented Kurdish from being used in education. The Kurdish language which consisted of several dialects, is related to Persian but heavily influenced by Arabic and Turkish as well. The official Turkish view is that Kurdish is not a distinct language but a border dialect. Kurdish was never a literary or administrative language under the Ottoman Empire and was spoken mainly in the countryside. In 1980 the public use of Kurdish dialects such as Kurmanji and Zaza were banned. The Turkification of surnames, the names of villages and the names of local places are other examples of assimilatory strategies. Another favoured method of assimilation was boarding schools. A large

number of boarding schools were established in the Kurdish region with the aim of educating Kurdish boys and girls in an atmosphere free from Kurdish influence. However, it has been argued that while non-Muslim citizens have been subject to discrimination, Kurdish citizens have been subject to assimilation. This according to Yegen was based on the idea that non-Turkish Muslims could be perceived as 'prospective' Turks, an idea that changed in the early 2000s when it was realized that despite the defeat of Kurdish resistance in the 1990s, many Kurdish citizens were not assimilated into Turkish society.[28]

In fact, attempts at assimilation had been under way since the transition to multi-party politics in the post-World War II era, when new patterns of political patronage became important where Kurdish landlords took advantage of the support they could render to political parties in Ankara. Both the CHP and the newly formed Democratic Party (DP) engaged with the local Kurdish landlords. While the CHP instituted steps like the return of the Kurdish nobility who had been deported, it was the DP which proved more successful in co-opting the influential Naqshbandi *sheikhs* who had gone underground since the official ban on Sufi sects in 1925. With the electoral victory of the DP in the 1950 elections, a number of measures for rural development and mechanization of agriculture was undertaken that had a significant impact on the south-eastern Kurdish areas. Large-scale landholdings remained the norm in these areas, and mechanization significantly increased profit margins for the landlords. This led to the migration of surplus labour but also significantly increased the influence of the landlords who exploited rival political parties at the centre. It was during the period of the DP that waves of Kurdish migrants to urban peripheries took place, that led to the emergence of politically active and ethnically conscious Kurdish communities in the 1960s and 1970s. In 1977 the PKK (Kurdish Workers Party or the *Partiya Karkeren Kurdistan*) was formed.

The era of political pluralism and ideological competition that began with the return of democracy in 1961 a year after the military takeover of 1960, led to the emergence of the first socialist party in Turkey, the Turkish Worker's Party (TWP). Many Kurdish intellectuals who shared the socialist tendencies of the party joined the TWP. Many of them shared the belief that the south-eastern region's poverty was the result of feudal structures and economic exploitation. The ideological polarization in the 1960s and 1970s meant that platforms for expressing ideological positions became relevant. Yet, the diminishing significance of Kemalism did not translate into relaxation

of the Kurdish taboo. Journals in the Kurdish language advocating cultural rights remained illegal. These forced ethnically-conscious Kurdish intellectuals, students and workers of the urban centres to join a multiplying number of underground political movements. The increasing political influence of the Kurdish intellectuals within the TWP led to the first recognition of the existence of a Kurdish minority by the party which led to its closure shortly after the March 1971 military ultimatum. This was followed by a wave of repression against ethnic separatism and thousands were arrested in the Kurdish cities of the south-east.

In the 1970s an increasing number of Kurds became dissatisfied with the way that their cause was being handled at the national level by the leftists, and the number of radical Kurdish organizations proliferated. It was not uncommon for the violence that erupted at this time to assume a sectarian character—Sunni *versus* Alevi. While most Kurdish Alevis identified with secular leftist parties, it was not uncommon for the conservative Sunni Kurds to identify with Turkish nationalists and religious conservatives. The military intervention in 1980 followed by the 1982 Constitution strengthened cultural and political suppression in the south-eastern provinces.[29] An important dimension of the military repression was the increasing numbers of Kurdish dissidents who sought asylum in Western Europe.

With the coming to power of Turgut Ozal's Motherland Party (*Anavatan Partisi*) in 1983, and the successful transition to democratic politics, it was assumed that armed dissidence had been crushed in Turkey. However, during the 1980s, the longest period of Kurdish insurrection was launched in Turkey. The increasing amassment of security forces to deal with the problem proved to be counter-productive. A breakthrough in the situation occurred in 1988 when Turkey was faced with the plight of a large Kurdish exodus from Iraq, following chemical attacks on the Iraqi Kurdish town of Halabja. Approximately 100,000 Kurds sought refuge in the Turkey's mountainous border with Iraq. Prime Minister Ozal believed that this provided an opportunity to win the hearts and minds of the disenchanted Kurds in south-eastern Anatolia. He persuaded the military to open the border to the refugees. The 1988 crisis triggered a change in Turkey's conceptualization of the Kurdish problem, and parliamentarians of Kurdish origin challenged the Republican taboo on Kurdish ethnicity. The second Kurdish refugee crisis in 1991 established a working relationship between Ozal and Kurdish leaders of Northern Iraq like Masud Barzani and Jalal Talabani. This was part of Ozal's strategic vision of an enhanced Turkish influence

over northern Iraq. By co-opting Iraqi Kurdish leadership Ozal hoped not only to marginalize the PKK but also to gain the confidence of Turkey's own Kurdish citizens for whom he envisaged cultural rights and a less centralized administrative system. Claiming partial Kurdish ancestry himself, he challenged the hitherto taboo ethnic issue.

In 1991 President Ozal legalized the usage of Kurdish in everyday conversation and folkloric music recordings by rescinding law no. 2932.[30] Usage of Kurdish in media, however, remains restricted, and literature in Kurdish remains under close official scrutiny. However, Ozal's economic and political liberalization processes opened new discursive spaces for a more organized Kurdish movement. The demands of this movement ranged from full democracy for all citizens of Turkey to an independent Kurdish state for the Kurds. The movement manifested itself in three distinct forms. It was first organized as a guerrilla group, the Kurdish Workers Party or the *Partiya Karkeren Kurdistan* (PKK), and a new form of self-consciousness among the Kurds. This new consciousness of Kurdish identity led to the formation of the first Kurdish political party in Turkey, the *Halkin Demokrasi Partisi* (HADEP). Kurdish opposition assumed a third form in new media opportunities such as MED TV, an television station established and run by diaspora Kurds.[31]

With the death of Ozal in April 1993, the reformist wing of the state lost an influential politician who believed that the Kurdish problem could not be resolved without cultural and political openings for the Kurdish community. During Suleiman Demirel's Presidency, the Kurdish question became the domain of the military which continued with Tansu Cillar. As a result, the conflict reached unprecedented heights. The radicalization of Turkey's military campaign against the PKK had important political repercussions. This, along with the closure of the PLP and DEP, destroyed a legitimate political middle ground for moderate Kurdish nationalism and enhanced the legitimacy of the PKK in the eyes of the Kurdish people. Similarly, the Welfare Party's sweeping victory in the south-eastern provinces in 1994 was seen as alarming by the Kemalist establishment. The WP's popularity was linked to the fact that it had a view of the Kurdish problem that was at odds with that of other parties as it assumed an Ottomanist tendency and considered the problem to be a creation of secular Turkish nationalism. The April 1999 elections once again brought to power two parties who tended to reduce the Kurdish problem to terrorism, the Nationalist Action Party, and the Democratic Left Party. Despite the heavy losses of the PKK, the

insecurity of the Kemalist establishment was compounded by the fact that there was growing support for Kurdish nationalism in the south-east.

It has been argued that the solution to this lies in accepting a more liberal platform of multiculturalism. In this connection the 'Document of Mutual Understanding' that resulted from a series of meetings between Turks, Kurds and members of the minority groups in Turkey, in the course of meetings between 1996 and 1999 is important. It emphasized that the Kurds wished for official acknowledgement of their existence as a unique cultural group.[32] They wanted this acknowledgement to extend beyond verbal assurances to include legal warranties having an effect on everyday life, including being counted in censuses and free exercise of their cultural identity. It states clearly that the Kurds do not wish for these rights in order to distance themselves from the state or to divide Turkey. Rather, they wish to preserve their cultural heritage and still live in safety as equal and respected citizens. The alternative that is suggested is for the installation of 'pluralistic nationhood' where reductionist nationalism based on ethnic identity and the religious creed of a majority or a privileged minority is not the norm since this carries within itself seeds of exclusion and segregation. Chief among the demands of the Kurdish nationalists is therefore a redefinition of citizenship in neutral terms with republican citizenship being emphasized instead of the Turkish. The need of the hour is stated in terms of institutionalizing respect for all ethnic and religious values and strengthening democratic institutions which would safeguard cultural diversities and political freedoms.

CONCLUSION

While many scholars ascribe the current politicization of Kurdish identity to the uneven and incomplete modernization of south-eastern Anatolia, it has been argued that the Kemalist conception of statist modernity and a state-led social and cultural transformation was in fact a major cause of the phenomenon.[33] Kurdish intellectuals used the economic and social gap between the western and eastern parts of the country to construct Kurdish ethno-nationalism. Thus excessive state-centric development along with an increase in literacy, led to the rise of Kurdish ethnopolitics. As the Republic moved away from a 'civic' nationalism to an ethnic-based Turkishness, between the 1970s-80s, Kurdish peoples were further alienated. The state's

refusal to recognize Kurdish cultural identity and its political repercussions during the 1980s military coup and its aftermath further reinforced the Kurdish people's impression that the state of Turkey is a state for the Turks not for the Kurds. This perception in turn undermined the legitimacy of the state. The 'other' of the Kemalist modernization project has always been a politicized Islamic identity. The powerful Kurdish representation within the pro-Islamic *National Outlook Movement* which was institutionalized as the *National Salvation Party* (1973-80) and then as the *Welfare Party* (1983-98) brought the state in direct opposition to both its enemies, Kurds and Islamists.

It also has to be kept in mind that the Kurdish question cannot be understood in isolation. The monolithic nature of Turkey's political culture, the military's role in politics, the uneven development of parts of the state and the incomplete integration of the country's Kurdish regions are all part of a complex phenomenon. Part of the 'democratic opening' is also in response to EU requirements. In fact, recognition by the EU of Turkey's candidacy for membership within the EU has made democratization a practical necessity.[34] The 'Kurdish opening' has important foreign policy implications. With US troops scheduled to complete their withdrawal by summer 2010, Turkey is set to indirectly fill in the vacuum in northern Iraq. Developments in Kurdish-controlled northern Iraq will provide Turkey with an opportunity to neutralize the PKK. Similarly, Turkey's policy of rapprochement with Syria and Iran, seen as part of a neo Ottomanist foreign policy is also in part aimed at dealing with the PKK as the two states' support for the Kurdish separatist movement is well known.[35]

The year 2009 opened with some major steps towards the politics of recognition. At the beginning of the year the state broadcasting agency TRT launched a 24-hour Kurdish language channel, TRT 6. Also the Higher Education Board resolved to establish Kurdish language and literature departments in universities. These are radical gestures on the road to the recognition of Kurdish identity in Turkish history. Additionally the AKP government announced in July 2009 that it was preparing a comprehensive plan to provide a solution for the Kurdish question. Whether these will be successful remains to be seen. In any case the fundamental dilemma of identity within the state will remain as long as the ideal is perceived in terms of a homogeneous monolingual political community. With its policies of 'democratic opening' the AKP government has embarked on an enterprise that will ultimately challenge the core identity of the Republic as a specifically 'Turkish' state. However, critics note that

the opening that the AKP government is offering and the reforms that have been set in motion are propelled by the need to create space for Islamic identity within the state rather than any commitment towards cultural plurality. President Abdullah Gul had stated in an interview in the late 1990s about 'a convergence between the aspiration of the Kurds and us (the Islamic movement)' hinting at a basic antagonism towards the founding ideology of the republic with its emphasis on secular Turkish nationalism.[36] Yet it is also true that the two sides remain rivals. While the Kurdish democratic opening of the AKP government is encouraging, yet it would be a challenge to accommodate Kurdish aspirations without provoking a Turkish nationalist backlash.

NOTES

1. There are alternative interpretations of this that claim that the phrase prioritized a personal identification with 'Turkishness' rather than an ethnic or racial scrutiny of individual citizens. See Omar Taspinar, *Kurdish Nationalism and Political Islam in Turkey,* New York and London: Routledge, 2005.
2. Sinan Ciddi, *Kemalism in Turkish Politics: The Republican People's Party, Secularism and Nationalism,* London and New York: Routledge, 2009.
3. Cited from Feroz Ahmad, *The Making of Modern Turkey,* London and New York: Routledge, 1993.
4. J. Habermas, 'Modernity versus Postmodernity', *New German Critique,* no. 22, 1981.
5. Ciddi, *Kemalism in Turkish Politics*, op. cit.
6. See for instance, Menderes Cinar, 'The Justice and Development Party and the Kemalist Establishment', in Umit Cizre (ed.), *Secular and Islamic Politics in Turkey: The Making of the Justice and Development Party*, London and New York: Routledge, 2008.
7. Ciddi, *Kemalism in Turkish Politics*, op. cit.
8. Murat Somner, 'Defensive and Liberal Nationalisms: The Kurdish Question and Modernization/Democratization', in E. Fuat Keyman (ed.), *Remaking Turkey: Globalization, Alternative Modernities and Democracy,* Lanham: Lexington Books, 2008.
9. Andrew Mango, 'Introduction: Ataturk and Kemalism throughout the Twentieth Century', in Celia Kerslake, Kerem Oktem and Philip Robins (eds.), *Turkey's Engagement with Modernity: Conflict and Change in the Twentieth Century*, Basingstoke, Hampshire: Palgrave Macmillan, in association with St Antony's College, Oxford, 2010.
10. Halil M. Karaveli, 'Could Turkey's Glasnost Establish Equality as the Founding Principle of the State?', *Turkey Analyst*, vol. 2, no. 23, 21 December 2009.
11. Kemal Karpat, *The Politicization of Islam: Reconstructing Identity, State, Faith and Community in the Late Ottoman State*, Oxford: Oxford University Press, 2001.
12. *Tanzimat* referred to a period of modernizing reforms instituted under the Ottoman Empire from 1839-76, when the edict entitled *Hatti-i-Sharif* of

Gulhane laid out the fundamental principles of *tanzimat* reform. Foremost among the laws was the security of honour, life, property for all Ottoman subjects, regardless of race or religion. Other reforms sought to reduce theological dominance, including the lifting of monopolies, fairer taxation, secularized schools, a changed judicial system and new rules regarding military service. *Tanzimat* ended in 1876, under Abd al Hamid II's reign, when the ideas for a Turkish constitution and parliament promoted by the vizir Midhat Pasha were rejected by the Sultan. Under Mustafa Reshid Pasha (1800-58), a programme of reform was steadily developed. Abuses in the taxation system were to be eliminated and provincial representative assemblies were created. New codes of commercial land and criminal law based on French models were introduced with new state courts, separate from the Islamic religious courts.

13. On 3 November 1839, Sultan Abdulmejid issued an organic statute for the general government of the Empire named Hatti-i-sharif of Gulhane (the imperial palace where it was first proclaimed) and sometimes called the *tanzimat fermani*. In this document the Sultan stated that he designed to attempt by new institutions to obtain for the provinces composing the Ottoman Empire the benefits of a good administration, and that these institutions would principally refer to these topics: (1) guarantees which will ensure all subjects security of life, honour and property; (2) a regular method of establishing and collecting taxes; (3) an equally regular method of recruiting, levying the army and fixing duration of the service. This edict was followed by the Hatti-i-Humayan of 1856 which promised full equality of religion and the Nationality Law of 1869 that created a common Ottoman citizenship irrespective of religious or ethnic divides. The reforms peaked in 1876 with the implementation of an Ottoman constitution checking the autocratic powers of the Sultan. While the new Sultan Abdul Hamid II signed it, he also quickly turned against it.
14. Taspinar, *Kurdish Nationalism and Political Islam in Turkey*, op. cit.
15. Ibid.
16. Ciddi, *Kemalism in Turkish Politics*, op. cit.
17. Bernard Lewis, *The Emergence of Modern Turkey*, New York, Oxford: Oxford University Press, 1961.
18. Cited from Gerassimos Karabelias, 'The Military Institution, Ataturk's Principles and Turkey's Sisyphean Quest for Democracy', *Middle Eastern Studies*, vol. 45, no. 1, January 2009.
19. Kemal Karpat, *Turkey's Politics: The Transition to Multiparty System*, Princeton, NJ: Princeton University Press, 1959.
20. Fotios Moustakis and Rudra Chaudhuri, 'The Turkish Kurdish Relations and the European Union: An Unprecedented Shift in the Kemalist Paradigm?', *Mediterranean Quarterly*, Fall 2005.
21. See for instance Mesut Yegen, 'Prospective Turks or Pseudo Citizens: Kurds in Turkey', *Middle East Journal*, vol. 63, no. 4, Autumn 2009, where he cites from meetings of the Grand National Assembly and minutes of Parliament in the early years of the inception of the Republic, to show that the Kurds were perceived as a particular ethnic community with group rights.
22. Cited from Mesut Yegen, 'Citizenship and Ethnicity in Turkey', in Ali Carkoglu and William Hale (eds.), *The Politics of Modern Turkey*, London and New York: Routledge, 2008.
23. Ibid.

24. *Records of the Assembly on 1924 Constitution* cited from Yegen, 'Prospective Turks or Pseudo Citizens: Kurds in Turkey', op. cit.
25. For details see Yegen, 'Prospective Turks or Pseudo Citizens: Kurds in Turkey', op. cit., pp. 597-615. See also Mesut Yegen, 'Banditry to Disloyalty: The Kurdish Question in Turkey', www.setav.org/ups/dosya/16058.pdf.
26. Dogu Ergil, 'The Kurdish Question in Turkey', *Journal of Democracy*, vol. 11, no. 3, July 2000.
27. Cited from Feroz Ahmad, *The Making of Modern Turkey*, op. cit..
28. Yegen, 'Prospective Turks or Pseudo Citizens: Kurds in Turkey', op. cit.
29. For instance Articles 26 and 28 of the Constitution prohibited the expression and dissemination/publication of thought in any language prohibited by law; and Law 2932, that followed a year later reiterated that the mother tongue of Turkish citizens is Turkish and it is prohibited to use as a mother tongue any other language. For details, see Taspinar, *Kurdish Nationalism and Political Islam in Turkey*, op. cit.
30. Law 2932 was passed in 1983 declaring the mother tongue of Turkish citizens to be Turkish, thereby prohibiting the use of Kurdish language.
31. For details see M. Hakan Yavuz, 'Search for a New Social Contract in Turkey: Fethullah Gulen, the Virtue Party and the Kurds', *SAIS Review*, vol. 19, no. 1, 1999.
32. From Excerpts from the Document of Mutual Understanding, cited from Ergil, 'The Kurdish Question in Turkey', op. cit.
33. Hakan Yavuz, 'Search for a New Social Contract in Turkey: Fethullah Gulen, the Virtue Party and the Kurds', *SAIS Review*, vol. 19, no. 1, 1999, pp. 114-43.
34. For details see, Moustakis and Chaudhuri, 'The Turkish Kurdish Relations and the European Union: An Unprecedented Shift in the Kemalist Paradigm?', *Mediterranean Quarterly*, vol. 16, no. 4, 2005, pp. 77-89.
35. M.K. Kaya, 'The AKP Seeking to Reinvent Turkey, is Forced to Tread Carefully', *Turkey Analyst*, vol. 2, no. 21, 23 November 2009.
36. Halil M. Karaveli, 'Ankara's New Kurdish Opening: Narrow Room For Maneuver', *Turkey Analyst*, vol. 2, no. 14, 17 August 2009.

11

One Size Fits (not) All! De-hyphenating Chechen Nationalism from Kremlin's Rhetoric of 'War on Terror'

ANTARA MITRA

INTRODUCTION: RETHINKING NATIONALISM AND ETHNICITY IN AN ERA OF 'GLOBALIZATION' OF JIHAD

Dear Chechnya is filled with blood
And became blood-red.
Our sisters are dead in flames of fire,
But these sacrifices will not be useless.
Jihad is happening,
For rescuing our homeland,
Maybe the whole nation will become shahid!

–Epigraph to Khava Baraeva, the first Chechen suicide-bomber

Ethnic and cultural fragmentation and modernist homogenization are not two arguments, two opposing views of what is happening in the world today, but two constitutive trends of global reality.[1]

Notwithstanding de-territorializing consequences of globalization, regional integration and an increasingly vociferous paradigm anticipating 'death of geography' and a transitory shift of international politics to a 'post-modern' era, nations remain fundamental geo-cultural referents of ethno-cultural identity and geopolitical reasoning in international politics.[2] Historically, nations, in their symbolic and affective dimensions, have been highly contentious discursive sites where contending discourses of *geopolitical culture*, *geopolitical traditions and geo-cultural imaginations* are inter-subjectively constructed by various competing actors and networks of power and juxtaposed against each other.[3] Embedded within these discursive spaces of nation states, thus, is a strong undercurrent of power-play

in which dominant groups legitimize and reinforce their privileged *status-quo* and hierarchical social relations of power *vis-à-vis* 'others'—religious-ethnic minorities, economically marginalized groups or political voices of dissent challenging the prevalent *status-quo*—through control of institutional tools of coercion and dominance, as well as command over knowledge-production and cognitive tools of *hegemonic narratives*.[4] Dominant socio-political interest groups and actors thus reinforce their power positions and replicate hierarchical social relations of power not only through institutional-coercive tools of control but also entrenched control of knowledge-production within the discursive space of nation states. Their discursive power significantly determines their institutional power reducing socio-political groups with little political means to challenge state exclusionary agenda into mere faceless *subjects* at clearly disadvantaged position.[5] As Shabot succinctly points out,

> . . . intersubjectivity turns out to be one of the key concepts for comprehending identity. The postmodern subject must be understood as constantly re-emerging anew from its intersection with the outside world and its Other. . . . The post-modern subject is an embodied subject, but it is also historically, socially, and culturally defined.[6]

Indeed there cannot be a more blatant illustration of subjective paradigms, as propagated by dominant power cliques, becoming standardized expressions of knowledge than the post-9/11 triumph of Samuel Huntington's fallacy-ridden thesis of *clash of civilizations* and *securitization* of Islam.[7] While Huntington does not claim that fault line conflicts exist exclusively in relations between predominantly Islamic states and their neighbours, he does point out that:

> Islam's borders *are* bloody, and so are its innards. . . . Wherever one looks along the perimeter of Islam, Muslims have problems living peaceably with their neighbors. The question naturally rises as to whether this pattern of late-twentieth-century conflict between Muslim and non-Muslim groups is equally true of relations between groups from other civilizations. In fact, it is not. Muslims make up about one-fifth of the world's population but in the 1990s they have been far more involved in inter-group violence than the people of any other civilization. The evidence is overwhelming.[8]

National demography, all over the world, in this age of globalization, has become ethno-racially more differentiated. Multiple identities and ethno-religious-linguistic pluralism within such singular national identity discourses, and concomitant ethno-linguistic imbalance in national power-sharing have spurred intra-state separatist 'little nationalisms' at regional and sub-regional levels, civil wars have widened discursive, spiritual and ideological vacuums in ideology

and identity. A multitude of indigenous or external groups, especially militant religious radicals have opportunistically rushed in such politico-ideological voids not out of 'civilizational concerns, but purely pragmatic agenda of quest of safe, logistical havens and mobilization of grievances. Post-Soviet conundrum in the Caucasus has opened the floodgate of myriad ethno-national struggle. Federal-units that sprang after Soviet implosion, within the extensive post-Communist sphere, were not culmination of organized and collective, popular nation-building processes, but rather arbitrarily as a result of failure in consensual negotiation to accommodate the multiple identities and ethnicities of population within a single nation state.

This paper illustrates such broader trend of restorative standardization of flawed official geopolitical 'storyline' by existing dominant power structures at the state centre through deconstruction of Kremlin's official, militant doctrine of 'war on terror' *vis-à-vis* the long-drawn Chechen nationalism. The paper looks at Kremlin's brutal subversion of Chechen nationalist movement and argues that colonialism of a subversive Russian state is a *necessary* but not *sufficient* variable in explaining increasingly Islamized rhetoric of erstwhile secular Chechen nationalism.[9] The Chechen dilemma is a bold illustration of the old saying 'One man's freedom fighter is another man's terrorist'.

The paper analyses Kremlin's official discourse on Chechen policy. He links it to international terrorism after 9/11, and on the other hand, heterogeneous, shifting discourses of nationalism and finally, 'global Jihad' by that of the Chechen nationalists. The article probes into a relatively less-explored but increasingly salient conceptual *terra incognita*—changing rhetoric and shifting trends in discourses of ethno-nationalism in a world confronting the menace of 'global Jihad' and normative contradictions in securitization of Islam. The rhetoric of 'war on terror' has rapidly diffused across the world, having been increasingly usurped by political elites and subversive states to legitimize their minority-incarceration and asphyxiation of elements of internal dissent. Contextualized within diffused geopolitics fraught with newer amorphous actors and threats, post-9/11 international existential concern for global jihad has exacerbated certain complex, problematic trends in traditional discourses on ethnicity, nationalism and anti-colonialism. Amidst territorial export of calibrated military violence to Global South, and its vicious spill-over into increasing militarization of pre-existent regional ethno-national movements and asymmetric insurgencies, there emerged a discursive proclivity to thrust dynamics of ethnicity, nationalism

and anti-imperial, anti-hegemonic identity-politics into monolithic rubric of global jihad. In the Eurasian context, this blatantly de-historicizes nationalism and de-colonization movements, ignoring region-circumstantial, historical and socio-cultural specificities which contoured differential interactive patterns between Islam and indigenous ethno-cultural settings. This was further exacerbated by de-fragmentation of Al-Qaeda into splinter, sleeper cells and an increasingly northward shift on their heals to Trans-Caucasus. Post-9/11 era witnesses different *localized* forms of Islam which stand out due to their complete merger with criminal groups so as to sometimes prioritize *profit* over *vindication* or inextricably combine these two motivations. Against such backdrop, rhetoric of existential threats and international security emergency often offered a conceptually malleable, politically correct rhetoric of 'war on terror' has been a political cloak to justify subversive states' minority-incarceration, asphyxiating elements of internal dissent. International isolation left the Chechens susceptible to a non-indigenous, imported Salafi-Wahhabist mobilizing agenda. This radicalization in a form of *New Chechen Jihad* fundamentally deviates from the original secular-nationalist agenda, subordinating national Chechen identity to a meta-Islamic brotherhood in global Islamic *Ummah.* This, especially, post-Beslan tragedy, has eroded its pure ethno-nationalistic appeal and its representative legitimacy among common Chechen population, in their collective quest for nationhood.

This article attempts a deconstruction of such discursive trends in context of Kremlin's brutal subversion of the Chechen nationalist movement and argues that colonialism of a subversive Russian state is a *necessary* but not *sufficient* variable in explaining increasingly Islamized rhetoric of erstwhile secular Chechen nationalism.

SECURITIZATION OF IDENTITY-POLITICS, JIHAD AND NEO-IMPERIAL 'HEGEMONIC GLOBALITY' IN POST-9/11 ERA

Security and politics of security are linked closely with identity politics. The will to secure the Self has as its corollary the will to make insecure the Other, the desire to control and use violence. How we define ourselves depends on how we represent others. This representation is thus integrally linked with how we 'secure' ourselves against the Other. Representations of the Other as a source of danger to the security of the Self in conventional understandings of security are accompanied by an abstraction, dehumanization,

depersonalization and stereotyping of the Other. The Other gets reduced to being a danger and hence an object that is fit for surveillance, control, policing and possibly extermination.[10] This logic of the discourse of security dictates that the security of the Self facilitates and even demands the use of policing and violence against the Other. The Productive Discourse of Security is a central concept in the theory and praxis not only of international relations but of local, inter-local and trans-local relations. Thus, Jihad and Islam are discursively constructed as sites of dread, abomination desires of abjection and/or extermination. The desire of emulation, abjection, and extermination is inextricably linked to certain threatening representations of 'the Muslim'. According to this school of thought, security as a concept has little a priori objective meaning and is largely an inter-subjective socio-political construction. Thus securitization is the process which identifies a certain socio-political or economic issue invoking its threat potential *vis-à-vis* a particular referent object and formulates emergency policies to alleviate the threat to ensure the survival of that particular referent. Thus, it involves the ascent of an issue from the realm of normal politics to emergency politics on the plea of security, even if it demands circumvention of democratic and normative principles. Thus, a *securitized issue* is essentially different from a *political issue*. As Barry Buzan succinctly summarized this:

> Threats . . . have to be staged as existential threats to a referent object by a securitizing actor who thereby generates endorsement for emergency measures beyond rules that would otherwise bind. In other words, issues become securitized when leaders (whether political, societal, or intellectual) begin to talk about them—and to gain the ear of the public and the state—in terms of existential threats against some valued referent object. The securitizing formula is that such threats require exceptional measures and/or emergency action to deal with them. Securitization classically legitimates the use of force, but more broadly it raises the issue above normal politics and into the realm of 'panic politics' where departures from the rules of normal politics justify secrecy, additional executive powers, and activities that would otherwise be illegal. Securitization can thus be seen as a more extreme version of politicization. It is the intersubjective establishment of an existential threat with a saliency sufficient to have substantial political effects.[11]

Discourses, in critical, positivist theoretical perspectives, are inter-subjective constructs fraught with ontological-existential implications. Narrowing down to those on 'danger' and 'insecurity', they are *productive, representative* as well as *reproductive* of operational concepts, and existential categories of security-referents, insecurity-boosters, and the 'Self/Other' binary.[12] Thus, discourses of insecurity

are about 'representations of danger'.[13] Overly broad geopolitical interpretations of the conflict have also confounded efforts to answer critical economic questions.

In the context of post-9/11 geopolitical evolution of post-Soviet space, the 'exogenous shock' radically transformed global discursive environment within which competing political elites within states defined their positions, articulated their differences and elaborated clashing visions of state identity and national security. Islam in Eurasia has been a predominantly *localized phenomenon* often divorced from the global jihadist ideology. In the Volga-Urals, Trans-Caucasus and the Ferghana Valley a distinct political and socio-economic-cultural microcosmic has crystallized over centuries which impart a considerably different ethno-cultural dimension to the Islamic radicalism in the post-Soviet *ummah* (Islamic communities). Due to centuries of Russification, industrial urbanization, and sustained communist secularization, orthodox political Islam has been less pervasive in this region. After the collapse of the Soviet Union, religion, in particular Islam, has come to play an important role in Russia's regions. Two simultaneous processes of de-secularization of political elites demanding autonomy and organizational de-centralization of insurgency have rendered momentum to salience of religion in identity-building.[14]

The first process is the product of the ideological vacuum created by the collapse of the Soviet Union. It stems from a frustration with non-religious values, culminating in the shedding of one ideology and the adoption of another. The desecularization of society brings with it the potential for conflict both within religions and within society as a whole. The fact that religious identities remained dormant during Soviet times makes the situation even more unstable as religious consciousness bursts onto the scene. Previously, secular nationalist movements, such as the one in Adigeya, are beginning to use Islamic slogans. Moreover, residents of the North Caucasus are turning to religious organization as a provider of social, not just spiritual goods.

Because the war in Chechnya began as an ethnic separatist conflict, narratives about Russian subjugation of the native people and the possible spread of separatism to other regions predominate. The conflict has been interpreted as a clash between imperial (Russian) forces and a Chechen national liberation movement. The dominant view coming from this camp has been that Chechnya—even the entire North Caucasus—is not historically a part of Russia. As Ronald Suny has noted:

> Though the Russian Federation is even more artificial a state than was the old USSR—it had never existed in history in its current borders except as a creation of Soviet power—its claim to be the heir to historic Russia has been recognized by the whole world and given a legitimacy that permits statesmen to excuse the Chechen war as an 'internal problem.' . . . Whatever Russia becomes internally, its relationship with Chechnya can hardly be seen as anything other than imperial.[15]

It is important to understand the ethno-religious dimensions of the Chechen nationalist struggle. The Chechens give primacy to their ethnic identity. Thus the ritual, mythic/narrative, experiential/emotional, ethical, legal, social, material, and political dimensions of life are all interpreted and perceived through the lens of ethnic identity. Ethnicity is mixed with religion, resulting in the formation of an ethnicized view of Islam. The Chechens resist permanent integration into Russia primarily because of their apprehensions of their distinct ethno-cultural disintegration. That is why initially the Chechen separatist movement hardly hinged on any religious propaganda or mobilization of the belief in irreconcilability between Russian and Chechen denominational and cosmological orientation.

According to Russian official circles:

> The North Caucasus is a major center of diverse but united Russian spiritual culture. Any attempts to break this unity have always met with resistance, including from the Caucasus peoples themselves. The people of Russia and the peoples of the Caucasus share a common destiny . . . for Russia, the Caucasus is not just another region, and this is well known throughout our country. There is a special fondness for the nature of the Caucasus. The Caucasus and its history is something close to us from our time as schoolchildren.[16]

'SPATIALIZING' NATIONAL IDENTITY: THE 'MAKING OF CHECHEN MARTYR'

The post-colonial conundrum syndrome has opened the floodgates of myriad ethno-national struggle in the post-Soviet North Caucasus. Nation states that sprang after Soviet implosion within the extensive post-Communist sphere, were not culmination of organized and collective, popular nation-building processes, but rather arbitrarily as a result of failure in consensual negotiation. Do nation states aim, in their dominant, officially centralized national meta-identity narratives, at throttling pluralities of distinctive voices of ethno-religious 'minorities'? This de-historicizes nationalism, especially in Eurasia, ignoring region-specific circumstantial contexts which contoured different patterns of intersection of Islam with indigenous

ethno-cultural nationalism at different times. The nation states in North Caucasus have not emerged as a culmination of a political process, but rather from a failure to negotiate and accommodate the multiple identities and ethnicities of population within a single nation state.

IMPORTED JIHAD, EXPORTED UMMAH

One of the things that must be understood regarding the current mentality of the Chechen al-Qaeda affiliates that is frequently misunderstood by Western analysts is that they are not simply fighting for their independence against Russian occupation of their homeland—they plan on spreading Wahhabism throughout the Caucasus. Nowhere is this better highlighted than in a *K avkaz Interview* with Amir Ramzan, the commander of one of Chechen *jamaats* (Chechen Al-Qaeda contingents) fighting in the North Caucasus, which makes this much clear:

> Not only we carry out raids to various areas in the Caucasus, but we also form local Jamaats, militant sabotage groups locally. We are joined by a lot of Kabardinians, Dagestanis, Karachaevans, Ingushetians and even Ossetians (Muslims). . . . Next year the war will seize the entire Caucasus from the Caspian Sea to the Black Sea. Apart from Ossetia and Ingushetia, this year another guerrilla war has already started in two areas of Dagestan bordering Chechnya. I swear by Allah, this is only the beginning. Russian authorities are well aware of this and this is why they are trying to organize formations of the local residents in the area who could resist us effectively. Similar process is taking place in Chechnya. But it will come to absolutely nothing. Having reached a certain level of confrontation inside Chechnya, Russia will sooner or later have to withdraw its troops beyond the Terek River, for instance. In that case we will need no more than two weeks to destroy all the pro-Russian puppet formations.[17]

Islamic radicalism in Eurasia has been a predominantly *localized phenomenon* often divorced from the global jihadist ideology. In the Volga-Urals, Trans-Caucasus and the Ferghana Valley a distinct political and socio-economic-cultural microcosmic has crystallized over centuries which impart a considerably different ethno-cultural dimension to the Islamic radicalism in the post-Soviet *ummah* (Islamic communities). Due to centuries of Russification, industrial urbanization, and sustained communist secularization, orthodox political Islam has been less pervasive in this region. This paper seeks to underscore a worrying functional *convergence* between the criminals and terrorists through cooption and coordination of cross-organizational skills that would compound and mutuate their

traditional skills, generate funds to sustain the jihad for a Central Asian *Valallah.* Geographically close to both the Golden Triangle and the Golden Crescent, the Trans-Caucasus has become a dumping ground for huge stockpiles of narcotics and a proliferating ground for small arms, light weapons and allegedly, illegal diversions of chemical and biological weapons, meeting the demands from the warlords, guerillas and radical Islamic terrorists to sustain their organizational agenda and separatist conflicts. The US-led Operation Enduring Freedom (OEF) in Afghanistan, Putin's centralization policy in Northern Caucasus and Kyrgyzstan's Tulip Revolution have further exacerbated the situation. The active engagement of the Northern Alliance and the Shura leadership in the unprecedented drug trade is heavily compromised by the US and the international community, as the former is instrumental in hunting down the vestiges of the Taliban and Al-Qaeda in Afghanistan, and maintaining a semblance of political stability.

Principles of multilateralism, mutual non-interference and non-aggression, peaceful coexistence and a shared politico-economic space in international order had already foreshadowed the imminent crystallization of a new world order to gradually relegate the principles of national sovereignty and territorial integrity to desuetude. In the wake of decolonization, the Third World countries experienced unprecedented politico-economic dislocations within the states that turned the realist model of inter-state resource conflicts upside down.

Apart from the infamous Chechen Mujahidin group, another recent network called Al-Ansar Mujahidin seems to have sprung up in Chechen under the tutelage of the late Iraqi Jihadist leader Al-Zarquawi, and now functions as a regional proxy of Al-Qaeda with intimate associations with Moro Islamic Liberation Front (Philippines), Jemaah Islamiah (Southeast Asia), Egyptian Islamic Jihad (merged with Al-Qaeda in 2001), Alal-Gamaa al-Islamiya (Egypt, and has a worldwide presence), Abu Sayyaf (Philippines), the Islamic Movement of Uzbekistan, and Harakat ul-Mujahidin (Pakistan/Kashmir) and other splinter-groups. Some experts see increased reliance on connections to other groups as a sign of Al-Qaeda's weakness; others point to enhanced cooperation with other groups as a worrisome indicator of strength, especially with groups that formerly focused on local issues and now display evidence of convergence on Al-Qaeda's international anti-US, anti-West agenda. An important question is whether Al-Qaeda might

be evolving further into a new form, more like a movement than a formal organization, increasingly diffuse internationally and less reliant upon its own membership.[18]

CONCLUSION

As for the securitization of immigration in post-9/11 era is concerned, it can be stated, following Tomas Faist, that the meta politics of anti-immigrant militant democracy only exaggerates the forces of *vicious transnationalization*, or import-export cycle of security threats across national boundaries while downplaying the positive and ameliorative potential of *virtuous transnationalization.* The post-Kantian order can now be described more as a 'world of societies' or even a 'world of cultures' rather than a 'world of states', thanks to the rise of prominent civil societies, ethno-culturally heterogeneous society, transportability of culture through diaspora and ensuing multiculturalism and pluralism of identity. Against this backdrop, transnational diaspora also include forces of *virtuous transnationalization* for diffusion of human rights across the borders, institutionalization of an international human rights regime and politics of multiculturally inclusive social citizenship.

Most significant perhaps is the fact that the ever-increasing privatization and exclusive social citizenship and welfare measures of the European states today have veritable boomerang effects on the citizens themselves also. When the lowest common denominator and referent of security has now become the individual human being and not sovereign-states, demographic governance in European states, paradoxically, impairs the doctrinal and practical basis of human security. Not only do the contributory-welfarism and militant democracy directly impinge upon the individual liberty and socio-economic security of the citizens also (especially those concentrated in semi- and low-skilled labour sectors), the securitization of immigration also hinders the socio-cultural assimilation of the second and third generation immigrants. The crisis that Europe today represents is thus a *de-humanization* of social citizenship that breeds a sense of alienation which can act as a sufficient condition for resurgence of centrifugal forces of *reactionary modernism* like that in the Weimar era. A growing trend of Islamic conversion of many Westerners and the thorny debate of Euro-Islam and involvement of numerous formerly non-Muslim Western citizens converting into Islam and actively participating in the global terrorist jihad can be taken as

symbolic politics of vindication against the alienating effects that the socio-economic and security governance of the Western democracies.

Europe's long-standing debate on 'democratic deficit', primarily being understood from a political perspective claiming an increasing disengagement of European people from the Europeanization and integration process, however, is inextricably interlinked with an alarming 'social deficit' also. And without redressing this social deficit and social problematique, Europe cannot aspire to transcend the problems of 'democratic deficit'. Europe's social models with the institutions of social citizenship and welfarism are organic constituents of an European culture, and any erosion and abandonment of that threatens to usher a fundamental crisis of decline of the West.

NOTES

1. Bateson, quoted by Thomas H. Erikson, *Ethnicity and Nationalism: Anthropological Perspectives*, London: Pluto Press; USA: Sterling, 1993, p. 1.
2. John Gaventa, *Power and Powerlessness: Quiescence and Rebellion in an Appalachian Valley*, Chicago: Chicago University Press, 1980.
3. Critical geopolitics provides a series of concepts by which we can study the contested geopolitical meaning of regions like the North Caucasus. Ó Tuathail (2006) distinguishes between geopolitical cultures, popular geopolitical imaginations and elite geopolitical traditions. Along with Kolossov, he succinctly defines *geopolitical culture* as:

   '. . . the practices by which states make sense of their identity, position, and role in a world of states. This culture is formed not only by the institutions of a state, its historical experiences, and geographical embeddedness, but also by networks of power within society and how these condition debates over national identity, prevailing geopolitical imaginations, codified geopolitical traditions, and the institutional processes by which foreign policy is made in the state. *Geopolitical imaginations* include the prevalent images, conceptualizations, and discourses in popular culture and among the general population of where that state is positioned and located within the world's community of states. Geopolitical imaginations are a mix of popular culture geopolitics and the geopolitical orientations of a state's population. *Geopolitical traditions* are the range of relatively formalized and competing schools of geopolitical thought that comprise the "high culture" of a state's geopolitical culture. Each tradition is a canon of thought on state identity, the national interest, and normative foreign policy priorities'. For a detailed discussion of this issue see Vladimir Kolossov and Gerard Toal (Gearóid Ó Tuathail), 'An Empire's Fraying Edge? The North Caucasus Instability in Contemporary Russian Geopolitical Culture', *Eurasian Geography and Economics*, vol. 48, no. 2, 2007, p. 203. Also see Andrei P. Tsygankov, 'Rediscovering National Interests after the "End of History": Fukuyama, Russian Intellectuals, and a Post-Cold War Order,' *International Politics*, vol. 39, no. 4, 2002, pp. 153-73. See also Andrei P. Tsygankov, 'Mastering Space in Eurasia: Russia's Geopolitical Thinking after the Soviet

Break-Up', *Communist and Post-Communist Studies*, vol. 35, no. 1, 2003, pp. 101-27, and Denis Tukmakov, 'Parad Separatistov (The Parade of Separatists)', *Zavtra*, 31 May 2006.

4. For a nuanced account of how ideological frameworks of knowledge and political construction of contextual meanings and implications intimately interacts with power-dynamics, see John Gaventa, op. cit.
5. Dominique Dijck, *Is EU Policy on Illegal Immigration Securitized?*, paper presented at the 3rd Pan-European Conference on EU Politics, Istanbul, 21-3 September 2006.
6. S.C. Shabot, 'The Grotesque Body: Fleshing out the Subject', in S. Horskotte and E. Peeren (eds.), *The Shock of the Other: Situation Alterities*, Amsterdam: Rodopi, 2007, p. 57.
7. Samuel Huntington, 'The Clash of Civilizations?', *Foreign Affairs*, vol. 72, no. 3, 1993, pp. 22-49. For a detailed account of this cultural thesis, see Samuel Huntington, *The Clash of Civilizations and the Remaking of World Order*, New York: Simon & Schuster, 1996. For a general picture of how this thesis influenced the understanding of 9/11 and subsequent surge in radical terrorism see Samuel Huntington, 'The Age of Muslim Wars', *Newsweek*, 3 January 2002; Barbara Crosette, 'Survey of Islamic World Finds Few Democracies', *New York Times*, 23 September 2001; Ian Fisher, 'Democracy in the Muslim world', *New York Times*, 23 November 2001; John Tierney, 'Fantasies of Vengeance Fed by Fury', *New York Times*, 18 September 2001; Alan Schwartz, 'Getting at the Roots of Arab Poverty', *New York Times*, 1 December 2001; Joseph Kahn, 'A Business Plan for Islam Inc', *New York Times*, 30 December 2001; Kahn, 'How Islam Won, and Lost, the Lead in Science', *New York Times*, 30 October 2001; Neil MacFarquhar, 'Anti-Western and Extremist Views Pervade Saudi Schools', *New York Times*, 19 October 2001; Thomas Friedman, 'Hamas Rules', *New York Times*, 15 September 2001; Friedman, 'Yes, but What?', *New York Times*, 20 September 2001; Thomas Friedman, 'Bush to Bin Laden', *New York Times*, 12 October 2001; Friedman, 'Drilling for Tolerance', *New York Times*, 20 October 2001; Friedman, 'We are all Alone', *New York Times*, 26 October 2001; Friedman, 'In Pakistan, it's Jihad 101', *New York Times*, 13 November 2001; and Friedman, 'Rights in the Real World', *New York Times*, 2 December 2001; Alan Krueger, 'To Avoid Terrorism, End Poverty and Ignorance. Right: Guess Again', *New York Times*, 13 December 2001; Mark Danner, 'The Battlefield for the American Mind', *New York Times*, 16 October 2001; Reuel Gerecht, 'The Future of bin Ladenism', *New York Times*, 11 January 2002; Lamin Sanneh, 'Faith and the Secular State', *New York Times*, 23 September 2001. However, it should be noted that this list of suggested reading is, in no sense, an exhaustive one.
8. Huntington, *The Clash of Civilizations and the Remaking of World Order*, op. cit., 1996, pp. 256-8.
9. For a general overview of Kremlin's portrayal of Chechen rebels as 'Islamic Terrorists' refer to the following literature list: I. Bremmer and A. Zaslavsky, '2001/2002 Bush and Putin's Tentative Embrace', *World Policy Journal*, vol. 18, no. 4, pp. 11-17; J. O'Loughlin, 2001, 'Geopolitical Fantasies, National Strategies and Ordinary Russians in the Post-Communist Era', *Geopolitics*, vol. 6, no. 3, pp. 17-48; J. O'Loughlin, Ó. Tuathail and V. Kolossov, 'A Risky Westward Turn? Putin's 9-11 Script and Ordinary Russians', *Europe-Asia Studies*, vol. 56, no. 1, 2004, pp. 3-34. Ó. Tuathail, 'Theorizing Practical Geopolitical Reasoning: The

Case of U.S. Bosnia Policy in 1992', *Political Geography*, vol. 21, no. 5, 2002, pp. 601-28.

10. Michel Foucault, *Discipline and Punish*, New York: Vintage Press; and 'Technologies of the Self, in L.H. Martin, H. Gutman and P.H. Hutton (eds.), *Technologies of the Self*, Amherst: University of Massachusetts Press, 1988.
11. Tony Buzan, *Mind Mapping*, London: Buzan, 1997, pp. 11-12.
12. For a preliminary overview of critical security theories, refer to D. Campbell, *Writing Security: United States Foreign Policy and the Politics of Identity*, Minneapolis: University of Minnesota Press, 1998; K. Krause and M. Williams, (eds.), *Critical Security Studies*, Boulder, CO: Lynne Rienner; R.D. Lipschutz, *On Security*, New York: Columbia University Press, 1995; J. Weldes, M. Laffey, H. Gusterson and R. Duvall (eds.), *Cultures of Insecurity: States, Communities, and the Production of Danger*, Minneapolis: University of Minnesota Press, 1999.
13. Lyle Campbell, *Historical Linguistics: An Introduction*, Cambridge, MA: MIT Press, 1999; Dillon, 1996.
14. Martha Brill Olcott, Aleksei Malashenko, Igor Semeonov, Damir Shagaeviev, Igor Dobaev, Tatiana Kostykova and Ahmed Yarlikapov (eds.), *Islam and Russia's Regions* [Proceedings of Carnegie Endowment for International Peace working meeting on *Islam and Russia's Regions*], 17 November 2006.
15. Suny, 1995, op. cit., p. 195.
16. Vladimir Putin, 'Zaklyuchitel'noye slovo na obshchestvennom forume narodov Kavkaza i yuga Rossii' (Speech at the Public Forum of the People of the Caucasus and Southern Russia), 26 March 2004 [http://www.kremlin.ru/].
17. Dan Darling, 'Al-Qaeda in Chechnya', 22 April 2004, Analytical Briefs, Windsofchange.net.
18. For further information, see CRS Report RL31119, *Terrorism: Near Eastern Groups and State Sponsors, 2002,* 13 February 2002, and Kenneth Katzman, David Johnston, Don Van Natta, Jr. and Judith Miller, 'Qaeda's New Links Increase Threats From Far-Flung Sites,' *The New York Times*, 16 June 2002, p. A1; 'President Bush Announces Combat Operations in Iraq Have Ended', Remarks by the President from the USS *Abraham Lincoln* At Sea Off the Coast of San Diego, California, 1 May 2003, accessed at: [http://www.whitehouse.gov/news/releases/2003/05/iraq/20030501-15.html] on 16 May 2003. International Institute for Strategic Studies, *Strategic Survey, 2002-2003*; and Bruce Hoffman, 'The Leadership Secrets of Osama bin Laden: The Terrorist as CEO,' *The Atlantic Monthly*, April 2003, p. 26.

V. TRANSNATIONAL IDENTITIES

12

Comparing Zionism with European Nationalisms

PRIYA SINGH

ETHNO-CULTURAL AND CIVIC NATIONALISMS

Historians and sociologists broadly categorize nationalist ideologies into two main types: ethno-cultural and civic nationalism.[1] According to the former category of ideology, members of groups sharing a common history and culture have fundamental, morally significant interests in adhering to their culture and in sustaining it for generations. Moreover, these interests warrant political recognition and support, primarily by means of the right to national self-determination. In other words, ethno-cultural nationalism, sometimes denoted as ethnic or cultural nationalism, is one in which the nation is portrayed as a community united by its ethno-cultural similarities, which stems from the common ancestry of its members. A defining character of ethno-cultural nationalism is that the nation chronologically precedes the state that is subsequently established by that particular nation.[2] The ideology of civic nationalism, by contrast, mainly argue that the citizenry of the state has an interest in sharing one homogeneous national culture. The interest is not derived from people's interest in adhering to their original culture, rather it originates because cultural homogeneity facilitates the implementation of universal values such as democracy, distributive justice and economic growth. According to civic nationalism, when the state citizenry's interest in cultural homogeneity conflicts with people's interest in adhering to their own culture, the former should prevail. The nation, in this formulation, is defined in terms of a shared commitment to, and pride in, the public institutions of state and civil society, which connect the people to the territory that they occupy. The nation is thus depicted as united by a common public culture, a way of life, a national character, which is shared by all

citizens irrespective of ethnic origin. A defining characteristic of civic nationalism is that the state chronologically precedes the nation, which is then forged as a result of people's affiliation with this state.[3] Hungarian nationalism and Serbian nationalism are considered to be prime examples of ethno-cultural nationalism whereas the nationalisms of France and Britain are regarded as typical examples of civic nationalism.

ZIONISM: A CASE OF ETHNO-CULTURAL NATIONALISM

Zionism is usually looked upon as essentially constituting a case of ethno-cultural nationalism. The pioneering Zionist ideologues, leaders and activists were of the view that they were members of an ethno-cultural group that was stateless and therefore aspired to self-determination as a means of promoting the interests of the members in adhering to their culture and sustaining it for generations, and protecting its members from persecution. However, certain concepts propounded by the Zionist ideologues and some of the processes that occurred in the history of Zionism could be categorized as constituting the elements of civic nationalism—some of the ideas and initiatives espoused by a few prominent Zionists and the motivation behind them are in fact, considered to be similar to those associated with civic nationalism.[4] For instance, both Theodor Herzl, the founding father of Zionism and Leo Pinsker, a precursor to the Zionists, prior to becoming Zionists had advocated Jewish cultural assimilation to the majority populations of the host states, hoping that these states would eventually place less emphasis on their ethno-cultural characteristics and they would become increasingly civic. The change in their thinking was primarily the consequence of the persecution of Jews in Europe rather than an outcome of their desire to ensure the continuity of the Jews as a distinct ethno-cultural group. Moreover, in their quest to create a Jewish state, they strove to implement the principles of civic nationalism rather than establish a framework within which they could nurture and promote the ideas of ethno-cultural nationalism for the preservation of Jewish culture. This is particularly true in the case of Theodor Herzl, and authenticated in both his books: The *Jewish State* and *Altneuland*[5] (by the proposal to establish a Jewish state in Uganda), and the vision expressed in *Altneuland*, which reflects Herzl's ambition to realize the universal value of liberalism and progress within the framework of the Jewish state. For instance, Herzl envisioned German rather than Hebrew, as the language of the Jewish state, thus reiterating the opinion

that Herzl's thinking fell within the conceptual framework of civic nationalism. Herzl did not consider language as a distinct component of cultural identity to which the members of the ethno-cultural groups adhere precisely because they perceive it as such. Moreover, in the Jewish State, Herzl argued that the Jewish people's immediate requirement was for a place where they could establish that state but this necessarily did not have to be the Land of Israel, as attested to by his Uganda Plan. In his opinion, a specific territory for the Jews was merely a haven from persecution. He did not consider territory to be a constituent of a people's cultural identity, which would have to be adhered to merely because it formed a component of their identity.[6]

Moreover, Zionism also revealed a few characteristics of civic nationalism in the form of some practices instituted by the State of Israel. The foremost being the melting pot ideology, which influenced the Israeli policy makers in the initial decades of its existence in the process of forging a homogeneous culture as the diverse Jewish communities that had arrived in Israel differed from one another in terms of language, lifestyles, customs and their respective histories. In this way, the Zionist movement aspired to build a new nation, therefore the state preceded the nation one of the salient features of civic nationalism.

Another feature that could lead to the possible association of Zionism with civic nationalism is the fact that the actuality created by the Zionist movement facilitated the emergence and development of quasi-civic and civic movements like the Canaanite movement,[7] which have argued for a State of Israel in the form of the nation state of 'Israelis', irrespective of whether they are Jews, Arabs or Druze. In other words, the aim of this movement was the creation of a state by ethno-cultural Zionism, which would be a stepping-stone in the formation of a new nation that would integrate all the inhabitants of the Land of Israel. The intention was to create a culturally homogeneous state, an attribute of civic nationalism. The Canaanite movement attempted at the assimilation of the distinct ethno-cultural groups that dwell in Israel into a nation with one culture and one citizenry. The Canaanites contented that Israel should be regarded as the state of the nation it created—the Israeli nation and not the state of the nation that created it, the Jewish people.

Despite these manifestations of civic nationalism, the ethno-cultural nature of Zionism is validated by the fact that (a) The Zionist movement did not consider any language other than Hebrew as the language of the Jewish State even though the idea had been entertained by a leader as eminent as Theodor Hegel, (b) Similarly,

Hegel's proposal for the creation of a Jewish State in East Africa (Uganda Plan) was not fundamentally acceptable to the Zionist ideology and as such was rejected by the Seventh Zionist Congress in 1905.[8] Finally, the fact that the State of Israel was formed as a melting pot from a concoction of dissimilar cultural groups that had little in common with each other does not imply that Zionism is a category of civic nationalism because Israel has applied the melting pot policy to the Jews only and not to any other ethno-religious and cultural group dwelling in the state. The melting pot policy was never used to facilitate the realization of universal democratic values of democracy and distributive justice for its entire population.

While Zionism is a Jewish version of ethno-cultural nationalism, it differed initially from other Jewish and non-Jewish ethno-cultural ideologies by virtue of its aspiration to realize the nationalist ambitions of the group it represents not in the places in which the members of this group were currently living, but rather in the historical homeland from which the Jewish people had been cut off since antiquity. Since the inception of Zionism, this homeland was and continues to be the homeland of another ethno-cultural group. Despite this, the Zionist movement resorted to the historical rights argument to justify the Jewish return to the Land of Israel.[9]

ZIONISM AND EUROPEAN NATIONALISMS

It is only in the recent past that studies on Zionism as a nationalist movement from a comparative perspective has been initiated. Yet there is no one model of nationalism by which Zionism can be tested. Nor has there been a single concept of Zionism accepted by all. For some it was primarily political, for others cultural, social or religious. Any comparative study should entail questions such as: Is the Zionist claim based on common territory, language or descent, like the nationalist movements of the Czechs or Hungarians? And the answers vary, while some state that there is a myth of common descent from the ancient Hebrews, there is a homeland, Palestine and there is a common language, Hebrew, the language of the Bible, which has been preserved as the language of religion and prayer, others refer to and emphasize on the aspect of the dispersion of the Jews all over the world, the variety of languages and cultures in which the Jews live and function and the apparent ethnic differences between the various dispersions. Other queries allude to the combination of conservative and revolutionary aims inherent in Zionism but which are also typical of many national movements albeit in a variety of

manifestations (e.g. whether the ideology of Zionism revealed the recurring combination of a wish for modernization with a romantic yearning for reviving the past?)[10]

The essay contends that while such comparisons abound yet at the same time they enrich historical research and at the core of the basic comparison of Zionism with the other national movements lies the deep belief or disbelief in the uniqueness of the Jewish people and the divine purpose for which it exists. Thus, there is simultaneously, on the one end, (i) a claim for uniqueness and at the other extreme, (ii) an equally strong aspiration to be like the other nations. Both the views are genuine expressions of Jewish nationalism.

Zionism is a mixture of contradictory/antagonistic standpoints, one which stresses upon the overwhelming primacy of the existence of Judaism over the well-being of the Jews and the other which deals with the normalization of the life of the Jewish people as a nation like others. The doctrine of nationalism in Europe arose as part of the drive for freedom and self-rule inspired by the French Revolution. Once the principle of sovereignty of people was recognized, it was imperative to lodge sovereignty in a group of people that would act as the source of authority. Naturally groups evidently distinguished by centralized rule, location, language, culture and history were chosen by themselves for that purpose. Therefore human collectivities (ethnic groups) declared themselves to be nations with political rights of self-governance.[11]

There were disagreements within national movements between those who aspired for full independence and those who believed they could get some form of autonomy. However, the latter often turned to the demand for independence when conditions seemed appropriate. (For example, the Czechs within the Hapsburg Empire until World War I.) Therefore there existed marginal groups of people who were convinced anti-nationalists. (Marxists, in England for example, who refrained from joining thee Boer War and World War I.)[12] The phenomenon, however, of large and influential groups within a people declaring that their people did not form a nation and should not have an independent state is uniquely Jewish and has proven to be excessively divisive. In recent history, there have been times when by force of colossal events like the *Shoah* (Holocaust) or the establishment of Israel, an appearance of unity and solidarity seemed to emerge; but in fact the underlying ideological diversity is as strong today as it ever was.

The fathers of Zionism, Herzl, for example, believed that Jewish people could follow the example of the European nations and

arrive at the territorial concentration and political independence of a progressive society guided by the principles of the European Enlightment. The precursors of Zionism mentioned inspiring examples of Greece, Belgium, Serbia, Italy, etc. Herzl often emphasized upon the comparative aspect, thus the attempt of political Zionism to fit the Jews into the general picture was natural and logical at that time[13] (late nineteenth-century Europe).

Zionism demanded a conceptual revision from both Jews and gentiles. In the course of the nineteenth century, for decades, Jews had tried to integrate into the surrounding societies on equal terms, renouncing separate national loyalties. At the same time, liberal and progressive forces in Europe pressurized their governments to accept the Jews living amongst them as English, French, German, etc. At the end of the century, before the people of Europe had internalized this innovation, they were required by the Jewish spokesmen to adopt an opposite conceptual innovation, that the Jews were after all a separate nation with a right to their own state.

There were also similarities between anti-Zionist arguments of Jews and non-Jews, as for instance, the claim that Judaism was a religion and not a nation and accordingly the expression of a preference for the goal of equality in a multi-cultural society over Jewish particularism was shared by both Jews and non-Jews. There was a parallel Jewish claim that the fate of the Jews to be eternally dispersed among nations was the result of divine punishment. Or alternatively the Jews were the divine instrument for the redemption of the world. There were Jews who agreed with the Jewish settlement of Palestine for humanitarian reasons, claiming that they would improve the lot of the Jews, and at the same time, divert the pressure of Jewish immigration form Western countries. Thus both Zionism and anti-Zionism was primarily based on European ideas and inclinations.

Present-day research has overcome the tendency to classify types of nationalism for a comparative study and has learned to recognize the culturally individual character of each national movement. However, civil nationalism with the French example, motivated by the principles of equal citizenship and freedom and ethnic nationalism as exemplified by German nationalism that arose as a result of French conquest, based on an emphasis on the ethnic nation, the autochthonic culture, historical continuity, pure language and tradition, are the two prototypes.[14] However, these terms do not represent mutually exclusive types. When investigated most movements

reveal both elements in varying proportions.[15] The emphasis on a civil or ethnic ingredient depends on the historical circumstances and on the prevailing views at different times.

The sources on which nationalist theories are based are mostly literary.[16] For example, the German Herder is connected with cultural, ethnic and organic nationalism. Fichte is associated with an exclusive and militant nationalism. Mazzini, the father of Italian nationalism, became known for a theory that combined individual and national freedom with the construction of an internationally harmonious world society. Dostoevsky appropriated the idea of God's chosen people exclusively for Russia. Themes of national martyrdom and self-sacrifice are abundant in the nationalist Hebrew poetry of Uri Zvi Greenburg. However, nationalist literature is not a reliable documentary source for analysis and categorization of types of nationalism and for classifying particular countries as reflecting this or that type. Literary creativity is not subject to logic and the history of Zionism is rich with examples of logical inconsistencies.

In fact, it was Achad Ha'am, the father of spiritual Zionism, the advocate of a minimalist political programme and of accommodation with the Arabs, who gave nationalism an organic, ethnic and culturally exclusive definition.[17] He followed the example of German thinkers like Herder, Fichte and Hegel, who saw the national spirit as an historical entity forming the nation and its culture from within by means of ethnic and organic continuity. The question which arises is that was Achad Ha'am a minimalist Zionist or an ultra-nationalist? He was a creative and eclectic thinker and not a systematic theorist of nationalism. Brit Shalom, a group inspired by Achad Ha'am was extreme in their demand for equality and justice among nations and particularly between Jews and Arabs in Palestine, at the same time, it was they who openly and demonstratively based their world view on an absolute certainty in the moral superiority of Judaism over all other religions and the imperative duty of the Jewish people because of their superiority to save the entire world with love and compassion, a concept similar to Kipling's famous phrase, 'the white man's burden', hailing the duty of the superior white race to serve the rest of the world for its own good.

The Herzilian stream of political Zionism, whose starting point is the revolutionary demand that the Jews be recognized as a political nation with the right to a sovereign state in Palestine, did not give too much thought to the specific national content of that state, culturally or religiously. Herzilian nationalism was almost formal, a matter of

rights and laws and recognition. He accepted the nation as produced by history, multi-cultural, multi-lingual and multi-attitudinal towards religion and expected this state of affairs to continue.[18]

The paradox here is that the very stream of Zionism, which was extreme in its political demand for international recognition of the Jewish people's right to a sovereign state in Palestine, was almost indifferent to the cultural content of the state and in fact, planned a modern civil society that would be progressive and pluralistic. It would be difficult to say which of these opposite streams belongs to the supposedly moderate civil type of nationalism and which to the self-centred ethnic and exclusive type.[19]

ZIONIST BINATIONALISM: THE INFLUENCE OF CENTRAL EUROPEAN NATIONALISMS

> The problem with Israel. . . is not—as sometimes suggested—that it is a European enclave in the Arab world; but rather it arrived too late. It has imported a characteristically late nineteenth century separatist project into a world that has moved on, a world of individual rights, open frontiers and international law. The very idea of a Jewish state—a state in which Jews and the Jewish religion have exclusive privileges from which non-Jewish citizens are forever excluded—is rooted in another time and place. Israel, in short, is an anachronism.
>
> TONY JUDT [20]

Judt offered a binational solution as a desirable outcome of the Israel-Palestine conflict. The idea of binationalism is within Zionism and can be traced to the early 1920s to the Brit Shalom organization,[21] which was an advocate of binationalism in Palestine. A small group, it believed in binationalism as a solution to the protracted national conflict. In spite of its small numbers, the organization was significant because it offered a fundamental alternative to all Zionist programmes. Renowned members of the group included Hans Kohn, the scholar of nationalism, Robert Weltsch, editor of the most important Zionist newspaper of that period, philosopher Hugo Bergmann, Arthur Ruppin, one of the first sociologists in mandatory Palestine. The central European influence on the organization was tremendous, in terms of membership and support overseas. A certain degree of ideological cohesiveness among those with central European backgrounds together with a willingness to get carried away in their quest for a compromise between Zionist aspirations and the demands of Arab nationalism, led to the identification of Brit Shalom's positions with a central European heritage. Thus, for Lavsky, central European traits such as 'liberal humanism of the enlightened Middle European Bourgeoisie', 'liberal tolerance and openness . . . a tendency to political

skepticism, openness to new ideas and progress, the social sensitivity and distaste for a narrow self-serving approach',[22] explain the genesis of the Brit Shalom's personality. However, the events of World War I, 'confronted German Zionists with a nationalism that had degenerated into aggressive chauvinism'.[23] Germany's Zionists had to shape their Zionism as it grew stronger, establishing itself as a form of moral nationalism in no wise resembling German nationalism. For example, Hans Kohn forcefully criticized the Zionist aspirations to become a majority in Eretz Israel, arguing that the Zionist view had already been divorced from the 'majority question'.[24] Kohn saw a striking similarity between the dilemma of majority-minority relationships that was beginning to develop in Mandatory Palestine and similar dilemmas in Czechoslovakia, Poland, and Romania. In a different context, Kohn asserted that the Zionist idea should not be limited to the political issue, that the Zionist movement should not be seen as a response to anti-Semitism or as a national movement along the lines of the Czechs, Arabs, or the Germans. What especially troubled Brit Shalom's members was precisely the Zionist circles' aspiration to achieve a Jewish majority in a future Israeli-nation state. From the point of view of the society's members, the demographic question became a seismograph for Zionism's sensitivity to the status and rights of minorities. Hungary, Romania, Poland, Czechoslovakia, the Ukraine and Germany formed a threateningly dense constituency among the diverse gamut of the members of Brit Shalom. All these nations seemed to be imposing themselves on the Jews, threatening to erupt as a kind of revival of the repressed at the same time that the Jews were seeking to find a form for their own nationalism in Mandatory Palestine. In other words, the only way in which central and eastern Europe could be considered a political and ideological infrastructure for Brit Shalom members is in the negative sense as an example of the ever-present threat posed by ethno nationalism and it was not the liberal spirit of central Europe but the liberal Jewish criticism of the illiberal turn to ethno-nationalist practices in that geopolitical sphere which gave rise to a synthesis in the spirit of conciliatory Zionism.

From the perspective of Zionist studies, central Europe comprised those areas where German-speaking Jews lived—Germany and German-speaking parts of the Hapsburg Empire, Vienna and Prague. Therefore greater emphasis is attached to the principle of language and culture than to geo-political divisions, defining Jews of various states as falling within a single area. In Zionist historiography, Brit Shalom Society is a central European association, representing the

central European heritage because its members and supporters were part of the German cultural sphere. This central European heritage was represented in the works of Hans Kohn and Arthur Ruppin, the two key figures of the Brit Shalom Society.

HANS KOHN

In his memoirs, Kohn wrote, 'I was born in Central Europe at the beginning of the last decade of the nineteenth century.'[25] From Prague, Kohn gained insights that later determined his approach to Zionism. 'The German-speaking minority among whom I grew up maintained a fully developed, separate cultural and social life of its own. We did not feel isolated. We felt at home in Prague and in the Czech countryside around the city. All this was our land; too, we breathed its air and loved its contours.'[26]

As depicted through Kohn's eyes, this taken for granted existence took place in a segregated environment rather than an integrated one, 'In all fields of life and activity there reigned a voluntary segregation, a kind of tacitly acknowledged iron curtain which separated two worlds living side by side, each one self contained, scarcely communicating.'[27]

Kohn's attachment to the binational concept as the right and only possible solution for Jewish-Arab relations in Palestine cannot be attributed solely to nostalgia for the multinational empire in which he grew up. He examined the empire in terms of the states that emerged out of its ruins. The new states by which Kohn meant 'Czechoslovakia, Poland, Yugoslavia and Romania', regarded themselves, in spite of their multi-ethnic composition, as nation states, with one nationality native to the state and the others being tolerated more or less as unwelcome guests.[28] It has been argued that Kohn's outlook from his life in Prague up to and including his Palestine period was characterized by a fundamentally modern approach to ethnic nationalism.[29]

The danger that as Kohn learned is to be found in a rigid insistence in central Europe in the wake of World War I, in areas with mixed populations it is impossible to establish nation-states; instead, they became *de facto* multinational states. These states, Kohn contended, overlook their *de facto* situation, disregarding the situation and rights of the minorities within their borders. Kohn's insights with respect both to *de jure* multinational states and to nation states that are *de facto* multinational states were shaped by his personal experience as

somebody who belonged to the Jewish minority within and alongside the German linguistic minority in Czech-speaking areas.

Kohn came to Zionism during his Prague years, and his Zionist sympathies continued for some 20 years from the pre-World War I years to the four years (1925-9) that he spent in Jerusalem. His attraction to Zionism was not merely intellectual; during his period in Palestine he occupied a senior administrative position and he developed his views of the future autonomy of the two peoples, Jewish and Arab, in a unified Palestine, were the direct result of his European insights.

The riots of 1929 in Palestine, marked a watershed in the attitude of Kohn to Zionism and a number of Brit Shalom members who decided to establish a parallel association in Germany, the objectives of which were: to bring pressure to bear on the world Zionist leadership to adopt a different strategic policy and to undertake a struggle within the Zionist movement against the slide to the right.[30] In the wake of the 1929 riots in Palestine, Kohn chose to leave Palestine and for all intents and purposes turned his back on Zionism—this was a significant breaking point, one that influenced Kohn's historical interpretation of modern nationalism and especially his energetic opposition to ethnic nationalism. 'Zionist nationalism went the way of most Central and East European national movements. But whatever the present or the future was to hold, my participation, for almost twenty years, in the Zionist movement enriched my life in many ways. It gave me a better understanding of the pitfalls and self-deceptions inherent in most national movements and political activities.'[31]

Kohn viewed Palestine in the late 1920s through his experience in central Europe in the first quarter of the twentieth century; conversely, his reading of modern European nationalism was shaped in light of his Zionist experience in Palestine. Kohn consequently developed a binary model of nationalism. According to this bifurcation, the Western nation state was perceived as representing universal, inclusive elements that focus on territory but are indifferent to ethnic composition. In central and eastern Europe, however, matters were found to be conducted on the basis of long historical (ethnic) memories, so that this part of the world was viewed as the cradle of particularistic exclusive nationalism. In this context, Western nationalism is rational and good, whereas the central and eastern European version is nostalgic, emotional, eruptive, irrational and as such bad.

In Kohn's understanding, the 1929 riots denoted the dangers latent in nationalism that eventually brought the Zionist chapter in his life to end. Others like Anita Shapira, in her book, *Land and Power*,[32] has pointed out that it was Hebron and Safed, the two mixed towns were Jews and Arabs had lived side by side for generations that the worst attacks were perpetrated against the Jews. These riots 'exercised a major formative impact on the future map of Jewish colonization in Palestine. The configuration would serve as a basis when the day arrived for a partition plan.'[33]

ARTHUR RUPPIN

Arthur Ruppin came to Zionism and Brit Shalom from a different corner of central Europe; his roots were in the traditional Jewish community of Posen in western Prussia. He came to Palestine at the age of thirty-two, and his world was deeply influenced by his personal, academic and professional experiences in Germany.[34] Derek Penslar in *Zionism and Technology* highlights the fact that Ruppin began to form his views of the relationship between the individual and society in his book *Darwinism and the Social Sciences* with a view to improving the German race.[35] However, his exposure to anti-Semitism led him to conclude that he had to devote his life to the Jewish people. Once the decision was made, Ruppin began to put into practice the view of renewal that he had developed in Germany, in Jewish society. Ruppin, the demographer had come to Palestine with an anti-assimilation stance that is, separation of populations—Arabs and Jews. Over the years, Ruppin was forced to contend with the Palestinians' hostility to the Zionist settlement enterprise and after 1910; he began to recognize the beginnings of a national conflict. Agriculture played an important role in Ruppin's conception of Zionist renewal. Agriculture needs land and in the Zionist setting such areas were destined to become disputed territory. Penslar argues that the Zionists application of the Prussian model to Palestine was more instrumental than substantive.[36] Ruppin did believe that the Jews and Arabs were caught up in a life-and-death struggle for one and the same territory.

Both Kohn and Ruppin advocated separate existence and autonomy as two models of coexistence and binationalism—models that also functioned as strategies for the survival of Zionism. While Kohn developed a cultural model of separation, Ruppin translated his concept into a territorial/spatial framework. He based his rejection of plans such as the Balfour Declaration on a position that he ascribed

to east European Zionism. So, for Ruppin, the most that the Arabs were prepared to grant to the Jews were the rights of a minority in an Arab state, following the east European pattern and past experience revealed that rights granted by the majority are worthless and would certainly not satisfy the east European Jews, who constituted an overwhelming majority of Zionist. This would result in a decline of enthusiasm for Eretz Israel and such a Zionism would mean Zionism without Zionists.[37]

THE BRIT SHALOM MOVEMENT

The standard historiographic reading ascribes to the Brit Shalom members the attributes of central European liberalism and moderation. However, a more in-depth analysis of the formative experiences of representatives of Brit Shalom's two wings—Kohn standing for the radical wing and Arthur Ruppin as spokesman for the consensual position reveals the view to be superficial and general. Hans Kohn was the champion of the dichotomous division between ethno-nationalism in central Europe and state nationalism. According to Will Kymlicka, 'this misleading view, resting on the dubious historical distinction made by Kohn between western territorialism and eastern ethnicism has been reinforced by the myth of the ethno-cultural neutrality of liberal-democratic western states'.[38] Kymlicka rejects the geographic distinction, emphasizing that ethno-nationalism is related to the process of nation-building, and not to any essentialist geographical trait or quality. He argues that, in Eastern Europe, models suddenly appeared that involved a genuine attempt at solving the problems of multithnicity. Geographical location does not determine political outlook, geography is neither fate nor essence, it provides a fabric on which agile minds can move in various directions. Even the most progressive Zionists were not able to articulate binationalism effectively.[39]

JEWISH NATIONALISM: ITS DISTINCTIVENESS

Nationalist movements differ from one another, the common denominator, is usually reduced to the aspiration of a collectivity, conscious of its particular identity, to govern itself and nurture its culture. National movements reveal an enormous variety of historical features, each resulting from a separate culture, history and set of circumstances. This is particularly true of the Jewish case because of the variety of Diasporas. Jewish nationalism was particularly careful to

guard the borders of Jewish identity and Jewish nationalism always appeared as an eminently particularistic nationalism that closes in on itself, keeps itself apart and rejects outsiders. The impression of Jewish national identity remained that of a closed society, often considered to be similar to German nationalism, which emphasized the importance of kinship above all other tests of identity.[40]

There is also a tendency to trace a close connection between the Jewish people and the very appearance of nationalism. Rousseau singled out the Jewish people as an extraordinary case of a people that had survived through dedicated preservation of its culture and laws, even in times of adversity. Hans Kohn,[41] Adrian Hastings,[42] developed the idea that the example of the biblical Israelites was the first historical example of a nation proper and of nationalism.

If the principles of European nationalism are applied to Zionism, it can be said that when Herzl received the principle of modern nationalism from Europe and sought to apply it to the Jewish people, he adopted a modern, secular and foreign principle. It was, however, a principle whose remote roots sprang from within the ancient Jewish people before being transmitted to Christian Europe. It was also a principle which did not remain secular and foreign for long as it was quickly converted taking on central and symbolic Jewish traits.[43]

The Zionists were endlessly grappling with the abstract problems involved in defining their goals. The need of the Jewish thinkers to harmonize their world-view with their attitudes toward Zionism is very striking. It is as if an aspiration for national independence resulting from a feeling of belonging may be enough for other national movements, but not for Jews. The different streams of Zionism loaded their ideological agendas with religious, social or universalistic aims. During the mandatory period, a group of Hebrew University professors,[44] emphasized the duty to act according to the moral laws of Judaism, which they interpreted as being universal moral laws objectively applied. They were also keen to apply intellectual conclusions derived from historical or philosophical research to the problems that Zionism raised. Descent, origin, belonging, collective interest were to them irrelevant as motives. Jewish wisdom and morality dictated to them cooperation with the Arabs, the setting up of a bi-national pacifist and disarmed state, a model society based on the Jewish heritage of justice and equality.

Contrary to the European and American reform movements, the Jewish reform movements did not shake off Jewish nationalism but gave it their own definition. They believed in setting up a Jewish

community in Palestine, imbued with Jewish culture, as part of a bi-national Palestinian state. The university was to be the place where the revival of Jewish culture and its enrichment through the study of humanities and the sciences would take place. The plan for a binational state resulted from a conviction that morally and realistically it was the only option. The aspiration of a Jewish state was bound to lead to endless war. This group was troubled by questions concerning the essence of nationalism and its good and bad ways of expressing itself. Judaism dictated to them a spiritual kind of nationalism—moral, just, pacifist—whose horizons would cover the whole of humanity.

In Israel, universalism was adopted by some of the peace movements. Brit Shalom movement in the mandatory period was influenced by the American model, but its remarkable feature was its claim that the inspiration and authority for a morally universalist and internationally peace-oriented nationalism was to be found in Judaism and in the teachings of the biblical prophets. An inherently strong Jewish element was evident in the early peace movements derived partly from the European Jewish scholars who interpreted Judaism for themselves and for the outside world as an eminently moral, pacifist and universalist religion.

In contemporary Israel, the transformation that was supposed to turn the Jewish people into a normal nation whose identity would be taken for granted and therefore ignored as an issue, has not taken place. The tendency to grapple with questions of identity and goals has grown more intense. Two thousand years of deeply diverse developments cannot apparently be ironed out easily. The debate within Zionism between saving the individual or saving the collective existence between particularism and universalism; between ordinary nationalism or a Zionism imbued with aspirations of saving the world; between 'like other nations' and the idea of a model nation; between Judaism as a product of the national culture or the notion that Judaism is the purpose for which the Jewish people exist—all of these debates continue till date and continue to influence the practical choices that individuals and groups make.[45] The language of the debate has changed as new vocabularies are introduced that fit the historical experiences and intellectual discourses of the present generation; but the need for them springs from the predicaments that have resulted from the torturous paths of Jewish history. These deep ideological rifts have accompanied Zionism since its inception and even after the fulfilment of its political objective that distinguish Jewish nationalism from all others.

NOTES

1. The classification of nationalism into ethno-cultural and civic has been advocated by the likes of Hans Kohn, Anthony D. Smith and Chaim Gans. See Hans Kohn, *Nationalism: Its Meaning and History*, N.J., Princeton: D. Van Nostrand Company, Inc., 1965. Also see, Anthony D. Smith, *Nationalism: Theory, Ideology, History*, N.J.: Wiley-Blackwell, 2001 and Chaim Gans, *The Limits of Nationalism*, Cambridge: Cambridge University Press, 2003.
2. See Gans, *The Limits of Nationalism*, op. cit., introduction, pp. 1-6 and ch. 1, pp. 7-38, for a detailed definition of ethno-cultural nationalism.
3. See ibid., for a definition of civic nationalism and for drawing a contrast between civic nationalism and ethno-cultural nationalism.
4. For an account of the debates on whether Zionism should be regarded as an example of ethno-cultural nationalism or as civic nationalism, see Chaim Gans, *A Just Zionism: On the Morality of the Jewish State*, Oxford: Oxford University Press, 2008, pp. 9-24.
5. Theodor Herzl, *The Jewish State*, tr. Sylvie d' Avigdor, New York: Dover, 1988, Theodor Herzl, *Altneuland*, tr. Lotta Levensohn, New York: Bloch, 1941.
6. For a detailed discussion on aspects of civic nationalism and ethno-cultural nationalism within Zionism see Gideon Shimoni, *The Zionist Ideology*, Hanover: Brandeis University Press, 1995. See also Anita Shapira, *Land and Power: The Zionist Resort to Force, 1881-1948*, New York: Oxford University Press, 1992.
7. For an understanding of the Canaanite movement, see James S. Diamond, *Homeland or Holy Land?: The Canaanite Critique of Israel*, Bloomington: Indiana University Press, 1986.
8. For details on the Uganda Plan and the Seventh Zionist Congress, see Shimoni, op. cit.
9. Gans, *A Just Zionism: On the Morality of the Jewish State*, op. cit., pp. 15, 24.
10. Kidron Hedva Ben-Israel, 'Zionism and European Nationalisms: Comparative Aspects', *Israel Studies*, vol. 8, no.1, Spring 2003, pp. 91-104.
11. Ibid., p. 94.
12. See Alan John Percivale Taylor, *English History 1914-1945*, Oxford: Oxford University Press, 1965, pp. 51-2.
13. See Shimoni, *The Zionist Ideology*, op. cit. Also see Arthur Hertzberg, *The Zionist Idea: A Historical Analysis and Reader*, Philadelphia: The Jewish Publication Society of America, 1997.
14. See Gans, *The Limits of Nationalism*, op. cit., introduction, pp. 1-6 and ch. 1, pp. 7-38, 2003 for detailed definitions of ethno-cultural and civic nationalisms.
15. See Anthony D. Smith, *The Nation in History: Historiographical Debates about Ethnicity and Nationalism*, Hanover: Brandeis University Press, 2000.
16. See Hans Kohn, *Prophets and Peoples: Studies in Nineteenth Century Nationalisms*, New York: Macmillan, 1952.
17. For Achad Ha'am, see Shimoni, *The Zionist Ideology*, op. cit., pp. 80-96.
18. See Shimoni and Wistrich, *Theodor Herzl: Visionary of the Jewish State*, Jerusalem: The Hebrew University Press, 1999, pp. 240-64.
19. Kidron Hedva Ben-Israel, 'Zionism and European Nationalisms: Comparative Aspects', *Israel Studies*, vol. 8, no. 1, Spring 2003, p. 98.
20. See Tony Judt, 'Israel: An Alternative Future', *New York Review of Books*, 23 October 2003.

21. See Hagit Lavisky, 'German Zionists and the Emergence of the Brit Shalom', in *Essential Papers on Zionism*, ed. J.Reinharz and A. Shapira, New York: New York University Press, 1996, p. 654.
22. Ibid., p. 655.
23. Ibid.
24. See Yfaat Weiss, 'Central European Ethno-nationalism and Zionist Binationalism', *Jewish Social Studies* 11, no. 1(Fall 2004), pp. 93-117.
25. See Hans Kohn, *Living in a World Revolution: My Encounters with History*, New York: Simon and Schuster, 1964, p. 1.
26. Ibid., p. 9.
27. Ibid., p. 10.
28. Ibid., pp. 18-19.
29. See Weiss, 'Central European Ethno-nationalism and Zionist Binationalism,' op. cit., p. 101.
30. See Havit Lavsky, *Before Catastrophe: The Distinctive Path of German Zionism,* Detroit: Wayne State University Press, 2002, pp. 191-5.
31. See Hans Kohn, *Living in a World Revolution: My Encounters with History*, New York: Simon & Schuster, 1964, p. 53.
32. See Anita Shapira, *Land and Power: The Zionist Resort to Force, 1881-1948*, New York: Oxford University Press, 1992.
33. Ibid., p. 176.
34. See Derek Penslar, *Zionism and Technocracy: The Engineering of Jewish Settlement in Palestine, 1817-1918,* Bloomington: Indiana University Press, 1991, pp. 80-1.
35. Ibid., p. 88.
36. Ibid., pp. 95-8.
37. See Weiss, 'Central European Ethno-nationalism and Zionist Binationalism', op. cit., pp. 110-11.
38. See Will Kymlicka, ' Nation-building and Minority Rights: Comparing West and East', *Journal of Ethnic and Migration Studies*, vol. 26, no. 2, 2000, p. 186.
39. See Weiss,' 'Central European Ethno-nationalism and Zionist Binationalism', op. cit., pp. 112-13.
40. Kidron Hedva Ben-Israel, 'Zionism and European Nationalisms: Comparative Aspects', *Israel Studies,* vol. 8, no. 1, Spring 2003, pp. 98-9.
41. See Hans Kohn, *The Idea of Nationalism*, New York: Macmillan, 1944.
42. See Adrian Hastings, *The Construction of Nationhood: Ethnicity, Religion and Nationalism*, Cambridge: Cambridge University Press, 1997.
43. See David Vital, *The Origins of Zionism*, Oxford: Oxford University Press, 1980, pp. 339-45.
44. They include the likes of Judah Leon Magnes, Martin Buber, Hugo Bergmann and others.
45. Kidron, Hedva Ben-Israel, 'Zionism and European Nationalisms: Comparative Aspects', op. cit., pp. 91-104.

13

Shiva's Children in Prophet's Land: The Story of Indians in Malaysia

BINODA K. MISHRA

INTRODUCTION

Culture has emerged as an interest area of study for scholars interested in a wide variety of subjects ranging from sociology to international relations. One reason for its increasing demand as a subject of study is its being perceived as a cause of conflict in various parts of the world. In the last few decades, in conflict after conflict based on identity and identity politics, it is assumed by both the participants and the observers of such conflicts, that such identities are deeply rooted in a distinctive 'culture' that must be preserved and defended. The culture in question is said to be larger than civilization, which travels with man when he transgresses the civilizational boundaries in terms of time and space. Such notion of fixed cultures and fixed identities emerging from them, is a product of the recent discourse that names cultures and divides societies. This paper intends to argue that culture is not fixed, rather it changes in terms of its connotations. Culture demonstrates its static potential only as a form of strategic essentialism. Culture becomes rigid and backs or creates rigid identities only when the culture in question is purposively targeted and the identities associated with that culture are forced to evaporate. The culture then becomes crystallized and the identity it supports becomes a jealously guarded objective. In other words, only when the political system, within which a particular culture tries to survive or exist, tries to create a society based on hierarchy of identities and cultures, that culture and identity get fixed. I look at the identity politics in Malaysia in which Indians are struggling to survive and locate the utility and role of culture and show how the connotation and role of culture has changed in response to non-cultural, particularly, political stimuli.

Malaysia is trying hard to refute its own history and create a homogeneous state of the historically constituted composite society. An attempt is being made to deny the civilizational contact that Malaysia had with Indian civilization. This is not a natural development, and not in line with natural evolution of societies. It is just a matter of political expediency. The political actors dealing with the history of Malay nationhood are undoubtedly aware of the adverse impact of such actions on the natural evolution of the nation state. The story of the Indians in Malaysia is altered/re-written by some scholars and people at large. In this case, this created/re-created identity which becomes the reference point, is highly parochial and exclusive. If the alteration of/assault upon this identity is at the level of sumum genus, then the identity that emerges is highly inclusive among the diaspora. Divisive lines among the diaspora merge to create an identity based on the lowest common denominator and acts as a binding force for the diasporic community in the distant land, working against the attempt of subjugation and elimination.

INDIAN DIASPORA AND THE INDIAN IDENTITY IN MALAYSIA

Identity may have emerged as a focal interest-area for academics fairly recently, but its genealogies are embedded in histories of communities. The intensity of attachment of the community to its primordial identity varies with the community's physical proximity to the sources and symbols of their primordial identity. Thus, identity becomes an issue more for the diaspora who move away from the source of identity and culture carrying nothing but the culture of their native lands when they travel away from their homelands. Culture provides them the nucleus and social space they need during the process of integration into the alien society within which they are placed, sometimes forcibly. The longevity of the carried culture, in its pure form, depends on the environment of the host society. If the host society is accommodative in every sense, then the carried culture soon fades away leading either to complete integration of the diaspora community into the host society, or at the least to the creation of a unique culture having traits of both the native and host societies. But in case the host society is non-accommodative or turns hostile before the process of integration is complete, friction results and the carried culture solidifies into a boundary that the diaspora dares not to cross. On the contrary, the diaspora fight to protect the boundary. The story of Indians in Malaysia closely resembles the second scenario.

The present people of Indian origin in Malaysia largely originated from the labour migration under the British colonialism. Mercantile and religious travels to Southeast Asia in general predated the labour migration under the colonial masters, but nineteenth-century labour migration to Malay formed a foundation for an evolving Indian community in the country. Indian population in Malaysia, despite having ancient contacts, was not substantial till the involvement of the British in both India and Malaysia. 'By 1833, there were no more than 15,000 Indians,[1] and many of these had been recruited by the colonial government to fulfil roles in the administration such as clerks and policemen, who were generally Punjabis.'[2] A large number of Indians travelled to Malaysia under the indenture system to fill the labour shortage created by the abolition of slavery in 1833. With the introduction of sugar and coffee plantations in Malaysia, the demand for Indian labourers increased. Indians were transported either directly by the British owners or were sent by *kanganis*.[3] The system of recruiting Indian labourers (coolies) became so exploitative that the Indian government banned the practice, but the desperate need for labour led to flagrant violation of this ban. After negotiations between the governments of India and of the Straits, free movement of Indian labour was allowed from India to Malaysia. The need for Indian labour got a further boost with the introduction of rubber plantations in Malaysia in 1905. The need was so intense that the colonial government in India became directly involved in the process of labour migration.[4]

The process of Indian labour migration continued to Malaysia freely till the 1931 census of Malaysia revealed that the indigenous Malays had been outnumbered by the combined population of the Indians and the Chinese. Some time before this census, when the Malay minority in Malaysia seemed eminent, the British articulated a policy of discrimination, abandoning their advocated democratic approach. Under the discriminatory policy, the Malays were to get preference over the non-Malays in matters of land, political opportunities, education, citizenship, etc. To arrest further dilution of Malay population profile, restrictive acts such as 'Aliens Ordinance' (1933) were promulgated to restrict migration into the country. In order to ensure facilities for the indigenous Malays, the term 'Malay' was defined to exclude the Indians and the Chinese even though they had been living in Malaysia for a few generations. 'Malay' was defined to be someone who belonged to Malay race, spoke Malay language, and professed Islam.[5]

By the time Malaysia attained independence, a grand alliance among the ethnic Malays, the ethnic Chinese, and the ethnic Indians represented respectively by United Malays National Organisation (UMNO), Malay Chinese Association (MCA), and Malaysian Indian Congress (MIC) were working towards the independence of Malaysia. A compromise was struck among the three political parties representing the three main races that constituted the Malaysian nation: namely, the Malays, the Chinese, and the Indians. According to this compromise, the Chinese and the Indians would accept the special political privileges of the Malays, in return of Malays acknowledging the rightful business interests and liberal citizenship rights for the Chinese and the Indians. This compromise was supposed to give political power to the Malays and economic power to the Chinese and the Indians, and there would be a peaceful coexistence of the three main races in the newly independent Malaysia. The riots of May 1969 proved the lack of equal commitment of all parties to the compromise of 1957. The immediate fallout of the riot was an attempt to tighten the Malay control not only over politics but also over the economy of the country through the introduction of the New Economic Policy (NEP) of 1971. Before going into the discussion as to how the new economic policy of 1971 affected the Indians, it would be apt to discuss the profile of the Indians who travelled to Malaysia and their socio-cultural and economic status till the introduction of this NEP.

The Indians who travelled to Malaysia were primarily from the southern part of the India, but also contained people from other parts of the country. The labourers recruited from India were drawn primarily from socio-economic backward classes of the society and were mostly illiterate and parochial. The labour recruitment policy of the British ensured that the labourers could be manipulated easily and prevented from getting assimilated into the host society. In the words of Kernial Sandhu:

> The south Indian labourer was preferred because he was malleable, worked well under supervision, and was easily manageable. He was not as ambitious as his northern Indian compatriots and certainly nothing like the Chinese . . . he was the most amenable to the comparatively lowly paid and rather regimented life of the estates and government departments. He had fewer qualms or religious susceptibilities, such as aversion to crossing the dreaded *kalapani* and food taboos . . . and cost less in feeding and maintenance.[6]

Contracted for a period from one year to three years, the Indian labourers ventured abroad under the indenture system. One of the reasons for Indians opting to migrate in large numbers was the lack of economic opportunity for the economically lower stratum of the

society and the lower social status of the backward castes. This exodus (migration to a foreign land/lands) was a logical extension of the internal migration that was widespread throughout India during the nineteenth and first decades of the twentieth century. By the time Malaysia attained independence, Indians constituted the third largest ethnic community of the country accounting for 14 per cent of the population of Malaysia. As mentioned earlier, the migrants mainly came from southern part of India though it was estimated that nearly 50,000 north Indians had also made their way to Malaysia under various systems of recruitment, mostly voluntary in nature.

However, the control of the British government over the entire process was directed not to allow the migrants getting integrated into the local community since this needed allowing some rights to the Indians. The process was often so harsh that they lost the habit of taking on adventurous plunges into uncertainly. This segregation at the psychological level prevented Indians from breaking away from their 'mythical' Indian identity and create a unique identity, in which being Malay would be equally reflected. I call the Indian identity mythical because there is a difference between actuality and its perception from afar. This became prominent among the second generation onwards. The identity that emerged among the first and the second generation, in the words of Shanthini Pillai, was a 'suspended' identity created on the basis of the symbols preserved and passed down generations as the only representative of the identity they are supposed to protect lest the pain would be much more than the [then] present. There are interesting descriptions of the boundary that separated the mythical Indian identity and the identity of the adopted homeland. It has been described as the magical line drawn by Laxman around Sita when he was forced to follow Ram during the chase of the deceptive and illusory *Swarna Mriga* (golden deer). Indians lived in the peace of security within that boundary as Sita was meant to stay. The most important implication of this analogy/description is the warning against violation, the results of which are well known. 'Denied their humanity and self-respect, it is therefore not surprising that their ability to retain aspects of culture connected to the motherland was seen as a triumph for the Indian immigrants, as it forged their own emblem of an undiminished Indian self. Anything that was seen as likely to fracture this "intact" self was shunned.'[7]

The culture that became the reference point for such suspended identity was not inclusive even within the community. The earliest effort to keep the Indians separated from the indigenous community was prevention of mobility, even among Indians. The segregation

of Indian migrant labourers into smaller groups, often belonging to smaller known groups or communities, the origins of which may have been as traced to meetings in the ship during the voyage to the unknown, resulted in highly parochial cultures in various parts of Malaysia. The fragments have also been accused of fighting amongst each other, though not with arms. The fractured and contested identities included markers such as language, region, caste, etc.

ISLAMIZATION OF MALAYSIA

The British economic and political objectives were well served by ensuring that the suspension did not end. In order to perpetuate this suspended position of the Indian migrant labourers they practised their usual policy of divide and rule. The British were quick enough to realize the inherent potential of Malaysian society to cause the division on ethnic lines. Comprising three ethnicities—Malays, Chinese and the Indians, the society could be easily divided, and one could be set against the other. The situation was expected to change after Malay independence in 1957. The alliance that was formed on the basis of an understanding between the three racially represented political parties, was supposed to make Malaysia a modern composite nation. The riot of 1969 was the first major indicator of the uncomfortable juxtaposition of the three major races in Malaysia. And the situation became complex with Islam being inextricably enmeshed with, and connoting the Malay identity. During the initial years of independent Malaysia, Islam was being promoted by Persatuan Aislam Sa-Melayu (PAS), which later came to be known as Partai Islam Se-Malay. PAS objected to the ethnic compromises and strongly pressed for the idea of 'Malaya belonging to Malays'. 'It campaigned for enforcing Islamic principles and supported the application of *Sharia* law in matters relating to criminal, public and commercial law.'[8]

The riots of 13 May 1969 were regarded as a result of the backwardness of indigenous Malays in Malaysia. Thus, the NEP spelled out the target of ensuring 30 per cent of Malay and indigenous ownership in all industrial and commercial activities by 1990. This was to be achieved though the system of 'special rights to Bumiputeras'. Along with the introduction of NEP of 1971, there was a strong articulation of Islam as the foundation and marker of Malay identity. Around the same time, a movement swept Malaysia that 'summoned' or 'called' the lapsed Muslims to restore faith in Islam, and accelerate conversion to Islam.[9] Islam was used as a political tool by political parties. But it slowly became a tool to craft

Malay nationalism. In the words of Dr Mahathir Mohamad: 'The inculcation of Islamic values into the country's administration will create a Government which is more just and effective. All citizens irrespective of race or religion will benefit from an administration based on Islamic values.'[10] This statement was in sharp contrast to what Tunku Abdul Rahman, the first prime minister of Malaysia, articulated in 1958. He said: 'There is no way we should have an Islamic state here . . . we cannot force the non-Malays and non-Muslims to follow our way of life. Our slogan "live and let live" must be maintained because it is the only practical solution in a multi-racial society like ours.'[11]

This departure was an indication of growing Islamization of Malaysia which was directed against the interests of the non-Malays. This exclusion of non-Muslims rested on/derived from the pretext of preserving Malay identity and preserving Malay (Muslim) dominance in Malaysia.[12] The approach had its manifestations in economy, politics, and culture. The demography of Malaysia over the years reveals the impact of Islamization. From 1980 to 2000 there have been contrasting changes in the religious configuration of Malaysia. The Muslim population increased from 53 per cent in 1980 to 60.4 per cent in 2000.[13] In contrast, the Hindu population decreased from 7 per cent in 1980 to 6.3 per cent in 2000. Another indication of demographic change was the reduction in Buddhist population from 28 per cent in 1970 to 19.2 per cent in 2000.[14]

The most important reflection was in culture, which resulted in social alienation of the non-Malays, particularly the Shaivite Indians. Islam was deployed and publicized to be the base of Malay civilization and culture. The aim was to undermine and later eliminate the ancient Hindu influence on Malay culture and civilization.[15] This gradual approach of eliminating Hindu influence took on a more aggressive tenor.

Empirical evidence shows the gradual subjugation of non-Malays over the years. During the period 1968-2000, 2,637 Malay primary schools have been built, while 48 Chinese primary school, and 144 Indian primary schools have been closed down.[16] Indian schools receive only 1 per cent of the education budget in comparison to 96.5 per cent that goes to the Malay schools.[17] Non-Malays constituted 70 per cent of the university lecturers in 1965. This number stands at 5 per cent in the year 2004.[18] 'Since 1970, at least 3000 mosques were built in all housing estates throughout Malaysia whereas no temples are required [*sic*] to be built in housing estates.'[19] By 1992, the ratio of mosques to Muslim worshippers was 1:800 in certain

parts of Malaysia, and the ratio of non-Muslim worshippers to their place of worship was 1:4000/1:5000 in the same area.[20] Restrictions were placed in 1981 on the importing of non-Islamic texts into Malaysia. The data shows clear subordination of non-Malay interests to the interests of the Malays. This systematic discrimination could be possible only because of the efforts of the political forces such as UMNO who tried to establish Malay hegemony in the country. The pro-Malay policy was never made obvious. But the political authority/government, determined to hold on to political power, did not adopt a more liberal policy that would create equal scope for the non-Malays to get assimilated into the Malay national mainstream. In the political sphere it was ensured that the Malays remained dominant. The consociational arrangement among the three ethnic political parties that was in practice since 1957, was changed in the aftermath of the 1969 riots to ensure UMNO dominance in the political domain of the country.[21] The MIC, formed in 1946 was the primary political organization responsible for articulating and protecting Indian interests. But in reality, the MIC could do nothing other than endorse the decisions taken by UMNO in return for personal favours to the MIC leaders and articulating seemingly well-meaning, but specious policies in regard to the interests of Malaysian Indians.

The economic impact of NEP along with increasingly aggressive Islamization of Malaysia is evident from the fact that 'since 1980, about 300,000 Indian plantation workers lost their jobs as a result of purchase of privately owned plantations by government-linked corporations or by sale of plantation lands for township development schemes'.[22] The loss was not only of jobs but also of property and housing for the Indians who were then forced to earn their livelihoods though lowest paid menial jobs in the urban centres. On pretexts of development, the Malay authorities started targeting the Hindu temples and demolished many of them. During 2006-7, a number of Hindu temples were demolished, including a 107-year old temple at Shah Alam.[23] This act of demolition angered the Indian population more than the economic and political deprivation they had suffered due to the 1957 bargain.

RE-ARTICULATION OF INDIAN (HINDU) IDENTITY

By the beginning of the twenty-first century, it was clear to the Indians that the solemn assurance given by the grand coalition—that Islam would not unduly intrude upon public and political life, was not kept. It was not going to be respected by the alliance led by Islamic

hegemonic UMNO. Indians, not alone though, started believing that Islamization posed a severe threat to both ethnic and religious integrity.[24] UMNO was perceived to be appeasing the Islamic radical extremism that would only weaken the status of the non-Muslims. In response to the discrimination by the Malays (Muslims) and the failure of the MIC, the principal political representative of the Indians in articulating and campaigning for Indian interests was the earlier divided Indian community. It started re-grouping itself. The cosmic dance of Nataraja was used by writers like K.S. Maniam to describe the destruction of the Indian identity. It tried to convey or reflect that the utopian concept of motherland, India, could not crystallize because of the assertiveness of the Sons of the Soil (*Bumiputras*) coterminous with Sons of Prophet (Allah). Thus, the re-grouped identity assumed a religious character.

To draw attention to the plight of the impoverished Indians, there emerged an organization representing the Indians. Hindu Rights Action Force (HINDRAF) stood up to protect the genuine interests of the Indians. Taking the issue of large-scale temple demolition during 2006-7 and the general socio-economic deprivation of Indians, HINDRAF conducted a peaceful rally to bring the plight of the Indians to the attention of the British crown, whom the Indian community held squarely responsible for bringing them to Malaysia and exploiting them for more than 150 years, and remaining unconcerned about their interests when they granted independence to Malaysia. Nearly 30,000 Indians gathered in the heart of Kuala Lumpur on 14 November 2007 to demand action by the British crown. HINDRAF demanded US $1 million as damage money for each Indian in Malaysia. This protest by the HINDRAF-led Indians was met with harsh response. Under the order of Prime Minister Badawi, the Malaysian authorities used extreme means to suppress the peaceful protest and arrested the top HINDRAF leaders, and sentenced them under the draconian Internal Security Act (ISA). It was claimed that they were 'spreading allegations against the government'. The organization was subsequently banned and the leadership is under constant surveillance.

What emerged from the 2007 protests was that the Indian community which remained divided from within, realized the futility of remaining divided. Ironically, Indians chose not to articulate their identity as 'Indian'. Rather, they chose to articulate it in terms of 'Hindu' religious rhetoric. This use of religion, to some extent, prevented the Indian government from responding in any effective manner, causing deep sorrow among the Indians in Malaysia for

most of whom the (rising) India was a glorious ideal reflecting pride and joy. Still regarded as 'outsiders' or the 'other' by the Malay hegemonic state despite having contributed to the country's prosperity for several generations, they always had a strong linguistic, cultural, religious and emotional bond with old India,[25] which were reconfigured in the early twentieth century through oceanic travels of the Indian literati—especially Rabindranath Tagore, Suniti Kumar Chattopadhyay and others.

CONCLUSION

Indians who travelled to Malaysia during the colonial times either voluntarily, or due to lure and pressure found themselves trapped in a situation of suspension till Malaysia attained independence in 1957. Being drawn from the lower rung of the Hindu society, these migrants had no other option but to live in their cocoons within the plantation estates. Their ignorance, and the deliberate efforts of the Malay authorities prevented them from taking advantage of the citizenship rights which were offered to them during the initial years of independent Malaysia. The resurgence of Islam as a force in Malaysia, and Islamic identity being made coterminous with Malay identity resulted in selective exclusion of non-Malays (defined as non-Muslims). Among the two major ethnic minorities, namely the Chinese and the Indians, the Indians suffered the most as they were not in control of the commercial sector which was, and is dominated by the Chinese. Within the plantation estates, the Indians were divided among themselves. There was no meaningful interaction among themselves and/or with other communities. Being uprooted from their plantations, the Indians were forced to come in contact with the rest of the Malay society. They then experienced selective discrimination at the hands of Malay authorities who were determined to establish an Islamic state in Malaysia. By attacking the Indian community in all forms such as economy, politics and culture, the Malaysian authorities created a condition for the fragmented Indian community to unite under the identity tag of 'Hinduism'. The protests of 2007 may have been suppressed for the time being, but if the UMNO and the MIC do not see the writing on the wall and get reconciled to the fact that the future of Malaysia lies in recognition of equal rights of the all Malaysian citizens of all ethnicities, these children of Shiva (the Hindus) may be determined to carve out a land for themselves in this land of the Prophet.

NOTES

1. Donald R. Snodgrass, *Inequality and Economic Development in Malaysia*, Kuala Lumpur: Oxford University Press, 1980, p. 24.
2. Loren S. Ryter, 'A History of Race Relations in Malaysia', available on http://www.huaren.org/diaspora/asia/malaysia/raceis.html, accessed on 28 June 2005.
3. The term *kangani* means overseer. The *kanganis* were the middlemen acting on behalf of the British estate owners to recruit Indian labourers. The system was called the *kangani* system and was often described as an exploitative system.
4. Michael Stenson, *Race and Colonialism in West Malaysia: The Indian Case*, Vancouver: University of British Colombia Press, 1980, p. 18, cited in Loren S. Ryter, 'A History of Race Relations in Malaysia'. The source for this is http://www.huaren.org/diaspora/asia/malaysia/raceis.html, accessed on 28 June 2005.
5. The term 'Malay' was defined in the Malay Reservation Enactment of 1930. See Leon Comber, *13 May 1969: A Historical Survey of Sino-Malay Relations*, Kuala Lumpur: Heinemann Asia, 1983, p. 23.
6. Kernial Sandhu quoted by Amarjit Kaur, 'Malaysia', in B.V. Lal (ed.), *The Encyclopaedia of the Indian Diaspora*, Delhi: Oxford University Press, p. 157.
7. Shanthini Pillai, 'Indo-Malaysians: Suspended Identities or Citizens of a New Serfdom', in Makarand Paranjape (ed.), *In Diaspora: Theories, Histories, Texts*, Delhi: Indialog Publications, 2001, p. 248.
8. Gordon P. Means, *Malaysian Politics: The Second Generation*, Singapore: Oxford University Press, 1991, pp. 123-31.
9. The movement that started in about 1970 was called the *Dakwah* movement. The term *Dakwah* means summon or call. For details see, Gordon P. Means, *Political Islam in Southeast Asia*, Salangor: Strategic Information and Research Development Centre, 2009, pp. 85-8.
10. Dr. Mahathir Mohamad's speech before the MNO General Assembly 1984. Quoted in Mohamed Aslam Haneef, 'The Development and Impact of Islamic Economic Institutions: The Malaysian Experience', in K.S. Nathan and Mohammad Hashim Kamali (eds.), *Islam in Southeast Asia: Political, Social and Strategic Challenges for the 21st Century*, Singapore: Institute of Southeast Asian Studies, 2005, p. 86.
11. Quoted in Lim Siew Foong, 'What Makes an Islamic State', *Berita NECF*, November/December 2001, p. 3.
12. 'Malaysia for Malays' was based on the concept of *Bhumiputras* (Sons of the Soil). The concept of *Bhumiputra* meant indigenous Malays, which slowly got transformed into Malay Muslims.
13. 'Malaysia Census Shows Minorities Dwindling,' *The Straits Times Interactive*, 8 November 2001.
14. Ahmad F. Yousif, *Religious Freedom, Minorities and Islam: An Inquiry into the Malaysian Experience*, Salengor: Thinker's Library, 1998, cited in Peter G. Riddell, 'Islamization, Civil Society, and Religious Minorities in Malaysia', in K.S. Nathan and Mohammad Hashim Kamali (eds.), *Islam in Southeast Asia: Political, Social and Strategic Challenges for the 21st Century*, p. 86.
15. B. Raman, 'Root Causes of Hindu Anger in Malaysia', *C3S Paper No. 83*, 6 December 2007. www.c3sindia.org, accessed on 7 December 2007.

16. Ramza, 'Discrimination in Malaysia', www.faithfreedom.org/oped/Ramza60224.htm. Accessed on 21 August 2008.
17. Ibid.
18. Ibid.
19. Ibid.
20. Ng Kiok Nam, 'Islam in Malaysia', in J.P. Rajsekhar and H.S. Wilson, *Islam in Asia: Perspectives for Christian-Muslim Enounter*, Geneva: Lutheran World Federation, 1992, p. 100.
21. P. Ramasamy, 'Politics of India Representation in Malaysia', in K. Kesavapany, A. Mani and P. Ramasamy (eds.), *Rising India and Indian Communities in East Asia*, Singapore: Institute of Southeast Asian Studies, 2008, p. 359.
22. Gordon P. Means, *Political Islam in Southeast Asia*, Salangor: Strategic Information and Research Development Centre, 2009, p. 355.
23. Ibid.
24. K.S. Jomo and Ahmad Shabery Cheek, 'Malaysia's Islamic Movements, in Joel S. Khan and Loh Kok Wah (eds.), *Fragmented Vision: Culture and Politics in Contemporary Malaysia*, Sydney: Asian Studies Association of Australia/Allen and Unwin, 1992, p. 104.
25. S. Nagarajan, 'Indians in Malaysia: Towards Vision 2020', in K. Kesavapany, A. Mani and P. Ramasamy (eds.), *Rising India and Indian Communities in East Asia*, op. cit., p. 388.

VI. GENDER AND IDENTITY MOVEMENTS

14

Gendering Dalit Identities: Retelling 'National' Histories of 1857

CHARU GUPTA

The past few decades have seen the emergence of a vast amount of popular Dalit Hindi literature. A section of this literature has represented the role of Dalits in the freedom struggle of the colonial period, particularly in the revolt of 1857, in interesting ways. An analysis of 1857 from a Dalit perspective throws a completely different light on it, and transforms it in substantial ways. It reflects competing and complementary dynamics of nationhood and identity politics. In this paper, I attempt to examine 1857 through Dalit feminist lens. I reflect on the contradictory Dalit voices on 1857, as reflected in contemporary debates, archival records and popular Dalit literature of north India. I relate these perspectives specifically to the representations of Dalit women in 1857 and examine whether that symbolizes a collusion or subversion of patriarchies, or both, or something more. While examining the historical consciousness of the revolt in the public memory of the Dalits, I wish to thus deconstruct present-day tracts written by Dalits on 1857 and its heroes, particularly the Dalit *viranganas* (heroic women). In the process, I also wish to interrogate conventional and historical writings on 1857, and search for possibilities of a radical gendered Dalit politics beyond the rubric of the nation, and one that is not tied just to the tyranny of 1857.

CONVENTIONAL HISTORIES: AMBIGUOUS DALIT GENEALOGIES

The outbreak of 1857 has been regarded as a memorable episode in Indian history. It was in a sense one of the first formidable revolt that had broken out against foreign domination. The recent festivities around 1857 invoked heated debates regarding the position and participation of Dalits in it. We mainly got two responses. On the one

hand, there was deep condemnation of 1857 from a Dalit perspective, and on the other, there was an assertion of Dalit contribution, particularly that of Dalit *viranganas*, in it. Both these viewpoints, however, need to be placed in a larger context.

Scholars have argued that subaltern political actions and consciousness revealed a great degree of autonomy from mainstream nationalism. It has been stated that Dalits particularly have had an ambivalent relationship with both Indian nationalism and colonialism, often contradictory with the views of dominant Hindu communities.[1] A Dalit intellectual argues that the British liberated the Dalit masses from the oppressions of Hindu society by providing Dalits with the most important tool of liberation, which is access to education. In UP, many of the activists within the Dalit movement had articulated similar ideas as early as the 1920s.[2] Dalits were neither fully convinced of the Congress-led agenda of nationalism, nor did they share universally the Indian nationalists' opposition to colonialism. Dalit activists, thinkers and intellectuals have thus often held positions at odds with those of mainstream caste Hindu historians and political leaders. These positions and mentalities have had a basis in their material and social realities. 1857 too cannot be isolated from these positionings. The upper-caste modes of thought and anti-Dalit biases of 1857 are well documented in the proclamations of Birjis Qadr[3] and Bahadur Shah.[4] Their derogatory statements reflect deep contempt for the Dalits in 1857, and also symbolize the authoritarianisms of pre-colonial caste formations. Their nostalgic yearnings for pre-British pasts have obviously not found any favour among the Dalits.[5]

Conventional and standardized histories of the revolt have stressed its upper caste character.[6] Scholars have also reflected on the overwhelmingly upper caste composition of the Bengal Army to underscore the internal caste contradictions within Indian society.[7] As these high caste personnel of the Bengal Army turned against the East India Company, the British mobilized a section of the low castes. The Awadh Police Force for example had a large component of Pasis, Bhungis, Chamars and Dhanuks, who participated in the suppression of the revolt.[8] It thus appears that Dalits did not have much to gain and only something to lose by being active allies in the revolt. It is not surprising that Jyotiba Phule congratulated the Mahars for aiding the British in suppressing the 1857 revolt.[9] In fact, from Phule to Ambedkar, a significant part of Dalit tradition has repeatedly celebrated the victory of British in 1857, which according to some Dalit intellectuals, was an antithesis of modernity, and was

retrogressive and narcissistically upper caste.[10] Dalit positionings thus point out to the limits of 1857, and by extension of nationalism. A part of Dalit politics has thus refused to bow down to the more powerful and inclusive categories of nation and nationalism, and have maintained a separate identity.

At the same time, it would only be a partial reading to end here. There were much more complex and contradictory pulls at this time, and the multilayered character of 1857 cannot be denied, and scholars too emphasize the popular and low caste basis of the revolt.[11] More important, post-independent India, particularly of the past three decades, coinciding with the meteoric rise of Dalit movements in north India, has seen a flourishing of popular Hindi Dalit literature, which is mass produced in thousands and sold through public rallies and *melas* of Dalits.[12] Given the imperative political assertions by the Dalits in present times, there has been a need felt to declare the nationalist credentials of the Dalits in a section of this literature.[13] Thus, Dalit histories have come out with copious volumes on their contribution and role in the independence movement.[14] 1857 especially figures in a major way here, converging histories, myths, realities and retelling of the pasts.[15] There has been an appropriation and a differential interpretation of 1857 here, taking on the character of a Dalit resistance, where alternative Dalit heroes—some constructed, some exaggerated, some 'discovered'—are represented as the real symbols of 1857. In these accounts, the armies of soldiers against British consist largely of Dalits. The focus of this literature is no longer on the sepoys or the greased cartridges, but on Dalits groaning under foreign oppression. As the famous Dalit poet Bihari Lal Harit says regarding 1857:

> *nai, dhobi, kurmi, kachchi/bharbhuje bhaat kumhaar lare.*
> *Lare khak rub mochi dhanak/sab daliton ke parivar lare.*
>
> (Barbers, washermen, gardeners, grain-parchers, bards and potters fought.
> Cobblers rolling in dust and cotton-carders fought. All Dalit families fought.)[16]

Dalit narratives of 1857 deploy an impassioned language, writing history with a mission by claiming a past and using it for the furtherance of their future. One of their purposes in writing inspirational histories of this kind is to stimulate Dalit nationalism, Dalit patriotic sentiment, and their pride. They are rewriting history to provide dignity to the Dalits.[17]

Present-day feelings are ascribed to Dalit heroes of 1857, and they are seen as teaching a moral lesson that the Dalits of today need to emulate the heroic deed of their past heroes, and fight for their rights now as well. The present circumstances have made new constructions and hitherto unimaginable imaginings possible for the Dalits. Through 1857, they are also seeking to win acceptance from the wider society by creating and legitimizing a space for themselves within the nationalist narratives.[18] However, these histories are not just reinventions of the past or inspirational histories. Dalits claim to be overturning the prejudices of mainstream historiography, be it nationalist, Marxist or Western, by retrieving lost histories. As says one:

yatra-tatra sarvatra milegi, unki gaatha ki charcha.
kintu upekshit veervaron ka—kabhi nahin chapta parcha.

(Here, there and everywhere, you will find discussions on their deeds, but the scorned [Dalit] heroes are never written about in papers.)[19]

This literature is representative of a Dalit imagined nation in search of its own historical narration. However, even in its inspirational and celebratory mode, it has an inherent tension within it, as it constantly grapples with its ambiguous genealogies of 1857 and Dalit relationships to the very character of the Indian nation.[20] However, it is significant that whether Dalits argue for an anti- or a pro-1857 stance, the social constructions of the role played by Dalits in 1857 have been changed by the Dalits themselves in tandem with changing social and political conditions in specific historical moments. Their literature underscores the disjuncture between a codified view of 1857 and its complex construction by Dalits.

More important, the paradoxical Dalit perceptions of 1857 signify the genealogies of ambiguous nationalisms, where the Dalits, from their own viewpoint, play with restrictive lineages of historical pasts. The contradictory politics of exclusion and inclusion, censure and celebration responds to the complex relationship that Dalits have had to both 1857 and nation-building at large, where they wish to be a part of the nation and yet cannot be. Dalits swing in their stances on 1857 because of their political compulsions about domains of power and nationalist assertions on the one hand, and their autonomy and resistance to a dominant and hegemonic nation on the other. Their discourse is thus marked by a complicated hybrid of shifting and selective appropriations, in which they can only have an incomplete and uneasy nationalist imagination with 1857.

POPULAR DALIT HISTORIES OF 1857 *VIRANGANAS*

1857 also emerges as a gendered arena from a Dalit perspective. Some of the scholars, while stressing the upper caste biases of 1857, have also accentuated how the revolt was an attempt to reinstate feudal patriarchies. Remarriage of widows and abolition of *sati* was condemned by many leaders of 1857.[21] A different kind of gendered tension, however, is visible in the popular Hindi Dalit literature of 1857, to which I now turn. When it comes to women, the memory of 1857 is inevitably tied to that of Lakshmibai, the Rani of Jhansi, with celebration of her valour in poetry, ballad, folk tale, drama, school textbooks and comics.[22] A chief feature of the popular Dalit histories of 1857 though has been an emphasis on the participation of their own Dalit *viranganas*, foreshadowing Lakshmibai and Begum Hazrat Mahal. In many popular Dalit histories, Dalit *viranganas* are being reinvented as part of a movement to define Dalit identities. Thus women like Jhalkari Bai of the Kori caste, Uda Devi, a Pasi, Avanti Bai, a Lodhi, Mahabiri Devi, a Bhangi, and Asha Devi, a Gurjari, all stated to be involved in the 1857 revolt, have become the symbols of bravery of particular Dalit castes and ultimately of all Dalits.[23]

Thus, for example, to take the case of Jhalkari Bai, there has been a proliferation of a number of popular tracts, and cultural invocations of her, including comics, poems, plays, novels, biographies, *nautankis*, and even magazines and organizations in her name. To name just a few, there is the comic *Jhalkari Bai*; poems variously titled *Virangana Jhalkari Bai Kavya*; *Jhansi ki Sherni: Virangana Jhalkari Bai ka Jeevan Charitra* and *Virangana Jhalkari Bai Mahakavya*; plays and *nautankis* called *Virangana Jhalkari Bai* and *Achhut Virangana Nautanki*; novels and biographies like *Virangana Jhalkari Bai* and *Achhut Virangana*; and a magazine called *Jhalkari Sandesh,* published from Agra.[24] Various Dalit magazines have published articles on her.[25] Similarly, on Uda Devi, there are poems, plays, stories and magazines penned and narrated on various occasions.[26] These representations of Dalit women as *viranganas* can be an important source of insight into gender politics from a Dalit perspective. They indicate certain ways in which 1857 is remembered and retailed by the Dalits, its relationship to their social and political positioning, and a sense of belonging to the nation.[27] Dalit women *viranganas* emerge here as objects of adulation. Their representations can signify contradictory voices, simultaneously asserting and subverting patriarchies.[28]

To take up some of the narratives briefly, Jhalkari Bai is depicted as an immortal martyr of 1857, belonging to the Kori caste, and hailing

from Jhansi. Her husband was an ordinary soldier in the kingdom of Raja Gangadhar Rao. Jhalkari Bai is shown as an ideal woman, stated to be brave since her childhood. Her face and body structure is said to resemble Lakshmibai. Slowly Jhalkari Bai and Lakshmibai become friends. Jhalkari was entrusted with the charge of leading the women's wing of the army. When the 1857 revolt began, and the British besieged the fort of Jhansi, Jhalkari fought fiercely. She urged Rani Lakshmibai to escape from the palace and instead she herself took on the guise of the Rani. She killed many British, and managed to hoodwink them for a long time, before they discovered her true identity.[29] Uda Devi is said to have been born in the village Ujriaon of Lucknow, and became an associate of Begum Hazrat Mahal. She formed a women's army. When the British attacked Sikandar Bagh in Lucknow under Campbell, he was faced with an army of Dalit women. At this point Uda Devi is said to have climbed over a tree and shot dead, according to some accounts 32 or 36, British soldiers, before she herself was shot dead.[30] Asha Devi Gurjari is portrayed as providing leadership to many women in 1857.[31] Narratives on Avanti Bai show how when surrounded by British soldiers, she decided to kill herself rather than surrender to them.[32] Mahabiri Devi belonged to the Bhangi caste and lived in a village of Muzaffarnagar. In 1857, she made a group of 22 women, killing many British soldiers. Finally she herself was killed by them and along with her, 22 other unknown women died.[33]

As a historian, when I started working on these Dalit *viranganas* of 1857, what concerned me was the absence of written historical evidence on them in the archives. At one level, Carlo Ginzburg reflects how an early manifesto on history 'from below' appeared in the form of an 'imaginary biography', where the intention was to salvage through a symbolic character, a multitude of lives crushed by poverty and oppression. The mixture of imaginary biography and historical documents makes it possible even for these Dalit histories to leap at a single bound over a threefold obstacle: the lack of evidence; the lack of importance of the subject according to commonly accepted criteria; and the absence of stylistic models. A multitude of lives that have been destined to count for nothing, find their symbolic redemption in the depiction of immortal characters.[34]

But this is not enough. Dalits themselves are keen to prove the historical credibility of their *viranganas*, and constantly cite sources from literary accounts, British narratives and oral histories. Their's is a conscious effort to suggest the existence of historical dimensions

that are hidden, in part (but not only) owing to the difficulties of documentary access, where gaps are filled with the use of memories, folksongs, oral accounts, and elements taken from larger present contexts. As says one:

aitihasik sandarbhon bhitar, ankit sari hai ghatna.
nahin kalpana se kalpit hai—amar humari yeh rachna.

(The whole incident is noted inside historical sources.
This immortal story of ours is not a figment of imagination).[35]

These Dalit histories of 1857 take recourse to historical events and intermesh them with subaltern renderings. The dim boundary between the imaginary and the real is the home terrain of these writings. They represent a practice of writing which neither disregards history nor, in its insistence on legitimacy, is completely oblivious of other myths and memories. The actual and the fictional coalesce here, pointing to further possibilities of 'truths' about 1857.

Scattered evidence is cited and quoted by Dalits repeatedly. Thus on Jhalkari Bai, a constantly quoted source is Vrindavan Lal Varma's *Jhansi ki Rani Lakshmibai.* It was published in 1946 after intense historical research.[36] Vishnu Rao Godse, who is said to have been present in the fort when the Rani had fought against General Rose, too had made a reference to Jhalkari in his Marathi book *Majha Pravas* (My Travels). Similarly on Uda Devi, Amritlal Nagar's *Gadar ke Phool* and William Forbes-Mitchell's *Reminiscences of the Great Mutiny* are often cited.[37] Other historical narratives sometimes substantiate these claims. Thus for example it is significant that W. Gordon-Alexander's account of the storming of Sikandar Bagh by British troops states:

> In addition . . . there were . . . even a few amazon negresses, amongst the slain. These amazons having no religious prejudices against the use of greased cartridges, whether of pigs' or other animal fat, although doubtless professed Muhammadans, were armed with rifles, while the Hindu and Muhammadan East Indian rebels were all armed with musket; they fought like wild cats, and it was not till after they were killed that their sex was even suspected.[38]

And today these stories stand as given truths, with stamps issued in their name, many statues constructed, public meeting organized, festivities conducted, and even colleges and medical institutions formed in their name.[39] With constant evocation, these names have become inscribed in popular Dalit memories. Different political parties have repeatedly used these *viranganas*, and made them an integral part of their electoral campaigns. The most successful has been the

Bahujan Samaj Party, who has used them to build the image of Mayawati particularly.[40]

These popular histories of Dalit *viranganas* are open to simultaneously persuasive and competing readings. There are of course limitations of this literature as a historical source. Their representation of Dalit women too needs to be questioned. As the main narrative plots have become more elaborate with time, they have also become more 'sure' of themselves, connected to larger purposes of Dalit identity. Elements of exaggeration have seeped into them. Jhalkari and Uda start as subordinates of Lakshmibai and Hazrat Mahal respectively, but now have acquired a larger than life status.[41] Alongside, Lakshmibai, instead of a model nationalist ruler, appears as a British agent.[42] It is Jhalkari Bai who is the real martyr. It is her name that ought to be written in golden letters. She was a Dalit woman, with no kingdom, no jewellery, and no silken clothes. She was neither a queen nor the daughter of a feudal lord, nor the wife of a *jagirdar*. She fought only for the love of her country, and thus her sacrifice far surpasses anyone else's.[43] Amplification and admiration are a hallmark in these stories. Mitchell's account has formed the most important source for Uda Devi, but it is selectively appropriated. After describing how the woman was shot dead, he clearly states:

> She was armed with a pair of heavy old-pattern cavalry pistols, one of which was in her belt still loaded, and her pouch was still about half full of ammunition, while from her perch in the tree, which had been carefully prepared before the attack, *she had killed more than half-a-dozen men.*[44] (emphasis mine)

However, all Dalit accounts of Uda Devi interestingly leave this out, and the number of soldiers killed by her has kept growing, ranging from 32 to 36![45] There are thus stresses and omissions, additions and subtractions in these tracts.

Mimicry becomes an important tool in these popular histories. Many of these *viranganas* appear to have the same features as reflected in popular memories of Lakshmibai. All of them are super brave and 'classic' beauties.[46] In these stories, songs occupy a central place. Again many of the narrative poems (*khand kavyas*) have cleverly appropriated the famous poem written by Subhadrakumari Chauhan on Lakshmibai. Thus goes one on Jhalkari Bai:

khub lari jhalkari tu tau, teri ek jawani thi.
dur firangi ko karne mein, veeron mein mardani thi.
har bolon ke mukh se sun hum teri yeh kahani thi.

(Jhalkari you really fought, your youthfulness was unique.

You were a man among the brave in ousting the British.
We heard your story from the mouth of warriors.)[47]

Most of these Dalit *viranganas* have Devi or Bai suffixed to their name. They are projected as Dalit female subjects of high moral fibre, who were fantastic nationalists. Many of the tracts appear didactic in their endorsement of certain patriarchal values as they are often replete with images of the obedient daughter, loyal wife and ideal mother, and of morally chaste women.[48] The moral language perhaps also allows Dalit men to police the behaviour of Dalit women in general. There is a fight against oppression, and yet certain hegemonic scripts get rewritten, where Dalits make their rubric of identity conform to somebody else's definition.

Almost all these popular histories of Dalit *viranganas* have male authors, catering in no small measure to masculinized political-public spaces. The gendered subaltern rarely speaks about herself in these histories. It has been argued that modern political arenas have been the 'natural' homelands of masculinity.[49] The images of these *viranganas* in the texts itself, and on the cover of these pamphlets spectacularize them as usually clad in 'masculine' attires. In all of them, they are expert in horse-riding, archery and sword fighting.[50] They are depicted as brave from their very childhood, and 1857 becomes the turning point which sparks them to accomplish great deeds. Through them, an embattled Dalit masculinity is asserting itself in the public-political sphere. It may be argued that the leadership of Mayawati provides a corrective to this, but she too fits into the mould of masculinity. Further, Uda Devi for example has become a figure to mainly promote the political aspirations of Ramlakhan Pasi, who is stated to have 'discovered' her.[51] Victimhood is replaced here by a new archetype of heroism. Although empowering, these images are not necessarily more representative of Dalit women. It may thus be argued from a Dalit feminist perspective that the emergence of popular Dalit male literature on 1857 has not altered much the images of Dalit women, often implying a mere transference, without radical transformation.[52]

At the same time, if we argue that the aim of such representations is ultimately coercive, then how can we use this space also for confrontation? Does their representation also have the scope of carving out more contingent and flexible modes of resistances?[53] For example, in these stories, in the very act of speaking back, of mimicry, new meanings are imparted. As remarks Homi Bhabha:

To the extent to which discourse is a form of defensive warfare, mimicry marks

> those moments of civil disobedience within the discipline of civility: signs of spectacular resistance. Then the words of the master become the state of hybridity—the warlike, subaltern sign of the native—then we may not only read between the lines but even seek to change the often coercive reality that they so lucidly contain.[54]

Even the representation of Dalit *viranganas* on a high moral and heroic ground can be seen as an appropriation of respectability and 'credibility', imparting Dalit participation in past histories new meanings. Moral codes have a different valence or connotation here. Through such portrayals, Dalits hope to garner greater opportunity and dignity to these *viranganas*, and through them to all Dalits.[55] These *viranganas* represent Dalits in service of freedom and Indian nationalism, also providing an appeal for redeeming images of Dalit humiliation. Their portrayal also covertly disrupts the usual dominant notions of Dalit female sexuality, and can be seen as a reaction to images of sexually immoral Dalit women. Here Dalit women are actors in their own right, are active and armed, and are transformed from victims to victors within the context of a narrative.[56] These are not just stories of brave Dalit women but of *all* Dalits, of their legacy, of their bravery, of their sacrifice in service of the nation.

At places the achievements of these Dalit *viranganas* are juxtaposed to the pathetic conditions of Dalit women in general.[57] Some Dalit women too are now trying to use these images to their advantage. Besides ways in which these symbols have helped build Mayawati, many have used these figures to question representations of Dalit women, as well as their exploitation in real life. Thus Meena Pasi stated,

> Uda Devi and Jhalkari Bai have shown to me that I too can resist all kinds of injustices. I do not have to take things lying down. These figures inspire me to question why I am getting less wages from the landlord, why I am beaten up by my husband when I do equal work. I can look up to Uda Devi and say that nothing is impossible if one has the will to resist and fight.[58]

These representations of Dalit *viranganas* may thus also be seen as 'positive engendering'.[59] The encounter with Dalit *viranganas* urges Dalits to produce a more critical and self-reflexive account of 1857, which reflects the limits but also the potentialities of gendered Dalit readings of the revolt. Rather than distilling hegemonic scripts from subversive ones, perhaps it would be more useful to see the lineages of these texts as more complex. They represent a hybrid and dynamic account of 1857 and Dalit *viranganas*, who in some ways reflect hyphenated bodies with various meanings.

CONCLUSION

What we are dealing with here are no ordinary, academic histories, but histories that wish to challenge conventional modes of thinking about 1857 and Dalit women. While they may not be inherently transformative, they can be seen to represent dissident voices, co-existing with and simultaneously challenging dominant ideologies. They also reflect Bakhtin's notions of dialogics and heteroglossia,[60] and Stuart Hall's concept of 'oppositional' decoding, challenging 'dominant-hegemonic' and 'negotiated' reading positions.[61] They may also be equated with Raymond William's useful paradigm of 'dominant', 'residual' and 'emergent' cultural practices, in constant interaction.[62]

Dalits are negotiating the tensions of being both within and outside 1857 through a simultaneous process of denunciation and glorification. They are offering subaltern Dalit gateways of 1857 through which the marginal enters the centre. They identify 1857 as an arena of Dalit suppression, of attempts to restore feudal patriarchies, of assertion of Dalit *viranganas*, of establishing masculinized Dalit political and public spaces. Their writings are caught in a dialectics of collusion with and subversion of notions of nationalism, and patriarchal and caste conceptions of 1857 and Dalit women. These simultaneously contradictory processes signify their multiplicity of identity positions and their dynamic relationships with the revolt. There is no single coherent story here, but a diological process that stands at the border between rejection and eulogization. Mainstream historiography of 1857 gives hardly any space to hierarchies of nationalism. However, the hybrid identifications of Dalits with 1857 signify the genealogies of ambiguous nationalisms, marking a third space, where the revolt is concurrently transformed and recouped, and its boundaries expanded and exploded.

NOTES

1. Eleanor Zelliot, *From Untouchable to Dalit: Essays on the Ambedkar Movement*, Delhi: Manohar, 1998.
2. *Police Abstracts of Intelligence of UP Government (PAI)*, 14 January, 28 January 1922.
3. He was raised to the throne of Awadh by the rebels on 5 July 1857 and he proclaimed: All Hindus and Mussalmans know that four things are held dear by every human being: (1) religion and faith; (2) honour and esteem; (3) life of self and relation; (4) property. These four were protected under the rule of the Indians, under whose government no one interfered with religion; everyone

followed his own faith and everyone's honour was protected in accordance with their position. No mean person (*paji*), for example, sweeper (*churha*), leather-worker (*chamar*), carder (*dhanuk*) or village watchman (*pasi*) could claim equality with them. But the English are the enemies of these four things. They have brought the honour of the high classes on a level with that of the lower people—sweepers and leather workers. In fact, the English show preference to the lower castes over the higher classes. On the complaint of a sweeper or a leather-worker, they seize the person of even a Nawab and a Raja and disgrace him.

4. On 25 August 1857, the proclamation of Bahadur Shah too read: 'It is evident, that the British Government in making zemindary settlements have imposed exorbitant *Zumas*, and have disgraced and ruined several zemindars, by putting up their estates to public auction for arrears of rent, in as much as, that on the institution of a suit by a common Ryot, a maid servant or a slave, the respectable zemindars are summoned into court, arrested, put in gaol and disgraced. . . . Such extortions will have no manner of existence in the Badshahi government.'
5. Virendra Yadav, '1857 ka Mithak aur Viraasat: Ek Punarpaath', *Tadbhav*, 15 January 2007, pp. 125-54.
6. S.B. Chaudhuri, *Civil Rebellion in the Indian Mutiny*, Calcutta: World Press, 1957; R.C. Majumdar, *The Sepoy Mutiny and the Revolt of 1857*, Calcutta: Mukhopadhyay, 1963; Tara Chand, *History of Freedom Movement in India*, vol. II, Delhi: Government of India, 1967, pp. 42-3; Thomas R. Metcalf, *The Aftermath of the Revolt: India, 1857-1870*, Princeton: Princeton University Press, 1964, pp. xiii-iv; Eric Stokes, *The Peasant Armed: Indian Revolt of 1857*, New York: Oxford University Press, 1986, pp. 50-1.
7. For details, see Douglas Peers, 'The Habitual Nobility of Being: British Officers and the Social Construction of the Bengal Army in the Early 19th Century', *Modern Asian Studies*, vol. 25, no. 3, 1991, pp. 551-2; Kaushik Roy, 'Recruitment Doctrines of the Colonial Indian Army, 1859-1939', *IESHR*, 14 (1997), pp. 345-6; Seema Alavi, *The Sepoys and the Company: Tradition and Transition in Northern India, 1770-1830*, Delhi: Oxford University Press, 1995, p. 51; Dirk Kolff, *Naukar, Rajput and Sepoy: The Ethnohistory of the Military Labour Market in Hindustan, 1450-1850*, Cambridge: Cambridge University Press, 1990.
8. Kaushik Roy, 'The Beginning of "People's War" in India', *Economic and Political Weekly*, vol. 42, no.19, 12 May 2007, p. 1725.
9. Rosalind O'Hanlon, *Caste, Conflict and Ideology: Mahatma Jotirao Phule and Low Caste Protest in Nineteenth-Century Western India*, Cambridge: Cambridge University Press, 1985.
10. Vibhutinarayan Rai, 'Kalkatiya Paltan ke Bahane 1857 ka Dalit Bhashya', *Vartman Sahitya*, no. 23, November-December 2006, pp. 25-31; Kanval Bharti, '1857 ka Bahujan Drishtikon', *Vartman Sahitya*, Year 23, November-December 2006, pp. 79-83; Mudrarakshas, 'Azadi ke Purvagrah', *Rashtriya Sahara*, Delhi, 25 February 2007; Yadav, '1857 ka Mithak'.
11. Rudrangshu Mukherjee, *Awadh in Revolt 1857-1858: A Study in Popular Resistance*, Delhi: Oxford University Press, 1984; Tapti Roy, *The Politics of a Popular Uprising: Bundelkhand in 1857*, New York: Oxford University Press, 1994.
12. Badri Narayan, *Documenting Dissent: Contesting Fables, Contested Memories and Dalit Political Discourse*, Shimla: Indian Institute of Advanced Study, 2001, pp. 104-12; Badri Narayan and A.R. Misra, *Multiple Marginalities: An Anthology*

of Identified Dalit Writings, Delhi: Manohar, 2004, pp. 13-36; R.K. Kshirsagar, *Dalit Movement in India and its Leaders*, Delhi: MD Publications, 1994, pp. 74, 135-6, 346-7; Charu Gupta, 'Dalit "Viranganas" and Reinvention of 1857', *Economic and Political Weekly*, vol. 42, no. 19, 12 May 2007, pp. 1739-45.

13. See for example, D.C. Dinkar, *Swatantrata Sangram mein Achchuton ka Yogdan*, Lucknow: Triveni Press, 1990, 2nd edn.; Mohandas Naimisharay, *Swatantrata Sangram ke Dalit Krantikari,* Delhi: Nilkanth Prakashan, 1999.
14. Badri Narayan, 'National Past and Political Present', *Economic and Political Weekly*, vol. 32, no. 31, 31 July 2004, pp. 3533-40.
15. Badri Narayan, 'Inventing Caste History: Dalit Mobilisation and Nationalist Past', *Contributions to Indian Sociology*, vol. 38, nos. 1&2, 2004, p. 199.
16. Quoted in Rajni Disodiya, 'Virangana Jhansi ki Jhalkaribai', *Apeksha*, vol. 3, no. 9, October-December 2004, p. 89.
17. Ram Dayal Verma, *Virangana Uda Devi,* Hardoi: Mahendra Printing Press, 1996; idem, *San 1857 ki Amar Shaheed Virangana Uda Devi (Khand Kavya)*, Hardoi: Manoj Printers, 2nd edn., 2004, p. 15. Henceforth, I will be using this second edition. The writer is a Pasi.
18. Badrinarayan, 'Inventing Caste History', op. cit., p. 201.
19. Verma, *San 1857*, op. cit., p. 13.
20. Mohandas Naimisharay, *Virangana Jhalkari Bai*, Delhi: Radhakrishna, 2003, p. 5; Thamman Singh 'Saras', *Avantibai Lodhi: 1857 ki Amar Balidani,* Delhi: Hind Pocket Books, 1995, p. 8.
21. Yadav, '1857 ka Mithak', op. cit.
22. For details see Joyce Lebra-Chapman, *The Rani of Jhansi: A Study of Female Heroism in India*, Hawaii: University of Hawaii Press, 1986.
23. Scholar Badri Narayan in his book (*Women Heroes and Dalit Assertion in North India: Culture, Identity and Politics,* Delhi: Sage, 2006) has provided a comprehensive analysis on this subject from a contemporary angle. However, his emphasis is more on how these Dalit women heroes are being used by the Bahujan Samaj Party to build the image of its leader, Mayawati. I am on the other hand interested in how we view history from a Dalit feminist perspective and in that how we analyse the role of these Dalit *viranganas*.
24. To name a few, Ansuya 'Anu', *Jhalkari Bai*, Delhi: Publications Division, Indian Government, 1993; Bihari Lal Harit, *Virangana Jhalkari Bai Kavya*; Mata Prasad Mitra, *Virangana Jhalkari Bai*; Naimishray, *Virangana Jhalkari Bai*; Chokhelal Nirmal, *Virangana Jhalkari Bai Mahakavya*; Radheshyam, *Jhalkari Bai*; Mata Prasad Raj Vaidya Sagar, *Achhut Virangana Nautanki*; Mata Prasad Sagar, *Achhut Virangana*, Lucknow: Cultural Publishers, 1987; Jagannath Prasad Shakya, *Jhansi ki Sherni: Virangana Jhalkari Bai ka Jeevan Charitra*, Gwalior: Mukesh Printers, 1999; Bhavani Shankar Visharad, *Virangana Jhalkari Bai*, Aligarh: Anand Sahitya Sadan, 1988.
25. For example, Sheelbodh, 'Jhalkaribai: Ek Aitihasik Karvat', *Apeksha*, vol. 3, no. 11, April-June 2005, pp. 85-9.
26. Verma, *San 1857*, op. cit.
27. Shahid Amin, 'Representing the Musalman: Then and Now, Now and Then', in Shail Mayaram, M.S.S. Pandian and Ajay Skaria (eds.), *Subaltern Studies XII: Muslims, Dalits and the Fabrications of History*, Delhi: Permanent Black, 2005, p. 2.
28. Further, remarks Stuart Hall, different groups from different social circumstances perceive the same representations differently. Stuart Hall, 'Encoding/Decoding',

in S. Hall, D. Hobson, A. Lowe and P. Willis (eds.), *Culture, Media, Language: Working Papers in Cultural Studies, 1972-79*, London: Methuen, 1980, pp. 128-38.

29. Naimisharay, *Swatantrata Sangram*, op. cit., pp. 133-7; Dinkar, *Swatantrata Sangram*, op. cit., pp. 21-5.
30. Raj Kumar Pasi, *Pasi Samaj ka Swatantrata Sangram Mein Yogdan,* Lucknow: Pasi Shodh Evam Sanskritik Sansthan, 1998, pp. 7-20; Verma, *San 1857*, op. cit., p. 20.
31. P.S. Verma (ed.), *Dalit (Swatantrata) Pira*, Delhi: Vimukt Jati Trading Private Limited, 1992, p. 18.
32. 'Saras', *Avantibai Lodhi*, op. cit.; Naimisharay, *Swatantrata Sangram,* op. cit., p. 142.
33. Dinkar, *Swatantrata Sangram*, op. cit., p. 26.
34. Carlo Ginzburg, *The Judge and the Historian: Marginal Notes on a Late-Twentieth-Century Miscarriage of Justice*, tr. Antony Shugaar, London: Verso, 1999, pp. 111-14.
35. Verma, *San 1857*, op. cit., pp. 13-16.
36. Vrindavan Lal Varma, *Jhansi ki Rani Lakshmibai*, Jhansi: Mayur Prakashan, 1987, originally or initially published in 1946, pp. 92-5, 324. For an analysis of this work see Francesca Orsini, *The Hindi Public Sphere 1920-1940: Language and Literature in the Age of Nationalism*, Delhi: Oxford University Press, 2002, pp. 215-24.
37. William Forbes-Mitchell, *Reminiscences of the Great Mutiny 1857-59: Including the Relief, Siege, and Capture of Lucknow, and the Campaigns in Rohilcund and Oude*, London: Macmillan and Co., 1893, pp. 57-8. Quoted in for example, Pasi, *Pasi Samaj*, pp. 8-11; Verma, *San 1857*, p. 8.
38. W. Gordon-Alexander, *Recollections of a Highland Subaltern: During the Campaigns of the 93rd Highlanders in India, under Colin Campbell, Lord Clyde in 1857, 1858 and 1859*, London: Edward Arnold, 1898, p. 104.
39. I was present in the *mela* held in 2005. It is organized by an organization called 'Virangana Uda Devi Smarak Sansthan'. Every year they take out a 'Smarika' on the occasion. See *Smarika: Virangana Uda Devi Pasi Shaheed Diwas*, Lucknow: Virangana Uda Devi Smarak Sansthan, 16 November 2005.
40. Badrinarayan, *Documenting Dissent*, op. cit., pp. 138-54; Badri Narayan, *Women Heroes.*
41. Shakya, *Jhansi ki Sherni.*
42. Dinkar, *Swatantrata Sangram*, p. 21. Dinkar quotes S.N. Sen, *1857*, pp. 267-96, to prove the point about 1857 revolt beginning against Lakshmibai's wishes.
43. Naimisharay, *Viranganan Jhalkari Bai,* p. 5; Dinkar, *Swatantrata Sangram*, pp. 21-5; Naimisharay, *Swatantrata Sangram*, op. cit., p. 136; Verma, *San 1857*, op. cit., p. 18.
44. Forbes-Mitchell, *Reminiscences of the Great Mutiny,* op. cit., p. 58.
45. Pasi, *Pasi Samaj*, op. cit., pp. 10-11.
46. Shakya, *Jhansi ki Sherni*, op. cit., pp. 2, 6; Verma, *San 1857*, op. cit., p. 23.
47. Shakya, *Jhansi ki Sherni*, op. cit., pp. 1, 44.
48. Ibid., p. 4.
49. Stefan Dudink, Karen Hagemann and John Tosh (eds.), *Masculinities in Politics and War: Gendering Modern History*, New York: Manchester University Press, 2004.
50. Verma, *San 1857*, op. cit., p. 23.

51. For example, a number of poems and write ups in *Smarika: Virangana Uda Devi* are actually devoted to Ramlakhan Pasi.
52. Bell Hooks, *Black Looks: Race and Representation*, Boston: South End Press, 1992, p. 126.
53. Rajeswari Sunder Rajan, *Real and Imagined Women: Gender, Culture and Postcolonialism*, London: Routledge, 1993, pp. 11, 129.
54. Homi Bhabha, *The Location of Culture*, London: Routledge, p. 121.
55. Verma, *San 1857*, op. cit., pp. 5, 17.
56. Rajeswari Sunder Rajan, 'Introduction: Feminism and the Politics of Resistance', *Indian Journal of Gender Studies*, vol. 7, no. 2, 2000, pp. 153-65.
57. Verma, *San 1857*, op. cit., p. 21.
58. Personal interview with Meena Pasi on 16 November 2005 at Lucknow. She, along with many other women, was a participant in the celebration of 'Uda Devi Shaheed Diwas' on that day.
59. For elaboration, see Vidya Daheja, 'Issues of Spectatorship and Representation', in Vidya Daheja (ed.), *Representing the Body: Gender Issues in Indian Art*, Delhi: Kali for Women, 1997, pp. 1-21.
60. Mikhail Bakhtin, *The Dialogic Imagination*, tr. Caryl Emerson and Michael Hollquist, Austin: University of Texas Press, 1981.
61. Stuart Hall, *Encoding/Decoding* (1973), in Culture, Media, Language: Working Papers in Cultural Studies, 1972-79, London: Hutchinson, 1980, pp. 128-38.
62. Raymond Williams, *The Sociology of Culture*, Chicago: University of Chicago Press, 1981, pp. 203-5.

15

Identity Consolidation of Meitei Women: Reflections on Women's War

RAKHEE BHATTACHARYA

MEITEI: IDENTITY IMAGES

Manipur has a chequered history, and so has the Meitei, the predominant tribe among its inhabitants. Its history is mired in cobwebs of ethno-genealogy, of a struggle often interspersed with warfare and bloodshed. In tracing the Meitei roots and descent, the Manipuri scholar Chongtham Budhi finds dominantly Mongoloid and Tibeto-Burman roots and affinity.[1] While conceptualizing identity images of the Meitei community, the words of another scholar of the valley, Konsam Manikchand, are worth noting:

> Since the dawn of history, the Meiteis developed a monarchical form of government, and subsequently they extended their sway not only over the surrounding hill tribes but also over other kingdoms that lay beyond the hills. It was their high sense of ethnocentrism, inherent martial tradition, and soldierly qualities that led them to engage in frequent encounters even with their bigger neighbour and traditional enemy, the Burmese.[2]

Meitei identity images therefore strongly uphold the solidarity of Meiteis and their society through persistent struggle and protest against authoritarianism. This sense of identity, which imbibed their own culture, religion, commerce, economy, tradition and customs, had played a pivotal role in their existence over a very long period of time. Bidyut Chakrabarty narrates this identity as negotiated within a flow of such multiple influences. He argues that our identity is a constant and dialectical interplay between ontological and epistemological factors; and identity can never be seen as a fixed notion; rather it is in constant flux for socio-cultural and political reasons.[3] A comparison can also be drawn between the Meitei identity and Amartya Sen's

idea of identity of the human race, when he says that, identity can be a source not merely of pride and joy, but also of strength, confidence and warmth for neighbours and members of the same community. This can strengthen bonds and help to develop 'social capital'. But Sen has cautioned that the same sense of identity can exclude many people even while warmly embracing others. A well-integrated community in which residents instinctively perform absolutely wonderful tasks for each other with great passion and solidarity can also be the very same community in which bricks are thrown through the windows on immigrants who move into the region from elsewhere. The adversity of exclusion can be made to go hand in hand with the gifts of inclusion.[4] Meiteis in Manipur form a small and closely bonded community, who have the history of retaining their identity images through various struggles over a long period of time, dating back to pre-colonial days. Thus the writings and memoirs of many British frontier officers, like Pemberton (1835), McCulloch (1859), Dun (1886), Brown (1874) and Johnstone (1896) capture a fairly vivid traditional lifestyle of Meiteis in Manipur till 1762, until they came in contact with the East India Company. The Anglo-Burmese War of 1824-5 brought the British to Manipur. The British, over time, became genuinely interested not only in Manipur but in the whole of north-east India, both for economic as well as strategic and connectivity reasons. During the nineteenth century, a new history of Anglo-Manipuri relations began to serve their mutual interests, though Manipur never formally acknowledged the suzerainty of the British government.[5] In 1891 the British defeated Manipur in the Anglo-Manipur war, and Manipur lost its sovereignty, which marked another era in Manipuri history that bought structural changes in its socio-economic and political landscape. The British then started asserting their own imperial connections. Due to trans-regional inflow of people from outside the valley, the Meitei community gradually became marginalized in their own land in terms of their skills, livelihood and identity. They woke up to assert their right to self-determination and their distinctive ethnic identity. Therefore the colonial milieu and context were important signifiers for the invention and reinvention of the idea of constructing Meitei identity, and then conceptualizing a notion of a nation and political entity in Manipur.

BELLIGERENT MEITEI WOMEN

A large part of Manipur's history has been acted and wrought by its women, something almost unique in the history of the world.

By fighting social oppression and evils, as also against colonial occupation for the freedom of the country, Meitei women are among the bravest and most upright. They were always revered in society and remained actively involved in socio-economic activities. Meitei women were never subjugated in their society. On the contrary, their roles have remained very significant throughout history. 'The high social and economic status of women in Meitei society was frequently remarked upon by British colonial officers.'[6] As argued by Parrot and Parrot:

> Despite the dominance of Hinduism in the plains of Manipur, Meitei women suffered none of the humiliating oppression of their sisters elsewhere on the subcontinent. Above all, the women controlled the food supplies and the markets, and were therefore a dominant economic force. From the beginning of the British period they had showed themselves capable and organized enough to take mass action when occasion demanded.[7]

Manipuri women have an umbilical bond with the traditional market and its related practices since ancient time. The *ima keithal* or mother's market also referred to as *nupi keithal* or women's market of Manipur is especially famous for being one of the largest markets of Asia managed and run by women. It is distinctive—as mentioned by Indira Barua and Anita Devi, because of its function as a controlling institution of women that affects and contributes to the whole economy of the state. It shows how women play a pivotal role in the economy and society, which is a continuance of the earlier form of social structure.[8]

The women are special again in the sense that they have been involved in many of the revolutionary movements, not so much for the cause of 'woman' as for the causes of the society and community in general, a fundamental distinction of any gender-related movement that has ever happened within India or outside. In India, for example, an organized women's movement started in 1917, under the Women's Indian Association led by Annie Besant and others. But way back in 1904, Meitei women in Manipur had organized a unique revolutionary movement against the British Raj, which is known as *nupi lan*, meaning 'women's war'. And the very nature of this 'women's war' was different: it was not fought for asserting any rights for women in the society in particular, but it was a war against the colonial establishment, and its policies towards the Meitei community in general, its traditional customary laws and practices, and the *keithal* was the facilitating space for women's activism in the state.

NUPI LAN 1904: WAR AGAINST THE POLITICAL ASSERTION BY THE COLONIAL RULERS

The Manipuri scholar Joykumar Singh writes, 'one of the most important and interesting aspects in the character of the womenfolk of Manipur was that in spite of all psychological torture their morale was very high and they were always ready to fight for justice. The glaring example was the outbreak of 1904 movement.'[9] On 5 October 1904, the people of Manipur, long dissatisfied, angered and agitated by monstrous British policies, began their protest against such policies. About 3,000 women gathered in the compound of the Political Agent, demanding the cancellation of the punitive order of Colonel Maxwell that reintroduced *lallup*, a system of forced labour, which had long been abolished. He was also forcing the people of Imphal to rebuild the burnt-down house of the Assistant Political Agent. The women of Imphal rose up in protest. The agitations were mostly led by the trades women, similar to the women's agitation of 1939.[10] The Khwairamband Bazar, which was run mostly by women, remained closed for days. This outbreak of *nupi lan* was directly related to the existing political, social and economic conditions of the state which had prevailed after the institution of the colonial administrative system. The new administrative policy introduced by the British after 1891 had brought radical changes in every aspect of the life of the Manipuris, disturbing their normal way of life, in order to gain undue economic advantages for the colonialists from the common Manipuris.[11] The deep-rooted cause of the movement was directly related to the irregularities and malpractices in the administration of the state.[12] Thus, as rightly expressed by Parrot and Parrot, the first *nupi lan* in 1904 had effectively forced the former Political Agent to rescind the onerous demands he had imposed on the population, and this had actually resulted in a tradition of women's political protest—something history would witness time and again, even in our times.[13]

NUPI LAN 1939: WAR AGAINST THE ECONOMIC EXPLOITATION BY THE COLONIAL RULERS

The first war that the women of Manipur had fought against the colonial establishment marked the beginning of their arduous journey towards identity and freedom. Manipur has emerged and re-emerged in different shapes, but the women of the Meitei community still reflect the same image of belligerence, firmness and conviction on

the issue of their identity. The second time when they raised their voices against oppression was through the second *nupi lan*, which broke out after 35 years on 12 December 1939. This happened in a much stronger and more forceful manner than the first women's war of 1904 against colonial exploitation, and this was more economic than political in nature. The second *nupi lan* eventually became the most famous women's war, not only in the history of Manipur valley but in the history of women movements across the world. As rightly mentioned by Joykumar Singh, the nature and character of this movement was entirely different from the other women's movements in other parts of the world. The basic and prime objective of most of the women's movements was pivoted around the uplift or empowerment of women's status in the society, against their less than equal and under-privileged status compared to that of men, and the unjust and unfair treatment that they received from the society under existing social laws. The nature of the Women's movement in Manipur, on the contrary, emphasized the uplift of the overall economic condition of the state and challenged the colonial exploitative economic policies. In that sense, the movement of 1939 was unique in character, distinct from other women's movement in India.[14] *Nupi lan* thus deserves a special place. Parrot and Parrot further viewed that Manipur actually could conduct its first democratic election in the subcontinent primarily due to such remarkable movements by Meitei women. Beginning as a mass protest against economic exploitation by Marwari traders of rice who were aided and abetted by a corrupt king, and the opportunistic British, it developed into the single most important catalyst for democratic reform, providing a popular platform for political activism of the elites who eventually overthrew the old feudal order.[15]

The outbreak of such women's agitations was thus a turning point for the emergence of a new trend and space for political and national consciousness in Manipur. The colonial authority also regarded the outbreak of this movement as the most important event of 1939.[16] It was a fight against the feudal rulers who wielded power with the support of the British. Some writers like Sanamani Yambem categorically regarded the second *nupi lan* movement as a dividing line between the oppressive economic and administrative policies followed by the Maharaja and the Political Agent, out of which a new Manipur emerged.[17] Sanamani Yambem elsewhere mentioned that this movement had eventually resulted in generating a much larger range of political consciousness among the people of Manipur.[18]

The continued and unabated economic exploitation by the outside traders with the help of the colonial authority obliterated all prospects of economic development of the state. The inhuman nature of such oppressive exploitation perpetrated by the feudal rulers with the active support of the imperial forces posed a serious threat to the normal life of the common people. The *nupi lan* of 1939 was a spontaneous eruption against such exploitation.[19] Khwairamband Bazar, that played a crucial role in the outbreak of the *nupi lan* in 1939, is a place where over 2,000 women usually occupy regular stalls, while an even larger number are seated outside; it is reflective of the Meitei women's status in Manipur. This bazaar is women-dominated, and apart from economic activities, the market also serves as a place for active social and political interactions.[20] Rice, the prime source of livelihood for the majority, was a major lucrative product for the British and the Mayang traders; they hugely profited from its export. Initially this foreign involvement was not a threat to the livelihood to the Meitei women, primarily due to the demand and supply situation, which had remained within bounds. But due to the poor yield in 1939 as a result of excessive rainfall, prices continued to escalate unusually. The Marwari traders took advantage of the situation and immediately resorted to export and hoarding. The threat of famine loomed large in the state and the situation started deteriorating fast, before actual riots broke out.

This rice issue was the culmination of many other oppressive economic issues that were prevailing in the state at that time. Finally on 12 December 1939, over 4,000 women of Manipur gathered to resolve the issue with the Political Agent Gimson for introducing a ban on rice export. The gathering grew in strength to around 10,000 in no time, and decided to destroy the Marwari rice mills. Gimson made all efforts to control this agitated crowd through negotiations but failed. This episode also drastically changed the image of the Maharaja and Durbar of the state, who technically had the responsibility to resolve the situation. Parrot and Parrot clearly remarked on this:

> Relations between the common people and those supposed to uphold law and order had deteriorated to mutual animosity and mistrust. No help could be expected from Maharaja: when he was not conveniently out of the country on pilgrimage he virtually secluded himself because of the illness of one of his daughters. Those rare occasions when he did agree to meet delegations from his people only reinforced their conviction that he was hand in glove with the Marwari traders and seeking to line his own pocket with their bribes. Nor did they have any confidence in the Durbar, which consisted only of the Maharaja's hand-picked henchmen.[21]

Another Manipuri scholar viewed that, while the economy and administration were in the hands of Marwaris and the British people, Manipur was also garrisoned by hordes of Mayang armies like Assam Rifles, Gurkha Rifles, Bombay Pioneers and Burma Military Police. These Mayangs were looked upon as the agents of colonialism, furthering the cause of administrative, cultural and economic exploitation. They obviously became the prime targets of attack during the *nupi lan* of 1939.[22]

Arambam later rightly evaluated the spirit of Meitei women, when he commented that the British could destroy the political might of the Meiteis and the military potential of the aristocratic lineage, but not the spirit of its women, whose indomitable anti-colonial spirit was reflected in the women's wars of 1904 and 1939.[23] Both these wars are unique in the world; in no other colonial history, women had ever raised such a strong and united voice and protested against the establishment for securing their political and economic rights. It forced some British officers like Sir Robert Reid, the then governor of Assam to remark once that 'Manipuri women are notorious for their independence and their proneness to take direct action to get their own way.'[24] The movements led by the women had actually led to important administrative reforms in the state by the colonial rulers in respect of revenues, laws and justice. Eventually a new Manipur had emerged after the World War II as a result of these movements. Joykumar Singh has rightly remarked that the very idea for the establishment of a responsible government was successfully planted by the women on the fervent soil of the state. The suffering, yet fearless women of this land who were at the vanguard of these changes.[25] Parrott and Parrott also viewed that whatever complex political life the state has, it owes it to the *nupi lan* of 1939, which acted as the main catalyst for the movement, which after a protracted struggle, eventually succeeded in displacing the ancient feudal regime, bringing about democratic elections of 1948, four years before the first democratic elections in India itself. By the end of that year, this small state of Manipur had replaced the rule of the Maharaja and his appointed Durbar with a form of 'responsible government' elected on the basis of full adult franchise.[26] But the struggle of Manipur did not end here, its journey continued with the tradition of *nupi lan* even after Independence with the lingering shadow of colonialism all over the state. The democratic government of Manipur was swept away when Indian Union absorbed it in 1949 and Manipur had to enter into a different history of struggle for its identity and nationhood.

MEIRA PAIBEE 1980: WAR AGAINST 'STATE TERRORISM' BY POST-COLONIAL ADMINISTRATION

Women's wars in Manipur during the colonial period has certainly bestowed upon the Meitei women an image of belligerence, independence and solidarity, and a spirit to fight against atrocities and injustice. It is remarkable to see that the image has not altered even in the post-colonial era. Manipur is a cauldron of many unresolved issues even today and has been in a perpetual state of turmoil since decades. It signifies the failure of the Indian administration to win the hearts and minds of the Manipuris, despite all its desperate attempts to put it in the 'right order'. Several measures were introduced to deal with the unceasing underground activities and insurgency within the state. The Armed Forces Special Power Act of 1958 was one such step, which was introduced in some parts of the state in 1960 and then to the entire valley (except Imphal municipal area) in 1980 as the disturbed area, in which the Army has been exercising, and often misusing almost unrestrained power over the hapless population of the state. The people of Manipur call this counter-insurgency measure as 'State Terrorism', which has actually intensified the trauma of the common citizens, who are trapped in a cycle of deprivation and violence, having no resolution in sight. Manipur presently is faced with a plethora of problems and conflicts, uncertainties and violence. Women are particularly vulnerable to violence and intimidation by the military at gunpoint, often used deliberately to frighten the populace into submission and surrender. Women and girls continue to be abused, tortured, raped and even killed with almost total impunity and are often the victims of human rights violation. Fifty years of such draconian laws have scarred the Manipuri society beyond recognition and shaken their faith in Indian democracy and the Indian army. As shown by Deepti Mehrotra, the violation list within 1980 to 2,000 includes fourteen major massacres, killing many innocent people, several tortures, rapes and other mental harassment.[27] To fight against such 'state terrorism', women of Manipur once again stood up *en masse* and raised their voices. After 41 years of the second *nupi lan*, in 1980 another women's movement broke out in Manipur known as *meira paibee* or women torchbearers to protect women's dignity, and safeguard them from abuse by the Indian armed forces. It started way back in 1970s as an anti-alcoholism protest, popularly known as *nishabandh* movement. Women raided liquor shops even at nights carrying flaming torches, and people informally called them *meira paibees*, and

this same movement eventually took up the issue of militarization in the state. Ningthouja rightly observes that the *nupi lan* of 1939 was an event of the past, yet the objective conditions under which women waged the struggle remained more or less unchanged until much later, and even in contemporary times. She firmly believes that if neo-colonialism has to be continuously superimposed upon Manipur, history would be an eyewitness to a series of *nupi lans* in the years to come.[28] Ningthouja mentions elsewhere that *meira paibee* movement reveals the contemporary state of the political structure in Manipur which perpetuates undemocratic rule through the use of military force by the State.[29] She defines *meira paibee* as women torchbearers. The term *meira* connotes initiative, progress and achievements or signifies a means to enlighten darkness. Thus *meira paibee* as an activist is defined as the repository of enlightenment whose utmost obligation is to defend and save society. Such an embellishment of the term reveals a new development of the *meira paibee* movement as an integral part of the national movement in Manipur, where the genealogy of women's roles can be traced back as revolutionaries and defenders of society at crucial junctures throughout history.[30]

The struggle of Irom Sharmila is part of this *meira paibee* movement. She is known as the 'Iron Lady' of Manipur, and is on fast for the last ten years since 2000, demanding the removal of AFSPA and restoration of peace in the state. She is an icon and a beacon of hope to the women of conflict-ridden Manipur today. The Malom massacre in November 2000, which killed one hundred civilians in a shoot-out by Assam Rifles in the aftermath of an insurgency operation made Sharmila start her battle against AFSPA. The other historic nude protest by dozens of Manipuri women in front of Assam Rifles headquarters at Kangla Fort in Imphal on July 2004 to condemn the alleged rape and custodial death of 32 year old Thangjam Manorama Devi is also a part of *meira paibee* movement. In this, women have considered the body as a weapon to protest against such atrocities of the Assam Rifles personnel.

CONCLUSION

The women's war in the colonial times and the subsequent women's movements in the post-colonial times in Manipur are unique, and cannot possibly be compared with any other women's movement across the world. women movements which have evolved around the world at different times are basically feminist movements trying to assert the rights and independence of women, and seeking

socio-economic and political rights and equality with men. Gender inequality that normally prevails in a society becomes the root cause of women movements anywhere, which gradually flows into different identity formations and manifestations. But the women's movements in Manipur were political in nature, which according to Ningthouja had followed a trend occurring in space and time within the parameters of an over-arching state structure.[31] In Manipur, the continuous war that the women of the state, primarily the Meitei women, have been fighting for the last century has not necessarily been for asserting any rights for gender equality in any skewed and discriminated society. Rather, women within this society have traditionally enjoyed high status and respect in the economic, social and commercial orders, and they occupy important roles in the traditional marketplaces as well. It was only when the outside forces tried to reform or change their society, and upset their traditional economic order that the Meitei women became belligerent, and protective about their liberty and power in the society. By fighting against such odds and against such discourse and challenge, Meitei women have actually consolidated and reinforced their identity in the society. Comparing with the idea of gradual consolidation of Sikh identity with ethnic factors constructed by Bidyut Chakrabarty,[32] one can say that during the last century Meitei identity has been consolidated which underlies the significance of 'womanhood' as a factor in the formation of a community that transcends regional boundaries. The role of woman as a powerful determinant of identity is undoubtedly refreshing in the sense that it is a break from the past in which the basic thrust mostly and primarily revolves around man as the ascriptive denomination of human existence. Though man continues to be the dominant gender in Meitei community in several important arenas, yet women share strikingly significant position in their identity images, and there exists no hyper-masculinity factor in the society. And this image is reflected vividly when Ningthouja says that the two *nupi lans* of colonial period reflect the women's desire for liberation. Women had involved themselves in war at the crucial junctures when men were paralysed and succumbed to colonial repression. There were even physical confrontation between women and the army, and their courage, rational approach, collective might, sacrificing spirit, organizational skill and tactics were all strongly reflected. British rulers were condemned for the crimes of inflicting torture and killing unarmed women agitators who had taken to the street for just causes. Later, in post-colonial times also, the Indian administration has been characterized and situated at par with the

British rulers, and Manipuri women have continued their wars against such injustice till date. Women condemned human rights violations by the state and launched action against undemocratic, repressive acts, sexual harassment, destruction of life and property and torture by the Indian army and paramilitary forces.[33]

Though the women of Manipur have been struggling hard for over a century to preserve their identity and position in the socio-economic space, more tangibly in the marketplace, the question that surfaces is: How have such persistent struggles been fruitful, and how far have they achieved success in meeting the challenges? The 1939 women's war, which was primarily fought for their economic justice has not achieved much benefit for the women of the state, though it led to overall administrative reforms. In the words of Chishti, the year-long agitation of the Meitei women died down and very soon they realized that their economic interest was solely rooted only in the Khwairamband *keithal* or market, the provider of their livelihood, and not much beyond that space. There was also lack of leadership in this movement, and a split in the Working Committee of the Nikhil Manipuri Mahasabha during 1939, which supported this war, disheartening the agitators to a large extent. Chishti thinks that such lack of both political and moral guidance along with persistent economic pressure led to the failure of the movement in 1939.[34] In more recent times also, in the tireless fights against 'state terrorism', voices of the women of Manipur are barely audible, the only exception being the persistent demand for the withdrawal of the Armed Forces Special Power Act and the unbroken and non-violent agitation by the iconic lady of Manipur: Irom Sharmila. Thanks to the media, scholars and human rights activists across the world and their reports and works support her cause.

But these in reality have failed to get justice of the Manipuri women, who till today dominate the markets and are integral to the food security link for the entire population and thereby are inextricably linked to the state's local economy, culture and society. But of late, the state government in collusion with the union Urban Development Authority has been trying to demolish such local markets by bringing in multi-storied malls, an embodiment of the so-called liberalized/open economy. This has brought another threat to women's economic domain and their livelihood. But amazingly, the women of Manipur still have not lost their will to fight, and have persistently refused to be displaced and dissociated from their roots, which is none but the *keithal*, the market. *Keithal* is the place from where Manipuri women have derived their identity since time immemorial. To protect it,

and along with it, their own identity, Meitei women would certainly not shy away from interminable wars and sacrifices. As rightly said: 'identity is formed out of contestations and can never be static but is constantly redefined, keeping more or less intact the core values on which it is grounded'.[35]

NOTES

1. Chongtham Budhi, 'The Ethnonym Meitiei', in Naorem Sanajaoba (ed.), *Manipur: Past and Present*, vol. 1, Delhi: Mittal Publications, 1988, p. 72.
2. Konsam Manikchand, 'The Evolution of the Meitei State: A Confederacy Through the Last Two Millennia', in Naorem Sanajaoba (ed.), ibid., p. 147.
3. Bidyut Chakrabarty, *Indian Politics and Society Since Independence: Events, Process and Ideology*, London: Routledge, 2008, p. 37.
4. Amartya Sen, *Identity and Violence: The Illusion of Destiny*, London: Penguin Books, 2006, pp. 2-3.
5. N. Lokendra Singh, *Unquiet Valley*, Delhi: Mittal Publications, 1998, pp. 1-26.
6. Among others, by W. McCulloch, *An Account of the Valley of Munnipore and the Hill Tribes*, Calcutta, 1859; R. Brown, *Annual Report on the Munnipore Political Agency*, Calcutta, 1874; and J. Shakespear, 'The Religion of Manipur', in *Folk Lore*, 24 (1913), pp. 409-55, cited by Saroj N. Arambam Parrot and John Parrot, 'The Second Women's War and the Emergence of Democratic Government in Manipur', *Modern Asian Studies*, vol. 35, no. 4, October 2001, pp. 905-19.
7. Saroj N. Arambam Parrot and John Parrot, 'The Second Women's War and the Emergence of Democratic Government in Manipur', *Modern Asian Studies*, vol. 35, no. 4, October 2001, pp. 905-19.
8. Indira Barua and Anita Devi, 'Women Market of Manipur: An Anthropo-Historical Perspective', *Journal of Human Ecology*, vol. 15, no. 2, 2004, pp. 129-33.
9. N. Joykumar Singh, *Social Movements in Manipur*, Delhi: Mittal Publications, 1992, p. 75.
10. Ibid., pp. 80-1; and Sanamani Yamben, 'Nupi Lan: Manipur Women's Agitation 1939', *Economic Political Weekly*, 21 February 1976, pp. 325-31.
11. Joykumar Singh, *Social Movements in Manipur*, op. cit., pp. 76-7.
12. Ibid., p. 73.
13. Saroj N. Arambam Parrot and John Parrot, 'The Second Women's War and the Emergence of Democratic Government in Manipur', *Modern Asian Studies*, vol. 35, no. 4, October 2001, pp. 905-19.
14. Ibid., p. 73.
15. Ibid., pp. 905-19.
16. Administrative Report of Manipur, 1939-40, p. 1, cited in Joykumar Singh, *Social Movements in Manipur*, op. cit.
17. Sanamani Yamben 'Nupi Lan (Women's War 1939)', a paper submitted in the seminar on 'History of Manipur', held on 30-1 December 1975, at J.N.V., Center for Postgraduate Studies, Imphal, Manipur, and cited in Joykumar Singh, *Social Movements in Manipur*, op. cit.
18. Sanamani Yamben, 'Nupi Lan: Manipur Women's Agitation 1939', *Economic and Political Weekly*, 21 February 1976, pp. 325-31.

19. Joykumar Singh, *Social Movements in Manipur*, op. cit., p. 74.
20. Sanamani Yamben, 'Nupi Lan: Manipur Women's Agitation 1939', *Economic and Political Weekly*, 21 February 1976, pp. 325-31.
21. Saroj N. Arambam Parrot and John Parrot, 'The Second Women's War and the Emergence of Democratic Government in Manipur', *Modern Asian Studies*, vol. 35, no. 4, October 2001, pp. 905-19.
22. Malem Ningthouja, 'Nupi Lan: Women's War in Manipur' , *Reflections*, vol. 1, Issue 2, 2007, p. 27, available at: http://www.ghadar.in/Vol1_Issue2_PDF/v1_I2_Reflections .pdf.
23. Lokendra Arambam, 'Peace Process in Manipur: Armed Conflict, State Repression and Women', p. 348, cited in Anuradha Dutta and Ratna Bhuyan (eds.), *Genesis of Conflict and Peace*, vol. 1, Delhi: Akanksha Publishing House, 2007.
24. Cited by Saroj N. Arambam Parrot and John Parrot, 'The Second Women's War and the Emergence of Democratic Government in Manipur', *Modern Asian Studies*, vol. 35, no. 4, October 2001, pp. 905-19.
25. Joykumar Singh, *Social Movements in Manipur*, op. cit., p. 96.
26. Saroj N. Arambam Parrot and John Parrot, 'The Second Women's War and the Emergence of Democratic Government in Manipur', *Modern Asian Studies*, vol. 35, no. 4, October 2001, pp. 905-19.
27. Deepti Priya Mehrotra, *Burning Bright: Irom Sharmila and the Struggle for Peace in Manipur*, Delhi: Penguin Books, p. 69.
28. Malem Ningthouja, 'Nupi Lan: Women's War in Manipur' , *Reflections*, vol. 1, Issue 2, 2007, p. 27, available at: http://www.ghadar.in/Vol1_Issue2_PDF/v1_I2_Reflections .pdf.
29. Malem Ningthouja, 'The Women's Movement in Manipur as Reflected in the Text "Meira Paibee"'; The Women Movement in Manipur, 2003, available at: http://www.re-volutionarydemocracy. org/rdv9n2/women.htm
30. Ibid., p. 1.
31. Ningthouja, 'The Women's Movement in Manipur as Reflected in the Text "Meira Paibee"'; The Women Movement in Manipur, 2003, available at: http://www.re-volutionarydemocracy.org/rdv9n2/women.htm.
32. Bidyut Chakrabarty, *Indian Politics and Society Since Independence: Events, Process and Ideology*, London: Routledge, 2008, p. 50.
33. Ningthouja, 'The Women's Movement in Manipur as Reflected in the Text 'Meira Paibee'; The Women Movement in Manipur, 2003, available at: http://www.revolutionarydemocracy.org/rdv9n2/women.htm
34. S.M.A.W. Chishti, *Political Development in Manipur: 1919-1949*, Delhi: Kalpaz Publications, 2005, pp. 88-9.
35. Bidyut Chakrabarty, *Indian Politics and Society Since Independence: Events, Process and Ideology*, p. 53.

16

Bengali Muslims at Crossroads: Women and Encounters with Contemporaneity

SYED TANVEER NASREEN

Islam is often regarded as an immutable monolithic system; Muslims are consequently viewed as members of a single, undifferentiated community, their identity entirely derived from a religious commitment. This oversimplifies a complex and highly diverse religious terrain. Such a perception overlooks socio-cultural diversities, sectarian differences, cultural pluralism and specificities of historical contexts among Muslims, leading to the tendency of generalizing Muslims as a category 'separate' or 'different' from the rest. My objective here is to examine the responses and inherent contradictions in the lives and psyche of Bengali Muslims, particularly the women, from the second half of the nineteenth century.

'Bengali Muslims' as a socio-historical category are not the same as 'Muslims in Bengal'. The latter category comprises temporary migrants to Bengal, as well as those, who, in spite of staying in Bengal for several generations, either fail or refuse to imbibe the language and culture of the land. 'Bengali Muslims', on the other hand, are a category of Muslims, who also subscribe to the local Bengali identity sharing the regional language, culture and values with non-Muslims.[1]

Various sociological factors went into making Bengal a congenial home for Islam. The devising of a typical *Islami* or *Musalmani Bangla,* in which Bengali was profusely interspersed with Persian-Arabic words, was instrumental in its survival.[2] The Islamic syncretistic tradition, focusing on its accommodative and acculturating traits, was another important factor in the process.[3]

Sharafati or elitism was a coveted social ideal among Bengali Muslims. It attributed the ancestry of a person to immigration from, if not the classical world of Islam, then at least the more prosperous

seats of Mughal culture in north India. Dissociation from local language, culture and customs was thus a prerequisite to legitimize the claim to a purer and hence, more respectable lineage than conversion to one's ancestry. The controversy surfaced following the Census of 1872, wherein Henry Beverley, its compiler commented, 'The existence of Muhammadans in Bengal is not due so much to the introduction of Mughal blood into the country, as to the former inhabitants, for whom a rigid system of caste discipline rendered Hinduism intolerable.'[4]

This subtle hint at the base origin of Bengali Muslims, subscribing to what Richard M. Eaton later theorized as the Social Liberation Thesis,[5] did not go unprotested. Abu A. Ghuznavi reacted sharply, 'The majority of the modern Mahomedans are not the descendants of Candalas and Kaivartas, but are of foreign extraction, though in many cases it may be of a more or less remote degree.'[6] Ghuznavi subscribed to the theory of immigration; very popular among Muslims at that time.[7] Such claims of foreign descent came in spite of the revelation of the Census of 1881 that 62.81 per cent of Muslim men in Bengal were peasants.[8]

The aspiration for elitism and upward social mobility among the lower socio-economic groups was satirized in many popular rhymes in the rural world of Bengali Muslims. One such rhyme was:

Agey chhile ulla tulla/tarpor hole uddin
Dhire Dhire Choudhury Saheb
(or, Parer sekh agey jay)
Bhagya phirte jaddin.

You were nobody at first (*ulla-tulla*), then you acquired some prestige (became an *uddin*); gradually you will be addressed as *Choudhury saheb* (or, the 'sekh' used as a casual suffix to your name will be adorably prefixed), when luck favours you further.

The custom of women's seclusion, very politely termed *purdah*, was an integral part of this elitism.[9] Seclusion did not only imply restricting the visibility of the physical 'self' of women; it was also extended to include *purdah* of the voice and the handwriting. To prevent the public audibility of her voice, a girl was expected to roll a nutcracker over a brass plate to indicate her consent in marriage.[10] Women's education was usually confined to religious and domestic training; learning the ritualistic practices of ablution (*waju*), offering *namaz* and memorizing the Koran. Lack of knowledge of Arabic precluded the possibility of any meaningful comprehension of the text. Decency (*adab*) expected that a girl would not want to learn

to write. This was not only because of the 'fear' that she might then write letters to forbidden persons,[11] but also that her handwriting might be exposed (*be-purdah*) before the gaze of males outside the legitimate family circle (*par-purush*).[12] The patriarchal objection in this regard did not merely imply that a woman's writings reflected her personal point of view and enabled the reader to have a glimpse of her 'self' through the narration. Her handwriting was perceived as an inseparable part of her person and to prevent if from being exposed to public gaze, women were preferably kept uneducated.[13]

The craze for *sharafati* sometimes assumed ludicrous proportions. Hamida Khanam (b.1923) gives a humorous account of this in her autobiography, *Jhara Bakuler Gandha.* She writes,

> We used to meet Saburan's *dadi* (grandmother) on holiday mornings when we went for a stroll on the bank of the Padma river. We stopped to talk to her for some time. At one point we asked her where her *desh* (country, extended to mean 'home' or 'place of origin') was. In fact this is why we had stopped. Dadi used to exclaim, 'O our *desh* is not here, it is in Arab'.[14] Dadi, who was the mother of a local sweet-seller and washed her utensils by a roadside tap, apparently belonged to the lower socio-economic stratum. Young Hamida was amused, 'Dadi lives in Pabna, speaks in Bengali and says her desh is in Arab (Arabia)'.[15]

The pressure of *sharafati* assumed a different dimension for Begum Sufia Kamal (1911-99). She came from the Shaistabad nawab family in Barisal. Sufia told in an interview:

> Our family was very annoyed that I had learnt Bengali and that my Bengali writings had been published. Nobody in the family except my mother wanted me to write. Writing in Bengali, speaking in Bengali, mixing with Bengalis, stepping out of home for social work without a *burqa*, all that I did, was a matter of great dishonour and disrepute (*be-izzati*) for the entire family. Everyone seemed to be ashamed of me.[16]

Unlike Sufia Kamal, identification with the local culture came more spontaneously for Sofia Khatun, who actually belonged to an immigrant Afghan family. In 1922, Sofia Khatun wrote, 'My father is an Afghan, so is my mother. But my siblings and I have been born in Bengal. We have been nourished by the food and water produced in Bengal . . . I have never been to the Afghan land . . . my life is filled with the pleasant, auspicious memories of Bengal.'[17]

Women were expected to perpetuate the ideas of *sharafati* even in their lives within the zenana, through the languages, dress and ornaments, cosmetics and culinary practices.[18] The discontent against such impositions was explicit in the writings of women. Most of the women writers of the early twentieth century came from an elite

background. Many of them were very sarcastic about this elitism, often comparing their situation with birds, *tiyapakhi*, *totapakhi*, etc.[19]

It is also worth noting that they chose chaste, Sanskritized Bengali as their medium of expression. Fazilatunnessa (1905-76) was the first Muslim student of Bethune College in 1923, the first Muslim girl in Dhaka University to study Applied Mathematics and also first among Bengali Muslim women to go abroad for higher studies on a scholarship in 1928. She wrote,

> Muslims in India are Indians. They have nothing to be proud of in any other identity; they should be ashamed if they think of anything else. They must know that the language of the province in which they are born is their mother tongue, its dress their own, and at all times, in prosperity and in crisis, only an Indian shall stand by their side. Religion may be important in private life but in public life (*jatiya jivan*), it is not desirable at all.[20]

Theoretically a Muslim woman enjoyed a variety of rights as compared to others in the nineteenth century. She had a definite share in the property of her deceased parents or her husband. There were scriptural sanctions for widow remarriage or remarriage after divorce. The example of the 'other' community was, however, so deeply imbued among Muslims that even as late as 1931, one in eight Muslim women was a widow.[21] In spite of the Wahhabi *fatwas* against dowry, it continued to plague the Muslim society. The Bengal Muslim Marriage Expenditure Regulation Act was passed in March 1947, authorizing the provincial government to make rules 'prescribing the scale of dowry'.[22] Apparently, the practical implementation of the scriptural rights depended on the sense of justice of men, within the family, or in social leadership. Women were also deprived of their right to education for a long time notwithstanding the Koranic approval in this regard.[23]

Conscious efforts at educating women came to be taken up from the late nineteenth century. The *anjumans*, while these were 'generally formed by rich peasants and their activities included the social and economic improvement of rural Muslims',[24] also occasionally included professionals from the emergent middle class. The Dhaka Anjuman offers a example. It had decidedly established its composite identity in its dual name; the Perso-Arabic *Anjuman-e-Ahbab-e-Islamiya* had simultaneously extended itself to a Bengali identity in the *Dhaka Musalman Suhrid Sammilani*.[25] Abdul Aziz, one of its leaders, sent his granddaughter Samsun Nahar (1908-64) to school to set a social example. His bewilderment with the changing times and the dichotomy in his personality is evident when he withdrew Nahar from school at the age of nine and sent her for a secluded life.

Samsun Nahar was stubborn; how she was eventually appointed as a teacher in the Bengali department of Lady Brabourne College in 1939 presents a study of her engagement with contemporaneity at every point.[26] Rokeya Sakhawat Hossain (1880-1932) writes that her father, Abu Ali Saber, zamindar of the decadent Payraband estate in Rangpur district, was immensely pleased that his elder daughter, Karimunnessa (1855-1926), had learnt Bengali. The orthodoxy, *molla-murubbi*,[27] was furious and their scathing criticism finally prevented Abu Ali from making any advance in this regard. Karimunnessa was sent to her maternal grandfather's home and married away in a hurry. Taking a lesson from this experience, Ibrahim Saber, never ventured to teach his sister, Rokeya, during daytime. He thus evaded a confrontation with the orthodoxy and devised a pragmatic solution to achieve his purpose. Ibrahim was educated at St. Xavier's College, Calcutta. Exposure to the liberal metropolitan environment and the demonstration effect of the families of the more advanced classmates and colleagues introduced an element of social competition in the minds of people like Rokeya's brother, Ibrahim and her husband, Syed Sakhawat Hossain (1858-1909). With these factors that combined to create the 'pull', was the 'push' which came from the inherent urge for education among women themselves.

Prior to Karimunnessa, we have the instance of Faizunnessa (*c.* 1834/40-1903),[28] who was educated by her father, Ahmad Ali, a prosperous and powerful zamindar of Comilla. Ahmad Ali might have had a genuine concern for women's education; he might also have looked upon Faizunnessa as his successor in matters of administering his vast estate (both his sons were weaklings). However, the fact remains that Ahmad Ali was too powerful to be opposed by the orthodoxy. Faizunnessa also chose Sanskritized Bengali as her medium of expression.[29]

She was the first Bengali Muslim woman to establish schools for girls. She established two schools in Comilla and consequently in all the eleven *mouzas* of her zamindari.[30] According to a report, there were seventy girls in one of these schools in Comilla in 1902 but none of them was a Muslim.[31]

The early encounters between Muslim women and Western health care practices was not congenial. *Tamiz* demanded that the maidservant of a *sharif bibi* would place the stethoscope on her body according to the instructions of the doctor forbidding him to touch her.[32] In strict compliance with *adab*, a woman in labour had to complain of toothache to call the doctor.[33] At the same time, Faizunnessa established a zenana hospital in Comilla in 1893.[34]

Rokeya raised the demand for a separate medical college for women a decade later.[35] The conservative section of the society viewed such advancements on the part of women with apprehension. The 'fear' of possible social anarchy resulting from women's education and consequent empowerment was occasionally reflected in literature, as in the derisive portrayal of the *Begum Thakrun* in *Gazi Miyar Bostani* (1899) by Mir Mosharraf Hossain.

Though not the first of its kind, the Sakhawat Memorial Girls' School (1911) in Calcutta institutionalized the scope of education for Muslim girls. The school could not resolve all the situational dichotomies that existed. Despite her earnest wishes, Rokeya could not open the Bengali section of her school till 1927.[36] This was in the nature of a compromise with the *sharif* Muslims of Calcutta who considered association with Bengali in any form as demeaning to their status. The survival of the school depended on the support of this class to a great extent. Among Rokeya's students was nine year old Heera, whose father did not allow eyeholes in her *burqa,* considering it as a gross violation of purdah.[37] It was at the same time a positive indication that even such families had started sending their daughters to school.

Adding to prejudices prevalent in the nineteenth century, Hindu society about women's education resulting in possible widowhood and moral lapses was the last desperate attempt to delimit the scope of female education, by propagating the view that their educational achievements led to an inversely proportional ability to bear sons.[38] At the same time, education was sought to be legitimized on the grounds of equipping women in their future roles as ideal homemakers, good wives and noble mothers. The latter discourse was applicable to the Bengali Muslim society as well. Quite a few Muslim-edited journals published articles (by both men and women) justifying women's education on the ground of its domestic application. A number of booklets were also published on this subject. Samsun Nahar Mahmud's *Sisur Siksa* (Education of a Child, Calcutta, 1939) and Aziz Ahammad's *Lalana Suhrid* (Friend of Women, 24-Parganas, 1924) are examples. The author of *Lalana Suhrid* says that he engaged in writing the book because he could not find a suitable *Stripathyapustak* (primer meant for girls) for his daughter. Explaining the purpose of women's education in the preface, he postulated that this was neither acquiring a university degree as might result from the 'higher education of the Bethune College', nor enabling them 'to deliver lectures at the Town Hall'. Both these phrases are very significant. Only a year ago, in 1923 Fazilatunnessa had created a stir in Bengali

society as the first Muslim student in Bethune College. Rokeya had delivered a public lecture at the Calcutta Town Hall on 6 April 1920. Evidently, these achievements were considered too outrageous to be commendable.

Paradoxically, both Rokeya and Fazilatunnessa reverted to the ideologies of domesticity and motherhood to legitimize the scope of women's education in a generally orthodox and hostile social milieu. In 1903, Rokeya wrote, 'We shall do whatever is required to gain equality with men'.[39] Appreciating the necessity of a 'modern secular gender-neutral education which would prepare women for gainful employment',[40] Rokeya, at the same time, included subjects like nursing, cooking, sewing and religious training in the curriculum of her school. Her earlier secular and non-gendered view of education was thoroughly revised; she had to concede, at least ostensibly, that the purpose of education was to create 'obedient daughters, loving sisters, dutiful wives and instructive mothers'.[41]

By the 1920s, Bengali Muslims generally came to terms with the idea of their girls going to school;[42] the 1930s constituted the decade when they started going to college in large numbers and this necessitated the foundation of the Lady Brabourne College (1939). Hamida Khanam, who was one of the three Muslim girls in the MA class in Calcutta University in 1939, could perceive that the 'situation in the Muslim society was changing very fast and girls were beginning to show greater signs of awareness'.[43]

Realizing education as a means to employment, a few women were taking up the teaching profession though an exact statistics cannot be obtained. Anwara Khatun passed the MB Examination from the Calcutta Medical College in 1940. There were an increasing number of Muslim girls among those who passed the primary and final licentiateship examination from the medical colleges in the 1940s.[44] But the process of gradual advancement received a major setback with partition, a political event which sought to restructure the cultural history of Bengal.

In undivided Bengal until August 1947, Muslims formed the numerical majority in the population.[45] There are several possible reasons as to why middle-class Bengali Muslims started to move away from West Bengal at that time. Those who had faced the trauma of riots, whose persons and property were attacked, left their homes in search of security. This outflow started with the Calcutta Killings of August 1946 and continued till at least 1965 as a result of the recurrent riots.[46] Some people were not directly affected, but, nonetheless suffered from a certain fear psychosis due to recent

political events and also feared future communal attacks.[47] The idea of an Islamic nation about to be born fired the imagination of many educated Muslim youth. Some were ardent supporters of the Muslim League; some were simply inspired by religiosity.

The hope for better prospects and 'tremendous employment potential' in an environment where Muslim socio-cultural hegemony would be unchallenged, motivated many Bengali Muslim professionals to opt out of West Bengal at the initial stages. The entire infrastructure of Pakistan was new and meant to provide a platform free from Hindu competition. Along with the wives and daughters of the men who opted for Pakistan, many women who had attained considerable academic and professional renown also went away.[48] Many of these people who had come from various districts of East Bengal to study or work in Calcutta preferred to go back to their original homes in the event of an inevitable territorial separation. Fazilatunnessa was from Tangail, Hamida Khanam had come from Pabna, Samsun Nahar Mahmud had her ancestral roots in Noakhali and Chittagong. Perhaps a combined consideration of career and the 'call of the motherland' motivated them to go away to East Pakistan. It would be highly speculative to say whether these women would still have gone away if there was no Partition, or if they could still have made equally brilliant careers if they had stayed back in West Bengal.[49] The suddenness of the political change associated with Partition rendered a large section of middle-class Bengali Muslims psychologically unfit to confront it. Many of them initially suffered from an adjustment crisis. Under a growing minority complex, they initially recoiled into their community confines and yielded to the renewed social control exercised by the orthodoxy. Many women felt that there was a great deal of religio-social and familio-patriarchal monitoring over their activities at that time.[50] Of the Bengali Muslims who are found to have stayed back in West Bengal after Partition were a few secular people, with professed political commitments. Some, though not active in politics, were ideologically opposed to Partition. Some were not convinced of the viability of the new nation-state about to be born and thus preferred not to exercise their option. There was another section of the landholding middle class, whose strong sense of property and village identity prevented them from going away. Along with the emotional attachment to one's ancestral property which precluded the possibility of exchange, it was also practically very difficult to exchange such properties because these were jointly owned (in which case all the co-owners had to agree to

the terms of exchange). Hindu migrants from East Bengal also looked for urban property in non-Muslim localities.

Along with these categories, two new sections of Bengali Muslims emerged during the post-1947 period due to horizontal and vertical mobility.[51] The 'new' middle class among Bengali Muslims in post-1947 West Bengal, the socio-cultural counterpart of the Hindu *bhadralok*, was exposed to the social stress of competition from the Bengali Hindu middle class that was also undergoing considerable changes. Consequently, a section of the Bengali Muslims was forced to reformulate (even if partially) its social outlook, norms and ideals. Their achievements, in turn, inspired others within the community.

Post-1947 West Bengal was like a 'melting pot' in which the traditional social attitudes regarding women were being reformulated in the face of practical necessities. The old joint family was discarded,[52] many of the orthodox social customs were done away with,[53] and the traditional physical divide between the public and the private worlds also withered away.[54] All this restructured the social order, preparing the old for the new. Under dire economic stress, women of the migrant Hindu families in West Bengal had to take up jobs to sustain their families. As better academic qualifications would fetch better jobs, there was greater demand for education and the attendance of girls in the educational institutions of West Bengal increased considerably after 1947. Along with this was the initiative of the newly independent Indian nation to improve infrastructural facilities and give increasing importance to women's education. The Annual Reports on Progress of Education in West Bengal neither analyse the reason for the increasing academic interest of women, nor include any separate data on Muslim women.[55] One such Report for the year 1953-4 stated, 'demand for such education (of girls) is increasing very fast and the number of institutions is also rapidly increasing in almost all the stages of education'.[56]

The changing situation in the education of Muslim women is reflected in *Shahryar*, a novel by Syed Mujtaba Ali (Calcutta, 1969). Married to a descendant of one of the aristocratic families of Murshidabad, Shahryar is an upper middle-class housewife in Calcutta. She is an accomplished woman, with very strong roots in Bengali values and culture. Shahryar has acquired all this herself and in the process she realizes her crisis of not being able to relate with anyone around her. The author has a social observation, 'A decade ago, Muslim girls were so rare that Hindu professors treated them with greater care. It also included a bit of curiosity towards

the unknown, the new'. This indicates the initial post-Partition decline in the number of Muslim girl students in West Bengal. The gradual widening of the scope of education for them from the 1960s has been brought out in the character of Shahryar's niece. The 'new' woman gets a more concrete shape in her depiction. The Bangladesh Liberation War in 1971 also added to the confidence of some of these women as it established the primacy of culture over religion.

The widening scope of higher education is linked with the prospect of employment. It was with this objective in mind the Muslim Girls' Hostels were set up in Calcutta and other district towns. The change in mentality can be perceived by looking at girls who come from the villages. On the one hand, these hostels are indicators of a demand for higher education and greater urge of economic independence among girls. On the other hand, the establishment of separate hostels for Muslim girls in Muslim majority neighbourhoods segregates them from the mixed community environment, restricting their social interaction within the community to a great extent. Such attempts on the part of the community itself as well as the other community's refusal, for instance, to accept Muslim tenants, leads to ghettoization. Mixed habitations are on their way out over large areas of West Bengal and new settlements based on exclusive religious identities are growing.[57] With money accumulating in the hands of the new professionals, Muslim families have also shown an inclination to build houses in Muslim localities.

It is one of the queer contradictions in the present history of West Bengal that while the greatest similarities between Hindus and Muslims are noted in the socio-domestic sphere, yet this remains one of the areas where both strive their utmost to maintain the distinctiveness of their identities. From the point of view of Bengali Muslim women this gives rise to a complex phenomenon: a painful process in which middle-class women of the community have to balance themselves delicately among their socio-linguistic, religious and gender identities. Various conflicting patterns emerge from a study of the socio-domestic lives of Bengali Muslim women. Priority to the Muslim religious identity has chances of restricting the scope of interaction with other communities. A section of the Bengali middle class, both Hindu and Muslim, feel the necessity of increased interaction. Whether naturally achieved from a genuine commitment to secular Bengali values or diligently devised as a calculated step for acculturation in case of Muslim women, this alters their domestic pattern from the conventional Muslim type and changes the nature of their social interaction and attitude. It makes

greater socio-cultural interaction possible, with greater participation in each other's festivals and acceptance of occasional interreligious marriages. Religious differences are thus confined to the private domain and there is a conscious effort of building up a homogeneous Bengali culture, through secular socio-cultural idioms. In any case, the decisions are not autonomous; they are crucially conditioned by family values, male members in the family, personal experiences, etc.

It is a paradox that many women used to the *burqa* abandon it when they have to come out of the house more frequently than before. The *burqa* makes them anonymous in the public domain, providing a symbolic shelter in the separate world of Muslims. At the same time it also invites looks which identifies them as 'peculiar', different from the rest. If the *burqa* gives her anonymity, abandoning the *burqa* gives her a different anonymity. She cannot then be very easily identified on the basis of her religion. This is a very important part of the emerging middle-class structure and identity formation among Mu 'ims who refuse to be identified on the basis of their religion alone.

The construction of the *Musalmani Bangla* during the colonial period reincarnates itself in post-1947 West Bengal, the vocabulary sharply divided between the private and the public. Thus non-Bengali or Muslim kinship terms like *khala*, *fufi*, *chachi* are dropped in favour of Bengali Hindu terms like *mashi*, *pishi*, *kakima* in public. Sometimes the former set is altogether substituted for the latter in both private and public spheres. Gender as identity acquires importance in the domestic sphere as women face discrimination in matters of inheritance. When faced with crisis situations in family life, like polygamy (though very rare) and divorce, Muslim women realize how different and disadvantaged they are in comparison to women of other communities. Still they refrain from speaking in favour of a Uniform Civil Code since there is no clear picture of what such a Code is going to be like. Though they may not be orthodox themselves, these women resent the possibility of being hegemonized by 'others' in the name of uniformity.

With greater participation in public life and the widening sphere of interaction with other communities, there is a considerable break from the stereotypes about Bengali Muslim women, their world-views and family structure. Such changes are distinctly visible in the rising age of marriage among girls, declining rate of cousin marriages, rarity of the incidences of polygamy and divorce, general disapproval of the custom of widow remarriage, adoption of, or at least strong support for family planning measures, etc. Some of these changes, like reducing the contract of *mahr* at the time of marriage to a mere

formality and the growth of the custom of dowry, may be viewed as Hindu influence. But certain other features, like preference for nuclear families, indicate the growth of a new companionate marriage ideal among many Muslim couples.

The fact that many women reported that they have faced comments like, 'You do not look like a Muslim,' or 'I had mistakenly thought you were Bengali,' show that the idea about stereotypical Muslim women is still not altogether absent in popular perception and the mainstream culture is identified with that of a particular community. Such a perception is prevalent among members of both communities. It also establishes that a Bengali Muslim woman, culturally comparable to her Hindu social counterpart, is still not visible in significant numbers.

NOTES

1. The subject has been addressed in the works of Rafiuddin Ahmed, *The Bengal Muslims, 1871-1906: A Quest for Identity*, Delhi: Oxford University Press, 1981, Rafiuddin Ahmed (ed.), *Understanding the Bengali Muslims: Interpretative Essays*, Delhi: Oxford University Press, 2001.
2. Ibid.
3. This aspect has been focused by Asim Roy, *The Islamic Syncretistic Tradition in Bengal*, Princeton: Princeton University Press, 1983.
4. H. Beverley, *Report on the Census of Bengal, 1872*, Calcutta: Secretariat Press, 1872, p. 132.
5. Richard M. Eaton, *The Rise of Islam and the Bengal Frontier, 1204-1760*, Oxford: Oxford University Press, 1997.
6. Abu A. Ghuznavi, 'Notes on the Origin, Social and Religious Divisions and other Matters Touching on the Mahomedans of Bengal and Having Special Reference to the District of Maimensing', quoted in Eaton, op. cit., p. 120.
7. Another example of a similar text is Khondekar Fuzli Rubbee's *The Origin of the Musalmans of Bengal*, 1895, 2nd edn., Dacca: Society for Pakistan Studies, 1970.
8. Census of India, 1881, quoted in Peter Hardy, *The Muslims of British India*, Cambridge: Cambridge University Press, 1972, p.105.
9. The lives of secluded women within the *zenana* have been described by Sonia Nishat Amin, *The World of Muslim Women in Colonial Bengal, 1876-1939*, Leiden: E.J. Brill, 1996.
10. Rokeya Sakhawat Hossein, *Abarodhbasini*, Calcutta: Mohammadi Book Agency, 1931, episode no. 34.
11. This view was very popular in north India as pointed out by Gail Minault, *Secluded Scholars: Women's Education and Muslim Social Reform in Colonial India*, Delhi: Oxford University Press, 1998, p. 24.
12. Samsunnahar Mahmud, 'Begum Rokeya Sakhawat Hossain', *Prabasi*, vol. 33, pt. II, Phalgun 1339 BS, p. 688.
13. Identical fears initially prevailed in the Bengali Hindu circles as exemplified in Rassundari Dasi, *Amar Jiban*, 3rd rpt., Calcutta: College Street Publication, 2002, p. 57.

14. Hamida Khanam, *Jhara Bakuler Gandha*, Dhaka: Sahitya Prakash, 2001, p. 18.
15. Ibid.
16. Interview with Shaheen Akhtar, 6 and 20 September 1996, in Shaheen Akhtar and Mousumi Bhowmik (ed.), *Zanana Mahfil*, Calcutta: Stree, 1998, pp. 268-9.
17. Sofia Khatun, 'Bangalir Sahityanurag', *Bangiya Musalman Sahitya Patrika*, year 6, no. 2, Sravan 1330 BS (1923), pp. 121-5.
18. This identity crisis is brought out in the fictitious character of a young middle-class Muslim girl in the 1990s. While trying to use cosmetics on Id, Akashlina cannot choose between *surma* and eyeliner. The *surma* and the eyeliner are respectively the symbols of the sectarian and the mainstream female culture of self-decoration. Whereas she feels the eyeliner would be more effective as make-up, tradition insists that *surma* would be a more appropriate marker of her religious identity. The dilemma over a matter that apparently seems trivial is thus symbolic of larger problems of choice. Abul Bashar, *Akashlina*, Calcutta: Ananda Publishers, 1994.
19. Mrs M. Rahman, 'Amader Dabee', *Dhumketu*, Aswin 2, 1921 BS; Rokeya Sakhawat Hossain, 'Alankar na Badge of Slavery', *Mahila*, 1903 BS; 'Sourajagat' (short story), *Saogat*, Poush 1918 BS. It recurs in at least four other places in Rokeya's writings. Rassundari, interestingly had also referred to herself as *Pinjarbaddha bihangi* (caged bird), op cit., p. 53.
20. 'Muslim Nari Siksar Prayojaniyata', *Saogat*, Agrahayan, 1334 BS (1927).
21. *Census of India*, 1931, vol. VI, no. 1, p. 416.
22. *Calcutta Gazette*, Parts IA-VI, January-June 1947; Part IV-B, 6.3.1947, item 4(2) c, p. 30.
23. 'Lord, increase me in knowledge!' *The Koran*, 20: 114. 'They are losers who besottedly have slain their children by keeping them in ignorance'. Ibid., 6: 141.
24. Pradip Kumar Datta, *Carving Blocs: Communal Ideology in Early Twentieth Century Bengal*, Delhi: Oxford University Press,1999, p. 74.
25. This sort of composite identity may also be exemplified in the christening of a magazine as *Nabanur* and a primary school as Parapukur *Balika Maktab*. The Sanskrit *Naba* and *Balika* are combined with Persian words, *Nur* and *Maktab*. The name of *Srimati Bibi* Taherannessa, who wrote an article in the form of a letter to the editor of the *Bamabodhini Patrika* in 1866, may also be cited as an example.
26. Anwara Bahar Choudhury, *Samsunnahar Mahmud*, Dhaka: Bangla Academy, 1987.
27. Rokeya Sakhawat Hossain, 'Lukano Ratan', *Saogat*, Asarh, 1334 BS (1927).
28. Goutam Roy, *Nawab Faizunnessa Chaudhurani Muslim Nari Jagaraner Agradut*, Kolkata: Biswakosh Parishad, 2007. Also, Maniruzzaman, *Faijannechha Chaudhurani,* Dhaka: Bangla Academy, 1988.
29. Her 'protonovel', *Rupjalal* (1876) was the first book written by a Bengali Muslim woman, Sonia Nishat Amin, op. cit., p. 215.
30. Ekram Ali, 'Nawab Faizunnessa Chaudhurani', in Miratun Nahar (ed.), *Lukano Ratan,* Rokeya-Smarak Baktritamala, Kolkata: Suraha Sampriti, 2006.
31. Report published in *The Moslem Chronicle*, 1902, quoted in Ahmad Rafiq, 'Narisiksa Bistar O Samajkalyane Brati Faijannechha', in *Nari Pragatir Char Ananya*, Dhaka: Sahitya Prakash, 2006, p. 21.
32. Rokeya Sakhawat Hossain, *Abarodhbasini*, Calcutta: Mohammadi Book Agency, 1931, anecdote number 18.
33. Ibid., no. 38.

34. Sonia Nishat Amin, op. cit., p. 216.
35. 'Sugrihini', Article in *Motichur*, vol. I, Calcutta: Nabanur Karjyalaya, 1903.
36. Note of Dedication, *Motichur*, vol. II, Calcutta: The Author, 1922.
37. *Abarodhbasini*, op. cit., Episode no. 13, recorded as an incident of 28 June 1929.
38. An example of this is Nilkantha Majumdar's article 'Naridharma' in *Vedavyas*, Baisakh, 1296 BS (1889).
39. Rokeya Sakhawat Hossain, 'Alankar na Badge of Slavery?' first published in Girish Chandra Sen (ed.), *Mahila*, 1310 BS (1903) later edited and incorporated as 'Strijatir Abanati' in *Motichur*, vol. I, op. cit.
40. Ibid.
41. 'Educational Ideals for the Modern Indian Girl', *The Mussalman*, 5 March 1931, Mention may be made of Fazilatunnessa's articles: (a) 'Muslims Nari Siksar Prayojaniyata', *Saogat*, Agrahayan, 1334 BS (1927). (b) 'Muslim Narir Mukti', *Saogat*, Bhadra, 1336 BS (1929), which invoked a similar discourse.
42. This was in marked contrast with the attitude prevalent in the mid-nineteenth century social leadership. In the discussion which ensued following a paper read by Abdul Latif at a meeting of the Bengal Social Science Association on 30 January 1868, it had come out from Maulvi Abdul Haqim's reply to Pearychand Mitra that Muslim girls could not be allowed to go to schools like women of 'other' communities, disregarding purdah.
43. Hamida Khanam, op. cit., p. 61.
44. Notification from the State Medical Faculty of Bengal, Grosvenor House, Calcutta, 21 June 1945, *Calcutta Gazette*, vol. II, July 1945.
45. Though this was largely due to the preponderance of the agrarian masses in the Dacca, Chittagong and Rajsahi Divisions, Muslims formed 53.55, 54.43 and 54.29 per cent of the total population of Bengal as revealed in the Census of 1921, 1931 and 1941 respectively. Source: *Census of India 1921*, vol. V, pt. II, W.H. Thompson, Calcutta, 1923, pp. 28-9. *Census of India 1931*, vol. V, Bengal and Sikkim, Part II. Tables by A.E. Porter, Calcutta 1932, p. 220; *Census of India 1941*, vol. IV, Bengal, Tables by R.A. Dutch, Simla, 1942, Table XIII, pp. 44-5.
46. The politically committed family of Abul Hashim in Burdwan, for instance, which initially had no desire to migrate, left for Pakistan after their house was attacked in the riot of 1950. Apparently they had no plan of migration as the family had built a new house in the town after 1947.
47. Yaqub Ali, an Assistant Engineer in Nadia district, was not a direct victim of violence. Yet he preferred to migrate because his family was said to be 'eyed with silent menace' by some of his Hindu neighbours. Diary p. 2, MSS, Euro file no. C/188/8/AJ Dash Papers, India Office Library.
48. The alumni associations of the Sakhawat Memorial Girls' School and Lady Brabourne College were first informally organized in Dhaka before they could be formally launched in Kolkata.
49. Muslims were reduced to 19.85 per cent of the total population of West Bengal after Partition. *Census of India 1951*, vol. VI, WB and Sikkim; Part II by A. Mitra, Calcutta, 1953, p. 436.
50. All observations made in this section are primarily on the basis of a fieldwork conducted in West Bengal during 2002-4, as part of my Ph.D. work at Jawaharlal Nehru University. The fieldwork included extensive interviews of Bengali Muslim women.

    The dearth of written/published sources on the subject is remarkable, testifying to the observation '. . . for the social history of any minority group, the limitations

of written documentation are such that the use of oral sources introduces an entirely new dimension to the subject'. (Paul Thompson, *The Voice of the Past: Oral History,* Oxford: Oxford University Press, 1978, p. 88.)

51. 'Horizontal mobility' refers to the migration of the propertied rural classes to urban areas. 'Vertical mobility' refers to the upward socio-economic mobility of the lower groups in both rural and urban areas, by dint of academic and professional merit.
52. Kanti B. Pakrashi, *The Uprooted: A Sociological Study of the Refugees of West Bengal India,* Calcutta: Editions Indian, 1971, p. 72.
53. Gargi Chakravarty, *Coming Out of Partition: Refugee Women of West Bengal,* Delhi: Bluejay Books, 2005, p. 84.
54. Rachel Weber, 'Re(creating) the Home: Women's Role in the Development of Refugee Colonies in South Calcutta', in J. Bagchi and S. Dasgupta (eds.), *The Trauma and the Triumph: Gender and Partition in Eastern India,* Calcutta: Stree, 2003, pp. 59-79.
55. The idea regarding the backwardness of Muslims in education (treated as a homogeneous category irrespective of the socio-economic affiliations) is so commonplace that several scholars who have dealt with the topic have tended to make generalized statements. Examples: M. Indu Menon, *Status of Muslim Women in India: A Case Study of Kerala,* Delhi: Uppal Publishing House, 1981, p. 2; M.K.A. Siddiqui, *Educating a Backward Minority,* Calcutta: Abadi Publication, 1984, p. 16; *Towards Equality,* Report of the National Committee on the Status of Women in India, Delhi: Ministry of Education and Social Welfare, 1974, p. 96.
56. Report on the Progress of Education in West Bengal for the year 1953, Superintendent, Govt. Printing, W.B. Government Press, Alipore, 1958, p. 54.
57. This has also been mentioned in Saonli Mitra, 'Unmadanar Kaksapath', in *Mukure Mukh na Mukhosh,* Calcutta, 1997, pp. 45-6; Ranabir Samaddar (ed.), *Reflections on Partition in the East,* Delhi: Vikas Publishing House, 1997, p. 126, Chakravarty, *Coming Out of Partition*, op. cit., p. 119.

Book Reviews

The Trust Betrayed: Reflections on Diplomacy and Development

Jagat S. Mehta
New Delhi: Penguin/Viking, pp. 342, Rs. 550

KRISHNAN SRINIVASAN

Of the three score and more books written by former foreign secretaries, some are worthy, some mediocre, many self-serving, with one writer as sparing of the truth as the author was in real life. Jagat Mehta's four previous books have dealt less on his own considerable achievements but, rather with issues and policies.

Born with several silver spoons in his mouth but disciplined by a progressive father, he learned egalitarianism and social service from an early age. In a career spanning from independence uptil 1979, he was a fiercely independent thinker, derided by a senior ICS colleague, threatened with supersession, posted in Tanzania as a punishment, nearly superseded as foreign secretary, removed from that top position prematurely on the charge of being insufficiently 'pro-Soviet', and offered neither an Ambassadorship nor Raj Bhavan. His phone was tapped by Indira Gandhi, and despite, or perhaps because of all these tribulations, he is widely admired as a beau ideal, and was awarded the Padma Bhushan 23 years after retirement.

The present memoir compiled from memory is subjective but properly candid and controversial. He offers harsh criticism of what he sees as the consistent cowardice in rendering honest unsolicited advice in national interest to the political masters—'the one overriding weakness has been of us civil servants abdicating the obligation to volunteer advice in the long-term interests of the country' . . . 'honest opinion given in national interest has its own reward'. This book will therefore make most civilian and uniformed officials uncomfortable.

There is a moving chapter on his gifted late wife Rama, and one on the best and worst aspects of volunteerism in the Sewa Mandir, Vidya Bhavan and Environmental Education Centre of Udaipur, to which Mehta has devoted his life after 1985—he writes, 'the responsibility of ensuring a just democracy hinges on the activism of unselfish voluntary effort'.

There are interesting anecdotes of the early years in the foreign service and lively sketches of Indian and foreign dignitaries. A letter written in 1962 (from whom not mentioned) predicting the Chinese attack but never forwarded to Delhi was later found by him in a file in the Indian Embassy in Beijing. Nehru was 'generally misled or even deliberately deceived' on China. In 1964, Delhi wrongly assumed China would attack again. In 1965, Mehta anticipated from Beijing that China would not, despite threats and ultimata, intervene on behalf of Pakistan and told Delhi as much, which greatly impressed prime minister Shastri—this is Mehta's most cherished accolade.

As early as 1956 it was clear to Mehta that the superpowers were unwilling to use nuclear weapons and after Hungary, he feels Nehru should have pressed harder for détente and disarmament. He would have advocated an open mind on signing the NPT to press the then nuclear five towards disarmament, which would have been Nehru's approach. He notes that Indira Gandhi and Narasimha Rao defaulted on the chance to have closer relations with Asean in 1980 when they declined an invitation of observer status.

The tryst was betrayed by many, with the result that India has under-performed diplomatically. Noting that 'in the twentieth century nothing was as difficult as diplomacy between unequal neighbours', he opposes the *anschluss* of Sikkim, contrasting it with Nehru's handling of Bhutan. The diplomatic approach must be different from the military one: all too often the MEA had followed the projections of the defence and intelligence establishment whereas the objectives of diplomacy are different, namely problem-solving without conflict, and must at times override public opinion.

Mehta urges the recognition of the equality of nationalism: he regrets that India did not perceive the Cold War as mutually reinforced paranoia and that outside the Cold War, the Soviet Union would be neutral in South Asia; he feels that many of Nehru's years were wasted—Nehru wrongly assumed that countries like China would appreciate India's non-hostility through non-alignment. After 1980, mistakes by Indira Gandhi in India's Afghan policy alienated India from the Afghan nationalists. On Pakistan, Mehta advocates professionalism in preference to knee-jerk hostility; he urges shedding the view that tensions in the subcontinent are unique, and opposes the IPKF operation in Sri Lanka.

Some elisions in narrative, perhaps inevitable in the constraints of the author's recollection, will be difficult for readers unfamiliar with the subject. It is a pity that greater elaboration was not offered

on the more contestable propositions. Jagat Mehta's views will cause lively debate, especially among conformist circles and this is no doubt precisely what he has intended.

The Last Thousand Days of the British Empire

Peter Clarke
London: Allen Lane, 2007, ISBN 978-0-713-99830-6, pp. 513, £ 25

KRISHNAN SRINIVASAN

This is a history written mainly from secondary sources; the diaries of Colville, Cadogan, Moran, Dalton, Senator Vandenberg, Wavell, Alan Broke et al.; the memoirs and books of Churchill, Truman, Montgomery and many others. It is pacy and page-turning history, but lacks analyses of the motivations and the characters of the persons involved in the drama. The author, after reading so many first-hand accounts, obviously cannot make up his mind whether to praise or condemn the various actors.

Three out of four parts of this book and 365 pages out of 513 take us to the end of World War II. The text ends in August 1947, whereas the Empire extended well into the 1970s. Therefore the book's title is a misnomer. The Empire had made Britain great by defying demography, economy and geography, but the war was an unsuccessful imperialist war. It left bills to be paid and the independence of the Empire was one of them. The Empire had ceased to exercise influence in a world with two superpowers and Attlee played a losing hand in India and Palestine with cards already dealt. Britain could not defend its Dominions like New Zealand and Australia or even India without the help of the USA, and Canada stood alone in the Empire who could contribute dollars to the war efforts. In return for Lend Lease, Britain accepted the end of imperial preferences in favour of free trade. The Americans not only picked up the war tabs but also the British markets. In 1944 Britain's reserves were down to $600 million. The end of the Empire was due to extension of British commitments in an age of declining British power. India and Pakistan had to be given up along with great power pretensions.

USA resented Churchill's 'outworn imperialism'. The preservation of the Empire was not why US was fighting the war. In fact, it was the reverse, whereas 'hands off the British Empire is our maxim' said Churchill. That US's suspicions of imperialism influenced Roosevelt's policy and Churchill's view was reflected in the Atlantic Charter of 1941. US intervention after Pearl Harbour was to ensure Britain's survival but Britain was eclipsed militarily and economically by the USA. The Cripps Mission to India in 1942 was prodded by Roosevelt but failed. While Roosevelt continued to press for a nationalist interim Indian government, the Indian Congress and Gandhi lost sympathy in the USA with the Quit India movement that hampered the war effort. Roosevelt wanted to determine the fate of Palestine on his own terms and not by British imperialism, whereas Britain felt its strategic interests would be served by Zionism. The Americans were always wary of getting enmeshed in Britain's plans to protect the Empire and were suspicious of Churchill's war strategies, great power pretensions, support of monarchies in the Mediterranean and the Balkans and wishing to be a part of the final stages of victory over Japan. They felt that Britain had been unable to protect its Empire in Asia and deserved to lose it. As Churchill predicted, 'after the war, we shall be weak, we shall have no money, and no strength, and we shall lie between the two great powers of USA and USSR'.

At the heart of the matter was, of course, money. Lord Keynes, in charge of negotiations with the US, clinched Lend Lease II for the post-war stage, using the moral argument 'we threw good house-keeping to the winds but we helped to save the world', but the Americans were suspicious of being fleeced by the rest of the world and were not interested in 'equal sacrifice', with the result that wartime financial negotiations with the USA were always ambiguous or meaningless—Lend Lease, Bretton Woods, post-war free market for exports, free convertibility and imperial preferences.

After Roosevelt died, the changes in Truman's cabinet were less friendly to Britain. After VE Day there were cut-backs of Lend Lease and ships were recalled even on the high seas. With VJ Day now on the horizon, Lend Lease III and sharper cut-backs loomed. Keynes estimated that by VJ Day, Britain owed £3 billion, 50 per cent to India, and had a balance of payment deficit of £8 billion. With the exception of Canada the rest of the British Empire had benefited from the war at Britain's expense, and by 1945 Britain's role in victory over Germany was minor, with only 1 soldier in 10. At Potsdam Churchill had tried to set the stage for Lend Lease III after VJ Day—that debts

should not be measured only in terms of dollars—but the US public felt that US was treated as a milch cow that made everyone else rich. The atom bomb put an abrupt end to the war even before Lend Lease III. US critics spoke of greedy Britain wanting loans of $4.5 billion from World War I and $14 billion from World War II to be written off.

With Lend Lease III the US wanted Britain to dismantle imperial preference and exchange controls, to promote free trade and multilateralism. Britain got $3.5 billion as loan against a promise to eliminate imperial preference and make sterling convertibile in one year. All Britain's dues under Lend Lease were reduced to $650 million, only 3 per cent of the actual debt. But in 1946 Britain owed India as much as £1.3 billion: the Empire had provoked aggression but saddled Britain with the defence costs, and the British were left bewildered that war had enriched US and impoverished Britain. They were surprised to find themselves victims rather than victors after the war was over in 1945 with no reward for their fortitude or sacrifices, and post-war austerity and rationing replacing wartime austerity and rationing.

In 1947 defence expenditure was still 40 per cent of the budget and the US and Canadian loans were being drawn down at an alarming speed. Keynes wanted properly costed social investment at home along with drastic cuts in overseas spending. He said, 'we have had to accept during the war a post war financial burden entirely disproportionate to what is fair'. Marshall Aid came to the rescue of Britain's dollar crisis in the nick of time. Eventually, the loans from the USA and Canada were paid off by the UK only by the end of 2006.

Whitehall neither knew nor cared about India as much as Leo Amery, Secretary of State for India, Viceroy Wavell discovered. Churchill delayed any discussion about India with Amery and Wavell till March 1945; neither democratization nor independence had any attraction for him, and the Bengal famine of 1943-4 was ignored. Amery and Cripps eventually overcame Attlee's dislike of the bourgeois Congress party and pressed to give Wavell a chance to negotiate with Indian politicians. Until May 1945 Wavell had still been told nothing. But with elections looming Churchill did not want India to be a domestic issue, and a conference of all Indian leaders was accepted. Churchill was prepared to risk an Indian settlement rather than make India an election issue. US needed a reliable ally in the UN and that was Britain, since obstruction came from the Soviet Union and all the minor states were unreliable. So it was prepared to settle for self-government rather than full independence.

But Wavell's Simla Conference to find an executive council of equal members from the Congress and Muslim League failed. In Palestine there was pressure on Britain to allow 100,000 Jews to immigrate. In pressing for a Jewish Palestinian state, the US thought it was attacking the British Empire whereas for Arabs, the Zionists were aspects of Western imperialism. And paradoxically the US did not want to open its own doors to Jewish immigrants.

The commitment of Attlee and Cripps to Indian independence was crucial. Congress had withdrawn from the government in 1937, and the Quit India movement from 1942 to 1945 was political paralysis. It allowed the Muslim League to organize and become dynamic. Congress saw the independence issue as between it and Britain; the Muslim League saw it as between the Muslim League and Hindu Congress. Congress displayed a lack of realism for which Gandhi was responsible. Both Jinnah and Gandhi could block a settlement, and Cripps' compromise of a federal centre was rejected by both. The vision of non-violence perished due to the deficiency in political skill. Gandhi refused on principle any compromise on moral grounds, and Nehru and Patel deferred to him. The realities were therefore determined by the politics of the street. Strategically, economically and militarily India could not be afforded. Morally it was known that there would be violence, but it was agreed that the newly independent nation would have to make its own way.

In Palestine also, the Jews and Arabs could not agree and Britain became the butt of criticism from Jews and Americans. A statement from Truman was interpreted as favouring partition and wrecked British plans for an Arab-Jewish conference in 1946. From December 1946 onwards Churchill opposed all Labour moves for India but had no alternative to offer. So it was 'scuttle and skedaddle' in India and Palestine though Labour tried to take credit for the policy of withdrawal. In December 1946 when Zionists decided on direct action, Britain decided to hand back the mandate to the UN and the mandate ended in May 1948. The options for Britain were partition wanted by the Jews or a binational state. There was lack of support but no lack of interference from the US in favour of the Zionists. Because Britain chose the Arabs and the US chose the Jews, there is an Israeli state but no Arab Palestinian state.

India Since Independence: Making Sense of Indian Politics

V. Krishna Ananth

New Delhi: Pearson, 2010, ISBN 978 81 317 2567 2, pp. 435, Rs 750

KRISHNAN SRINIVASAN

This book is not as superficial as Ramachandra Guha's *India after Gandhi* nor as racy as Shashi Tharoor's *From Midnight to the Millennium.* It is a dour, stodgy lament by a die-hard leftist for the loss of Mahatma Gandhi's economic socialism, allegedly perverted by Nehru and all his successors at the altar of capitalist business to whom, according to Ananth, they were in thrall. It also lacks balance; of the 415 pages, the first fifty take us swiftly to the end of the Nehru era while the major narrative is about Indira and Rajiv Gandhi and V.P. Singh, an epilogue bringing the tale to 2004. Added to this are curious usages of the English language like 'sectarian agenda' (to describe Congress siding with pre-war capitalists), 'become big', 'hoisting' (to describe promotion), 'errand boy', 'poster boy', 'cheerleader', 'doghouse', 'swanky car', 'chaffing' (instead of searching), 'anointed' (instead of appointed), which are constant vexations and unacceptable in what professes to be a serious study.

The capitalist class saw freedom as a way to consolidate capitalism in India despite the Karachi Congress session of 1931 that sought 'to end exploitation of the masses' and freedom for the 'starving masses'. FICCI, by 1944, wanted a socialist framework that did not dilute capitalism, which Ananth calls 'the Bombay Plan'. Nehruvian socialism implemented this FICCI agenda instead of radical land reforms and elimination of feudalism. The author glosses over Gandhi's contribution to India's Partition due to his failure to compromise, but mocks Nehru's ideas of socialism, claiming that the socialist project and the secular ideal were 'abandoned' or implemented piecemeal. It was the decline of the socialist project that led to the decline of the Congress in the 1960s.

Ananth has obvious sympathy with Jayaprakash Narayan, Ram Manohar Lohia, Asoka Mehta, V.P. Singh, and the 'glorious chapters of the history of the communists'. Accordingly some characters on the periphery of Indian politics are given undue attention due to this bias. There is scant mention of Ambedkar's contribution, and Nehru's socialism is said to have skirted steps to reduce poverty. According to

him Congress did not nationalize the private sector units nor carry out any campaign against caste discrimination. Indira Gandhi's 'tryst with the socialist rhetoric' is sarcastically referred to, despite her nationalizing of coal, bank and general insurance, abolishing of privy purses and management agencies and MRTP. Indira's 'achievement' in Bangladesh strangely merits only inverted commas.

Ananth is more plausible when he is able at length to shed some of his socialist crusade and deals with straight narrative after the Emergency. In fact, this book should have started in 1971 and been much shorter with all the tedious details of winners and losers in federal and state elections and assenting and dissenting judges in constitutional cases. Nor was it necessary to give potted biographies of the main characters—coming up to 2009 in some cases. He claims that matters like the Nehru-Prasad tension and Shastri's economic policies were 'outside the scope of this book', but apparently tittle tattle about Feroze Gandhi, Kanti Desai, Dhirendra Brahmachari and Suresh Ram was not.

Where the book has some merit is in dealing with the details of the Emergency, the Nagarwala-SBI incident, the Mandal Commission, Bofors, Shah Bano and Babri Masjid, but there is little or nothing original here or on the problems of the north-east, Sikkim, and even Kashmir. The text could have been improved upon without repetitions of people's designations, constant reminders that the politicians initially opposed to Mrs Gandhi were known as 'the syndicate', and otiose summaries at the beginning and end of each chapter like a school textbook. The habitual use of the editorial 'we', is constantly jarring to the ears. Pearson has done a poor job of editing this work, and bloomers like 'quite' instead of 'quiet' shows below-par proof-reading. The index is incomplete and inadequate.

What emerges overall is a hugely depressing narrative about the lack of principles and ethics, with intrigue and rampant corruption in the body politic, it is amazing to learn how critics of Congress leadership, even after suspension and expulsion, re-emerge to high office at later stages; the total lack of scruple and accountability is breathtaking. Even more astonishing is the number of politicians in high positions accused or caught red-handed in acts of corruption, but who invariably survive to indulge in further malpractices in defrauding the public. Despite the title, this book does not make any sense of Indian politics. We are still waiting for a book that does.

India and China: The Battle between Soft and Hard Power

Prem Shankar Jha
New Delhi: Penguin/Viking, 2010, ISBN 9780670083275, pp. 398, Rs 599

KRISHNAN SRINIVASAN

Of the recent books on India and China, this is perhaps the best; a stimulating work written lucidly by Prem Jha, who is clear about what he wants to say and how to say it. It arrives at arresting conclusions, supported by a wealth of detail and statistics.

India did not take the first steps to dismantle the command economy long after China but even earlier. Neither country took the plunge without considerable hesitation and on the part of India, an elaborate pretence of continuity. Only in the early 1990s did both countries choose market-led growth, and opted for gradualism. Both countries experienced cycles of downturn and growth. While they blame the global recession for the latest slowdown, their economies had begun to decline well before the crisis. In attempts to cushion the poor from industrialization, both have used the redistribution route to social justice and have failed to incorporate the poor as stakeholders in development so that they can acquire power and share the fruits of development. With corruption rampant, the poor are powerless.

India and China are transforming into capitalist states, beset by economic and political conflict. China lacks political institutions; India has them but they are almost non-functional. Meanwhile social discontent is growing and Jha is sceptical about the rise of these two late starters in capitalism, who must resolve the clash between growth and equity. India suffers Naxalite protests, and China's conflicts are both regional and local. In China, investment is financed by the people, but recession makes the task of equity more difficult. China's fiscal stimulus package has only 9 per cent for household consumption and will widen the urban/rural gap. India wants increase in people's incomes, but has the worst infrastructure of any country with a comparable degree of industrialization. Whereas Beijing retains the power to force local cadres and institutions, India does not discipline its states or officials.

The gap between India and China in growth, asserts Jha, is not large. India has assets like non-controversial statistics, more efficient use of domestic and foreign investible funds, raw materials and energy,

a larger pool of youth and Rajiv Gandhi's vision of technological progress. The flow of investible funds to China after 1990 was not entirely due to policy changes but because of deregulation of capital flows, the search for cheap labour, Japan nearing the end of a growth cycle, and wages rising sharply in SE Asia. Jha warns against correlating growth with reform and privatization. India's public sector was less than 20 per cent of GDP—why was growth so slow till 1991? The struggle between vested interests in China is economic, in India it is political. In China there was competition between party cadres and local apparatchiks to preempt resources for investment, and in India an unholy coalition of industrialists and politicians. In China this tension led to more investment; in India the coalition had a vested interest in scarcities. In China nearly everyone benefited initially from transition to market economy, though with the downturn, the number of losers will increase, with incidents of mass protest. There are land-based protests in both India and China. Governmental efforts do not prevent rising prices, widening incomes, and confiscation of natural resources for development. Both India and China are essentially conservative governments who shy away from reform that will empower people.

China did not dismantle its statist system overnight and its faster progress was due to loss of control by the centre. Local cadres had unlimited risk-free funds and the earliest reforms were instituted by peasants and local cadres, not the state. But there is wasteful use of inputs; numerous plants all over China rather than a few very large ones, the result of a race to invest between the centre and the local cadres. There is excess capacity aggravated by recession. There is pollution from half a million small and medium coal-fired boilers. China consumes more than the US of everything except oil, and 2 to 7 times as much as India in all traded primary raw materials. The social consequences in China are corruption, inequality and unemployment that challenge the legitimacy of the political system, and prompt public opposition to corrupt practices. This forced the state, afraid of the backlash of discontent, to restrict the citizens' right to resistance. China has to prevent dissidents from organizing themselves; hence the harsh restraints on the media, the Internet, and religious movements like Falun Gong.

The Chinese centre attempted to reassert its control on investment but local cadres have almost absolute power and reducing the tax-receiving authority of local bodies also reduced their ability to provide services and subsidies. It is too early to say if the 'new socialist countryside' will be effective, and whether disturbances and

the abuse of power of the local bodies are containable. But this is unlikely, since the centre depends on local bodies to uphold order and the Party itself. The separation of the party from government proved impossible, greed could not be checked or accountability enforced. The solution could be an independent judiciary, elections to all local bureaucratic levels open to non-party members, and peasants' right to own and not merely cultivate their land. But the leadership is more anxious to reform the party and to suppress demonstrations. Perhaps they do not see any threat, and do not fear going the way of the USSR. There is toleration of public intellectual and student dissent, but not at local level or with party cadres. After Tiananmen, democratization of the party to purge corruption was never raised again.

India from 1947-57 was a relatively open economy despite the socialist pattern decreed in 1954, followed until 1991 by inward looking self-reliance brought about by a foreign exchange crisis. By 1981 domestic inflation and foreign exchange crisis forced Indira Gandhi to see the need to abandon the command economy but she lacked the courage to confront the vested interests that thrived on shortages. There were instances of industry running the government and not vice versa. The need for political funding created a black market and black money. It was politics that prevented investment, production and employment and bred shortages and corruption. The government attempted reform by stealth from 1974 till 1991 when 'the humiliation that Indians suffered made them finally recognize and reject the hollow ideological foundations of the command economy'.

Unlike the previous stealth, the reform programme was drawn up in full view and with a lot of noise. With demand growth, opposition to reform became muted and by 1997 the control regime had all but disappeared, though the labour law and public sector organizations defied reform or privatization. The Congress party always believed control of inflation more important than stimulating growth. The challenges for India are 'Maoism' and the end of the Green Revolution, the first being one result of the second. The centre lost control in framing and executing policy while political coalitions and state governments gained economic power. The income gap between states grew, and the poor were deprived of government relief measures by predatory states and officials. Possible solutions are to coincide with national and state elections and evolve a system for funding political parties.

For Indians familiar with our economic history, the sections on China are more absorbing. Are the US and West in such terminal

decline as the author supposes: do they fear China's rise? What soft power—a contradiction in terms—is, the author does not clarify, and the 'battle' debate in the title is not pursued. The impact of WTO membership on India and China is not discussed. But these are quibbles: this is a must-read book, with compelling narrative and case studies.

On the Brink

Hank Paulson
London: Headline, 2010, ISBN 978 0 7553 6054 3, pp. 458, Rs 599

KRISHNAN SRINIVASAN

Paulson, former head of Goldman Sachs, took over as Treasury Secretary under President Bush in August 2006 when economic outlook was strong and stocks trading high. But the US was borrowing too much and export driven countries like China were shipping capital to the USA that heightened income disparity and enriched Wall Street. Credit had been too easy for too long. Paulson claims he warned of disturbances in capital markets at his first meeting with the president's economic experts due to leverage and risks like credit default swaps which were basically insurance against banks' defaults or downgrading.

On 4 September 2008 the US government decided to take over Freddie Mac and Fannie Mae, the troubled housing finance giants who sold insurance guaranteeing payment on mortgages as securities. They owned $5 trillion in mortgages and mortgage securities, 50 per cent of the US market, but by this time they had $5.5 billion in net losses for the year. They had too much leverage and benefited from lax regulation and employed or enriched Washington insiders inside and out of government. Paulson, a free market believer, had not planned to inject the government into the private sector; he was anxious that it should not look like nationalization but he was aware foreigners might lose confidence in the USA and cause a run on the dollar.

The regulating system was poor and relied on the companies' own analyses. The oversight bodies were too fragmented and lacked powers while the financial institutions were entwined worldwide.

Federal Reserve, Treasury and the SEC disagreed about who should regulate the banks. The crisis burst due to an unregulated housing boom fed by low interest that led to subprime or less creditworthy borrowing. When the housing market ran down, the banks were in trouble. Borrowers missed even their first payments and refused to pay when they had negative equity, when the loan exceeded the value of the house. The packaging and selling on of these loans into collateral debt obligations was opaque and affected banks in the USA and Europe. There had been an erosion of standards in the corporate and consumer credit markets. The housing crisis led to a financial crisis and the economy 'hit a brick wall'. J.P. Morgan bought Bear Stearns and Federal Reserve lent $30 billion to a new entity to buy Bear Stearns' mortgage assets. There were accusations that the taxpayer was bailing out Wall Street, and some thought it was a bad precedent—Bear Stearns should have been allowed to fail.

Paulson learned a lot from the Bear Stearns incident because there was only one buyer—J.P. Morgan. Merrill and Lehman were the next to be short of capital and at risk. Lehman's assets were at least $20 billion less than its estimate, and filed for bankruptcy 6 months after Bear Stearns. Forty per cent of all consumer credit loans had been packaged and sold on as securities but that market had all but closed down. Depositors queuing up to withdraw money from banks was a haunting image of the Great Depression. Freddie Mac and Fannie Mae now again needed a new line of government credit of $2.3 billion and both were essential for housing and capital markets and Russia, Japan and China held shares in them. In September both were placed in 'conservatorship', i.e. government control. Merrill and AIG, which insured mortgages and retirements, were also now under threat. Government took 80 per cent equity in AIG. BoA agreed to buy Merrill but by now all the big firms were in acute distress as liquidity was evaporating.

Paulson asked President Bush to go to Congress for emergency powers to prevent collapse of money markets since Federal Reserve and Treasury could do nothing more on their own. If stocks dropped and companies like GM went bankrupt, unemployment would zoom. The word 'meltdown' started to be used. The amount asked from Congress was $700 billion to buy banks' toxic assets—the word trillion had to be avoided at all costs. The legislation was denounced as 'un-American' and 'financial socialism'; every Congressman was angry at bankers' high pay and perks. The difficulty was to convince Congress that there was a severe crisis without spooking the already fragile market.

Then Wachovia, the fourth largest in USA and third for deposits, was taken over by Wells Fargo. Goldman was saved by Warren Buffet and Mitsubishi bought Morgan Stanley. Washington Mutual, the sixth biggest in the USA, was bought by J.P. Morgan. The legislation was passed in October 2008 after intense partisan debates. Government injected $125 billion into the largest 9 banks against shares. The question was whether there was enough money to deal with the unfolding crisis even with $700 billion. AIG needed more bailout money but saving the company was essential despite public anger. GE Capital and Citibank were the biggest takers of government loans to guarantee their debts. Citi was the weakest of all US banks. It had, with a market value of $21 billion, at least $300 billion of toxic assets, an unwieldy organization, no unified culture, and no business strategy.

In December 2008 BoA, GM and Chrysler all needed bailouts.

As Americans admitted, 'this is a worldwide problem, but we own it'. Paulson claims his team had to work with inadequate tools, limited powers, and outdated legislation. Collective decision-making in Washington was very poor. 'No matter what the problem, large or small, there is no such thing as a quick solution when you deal with Congress'. He makes four major points; The US consumes more than it saves and borrows too much; the regulatory system was outmoded and a patchwork; there were inadequate cushions of capital and liquidity; the largest financial institutions were too complex and 'too big to fail'—US and UK banks held about four times the value of their countries' GDPs. His prescriptions are to reduce the deficit, keep markets open, fix the regulatory system, take government out of the private sector and combat protectionism. He was obviously too busy fire-fighting to undertake long-term remedial measures himself.

This is a subjective close-up view of the financial crisis of 2007-9 that led to the downturn. There is praise for Bush's support, work ethics and methods. Paulson reflects great empathy with the Chinese, a lofty attitude to Russia and dislike of EU non-cooperation. India is mentioned nowhere. Being an ex-Goldman head, he never acknowledges that Wall Street was corrupt and callous in preying on gullible and defenceless consumers, instead calling the bankers 'smart and tough businessmen'. We might choose to call them crooks.

Picturing the Nation: Iconographies of Modern India

Richard H. Davis (ed.)
New Delhi: Orient Longman, 2007, pp. xii, 274, $50.00

AMBALIKA GUHA

The idea of nation, as conceptualized and articulated in modern political theory, derives its theoretical succor from a plethora of written sources, mostly scooped out from the archives and libraries: a strictly scholarly domain, so to say. Such an idea of nation, albeit with few exceptions, is largely official and elitist; outside the purview of popular comprehension. There is, however, an alternative idea of nation, which lies deeply ensconced in popular conceptions of what constitutes 'motherland' and finds expression in a deluge of commonplace visual objects like maps, paintings, architecture, calendars, posters, postcards, etc. To put it otherwise, the 'popular' visual representation of nation reflects an embattled response to the complexities inherent in the very act of defining what constitutes nation, not only in the process of defying the forces of colonialism, but also in grappling with the cataclysmic challenges of 'communalism' and 'regionalism' in the post-colonial era. Notwithstanding its manifold complexities, it is a less traversed domain of intellectual scrutiny in recent times. Therefore, in choosing to trace the trajectory of nationalism in India through multifarious visual projections at popular/subaltern level, Richard H. Davis (ed.), *Picturing the Nation: Iconographies of Modern India*, promises to usher in significant paradigmatic shifts in the conceptualization of nation.

The book is a collection of eight essays by scholars of international repute, with an extensive introduction by the editor. All of these grope their way into the complex world of visuals, delving deep into the process by which the idea of nationhood is constantly debated, reworked and reconceptualized across vast cross-sections of the Indian society. Strikingly enough, the conceptual threads of the essays are not woven into a single unifying fabric of thought, nor does the editor claim to do so. On the contrary, one of the objectives of the book, as explicitly stated in the beginning, is to analytically illustrate the 'multiple iconographies' of India 'within a historically changing nation-state'. Each of the eight essays is supplemented with

a well-chosen collection of pictures which are sure to add to the readers' delight.

The first three essays deal with pre-Independence visual iconographies and their role in evoking patriotic sentiment among the people of an incipient nation. Sumathi Ramaswamy's essay 'Body Politic(s)' zeroes in on cartography as the most tangible expression of a nation, by drawing a clear distinction between state-sponsored scientific map as representing an impersonal geographical space, and popular cartography, which by the incorporation of the familiar image of mother-goddess (Bharat Mata), becomes an object of pious devotion. The emblematic value of maps as 'bodyscape' (a term floated by the author herself), is not only capable of inducing rabid patriotism but has the magnanimous effect of transforming the 'abstract territory' into a 'lived nation', a religious and gendered entity worth dying for.

The next essay 'The Body and the Bomb' by Christopher Pinney focuses on two curious aspects of 'popular' visual imagery, the body and the bomb. In doing so, he chooses to bring under scholarly inspection, one of the national heroes, Bhagat Singh, whose sartorial disguise was a conscious strategy to obliterate the very differences on which colonial rule was founded. Yet as the author argues, the image of Bhagat Singh in a British trilby hat has been in much wider circulation throughout India than Gandhi projected in his innate Indianness—an instance that reinforces an alternative idea of nationhood that had already begun to gain a toehold in the realm of popular imagination in the early twentieth century.

Ajay Sinha's essay 'Against Allegory' critically analyses 'Medieval Saints', the large mural painted by Binode Behari Mukherjee on the eve of independence. Sinha shows how the mural, hitherto perceived as a piece of art allegorically encapsulating a modernistic vision of nation, was, in reality, illustrative of a much more complex world of colonial domination which, if evaluated carefully, corresponded to Tagore's own critique of nation state. Sinha's essay is sure to fascinate art historians for its adept analysis of a seemingly abstract theme.

Moving into a more theoretical terrain of national imaginings, Sandria B. Freitag's essay 'More than Meets the (Hindu) Eye' offers insightful comments on the basic strands of visual history in South Asia, illustrating through the case study of Mysore, how the visual images while retaining their distinctiveness are, at the same time, reworked and redefined to 'express current understandings of the world.' She also takes up the instance of Islamic posters, in order to drive home the struggle of a minority community to retain its

distinctive Islamic identity and a niche for itself within the Indian nation-space.

Touching upon a similar theme, Catherine B. Asher's essay 'From Rajadharma to Indian Nationalism' investigates how religious monuments as potent symbols of visual piety can be deployed by a community to assert its identity, both within the urban city space and within the broader rubric of a nation state. She picks up the example of Jami Mosque in Jaipur to illustrate how the supposedly 'invisible' Muslim community carves out its legitimate place in the city by having the mosque built in the heart of the city and getting it designed in the 'traditional' Jaipuri style to convey a sense of conformity to the spirit of the city.

The last three essays have been woven by an overarching theme of Hindutva as a dominant ideology in redirecting attitude towards the nation. 'The Efficacious Image' by Kajri Jain highlights calendar prints as ubiquitous visual objects, embodying the commercial nexus between bazaar and Nehruvian vision of secular nation in the immediate post-Independence period and then representing an altogether different dynamics in an era of frenzied communalism through forging a nexus with the Hindu nationalist groups by building on the 'devotional ethos' of the bazaar. However, much of what the author has tried to communicate remains somewhat vague due to the use of unnecessary jargons.

Christiane Brosius's essay 'I am a National Artist' charts the career of two artists Balraj and Satya, within the overarching framework of a persuasive Hindutva ideology, thereby capturing some of the intricate dynamics that shape present-day cultural nationalism in India. The methodology (viz., the interviews of Satya and Balraj) used in the essay is indeed interesting inasmuch as it ventures into the inner world of Hindu fundamentalists.

The last essay 'Spectacles of Nationalism' by Raminder Kaur, examines the rich kaleidoscope of visual imageries that adorn the *mandaps* of Ganapati festival in Maharashtra, illuminating their role in buttressing India's Hindu identity against the 'other' in a global world of socio-economic and cultural networks and in contesting and explicating pertinent national issues by taking the viewers through a peripatetic journey from mandap to mandap. All said and done, the approach should have been more nuanced, as there has been a perceptible overlapping of ideas, thereby robbing the essay of its pithiness.

The essays, while opening new vistas, and enriching existing literature on nationalism, do not seem to address directly—the inter-

face between popular iconographies and the official ones in resolving questions pertaining to nationalism, communalism and identity movements in South Asia. Such an effort on the part of the contributors to this book, would have led to a more vivid understanding of the dialectics (if at all) between the two genres of visual representations (that is, the popular and the official) in defining the contours of an ever evolving discourse on nation and nationalism. Notwithstanding such shortcomings, it is overall a commendable effort and a must read for scholars of various disciplines.

Masla e Khilafat (in Urdu)

Maulana Abul Kalam Azad

New Delhi: Itihad Publishing House, 1987, pp. 336, Rs. 40

SAFOORA RAZEQ

In Islamic teachings, a distinction is commonly made between matters of religion (*ibadat*) and worldly matters (*mu'amalat*). 'Religious matters' connotes the relation between humankind and God, and 'worldly matters' connote the relation between Humans and [other Humans]. As it has been argued by the Islamic scholars, religion is a bilateral matter—as an analogy, it is the shortest distance between two points in a straight line. Thus religion brings humankind closer to God. Through religion, human beings realize the existence of the authority of God. Since through 'worldly matters' the existence of that 'noble truth' can be established, therefore the different sources leading to a single point acknowledge that different nations and different races are considered as members of the larger family of nations.

Maulana Azad's *Masla e Khilafat* is basically a simple explanation of the above idea where 'identity', 'nation' and a 'supra-national identity' are seen as distinctive points leading to a single focal point. Azad believed in the rights of individuals, as the bases for both religious and worldly salvation. His mastery over judicial sciences and formalistic casuistry (*fuqaha*) with his commitment to Islamic theosophy (*urafa*) made him 'truly guided' to address the very sensitive yet complex issue of the Caliphate. The Indian nationalist Muslims, from the days of their inception, were caught in the predicaments of

varying 'identities'. But for an erudite scholar like Maulana Azad, respect to religion, the responsibility of establishing the will of the people in its governance, and fighting to eradicate tyranny, are the objectives of the 'calipha'/khalifa?. It was from 1900 that such voices were raised in the Islamic world, by the Iranian constitutionalist, Arab nationalist and Syrian modernist. The construction of the new calipha was very much a component of the Qura'nic injunctions.

Maulana Azad was a hardcore Khilafatist and was in favour of obedience to the Ottoman Sultan, as 'Calipha'. Nevertheless, he was also the champion of its abolition, in the years when Mustapha Kamal (Ataturk)—the leader of Turkish nationalism, was all set to replace it with a secular state. *Maslah-i-Khilafat*, is a critique of the Ottoman Caliphate. It was not from the paradigm of a secularist but from that of his old 'identity' as a liberated person—a Sufi. He upheld the existence of 'noble-truth' (*nizam-i-Illahi*), which enforces the claim of the righteous in this earth and annihilates the wrong doers. Azad deprecates the logic of placing the Ottoman Caliphate, to the position of the Papacy. The hollow shell of pontifical honours of the Caliphate was a reality to Maulana Azad. That was the reason, why Maulana Azad was in favour of obedience to the Caliphate but not in the same degree as submission to God and Prophet. The Ottoman Caliphate failed to be consultative, democratic and divinely inspired. It had outlived its purpose and had survived by sheer force. Maulana Azad argues that the etymological origin of the 'Caliphate' is in the Holy Qur'an. Here multiple references are made to the use of the word 'Caliphate'. It is associated with the Prophethood of nations (*qaum*), i.e. spiritual leadership and also with the notion of territorial sovereignty. What is noteworthy is the fact that God appointed man as 'His Calipha' (vice-regent) on this earth. Therefore, in the absence of the Prophets and rightly-guided rulers, the 'general will' shall work in compliance with reason and universal justice, in the ordering of human life and politics.

As a Sunni, Maulana Azad believed that it was under the 'right-guided' (*Rashidun*), i.e. the four Caliphs, that the Caliphate was considered to be divinely ordained. After them, the Caliphate's importance diminished. Historically, there were no efforts until the eighteenth century, to revive the Caliphate. In the eighteenth century, the Sultan of Turkey made a concerted effort against the expansionism of imperialist powers under the banner of 'Holy-War'. The Ottoman Empire put aside all values and declared their Sultan as the 'Caliph'. In the years that followed, theologians provided support to strengthen the hands of the Caliphate. In the latter-half of the nineteenth century, the

Sultan consolidated his power with support from religious movements against Western domination. India and Russia, with large Muslim minorities, were the most active centres of pro-Ottoman campaigns. It was indeed the British colonial regime, which made the Ottoman Sultan a political figurehead in India. During the mutiny of 1857, the image of the Ottoman Sultan was boosted by the British who urged him to issue a proclamation instructing Indian Muslims to remain loyal to the British. There was further boost to Ottoman image when Turkey was idealized during the Crimean War. Abdul Aziz claimed to be the universal Khalifah of Islam and found generous support among the new Muslim leaders. This new leadership, challenging the loyalist attitude of their established leaders, found legitimacy in evoking the name of the Calipha, in organizing mass campaigns against the British colonial authorities.

Maulana Azad believed in the necessity to 'reconstruct' Islam. This, he believed, should be done to revive the claim of nations that mankind was the 'Caliph' of God. Thus the moral and political rights of the people were upheld by him against the autocratic right of the Caliphate. Maulana Azad's support was for Iranian constitutionalism or Arab nationalism while he was against Ottoman autocracy. This is indeed indicative of his commitment to the ideals of individual liberty, which is the very basis of esoteric Islam. *Jamat*, *ijtihad*, *jihad* and *ijma* were as important in the life of a nation as the divinely ordained right of the individual. This masterpiece work of Maulana Azad, which is a forgotten text, can be regarded as the work of a *sufi*, who hoped to build a nation of composite elements. And in doing so he refers to the Qur'anic principle that regards 'identity' and 'nation' as cognitive elements in the realm of religion and politics.

Dr Syama Prasad Mookerjee and Indian Politics: An Account of an Outstanding Political Leader

Proshanto Kumar Chatterji
Delhi: Foundation Books, 2010, pp. 381, $18.95

SOUMYA KANTI MITRA

This book leaves lasting impressions, chief amongst them being how Mookerjee and the Hindu Mahasabha (HM) did their best to avoid alienating Muslims during the fight to regain Independence,

endeavoured to ensure that India stayed unpartitioned and whole, and even attempted an united front with a Congress that was ambivalent.

A facet that also emerges is the British fondness of Muslims, which led to their being handled with velvet gloves, spared from numerous onerous imposts (while Hindus were not), and being preferred for official positions. Of a piece with those were the HM's insistent demands for Independence, and deliverance from Whitehall's harebrained, and panicked, 'scorched-earth' reactions to the (far-fetched) possibility of a Japanese advance into Bengal. Add the empty discussions of Independence with Stafford Cripps, and the cold-blooded connivance between police and ICS in the killing fields of the districts, and one gets a reasonably complete picture of the state of limbo that afflicted Bengal right from the 1920s.

Mookerjee felt deeply about every single one of these aberrations and did his best to involve, not just the HM, Savarkar, and his peers, but also the Congress. He wanted a united front for India's demands for participation in war, self-rule and Independence.

We shall chiefly scan the contents and purport of Chatterji's five main chapters. That is because there is a degree of overlap between their contents—dates, as well as event-wise.

Chapter one, for instance, recounts how he took up the issues outlined in the beginning with Viceroy Linlithgow. But he got no redress, had to be content with double-speak and false promises from Herbert, the governor of Bengal. Chatterji recounts just how dissatisfied were Mookerjee and the HM with the prospective partition of Bengal.

Chatterji usefully contrasts the HM's stance on such issues with the Congress party's (verily) *laissez faire* take on most of them. The latter at its plainest during the deliberations of the Bombay Congress Working Committee meet. On that occasion, the CWC remained ambivalent about partition, even resolved that only the dictates of 'free will' would determine if anyone would opt to stay on in India or emigrate to the nation about-to-be created out of India. Clearly, Congress thought it to be of far greater import to embark on Gandhiji's Quit India movement than to keep India unpartitioned and intact.

That was helpful for the rulers too. They started the machinery for arresting Congress' top-most leadership on 8 August 1942—which, readers might infer, was the best way to absolve them of blame if, and when, partition was decided upon.

Indeed, the fallout of incarceration on a lesser man might have been a feeling of vindication. For Mookerjee, however, his indignation

was at not having been being consulted prior to the act. Yet, he was practical enough to avoid taking umbrage: he neither quit his finance ministership, nor the various other capacities to which he had been officially appointed. (He did finally resign on 16 November but that was for a bigger slew of reasons.)

In sum, the first key aspect is how the British worked overtime to stoke an already uneasy communal divide in Hyderabad, Bengal and the NWFP. They did so in a way that Muslims were awarded the first fruits of any fallout from policy, legislation or ordinance. Secondly, Whitehall's terror of the imminence of Japan's invading from the east prompted the government to reduce the fertile rice basket of Bengal into a wasteland of famine-afflicted, homeless, and landless peasants. The main gainers of the shortages that ensued from the 'Denial Policy' were hoarders and sharp operators. Chatterji usefully relates the awful famine of 1943 to such policies.

These were excellent reasons for Mookerjee dissatisfaction with how things were progressing. They led the HM, led by Mookerjee, to advance proposals for 'an honorable Indo-British settlement'.

Adopted by the All India Hindu Mahasabha Working Committee of 31 August 1942, the proposals (ten in number) included the need for Britain to grant immediate freedom to India, mediated by an adequately empowered viceroy possessing the ability to negotiate with India's political parties. The HM wanted that the party concerned should possess the standing to make up, and run, the government.

It is notable that number six, of the ten, proposals was that neither the central government, nor those in the states, needed to be monolithic in character: coalitions would be acceptable at either level. The seventh proposal was novel too. Stressing the need to internalize external wisdom in the proceedings of legislatures, it urged the need for provisions that would allow influential 'outsiders' to participate, and contribute, to parleys—particularly since a war was being fought.

Proposal eight also cited hostilities, exhorting the need to industrialize, and economically uplift, India—the better to prosecute the collective war effort. The last point concerned the need to set-up a Constituent Assembly, and the need to contract an Indo-British treaty that would allow minorities to vet the Constitution and refer whichever part they think needs to be altered to an International Tribunal.

But the most glaring aspect of chapter one's narrative, really, is the unbroken strand of Imperial cruelty that runs through the skein of the narrative. That informed the Denial Policy, which reappeared in the executive's wanton callousness during the Midnapore disaster

(16 October 1942)—an added feature of that being deliberate information blackouts.

It is a tribute to Mookerjee's political probity that he felt impelled to finally dissociate himself from government directly he (and his political peers, including the chief minister) heard that there would be no British attempts to indemnify, or redress, the flood-afflicted. His resignation letter—the first one of many during his career—was dated 16 November 1942. (Chatterji notes the three proximate reasons that impelled Mookerjee to step down. They were, the delay in granting Independence, the servility expected of the Cabinet *vis-à-vis* Government of India, and misrule and maladministration under Bengal's Governor Herbert.)

Mookerjee's resignation letter was accepted on 20 November and he soon had a chance to air his views and reservations. That transpired on 12 February 1943, the date of the inaugural of the next Bengal Legislative Assembly.

A very similar occurrence was the one of 6 April 1950, when, Mookerjee again felt impelled to relinquish his position in the Nehru cabinet. He couldn't do otherwise owing to the latter's vacillation and inaction on the fate of Hindu refugees in East Pakistan.

Chapter two, on HM's ascendancy in Indian politics, is about the split in Congress, its reluctance to allow state units of the party to share power with the Muslim League or even the government that followed in Bengal (one led by the British and partnered by the League). But the chapter's key theme is the ill-feeling and discord between Gandhiji at the Centre, and Subhas Bose. Chatterji relates how the face-off climaxed on 11 August 1939 with the displacement of Bose from the position of president of the Bengal Provincial Congress Committee (BPCC).

Mookerjee, though, expressed himself as not unhappy with this turn of events: it allowed the Bengal Hindu Mahasabha to befriend both sides of the Congress party and patch together a united front *vis-à-vis* Britons. Yet, although he did open up channels of dialogue with the Boses, Chatterji reminds us how, all too soon, Subhas started intimidating and demonizing HM. Such acts were actually a help to the British: Subhas' fights with Gandhiji, his ouster from the Congress mainstream and his formation of the Forward Bloc, all served to divide and debilitate the Congress. Mookerjee's HM was, in that respect, an opposing force that endeavoured to protect Hindu interests and unite communities.

The Mahasabha was powerless, however, to either alter British

policy towards Hindus or dissuade the League-government from turning the screws on the majority community. Accordingly, the days of the League government were dark ones for Hindus. They were loaded down by numerous invidious imposts, terrorized by police—all with tacit ICS-gendarme understanding.

Congress, meanwhile, seemed unwilling to carry the fight to the enemy. Gandhiji, who 'went to Linlithgow' soon after the outbreak of hostilities in Europe on 3 September 1939, even commiserated with the average Briton's ill-fated existence following the start of Luftwaffe raids on London. Also, Congress offered unconditional help in the war. Chatterji comments that such offers were all part and parcel of Congress' attempts to soften Linlithgow: favours in exchange for Berlin-bashing, in short.

Contrasting Mookerjee's stand towards the British, the chapter relates that he wanted to aid the war only in order to accelerate India's industrialization, and militarization. He stopped well short of 'unconditional' support.

So, very soon, Congress's indeterminate attitudes impelled the HM to a stand-off with Congress. But the Mahasabha had also made its mark; its avowedly cross-community, pro-Hindu sympathies initiated a new chapter in funding. A new constituency of moneyed donors came into being—including many of Congress' rich patrons who started channelling substantial sums to the HM. Jugal Kishore Birla's is one example that Chatterji adduces. And, as the author says, there were many more 'Marwaris'.

One proximate fallout of that was, even the Bengali *bhadralok* class started appreciating HM's persistent call for 'undivided' India; they too began contributing to HM's coffers. Indeed, that was the interval when the Congress almost attained 'also-ran' status compared to the Mahasabha.

Such political shifts and cross-cutting strategies apart, Chapter two also provides an outline of Stafford Cripps visit, showing how—more than any other force of that time—the proposals he fielded were able to unite all of them into repudiating them.

But the next clear landmark for Mookerjee, and Bengal, materialized in the aftermath of the Noakhali killings, followed by Congress' continued and, by now all too familiar, ambivalence on how to act in its aftermath. That set Bengal politics on the boil. Thus, by December 1941, the picture following the ouster of the League government was one of a tripartite coalition ministry comprising the HM, Forward Bloc, and a section of Krishak Proja Party MLAs. Mookerjee played a preeminent role as catalyst for change.

The chief beneficiary of this fissiparous progression was, of course, Jinnah! An insistent voice amidst the cacophony, he succeeded in catching Linlithgow's ear and stepped up his (albeit, still ill-heard) call for a separate state for muslims. Not only did the idea take root thereafter, it found fertile soil in most Muslim-dominated areas of India. Indeed, Chatterji provides a telling account of how the issue of Pakistan was, in a way, predetermined in the top echelons of Congress and directed by C. Rajagopalachari's (CR) formula.

Mookerjee inferred that the CR formula had Gandhiji's acquiescence and support; that surmise became a certainty after his talks with the Mahatma in Wardha. But the crowning irony is that Gandhiji and Jinnah were at cross-purposes about the mechanics of Pak independence and self-determination!

Going by the CR formula, Gandhiji wanted self-determination to be awarded to Muslims by a provisional Hindu government. His preferred sequence was—Independence first, followed by the separation of Muslims. But Jinnah desired Pakistan first, with Independence to follow!

Chatterji rightly comments that Gandhiji let down the side by meeting Jinnah even half-way with the CR Formula. Subsequent events bear out that interpretation even though, later on, Gandhiji was at pains to convince Mookerjee that his support for the CR Formula was only 'a matter of expediency'.

The chapter ends with Mookerjee's new role as the Officiating President of the HM's Working Committee. Assuming that role in the 26th Session of the committee in Bilaspur, he expressed deep reservations in his Presidential address (of December 1944) about the likely fallout of the Gandhi-Jinnah talks.

Chapter three, on the supposed 'resuscitation' of the HM, ends with yet another reverse for Mookerjee and his party. Indeed, the history of the party was already a prior reflection of what was to come right until 1980. It was plagued, throughout, by the unwillingness to sacrifice ideals to expediency, insistence on plain-speaking, the desire to aid endangered expat Hindus and the wish to emerge Independent—but without preserving 'historical' Commonwealth links. It also demanded proportional representation so that Hindus might attain the level of political decisiveness that their numbers deserved. Those ideals neither enthused, nor were espoused, by the most important political grouping of the day, Congress.

The HM was also disadvantaged because Mookerjee did not endear himself to Wavell when he wrote to him that he was against the existing constitution (based on the Communal Award), the Simla

Proposals and the idea of Pakistan. Those apart, the HM's stated support for Nazi Germany and communalism offered the Viceroy good excuses to overlook HM while inviting the others to meetings on how to award Independence. (Jailed members of Congress were all released on 14 June 1945.)

It even came to such a pass that, by 1946, Mookerjee was reduced to saying that the HM's role should be active and distinct—but that it had better avoid clashing with the Congress. That was necessitated not only by the growing ascendancy of Congress in Bengal, it was hammered home when the party succeeded beyond expectations in the 1945-6 elections. (Chatterji explains how the Congress win was helped by the exploits of the INA, only to be rationalized away by Congress in its post-election stress on the difference between Bose's philosophy and Gandhiji's.)

Other factors assailing the HM at this time were the rise of internal (i.e. regional) dissensions, an acute shortage of funds and its inability to influence any of the decisions of the Cabinet Mission proposals of May 1946. The nearest that the HM got to influencing the Mission's deliberations was on 15 April 1946; it was on that occasion that Mookerjee presented HM's suggestions to the group. The only fallout worth stressing in this context was the Mission's reported unwillingness to create the separate nation of Pakistan. Indeed, such were the setbacks and catalysts which were to lead to the transformation of HM into the Bharatiya Jana Sangh and its alliance with the RSS and other cadre-based organizations. Chatterji shows how protean was the background against which they occurred.

Chapter four, after backtracking to 1942-3, revisits the famine of 1943 to expose the ineptitude of successive Bengal ministries to make a dent in it. Such slackness was very ably exposed by Mookerjee and HM. The chapter also recounts how, in February 1946, Mookerjee became a member of the state legislature, unopposed. Thereafter, the Congress nominated him to the Constituent Assembly which had been entrusted with the task of framing the Constitution. Thereafter, he was even invited by Sardar Patel to form a part of the Central Ministry—in which he was in charge of 'Industry & Supply'.

The narrative that follows goes into great detail about his philosophy on markets, private enterprise, industry, with numerous official units set up under him—but also with him having to face (needless) flak owing to a disproportionately large numbers of Bengali PSU-heads. He weathered that, but felt impelled to resign just two and a half years into his career as central minister. The sticking

point was Pandit Nehru's handling (bordering, Mookerjee thought, on appeasement) of the maltreatment of Hindus in Bangladesh and the unwillingness of the Centre to counter it in any way. So, what started small, as a letter of resignation to Panditji on 6 April 1950, snowballed into repeated entreaties to stay on by both the PM, Sardar Patel and HM co-travellers.

Mookerjee did not look back however: he was resolved on resigning and that is what he stuck to. He left for Calcutta on the morning of 20 April. The very next month saw him mulling the idea of forming a new party, which got christened Bharatiya Jana Sangh on 16 January 1951. The subject matter of Chapter five is the maturation of the new party, its tie-ups with other, like-minded, nationalist organizations like the RSS—and Mookerjee's ability to hold his own against the more hardboiled leaders of the latter.

What we have, in sum, is a book that tells of Mookerjee's high stature as a politician, scholar, and his sincerity, catholicism, adherence to principles, unwillingness to double-deal and honesty of purpose. Nor did he harbor hidebound beliefs. That gets established from his willingness to alter his stance on the issue of the creation of a separate Muslim nation out of India. But the sad sub-text that emerges is that he was no match for the wily ploys and ambiguous stances of Congress' top mentors and leaders. Not only were the latter able to upstage him systematically, the latter even carried the electoral battle into Bengal (his homeland) and swept the polls. The best way to recall him would be through his principled politics, and the industrial units he created.

Paradise Lost?: State Failure in Nepal

Ali Riaz and Subho Basu

Lanham MD: Lexington Books, 2007 and New Delhi: Adarsh Books, pp. 234, $75.00

MONIKA MANDAL

This book examines the factors behind the emergence of Maoist insurgency in Nepal and tries to map the future trajectories of Nepal's politics. It highlights the internal dynamics of developing societies by exploring the character of state formation, its transformation and

consequences of state failure. The study is empirical in nature and focuses on a single case study; but is also relevant for state-centric debates in general. Here, we see an attempt to situate the state-society relationship in the overall debate of state-building, taking into consideration the implications of such relationships especially at the policy-making level. The book is an indication of the intensity of the debates about the state in developing societies, which often, is erroneously perceived as a historical structure disconnected from its social context and which therefore can be reshaped by exogenous forces at will.

This book comprises an introduction and six core chapters. The first chapter traces the process of state formation in Nepal since 1769. The construction of Hindu identity in order to provide cultural legitimacy to the monarchical political order, that has existed since the state's inception in the eighteenth century to the democratic revolution in 1990, has resulted in the political alienation of the ethnic and social groups. By examining complex features of political and economic interaction, the chapter further argues that the unrepresentative process of state formation and the tradition of governance have contributed to the alienation of the citizens from the state and created a space for political violence, rebellion and state terrorism thereby exposing the fragility of emerging democratic institutions in Nepal. For nearly a decade, from the declaration of Maoist 'people's war' in January 1996 to the formation of the new alliance for the restoration of democracy in December 2005, Nepal has experienced a three-sided power struggle between Maoist insurgents who want a republic based on egalitarian principles, elected politicians who want an unfettered role in policy making and a monarch who is keen to restore his power as it was before democracy gained ground in Nepal. The first chapter seeks to identify the crisis by taking into account the historical context as well as the contemporary priorities that govern the making and unmaking of a state-society relationship.

Chapter two of the book discusses Nepal's geographical divisions: the Himalayas (Himal), the Hills (Pahad), and the plains of Terai (Madhes). Madhes-based parties have been demanding the incorporation of the adjacent Indian border on the south into a single Madhes state. Madhesi leaders define Madhesis as original inhabitants of Madhes who are not of Pahadi or Himali origin. This conceptualization seems to be based on the general perception among Pahadis of identifying the Madhesis as the people of the *terai* region or of Indian origin. The hill people traditionally have been calling the

people living on the plains as *madhesi*. But, not until recently was there any official definition or claim regarding who the Madhesis were. With the demand for a single autonomous Madhes State and 'wholesale' inclusion of Madhesis through reservation in all state organs emerged the controversy on the ethnological term 'Madhesi'. The present Nepali political and social life is, however, dominated by the socially privileged communities—the Brahmins, Chhetris and Vaisyas of Phada and Terai. The low caste and tribal ethnic communities as well as minority communities have not yet been able to secure themselves in the social and political domain. The demand for reservation for the weaker sections has been gradually gaining momentum as more and more organizations representing these communities started pressing for their due share in political, social, and economic life. By raising these demands they want to eliminate their sufferings and exploitation. Under the democratic system that the nation has adopted after 1990, *Jana Andolan* has given enough opportunity to organize such movements as pressure groups to influence the government and political parties.

Chapter three deals with external and internal factors that influenced Nepal's politics. The Nepali economy is dependent on external market demand and global politics that heightened during the Cold War. The internal factors include the absence of redistributive reforms, and the adoption of lopsided urban-centric development strategies. The ecological factors take into account the distinctive geography of Nepal and its peripheral position. The weak performance of the state authorities, especially the unremitting extraction of resources, has also weakened their position. There are other factors that have stemmed from the policies pursued by the Nepali elites, the monarchy and the political establishment.

Chapter four gives a framework for analysing the evolution of Maoist insurgency and its possible consequences. A decade-long insurgency movement developed into a People's War in February 1996, with the claim that only a communist state could solve the country's various social and economic ills. The insecurity of the people has enabled the Maoists to win considerable support in rural areas, especially from women and the marginalized caste and ethnic groups. The Maoists also suppressed opposition in rural areas with violent means and benefited from infighting within the political establishment. It is popularly believed that insurgency is the direct result of the feeling of despair among the poor and socially marginalized. While there is an element of truth in these analyses, evidence suggests that the

underlying causes of the insurgency movement, its rapid growth, and success are far more complicated issues. The study offers a different perspective of the political configuration in Nepal and reviews the brewing conflict as an offshoot of several socio-economic factors, trans-boundary issues, internal politics, etc. The overall political degeneration in Nepal led to the Maoist upsurge. Having assumed the throne after the death of his brother, Birendra, and his nephew, crown prince Dipendra, in the palace massacre of June 2001, Gyanendra quickly took a non-committal stance. Many perceived this stance as a veiled threat against the political parties. When the army (still under the direct command of the king) refused to help the police to flush out the Maoists, the Nepali people felt that the government was powerless to control the rebellion. The king and the army engineered the dismissal of the then-Prime Minister Girija Prasad Koirala (now the octogenarian head of the Seven Political Party Alliance or SPA) and replaced him with the more amenable Sher Bahadur Deuba. Deuba soon recommended the dissolution of the House of Representatives and was himself ousted by the King on 4 October 2002 for failing to contain the Maoist insurgency. He was reappointed prime minister in June 2004; but on 2 February 2005, Gyanendra dismissed Deuba for a second time, declared a state of emergency and named himself the chairman of the government. The brutality of Gyanendra's regime since then has prompted a popular uprising against him—an uprising that the political parties struggled to organize for the last three years, and the Maoists for the last ten years. At last, the people have sided with the SPA in a non-violent uprising which could yet become another inspiration for non-violent democratic change. Such a narrative also provides a general and wide-angle perspective of Maoist politics in South Asia.

The last and final chapter described as the uprising of 2006, has vindicated the argument that the Nepali state is a failed state characterized by patrimonialism and oppressive regime. It also has laid bare the uncertain future of the country. The international community, too, has a stake in Nepal's peace process. In retrospect, it can be said that Nepal has strategic importance not only for its neighbours, but also for the world at large. A peaceful and prosperous Nepal will be conducive to the maintenance of regional peace and security. We all know that instability in a country creates problems for others. In the present century, we are all sailing through troubled waters. That is why we expect constructive and positive response from the international community as well as from our regional partners.

Politics after Television: Religious Nationalism and the Reshaping of the Public in India

Arvind Rajagopal

Cambridge: Cambridge University Press, 2001, pp. 393, Rs. 1549

ABHIK SAMANTA

The author's selection of the title brings us directly into the methodology of his work. An attempt has been made to trace the impact of television on politics. Yet this work is not a summary depiction of how politics has been affected by the increasing popularity of television. The relationship between the two events lies at the heart of the explication of the relationship between politics and television. One is the broadcasting by Doordarshan of the television serial *Ramayan* and the other—the demolition of the Babri Masjid at Ayodhya by the militant Hindu nationalists. By no means is it suggested that the two events were the work of the same agency or related acts of doing. Rather, it is shown how the political movement culminating in the statement of demolition could occur in the context of the act of watching television. The word 'after' in the title: *Politics after Television: Religious Nationalism and the Reshaping of the Public in India* is significant here, since it conveys a sense of something following another as the provenance of the chief problematic. Through this, a boundary of the work is made explicit. Although the aim is to craft a general notion implied by the words 'politics' and 'television' or the effect of television on politics is, as the necessary subject of elucidation, the author achieves this through an exploration of the juxtaposition of the two events mentioned above. The danger here is that the search for the connection between two linear events cannot by itself be a theory which is non-linear. A theory would come about, if a replication of this connection can be shown which is thematically outside the scope of this work.

Perhaps at the heart of the contradiction suggested above, is simply the conflict between the conjuncture model of historical narrative and a theoretical one. The former form is evident in the way the author evokes the Nehruvian past in the opening chapter entitled 'Hindu Nationalism and the Cultural Forms of Indian Politics'. A perceived crisis of the Nehruvian state forms the background to the rise of Hindu nationalism as an alternative ideology of the state. The

crisis is perceived more than real because the idiom of a liberalized state *vis-à-vis* that of a planned state motivated by development is a deception. Akin to the state in the Reagan and Thatcher era, the opposite of a planning oriented socialist state was, in fact, a more authoritarian and interventionist one. Dismantling of the public sector and more flexible labour employment laws were signs of a global resurgence of capitalist state power. This is the context as well as the theory which explains the connection between two events which form the subject of this work. Thus, the conjuncture of declining employment opportunities, low growth rate, and production-centred state machinery fraught with corruption, formed the basis of the powerful critique of the Congress rule which could propel a political outcome in the destruction of the Babri mosque from an apolitical act of watching television. But the causality that the author depicts goes beyond this into the conceptual arena of late capitalism. Albeit the fact that the depiction in the following chapters is remarkable, two areas emerge as unclear propositions. One is the way the 'other' of lately resurgent capitalist order is depicted. Is the Nehruvian order a quintessentially non-capitalist order of politics and state formation? The other question also emerges from this uncertainty: How new is the structure of politics that emerges 'after television'? The examples that the author gives are not convincing enough, even though, he clearly demarcates the stages of growth of the Hindu nationalist combine since Independence. My contention here is that the political foundations of the Nehruvian regime, traced to the period of nationalist anti-colonial movement, display all the important aspects of politicization the author notes of the Hindu nationalist upsurge since the 1980s. As William Gould's[1] recent research has shown, the usage of Hindu religious ritual as political symbolism was intrinsic to the way the Indian National Congress generated mass mobilization against colonial rule.

The post-colonial state orchestrated a developmental regime which rested on a fundamental duality. It was liberal to those within the ambit of its laws but illiberal to those outside. 'A modernising state presumes an illiberal form of power; since liberal freedoms cannot be granted to those who are not yet modern.'[2] Such a stress on economics was prejudiced over matters of culture which were accorded a lower priority. This explains the lack of attention for decades towards broadcasting mediums such as radio or television. State monopoly, and rigidly enforced over these mediums, had the effect of removing these mediums from the sphere of politics.

Thus the modus Vivendi of the Nehruvian regime was to occupy a minimal common ground with respect to culture. This changed with the broadcasting of the *Ramayan* which occurred at a time when the Nehruvian state was attempting to address a situation of crisis through the New Economic Policy. There was thus a qualitative difference in the two orchestrations of state policy, one by B.V. Keskar (Minister of Information and Broadcasting, 1952-60) and the other by S.S. Gill, where the former had stopped the broadcasting of popular Hindi movie songs owing to their removal from Sanskritized classical culture and the latter who justified the broadcast of the *Ramayan* owing to, '. . . the fact of the matter that Hindus constitute eighty three per cent of the country's population. By and large, the Indian ethos is primarily Hindu and *Ramayan* is its centrepiece.'[3] This resort to the popular can be seen in the political realm as well as implied in the much discussed intentions of Rajiv Gandhi in the *Shah Bano* case and its complement in opening the Babri mosque to Hindu worship. Ashutosh Varshney described it as a 'politics of anxiety'[4] which is a fitting description of a time which revealed multiple fissures in a late Nehruvian order. 'Anxiety' thus straddles the economic, social and political realms and at the same time, does not assert the completion of any process of change. Rajagopal's narrative on the other hand, designates change as a point of closure which allows him to build a collage of depictions of the media and the politics. This collage, particularly visible in the last three chapters, cannot, in my view lead to the conclusion that he proposes for his work. This is expressed in the quote:

> The simulation of continuity with earlier forms of Hindu nationalist expression was misleading at the level of the movement's content, although important to its appearance. Hitherto organised Hindu communalism had avoided the use of specific religious content, both out of piety to its modernist ideals and for fear of dividing its ranks. The failure to recognize this shift has confused perceptions of the Ram Janmabhoomi movement.[5]

Here, I would like to point towards a misreading of the history of politics in India where we can see the use of 'specific religious content' not only by Hindu communalism but also by the Indian National Congress in the endeavour to launch mass movements against colonial rule. Going into details would be inappropriate here. Hence, I would like to conclude with the suggestion that the historical context of this work should be made clearer.

NOTES

1. William Gould, *Hindu Nationalism and the Language of Politics in Late Colonial India*, Delhi: Cambridge University Press, 2004.
2. Quoted in Arvind Rajagopal, *Politics after Television: Religious Nationalism and the Reshaping of the Indian Public,* Delhi: Cambridge University Press, 2004, p. 75.
3. Ibid., p. 85.
4. Quoted in Ashutosh Varshney, 'Contested Meanings: India's National Identity, Hindu Nationalism, and the Politics of Anxiety', *Daedalus*, vol. 122, no. 3, pp. 227-61.
5. Arvind Rajagopal, *Politics after Television*, p. 213.

Ah Q Archaeology: Lu Xun, Ah Q, Ah Q Progeny and the National Character Discourse in Twentieth Century China

Paul B. Foster

Lanham, MD and Oxford: Lexington Books: A Division of Rowman and Littlefield Publishing Group, 2006, pp. 401, £85.00

SUVRO PARUI

Luxun (Zhou shu Ren), one of the most prominent Chinese writers of the twentieth century, was considered to be the founder of modern Chinese Literature. His works exerted such an influence after the May Fourth Movement that he was lionized by the Communist regime after 1949. His writing comprising short stories, essays, novels lent new intellectual and artistic depth to an otherwise shallow corpus of literature of early May Fourth period. Son of Zhou Boyi, he wanted to become a doctor. With this objective in mind, he went to Japan studying medicine in 1904, but abruptly terminated his medical career and left Japan in March 1906, redirecting his interest on literature under the impact of the Russo-Japan war of 1904-5. He was deeply affected by the social condition of the Chinese and subsequently, devoted his literary skills towards the modernization of China which, in turn, became one of the powerful factors triggering the civil war in China. Luxun's warning through his writing is explicit and clear: 'You should change, change from the bottom of your heart. You

must . . . who was killed by the hunters! Just like insects'. Previously, access to literature was confined to the intellectual circles in the society, but it was Luxun who made it available to the common man. His skill in plot construction puts him at par with the short-story writers of the West. One of the hallmarks of his writings being his particular brand of satire, he was generally successful in admonishing his political and literary foes. However, Luxun objects to 'Laughter for laughter sake'. He chooses his satirical skill as a vehicle for social reform. As a reformer and critic, he clashed with radicals and conservatives alike, lashing out right and left at whoever stood in his way. The trend that he set in contemporary Chinese literature was followed by others, similarly dedicated to the idea of a realistic, socialist literature.

This book is based on one of the best creations of Luxun, i.e. Ah Q. It narrates the 'adventures' of a man, name Ah Q; who belongs to the rural peasant class with a bit of education, having no home, living in a temple, without a definite occupation; his personality is described in a very sarcastic tone, as thoughtless and short tempered, and experienced with an utter lack of self-awareness, a series of humiliation, and who is finally executed during the chaos of the republican Revolution of 1911. And Ah Q is considered the personification of the negative traits of the Chinese national character, while revealing Ah Q's weakness of will, the author has also shown his deep sympathy for his character. 'Spiritual Victory' depicts one thoroughly negative aspect of 'Guoming Xing' (Chinese national character). 'Spiritual Victory' is reinterpretation of Ah Q's story, which helps us to develop major aspects of Luxun and his critical approach towards the Nationalism, which made Ah Q as a hallmark. This method of psychological self-defence helped Ah Q to turn his defeat into victory. It has been depicted in particular chapter, where, Ah Q's victory is mentioned as a conflict: Ah Q *vs* village idlers. Ah Q is a bully to the less fortunate, but fearful of those, who are above his rank, power. He persuades himself that he is mentally and spiritually 'superior' to his oppressor while he succumbs to their tyranny and suppression. Writer exposed Ah Q with extra faults as symptomatic of the Chinese national character of his time.

The first chapter discusses nationalism issues, followed by the second which describes the imaging of nation and the essence of nationalism. The third chapter is more specific for it delves into the dynamics of Luxun's interest in nationalism, but the fourth deviates from the narrative to the critical and polemical, marking points of criticism in the ideological canvas of nationalism. Then, we have,

in the fifth chapter, a narration of Luxun's incisive assault on the national 'essence' and Chinese spiritual culture. It also delineates the method of Ah Q's spiritual victory. The last two chapters consider the core issue as a flashback—in other words, it deals with the very 'construction' of Ah Q, and the ironic inflections, critical spirals and meanderings of Chinese nationalism.

This book begins with a dilemma. The narrator claims he does not know which character is genuine/suitable and which character he and the readers should imagine and think about. What is aural and visual? The plot of this story is set in twentieth-century China, when there was a major clash between modern-capitalist-industrialist and traditional culture. The downfall of Qing empire, and the rise of Western capitalism have been emphasized. On the other hand, the author also said that, the ignorance of the masses in China, which was the root cause of its backward status, could not be remedied by simple changes of the government; so what the Chinese really asked for that is 'medicine of the spirit', which can be regarded as connoting modernized education, and the resulting changes in the social habits of the people. This story also strongly criticized the alleged historic-cultural burden of China at that time, which was formed by the long history of absolute authority of the feudal regime or system, and imperialistic oppression. As a result, enormous social pressure, group punishment, and the rigid civil service test—buttressed political and social hegemony in China. But the author Luxun has already pointed out that the people, moulded by this cultural environment were obsessed about saving their own face, being imbued with pride in their past. They had, in the past, accepted without questioning, the injustice imposed by the authority. But in modern times, 'Spirit of Ah Q' and Ah Q's mentality are commonly used as terms of mockery. The book tells a tale of the attack on national essence, Chinese spiritual culture, and the construction of Ah Q's discourse. Simultaneously, this discourse continued to thrive after the founding of People's Republic of China in 1949. Luxun was canonized by Chairman Mao. The character of Ah Q was re-interpreted and re-iconized as a Chinese peasant, whose negative behaviour reflected the mindset of the landlord gentry. But Ah Q never represented the national character. What this book does is to provide a detailed textual analysis revealing how the nation China was 'imagined' collectively. The 'True Story of Ah Q' is sometimes undermined by confusing organization and redundancy of important points. There are some illuminating chapters, which describe the historical conditions that gave rise to

a form of nationalism in China. It provides a useful discussion of a literature on the origins of nationalism and other issues also, which still has relevance: such as relationship with tradition, imperialism, print-capitalism and modernization. However, such essential information could have been more firmly, sharply and incisively dealt with in the book. For instance, the first chapter tells us that Ah Q is a prominent symbol of the Chinese national character in the modern Chinese intellectual consciousness, and that it is perceived as a negative symbol. But the author doesn't elaborate why the symbol is negative. Moreover, since this book deals with the concept of discourse and the method of archaeology, readers are surprised to see the omission of works by the other famous post-modernist theorists in the bibliography.

In conclusion, *Ah Q Archaeology* is an admirable piece of work, to weave together at least the three aspects, i.e. modern Chinese literature, modern Chinese theory, and the concept of nationalism or national identity. The final result is exceedingly rich, but readers might flit into digressive trajectories as some of the arguments diverge in different directions within a chapter. Ah Q as a reified and stereotypical image of the 'uncivilized' Chinese. It is a 'text' read, or re-read, and misread, often making the Chinese reflect on their weaknesses. In a sense 'Q' stands for self-imposed critical strategy for the Chinese people to find out their foe, and clearly conceptualize their own civilization and nation, and modernity. Lastly, ironically, as far as the aim of being 'completely' modern and civilized is concerned, unattained by the intellectuals in China, there does not seem to be a day when the 'Q' will come into full play and reality. But it is needed to historicize such interpretation, and to position Ah Q as symbolic of a national self in the larger historical context of colonial and imperialist expansion. With regard to the national character, the 'True story of Ah Q' turns into evidence integrated with Luxun's view of a vastly complex and critical analysis of Chinese nationalism. If Luxun's story is interpreted as a satire, the issue should not only be one of examining the satirical text, but also examining the manner in which it has been inscribed in popular imagination and narrative form over time.